West Chicago Public Library District
118 West Washington
West Chicago, IL 60185-2803
Phone # (630) 231-1552

American Icons

AMERICAN ICONS

An Encyclopedia of the People, Places, and Things that Have Shaped Our Culture

VOLUME ONE

Edited by Dennis R. Hall
and Susan Grove Hall

GREENWOOD PRESS
Westport, Connecticut • London

Library of Congress Cataloging-in-Publication Data

American icons: an encyclopedia of the people, places, and things that have shaped our culture/edited by Dennis R. Hall and Susan Grove Hall.
    p. cm.
    Includes bibliographical references and index.
    ISBN 0–275–98421–4 (set : alk. paper)—ISBN 0–275–98429–X (vol. 1 : alk. paper)—ISBN 0–275–98430–3 (vol. 2 : alk. paper)—ISBN 0–275–98431–1 (vol. 3 : alk. paper)
    1. United States—Civilization—Encyclopedias. 2. Popular culture—United States—Encyclopedias. 3. Americana—Encyclopedias. I. Hall, Dennis, 1942– II. Hall, Susan G., 1941–
E169.1 .A472155   2006
306.0973'03—dc22   2006006170

British Library Cataloguing in Publication Data is available.

Copyright © 2006 by Dennis R. Hall and Susan Grove Hall

All rights reserved. No portion of this book may be reproduced, by any process or technique, without the express written consent of the publisher.

Library of Congress Catalog Card Number: 2006006170
ISBN: 0–275–98421–4 (set)
     0–275–98429–X (vol. 1)
     0–275–98430–3 (vol. 2)
     0–275–98431–1 (vol. 3)

First published in 2006

Greenwood Press, 88 Post Road West, Westport, CT 06881
An imprint of Greenwood Publishing Group, Inc.
www.greenwood.com

Printed in the United States of America

The paper used in this book complies with the Permanent Paper Standard issued by the National Information Standards Organization (Z39.48–1984).

10 9 8 7 6 5 4 3 2

Contents

Guide to Related Topics	xi
Preface	xvii
Acknowledgments	xxi

VOLUME ONE

Alamo, *Richard R. Flores*	1
Muhammad Ali, *J. Peter Williams*	9
Amish, *David L. Weaver-Zercher*	15
Antiperspirant, *Jimmy Dean Smith*	22
Art Fair, *Mary Carothers and Sharon Scott*	28
Fred Astaire, *Michael Dunne*	35
Lucille Ball, *Rhonda Wilcox*	40
Banjo, *Jack Ashworth*	45
Barbie, *Dawn Heinecken*	51
Bear, *Richard Sanzenbacher*	58
Beats, *Jason R. Kirby*	65
Betty Crocker, *Pauline Adema*	73
Bomb, *Margot A. Henriksen*	82
Daniel Boone, *Richard Taylor*	90
Boy Scout Knife, *R. H. Miller*	101

Capitol, *Karelisa V. Hartigan*	107
Johnny Carson, *David Lavery*	114
Johnny Cash, *Don Cusic*	120
Cell Phone, *John P. Ferré*	128
Ray Charles, *Reginald Martin*	134
Julia Child, *Sara Lewis Dunne*	139
Computer Chip, *Michael Bertz*	145
Coney Island, *Judith A. Adams-Volpe*	151
Couch, *Dennis Hall*	159
Courtroom Trial, *David Ray Papke*	166
Joan Crawford, *Claude J. Smith*	173
Crayola Crayon, *Elizabeth Armstrong Hall*	180
George Armstrong Custer, *Michael C. C. Adams*	186
James Dean, *Geoffrey Weiss*	192
Dinosaur, *Mark A. Wilson*	198
Dollar Bill, *Heinz Tschachler*	205
Bob Dylan, *Edward P. Comentale*	213
Albert Einstein, *Anthony O'Keeffe*	220
Emergency Room, *Robert Wolosin*	226
Flea Market, *Michael Prokopow*	233
Ford Mustang, *Susan Grove Hall*	242
Gettysburg, *Randal Allred*	249
GI, *Michael Smith*	258
Golden Gate Bridge, *Kenneth M. Sanderson and Laura Kennedy*	266
Billy Graham, *David Fillingim*	271
Grateful Dead, *Nicholas Meriwether*	277

VOLUME TWO

Guardian Angel, *Scott Vander Ploeg*	285
Gun, *Michael C. C. Adams*	292

CONTENTS

Halloween Costume, *Sylvia Grider*	298
Hard-Boiled Detective, *Brendan Riley*	304
Harley-Davidson Motorcycle, *Wendy Moon*	310
Ernest Hemingway, *R. H. Miller*	316
Jimi Hendrix, *Joy Haenlein*	322
Audrey Hepburn, *Lucy Rollin*	329
Hershey Bar, *Dennis Hall*	336
Hollywood, *Thomas B. Byers*	343
Horse, *Barrett Shaw*	349
Indian Scout, *Tom Holm*	356
Martin Luther King, Jr., *Ricky L. Jones*	363
Evel Knievel, *Randy D. McBee*	369
Kodak Camera, *Richard N. Masteller*	375
Las Vegas, *Lawrence E. Mintz*	382
Rush Limbaugh, *Thomas A. Greenfield*	388
Charles A. Lindbergh, *Roger B. Rollin*	396
List, *Dennis Hall*	404
Log Cabin, *William J. Badley with Linda Badley*	412
Lorraine Motel, *Thomas S. Bremer*	419
Jessica Lynch, *Anna Froula*	425
Loretta Lynn, *Don Cusic*	431
MAD Magazine, *Charles Hatfield*	438
Madonna, *Diane Pecknold*	445
McDonald's, *Betsy Beaulieu*	452
Mexican-American Border, *Susana Perea-Fox and Iván Figueroa*	458
Miami, *Gary Harmon*	465
Mickey Mouse, *M. Thomas Inge*	473
Miss Manners, *Dennis Hall*	481
Marilyn Monroe, *Ann C. Hall*	486

Mount Rushmore, *Susan Grove Hall with Dennis Hall*	493
Muppets, *Robert Barshay*	501
NASCAR's Bristol Motor Speedway, *Barbara S. Hugenberg and Lawrence W. Hugenberg*	509
Niagara Falls, *Patrick McGreevy*	516
Jack Nicholson, *Thomas A. Van*	522
Olmsted Park, *Thomas J. Mickey*	530
One-Room Schoolhouse, *Ray B. Browne*	536
Oscar, *Robert Holtzclaw*	542
Patchwork Quilt, *Judith Hatchett*	549
Walter Payton, *Clyde V. Williams*	558
Polyester, *Patricia A. Cunningham*	565
Poster Child, *Mary Johnson*	572
Elvis Presley, *George Plasketes*	578

VOLUME THREE

Railroad, *Arthur H. Miller*	585
Robot, *Ira Wells*	592
Eleanor Roosevelt, *Maurine H. Beasley*	597
Rosie the Riveter, *Kathleen L. Endres*	601
Route 66, *Thomas A. Greenfield*	607
Babe Ruth, *J. Peter Williams*	614
Scrapbook, *Patricia Prandini Buckler*	621
Tupac Shakur, *Mickey Hess*	628
Spaceship, *Angela Hague*	634
Sports Bar, *William R. Klink*	641
Stadium, *Sylvester Frazier, Jr.*	648
Stonewall, *Thomas Piontek*	655
Suburbia, *Philip C. Dolce*	662
Superman, *P. Andrew Miller*	669

CONTENTS

Tara, *Diane Calhoun-French*	676
Tattoo, *Karen Aubrey*	683
Henry David Thoreau, *Daniel S. Kerr*	690
Tractor, *Robert T. Rhode*	698
Tupperware, *Judith Hatchett*	705
Underground Railroad, *J. Blaine Hudson*	713
Viagra, *Bennett Kravitz*	720
Video Game, *Ken S. McAllister and Judd Ethan Ruggill*	727
Vietnam Veterans Memorial, *Linda Marie Small*	733
Wal-Mart, *Richard Daniels*	739
John Wayne, *David Magill*	746
Whistler's Mother, *Elaine A. King*	752
Oprah Winfrey, *R. Mark Hall*	760
Witch, *Linda Badley*	767
Tiger Woods, *Michael K. Schoenecke*	776
Wright Brothers, *Roger B. Rollin*	783
Zipper, *Robert Friedel*	790
Selected Bibliography	797
Index	801
About the Contributors	849

Guide to Related Topics

Art and Architecture
Art Fair
Capitol
Coney Island
Crayola Crayon
Dollar Bill
Golden Gate Bridge
MAD Magazine
Mickey Mouse
Mount Rushmore
Olmsted Park
Patchwork Quilt
Whistler's Mother

Commerce, Consumers, and Marketing
Art Fair
Barbie
Betty Crocker
Coney Island
Crayola Crayon
Dollar Bill
Flea Market
Ford Mustang
Halloween Costume
Hershey Bar
Kodak Camera
Las Vegas
Log Cabin
McDonald's
Polyester
Poster Child
Elvis Presley
Scrapbook
Tupperware
Wal-Mart

Community or Civic Identity
Amish
Courtroom Trial
Dollar Bill
Albert Einstein
Golden Gate Bridge
Billy Graham
Gun
Harley-Davidson Motorcycle
Hollywood
Martin Luther King, Jr.
Rush Limbaugh
List
Log Cabin
Mexican-American Border
Miami
Mickey Mouse
Mount Rushmore
Olmsted Park
One-Room Schoolhouse
Patchwork Quilt
Stonewall
Suburbia

Femininity
Lucille Ball
Barbie
Joan Crawford
Hard-Boiled Detective
Audrey Hepburn
Horse
Jessica Lynch
Loretta Lynn
Madonna
Marilyn Monroe
Patchwork Quilt
Eleanor Roosevelt
Rosie the Riveter
Tupperware
Oprah Winfrey
Witch

Film
Alamo
Fred Astaire
Joan Crawford
James Dean
Hard-Boiled Detective
Harley-Davidson Motorcycle
Audrey Hepburn
Hollywood
Kodak Camera
Mickey Mouse
Marilyn Monroe
Mount Rushmore
Jack Nicholson
Oscar
Tara
John Wayne

Foodways
Betty Crocker
Julia Child
Coney Island
Hershey Bar
McDonald's

Generational Change and Counterculture
Muhammad Ali
Beats
Crayola Crayon
James Dean
Dinosaur
Bob Dylan
Ford Mustang
Grateful Dead
Harley-Davidson Motorcycle
Evel Knievel
MAD Magazine
Muppets
Rosie the Riveter
Stonewall
Tattoo

Hero
Muhammad Ali
Daniel Boone
George Armstrong Custer
GI
Hard-Boiled Detective
Ernest Hemingway
Charles A. Lindbergh
Elvis Presley
Babe Ruth
Superman
John Wayne

Home and Family
Betty Crocker
Couch
Flea Market
Log Cabin
Muppets
Patchwork Quilt
Rosie the Riveter
Scrapbook
Suburbia
Tara
Tupperware

GUIDE TO RELATED TOPICS   xiii

Wal-Mart
Whistler's Mother

Law

Courtroom Trial
Gun

Leisure, Travel, and Pilgrimage

Coney Island
James Dean
Flea Market
Gettysburg
Halloween Costume
Kodak Camera
Las Vegas
Lorraine Motel
Mount Rushmore
NASCAR's Bristol Motor Speedway
Niagara Falls
Elvis Presley
Railroad
Route 66
Stadium
Video Game
Vietnam Veterans Memorial

Literature

Beats
Ernest Hemingway
MAD Magazine
Tara
Henry David Thoreau
Zipper

Masculinity

Bear
Boy Scout Knife
Ernest Hemingway
Jack Nicholson
Robot
Sports Bar
Viagra
John Wayne

Medicine

Emergency Room
Viagra

Music

Banjo
Beats
Johnny Cash
Ray Charles
Bob Dylan
Grateful Dead
Jimi Hendrix
Loretta Lynn
Madonna
Elvis Presley
Tupac Shakur

Myth

Alamo
Amish
Daniel Boone
Boy Scout Knife
James Dean
Gettysburg
Hollywood
Indian Scout
Jessica Lynch
Route 66
Tupac Shakur
Spaceship
Tara
Henry David Thoreau
Underground Railroad
Oprah Winfrey
Witch

Nature

Bear
Daniel Boone
Dinosaur
Horse
Indian Scout
Niagara Falls

Olmsted Park
Henry David Thoreau

Race and Ethnicity
Alamo
Muhammad Ali
Banjo
Beats
Johnny Cash
Ray Charles
George Armstrong Custer
Jimi Hendrix
Indian Scout
Martin Luther King, Jr.
Evel Knievel
Lorraine Motel
Jessica Lynch
Mexican-American Border
Walter Payton
Tupac Shakur
Tattoo
Underground Railroad
Oprah Winfrey
Tiger Woods

Radio and Television
Lucille Ball
Johnny Carson
Julia Child
Emergency Room
Rush Limbaugh
Muppets
Oscar
Superman
Oprah Winfrey

Religion and Spirituality
Amish
Emergency Room
Billy Graham
Grateful Dead
Guardian Angel
Audrey Hepburn
Martin Luther King, Jr.

Poster Child
Witch

Science and Technology
Bomb
Cell Phone
Computer Chip
George Armstrong Custer
Dinosaur
Albert Einstein
Emergency Room
Gun
Charles A. Lindbergh
Niagara Falls
Polyester
Railroad
Robot
Spaceship
Tractor
Video Game
Wright Brothers
Zipper

Social Class, Sophistication, and Style
Antiperspirant
Fred Astaire
Couch
Joan Crawford
Audrey Hepburn
Hollywood
Miss Manners
Polyester
Tattoo

Sports
Muhammad Ali
Ford Mustang
Horse
Evel Knievel
NASCAR's Bristol Motor
    Speedway
Walter Payton
Babe Ruth

GUIDE TO RELATED TOPICS

Sports Bar
Stadium
Tiger Woods

War

Bomb
George Armstrong Custer
Gettysburg
GI
Gun
Indian Scout
Jessica Lynch
Rosie the Riveter
Vietnam Veterans Memorial

Preface

We can best introduce you to these entries by giving you the same description we sent to their writers, when asking them to contribute to the collection. We invited them to interpret a cultural "icon" in an essay for a wide readership, from casual readers in public libraries, to investigating students, to scholars researching patterns in American culture and popular culture. We asked for the essay to make cultural scholarship accessible to the general reader, and also to add to critical understanding of the subject and of its "iconic" character.

The term "icon"—as we pointed out to the writers—is now used everywhere. It has mushroomed in popular usage, coinciding with the growth of interest in popular culture and of popular culture studies. What does it mean when we say some person, place, or thing is an icon? We have speculated about features of people, places, and things commonly characterized as iconic. We have also tested lists of "icons" with various age groups, looking for patterns of recognition, understanding, agreement, and disagreement. We have surveyed scholarly research, studied the programs of recent conferences on popular culture and other fields, and attended many presentations, attempting to identify the popular phenomena which are now commanding attention, and to locate the best understandings of this attention. In the process of these discussions and research, we realized that "icons" generate strong reactions.

We gave writers our hypothesis about features that we came to associate with an icon. These qualities include the following:

—An icon generates strong responses; people identify with it, or against it; and the differences often reflect generational distinctions. Marilyn Monroe, for instance, carries meanings distinctly different for people who are in their teens and twenties than for people in their sixties and older.

—An icon stands for a group of related things and values. John Wayne, for example, images the cowboy and traditional masculinity, among many other associations, including conservative politics.

—An icon has roots in historical sources, as various as folk culture, science, and commerce; it may supersede a prior icon; it reflects events or forces of its time. The log cabin has endured as an influential American icon, with meanings and associations evolving from our colonial past through the present.

—An icon can be reshaped within its own image, or extended in updated images by its adaptations or imitators. The railroads and trains, for instance, have shifted from carrying associations of high technology and the modern, to conveying ideas of nostalgia and a retreat from high technology.

—An icon moves or communicates widely, often showing the breakdown of former distinctions between popular culture and art or historic American culture. Icons like "Whistler's Mother" and the patchwork quilt are both revered as high art and widely accepted as popular art.

—An icon can be employed in a variety of ways, and used in visual art, music, film, and other media. For example, references in text or graphics to Ernest Hemingway or to Mount Rushmore or to the gun add meanings to every artistic text in which they appear.

—An icon is usually successful in commerce. Every advertising campaign, every corporation, hopes to become the next Mickey Mouse, the next Las Vegas, the next Golden Arches.

In our invitations to the writers, then, we suggested that the essays should reveal an icon's origins and changes, its influences, and the meaning of its enduring appeal—and repulsive reactions. When the articles began to arrive, though, we found we had underestimated either the subjects or the authors, or both; the essays were fascinating for many reasons we had not anticipated. We have been surprised by the insights they offer, and pleased to learn much that we had not envisioned having importance, complexity, or charm. And as their numbers mounted to over a hundred, we continued to be surprised by what we learned, and increasingly curious, as the entries touched on related topics from differing viewpoints, and added to the attractive qualities of icons—and to their dubious qualities as well.

These items we call icons hold a depth of significance we had not foreseen; it's fortunate we did not attempt or request any definition of an icon, or of its appeal, because neither would have held true. We sought, instead, the range of meanings an icon holds for people. As we see it still, this range of meanings, plus people's disagreements about an icon's meanings and value, reflect the cultural resonance it holds, and provide the best indication of its character. In other words, a contest of possible meanings and values makes up the drawing power of an icon, and makes it dynamic, rather than static, evolving, rather than securely definable.

There are more icons than any three volumes could address. In making a selection, we have aimed at a representation of various kinds of icons, so that the entries treat principles and modes of differing types. Our arrangement of the icons into alphabetical order illustrates our idea of the equal, or random, relationship among icons, and the curious fact that out-of-the-way places,

PREFACE

and small items we take for granted, influence popular thinking as importantly as the hero or celebrity who is touted by media. The entries themselves illustrate a variety of approaches for understanding icons. Indeed, our basic purpose is to furnish useful demonstrations of how to "read" cultural artifacts, to make readers alert to such significant things around us, and to enable readers to interpret them.

Thus these writings should generate thought, not necessarily agreement. They are entries with lively variations in style and method, and often the writer rhetorically "animates" the subject. They present distinct viewpoints, but in ways that are thought-provoking and inviting of response. Icons may well be controversial in their very basis; these entries, separately, and much more in their convergences, should stir question and even dispute.

The entries provide a fund of themes and perspectives for study and scholarship. Among them are intriguing suggestions of possible patterns and modes among icons of differing types, related to such important concepts as identity, generational differences, and myths. Linking many of the essays are intersections of meaning, and webs of associations. To those who are or will be engaged in the study of icons, this collection will bring a wealth of resources, and make them accessible as subjects in the index.

Acknowledgments

We first thank the many people who shared their thoughts and opinions about icons with us as we developed our plans for this collection. These discussions—including the arguments—increased our understanding, stirred our curiosity, and encouraged our efforts to gather together the best voices for a worthwhile forum on the large but mysterious presence in our midst of those people, places, and things we call iconic.

We thank our writers for the help, encouragements, and pleasures they have given us. Some of the contributors we have known through many years of hearing their presentations at popular culture and literary conferences, and sharing critical discussions with them. Others we found as we searched for current writing, scholarship, and teaching on iconic subjects, or in the disciplines which study them; through subsequent conversations with them, we've enjoyed getting to know some very lively and original thinkers. We're appreciative that popular culture scholars ranging from the long-established to new contributors joined efforts with us, so the collection represents the flourishing vitality of popular culture studies. Our energy for this project has not flagged, because we kept hearing, from old associates and new, that they themselves looked forward to the finished volumes with great interest.

We are grateful to Eric Levy for asking us to consider editing a collection of essays on icons, whose suggestion started our thinking and investigation. Eric was then at Greenwood Press, where he was editor of *The Greenwood Guide to American Popular Culture*, essays on research and bibliography co-edited by M. Thomas Inge and Dennis Hall. Eric has moved to the Wesleyan University Press. Since then we have enjoyed having the attentive help of Lisa Pierce with the many questions and issues involved in bringing this collection to publication.

To the University of Louisville English Department and its chair, Susan M. Griffin, we are very grateful for the moral and material support they have given our efforts.

The University of Louisville Ekstrom Library and its librarians have provided help at every stage of our research on icons and preparation of this collection.

The Louisville Free Public Library has furnished many resources necessary for surveying and selecting popular icons, for finding books and articles with perspectives on them, and for fact-checking all kinds of matters from quotations to bibliographies. Their interlibrary loan and information services librarians have given us especially timely, needed help. Ruth Ellen Flint, information specialist at the Highlands–Shelby Park Branch, deserves our special thanks, because we took to her our problems of the most esoteric matters of fact, and she has never yet failed to devise a stratagem for finding the obscure detail which so often has seemed the key to correctness.

Alamo

Richard R. Flores

The Alamo in San Antonio, Texas, the site of the 1836 siege and battle between the army of Mexican general and president Santa Anna and the Texas forces led by William B. Travis, is the most visited site in Texas and one of the structures most established in American cultural memory. The stone façade of this early-eighteenth-century Spanish mission has struck an impression around the world, joining an idealized version of courage and valor to an even more idealized image of American heroism. The retellings of the Alamo story in song, art, theater, film, and television programs have contributed to making the names of Travis, Jim Bowie, and Davy Crockett, along with Crockett's coonskin cap, recognizable around the globe.

Film and television have played a major role in the popularization of the Alamo. From D. W. Griffith's production *Martyrs of the Alamo* in 1915 to John Wayne's 1960 version, as well as the recent film with Billy Bob Thornton as Davy Crockett, the story has been reproduced anew for every succeeding generation. Walt Disney's 1954–1955 television series *Davy Crockett: King of the Wild Frontier*, which reached fanatical heights of audience enthusiasm in only a few months, served to imprint Crockett and his death at the Alamo in the American imagination beyond even Disney's expectation. In creating a key site of American cultural memory, the shaping of the story of the Alamo has resulted in collapsing fact and fiction, and paring the complex events of 1836 into a myth of American liberty, heroism, and sacrifice.

The collapsing of historical narratives with those of myth is not in itself an issue: such blurring occurs in all kinds of myth-making. It is the effect of this blurring that, in the case of the Alamo, is of concern. One reason for concern is that this tale of freedom and valor emerged from a larger occurrence of racial bias that rendered Mexicans irreverent, contemptuous, and socially debased, in a widespread stereotype. That is, the myth of the Alamo took a political conflict of 1836 and turned it into a racial story to address the events of the early 1900s. This racialized story then served as the popular idiom through which the Alamo achieved its success in tourism and entertainment.

Finally, an element in the Battle of the Alamo controversy that seems quite overlooked is the men who died. The popular version claims that this was a battle between Texans and Mexicans, a categorization that merits special scrutiny because it collapses ethnic and political categories into an ambiguous binary. Ethnically, those who fought on the "Texan" side were anything but a homogeneous lot. There were thirteen native-born Texans in the group, eleven of whom were of Mexican descent. Of those remaining, forty-one were born in Europe, two were Jews, two were black, and the remainder were Americans from other states in the United States. Intermarriage between Anglo-Americans and Mexicans was common, with that of Jim Bowie and Ursula Verimendi, the daughter of the Mexican governor, serving as the closest case at the Alamo. On the Mexican side, Santa Anna's forces, as well as the local population in San Antonio, were an amalgamation of former Spanish citizens, now Mexican, Spanish-Mexican criollos and mestizos; and Santa Anna had conscripted numerous indigenous young men from the interior of Mexico to assist in battle. Politically, one has only to recognize that this was Mexican territory and "foreigners" were not citizens of Texas but affiliates of the Mexican state. Finally, one cannot forget that prominent Mexican citizens fought on both sides, dividing their allegiance along political and ideological lines. Neither side were the ethnically or nationally circumscribed identities popularized by the collective memory of this battle.

The historical events of 1836 are critical for a more rounded understanding of the Alamo. But it is the myth of the Alamo, I suggest, that offers more insight into the role of the Alamo as icon. It is the myth that captured the American imagination and that served as fictional fodder to nourish a growing nationalist ideology in the early twentieth century, and it is the story of the 1915 silent film.

Martyrs of the Alamo begins by introducing itself as a drama about the events that led to the independence of Texas, and making claims to its historical accuracy. Let me be clear. I am not expecting this film to follow the contours of the events of 1836. What interests me is how this film detracts from the past and, more importantly, why.

The film opens, incorrectly, with Santa Anna already in San Antonio, giving General Cos instructions as Santa Anna prepares to journey South to Mexico. It then moves to a depiction of the local Mexican population, both soldiers and civilians, as ill-mannered, slovenly, drunken, and lusting after women who walk before them. We find a Mexican officer stopping an Anglo woman, verbally accosting her and making suggestive advances. Upon returning home, the woman reports this to her husband, who proceeds to locate the Mexican officer and, after an exchange of words, shoot him dead. As a result of this incident, Santa Anna confiscates all weapons from the Anglo population, except for a cache of arms hidden beneath the floor by David Crockett and Jim Bowie.

These two projections—the maltreatment of Anglo women by Mexican men and the confiscation of weapons by Santa Anna—are depicted as the cause for

Crockett, Bowie, and other Anglo settlers to plot the taking of the Alamo. The opportunity to enact such a plan arises when, in the wake of Santa Anna's departure, the local Mexican population, including the military, take to the streets celebrating, drinking, and chasing women in wild debauchery. Finding this to be an opportune moment, Crockett, Bowie, and their followers gather their concealed weapons, storm the streets, take the Mexican army by surprise, and seize control of the city. With the Texans in charge, the local Mexican citizenry comport themselves very differently. After the text flashes "Under the new regime…" the film displays a scene where Mexicans are taking off their hats in deference to women, greeting each other and Anglos in a sober and respectful manner, and generally acting in a "civilized" fashion.

It is notable that up to this point, and throughout the remainder, the movie depicts an ethnic and racial divide between Texans and Mexicans. Although historians have demonstrated that those who fought on the Texan side were immigrants from both the United States and Europe as well as Mexican citizens, according to *Martyrs of the Alamo*, the conflict occurred between "white" Texans and "brown" Mexicans. The film's one exception is Bowie's "slave," portrayed by a black-faced actor who dutifully sits beside the ailing defender.

In the movie, General Cos, banished from San Antonio, reconnects with Santa Anna, who then calls his generals together to plan an attack on the Alamo. However, unsuspected by the Mexicans, "Deaf" Smith, one of the Texan leaders, is hiding in the bush, from where he hears the entire plan. He carries this information back to Bowie, Crockett, and now also Travis, who has been sent by Sam Houston to take charge of the former mission; preparations are made for Santa Anna's arrival and the battle.

After Santa Anna arrives and the actual siege of the Alamo begins, the Mexicans are portrayed as the more powerful, impersonal, villainous, and yet at times even inept, force. Perhaps one of the more disturbing images appears when the Mexicans have made their way into the Alamo. During a scene of hand-to-hand fighting, the scene shifts to a small, unarmed boy cowering behind a cannon, taking cover from the fighting around him. From nowhere appears the arm of a Mexican soldier, grabbing the youth by his neck and pulling him out of view. The next frame shows the dead corpse of the boy flying across the room, landing against the far wall.

The last scene I want to briefly address depicts Santa Anna camping near San Jacinto just before Houston's forces arrive. The film shows the Mexicans in their tents sleeping, drinking, and totally unprepared for battle. The text makes note of Santa Anna as a "drug fiend" who also engages in "orgies." With this, the film cuts to Santa Anna in his tent, in a drug-induced stupor, surrounded by scantily-clad dancing women. After a lengthy view of this image, the film shows the forces of Sam Houston arriving and Santa Anna, too inebriated even to hold his sword, fleeing for his life.

With Houston's forces shouting "Remember the Alamo," Santa Anna, hiding in a row of shrubs, is captured. Sam Houston, deciding the Mexican general is more valuable alive than dead, stops several soldiers from placing a noose around his neck and proceeds to sign a treaty with him that sets Texas free from Mexican rule.

How are we to understand this early film on the Alamo? In *Martyrs*, the impetus for Texas to secede from the Mexican Union is portrayed not as a political act but a social one, based on the depiction of Mexicans as disrespectful, uncivil, promiscuous, and sexually dangerous to Anglo women. Like the projection of arrogant reconstruction era blacks in Griffith's *Birth of a Nation*, these Mexicans, both citizens and soldiers, appear socially reprehensible and in need of control by Anglo rule. The film's biased representation results in the negation of history, as political difference is collapsed into social conduct, sexual morality, and representations of gender. Not only are Mexicans culturally to be feared in terms of future miscegenation, but their advances on Anglo women as objects of sexual desire require the saving presence of the Anglo male hero.

The fear of Mexicans that the movie implies extends to their behavior in regard to the norms of "civilized" warfare. The murder of the young boy cowering behind the cannon suggests unwarranted cruelty and accustomed savagery. Contrast this with the sparing of Santa Anna by Houston, as well as Cos's departure with sword in hand, and the noble character of the Anglo emerges quite clearly, in opposition. The portrayal of Mexicans as incapable of civil behavior posits their difference as the result of their social and cultural practice. It is Mexicans, according to this film, who are responsible for their particular plight in Texas.

The dominant narrative we find in this film, one that pits liberty-loving Texans against tyrannous Mexicans as the cause of the Battle of the Alamo, is incorrect, but it underlies today's accounts of the "hallowed ground" and "bastion of liberty" that range from histories to tourist promotions. Much earlier there were widely diverse stories of the choices made to remain in the Alamo, and of the men who made them. Moreover, the Alamo itself did not seem to stand as a hallowed bastion or even a site worth much interest until the 1890s. It was not tended or preserved, and became dilapidated; it was used for commercial purposes, for grain storage and even as a saloon. It became important for its significance to culture and history at last in the eyes of two women, who then campaigned to save it and give it public honor, and succeeded when the Texas Legislature purchased the property to entrust it to the care of the Daughters of the Republic of Texas in 1905.

For this change of attitude to happen, a new interpretation of the Alamo needed to emerge. A new historical vision of the place and its relationship to the surrounding culture developed, in response to changes that had occurred in Texas, and relevant to ideas and beliefs of modern Texas culture. The Alamo became a major icon early in the twentieth century because it responded to change by advancing a new mode of thinking, with a myth that appealed to people even far beyond Texas. How did this Alamo myth advance the changes in ideas and practices of this transition into twentieth-century modernism?

Tourists visiting the Alamo mission today. Courtesy of Shutterstock.

In brief, economic demands and needs changed radically in Texas with the introduction of the railroad in the 1880s, the closing of the range through barbed wire, and the beginning of industrial irrigation. The effects of these events saw Mexican workers and landowners lose status and jobs. The special skills of the Mexican ranch hand were becoming less important while the need for cheap labor to work newly irrigated land was increasing. Mexican workers and landowners, by 1900, became a landless class whose skilled labor was diminished if not obsolete.

These social and economic changes affected everyone. But the results of the alterations on the residents of the Mexican-origin community were disproportionate to their numbers. The Mexican and Mexican-American population of Texas experienced loss of status, economic stability, and rights during this period. For example, in 1850 over 60 percent of the Mexican-origin population in Texas were either landowners or skilled laborers. By 1900, this number hovered closer to 10 percent. With the arrival of the railroad, the skills of the Mexican vaquero—the foremost ranch workers in Texas—became nearly obsolete. Owners no longer needed to employ dozens of vaqueros to run their cattle north, and in their place hired only a handful of workers to get their cattle to the local depot. With irrigation, especially in deep South Texas, industrial farming required cheap and mobile workers. Mexicans were seen as the ideal population for this task.

The rebirth of the Alamo in 1905 coincides with the social changes going on in Texas. The mythic story of the Alamo that posits Mexicans as tyrannous and against liberty and freedom, those bedrocks of U.S. democratic ideals, serves to rationalize the Mexican community's increased segregation and economic erosion. The image of treacherous Mexicans produced by the myth of the Alamo story justified the racist establishment of Jim Crow segregation throughout Texas.

The myth of the Alamo that is represented in *Martyrs*, a myth constructed on the binary of good Texans versus evil Mexicans, or, in its least pejorative sense, the inaccurate representation of this history as one between Texans and Mexicans, has served as the foundation of all future tellings. The Disney stories of Crockett, artistic representations of the battle, and John Wayne's version of this story are all told through this same binary idiom. This mythic structure, one that collapses narrative features into a simple binary of us versus them, is one of the key reasons the Alamo as icon has been so popular. While Griffith's film tells the Alamo story as a means of exploiting and reproducing a racialized view of Mexicans, Wayne's film allows him to connect the Mexican threat to liberty with communism and the ideologies of the Cold War. For Griffith, Wayne, and the multiple other versions of this story, the Alamo as icon fosters a tale of American liberty and freedom against all odds and all enemies, regardless of the facts of history.

WORKS RECOMMENDED

Brear, Holly. *Inherit the Alamo*. Austin: U of Texas P, 1995.
Davis, William C. *Three Roads to the Alamo: The Lives and Fortunes of David Crockett, James Bowie, and William Barret Travis*. New York: HarperCollins, 1998.
De Zavala, Adina. *History and Legends of the Alamo and Other Missions In and Around San Antonio*. San Antonio: Privately published by the author. Rpt. edited and with an introduction by Richard R. Flores. Houston: Arte Público Press, 1996.
Flores, Richard R. *Remembering the Alamo: Memory, Modernity, and the Master Symbol*. Austin: U of Texas P, 2002.
Hardin, Stephen L. *Texian Iliad: A Military History of the Texas Revolution, 1835–1836*. Austin: U of Texas P, 1994.

Muhammad Ali

J. Peter Williams

When the April 1998 issue of *GQ* named their athlete of the century they printed his picture on their cover, but they felt no need to give their readers his name. The photograph of the most recognizable face on the planet was enough. They could have added that no other athlete, and likely no other public figure, more symbolized his time than Muhammad Ali.

Ali virtually defines the iconic: as well as any other individual, he "stands for" his historical period, which may be said to stretch from the time of John Kennedy to the onset of the Reagan era, from the period of individualism we loosely call the sixties to the shift, in the eighties, to a more corporate mindset. Like other icons who are also real people, however, Ali lived as a man as well as a symbol. He was always a performer, the lead in his own iconic drama, although it must be said that a role has seldom fit its player better.

Ali's career in the ring, like much great drama, has five acts. The first culminates in his initial defeat of Sonny Liston and his subsequent decision to change his name from Cassius Clay to Muhammad Ali; the climax of the second, after his suspension from boxing and his 3½-year absence from the sport, is his first loss, to Joe Frazier; the third act ends with Ali's spectacular victory over George Foreman in Africa, and the fourth with his defeat of Leon Spinks in their second fight, when Ali became the first heavyweight to hold the championship three times. Only in the final act does the story of the human individual diverge from myth. An aging athlete who stayed in the ring too long, Ali the individual was debilitated by Parkinson's Syndrome. As an icon, though, his final act could easily have been his best: his surprise appearance in Atlanta, when he held the torch that lit the Olympic flame.

Myth always trumps history. Although Ali himself is devoid of self-pity, some moralists might cluck at the sport that both made him and deprived him of coherent speech. Fortunately, however, we are here concerned not with the literal, but with the mythical, and, in this very real sense, the conclusion to Ali's drama cannot be called tragic.

Before his first fight with Sonny Liston, Cassius Clay seemed little more than an adolescent reveling in his first real spotlight, at times blustering like a bully, at others pretending to be terrified of the champion. As a result, when the match was finally scheduled for early 1964 in Miami, no one knew what to expect. At the weigh-in, Clay's eyes were fixed and glassy and he was so noisy and wild, once raising a fist and rushing Liston, that Morris Klein, the Commission's chairman, fined him $2,500. One reporter asked the Commission's doctor if Clay had been smoking "reefers," but the doctor said he just didn't know.

In retrospect, it's hard to see how easily everyone was so badly fooled. Clay had just invented the modern weigh-in, modeling his behavior—and he admitted this—on that of the flamboyant pro wrestler, Gorgeous George. He had posed for comic promotional photos with the Beatles just before the fight, and when one reporter begged for just one interview with Cassius when he wasn't onstage, Clay declined, saying that if the reporter wrote about what he was really like it would spoil his act. Clay was surprisingly blunt about his tactics. "When I become heavyweight champion, I probably will quit being a blabmouth," he said, asking if P. T. Barnum "could have been a great showman by saying nothing." Then he got serious. "My fighting is not an act," he said; "when I'm in the ring against an opponent, it's for real" (Bromberg).

The fight was every bit as one-sided as the writers had expected, but the dominant party was not the man they had picked. Clay's speed and reflexes so much outshone Sonny's that it became apparent after the first two rounds that Cassius's declarations had been more truthful than vain. Liston's frustration was turning to helpless rage, and he was cut so badly that he would later need six stitches. After six rounds, Sonny gave up. Sitting on his stool after the warning buzzer for round seven, watching the fresh and unhurt Clay standing and dancing in the corner opposite, he spat out his mouthpiece. Clay saw him do it and threw up his hands in victory.

After Clay won the fight, he was unemotional, even-tempered and calm, answering questions so quietly that reporters in the back row had to ask him to speak up. A few days later Clay discussed his tactics:

> It was an act, and I was quieter inside than all the suckers feeling sorry for me. And Liston, he was the biggest patsy of them all. When that doctor went along with it, saying I was deathly afraid of fighting, I was so happy I could have bust a gut laughing. (Bromberg)

All part of the plan; as with Prince Hal in Shakespeare's *Henry IV*, it turns out there had always been a *real* hero in that clown suit. Still, because Cassius had been a practitioner of hype for some time, why were normally skeptical journalists duped as easily as the Miami doctor and the Big Bear? Primarily, because most of them wanted to be.

In early 1964, the division of the country that we remember as the sixties had only just begun. Most adults who thought themselves responsible held the same dim view of a counter-culture still in its infancy as the reporter who wondered about "reefers" had of Clay. Almost everybody not only picked

Liston, but wanted him to win. Clay was viewed as a freak, just a Beatle with a haircut. One of the few writers who saw through Clay's deception was Leonard Schecter, who made the following perceptive comments:

> The weight of opinion against Clay has almost as much to do with his personality as with his ability. It's not a good thing to brag. Clay brags. Then there is the strong suspicion that Clay holds with the opinions of the Black Muslims. The revulsion in some quarters against the Beatles, noisy, irreverent, but basically decent young men, riding a tide of success, is similar to the reaction to Clay.

Schecter's remarks about the role Clay's image played in turning writers against him is very pertinent here; as the sixties began to grow increasingly volatile in the wake of the first Kennedy assassination, which had taken place very recently, different sides were being taken and new lines were being drawn. Liston had at first been considered an unpopular ex-convict; now he had become a popular champion for the first time, but only because he was opposed to Clay, who represented everything the threatened old order feared. Their fears were realized when, soon after becoming the new champ, Cassius made three announcements. Two of them can be summarized in the slogans of the sixties, even though this was not the precise language he used: "I want to do my own thing," and "Hell, no, I won't go." The third was that he had been a Black Muslim for about three months, or since roughly the time J.F.K. was killed. At first, in an interview in which he was photographed standing next to Malcolm X, he said his temporary name was Cassius X; a short while later, he said his permanent one would be Muhammad Ali.

This moment was arguably the most important event in the public life of the most prominent international athlete of the last part of the last century. What is *not* arguable is that it was the moment when the adult began to replace the teenager, when the icon began to supersede the individual. Put more accurately—and there is most truth in this—it was the

Muhammad Ali standing over a fallen Sonny Liston during their 1965 bout. Courtesy of the Library of Congress.

moment when that individual "came out," dropped his mask and, intuitively recognizing a certain destiny, put on the only attire that was ever designed to fit.

After he beat Liston, Clay had openly embraced Malcolm X; after he lost to Clay, Liston had said he hadn't felt so bad since he'd heard John Kennedy was killed, and you may remember that it was Malcolm X who called the J.F.K. assassination a case of "the chickens coming home to roost." To publicly ally yourself with Malcolm X a scant three months after the death of the Camelot president was impolitic; and Ali, who had been deferred from the draft because of his truly miserable math skills, was soon made eligible regardless. When he refused induction, claiming the status of a conscientious objector because of his Muslim faith, it took only twenty-four hours for the boxing authorities to strip him of his title and void his license; it would take nearly four years for our Supreme Court to advise us that we had punished someone for being, like so many others of his time, a sincere dissenter, and to convince skeptics (even black radicals like Amiri Baraka, who still called himself Leroi Jones) that his Islamic faith was genuine. By that time—at the end of Ali's Act II—there were few if any remaining who thought that the figure in question was *not* the iconic and legendary Muhammad Ali, and many who wondered if Cassius Clay had ever existed at all.

During the time he was out of the ring, Ali's iconic stature grew. The so-called counter-culture, by now healthier than ever, viewed him as the hero who had beaten not just everyone he'd ever faced in the ring, but also "The Man," the establishment that had tried to destroy his career. When he finally fought Joe Frazier for the title they had taken from him, "the fight" transcended sport; it was far more important on the symbolic level, a dramatic conflict between the old order and the new. Ali had not changed. He believed that blacks were not treated equally in our country, that the Vietnam War was a brutal mistake, and that Christianity in America tended more toward the hypocritical than the pious—and these were the same beliefs that had been espoused by Cassius Clay. The important difference was that, in the seven years since the Liston fight, Ali had been transformed from pariah to Galahad. The old guard that had run the country, made up of men like Richard Nixon, Spiro Agnew, and Chicago's Mayor Daley, had become as unpopular as the war itself and, like that war, was on the way out. Ali had not changed; the country had. Frazier, a change-resistant flag-waver, represented everything Ali had always fought, but he didn't see that now the country was in the other man's corner, and that the only place he could possibly win was in the ring.

Frazier did win, as everybody knows—or so it seemed at first. The war for the heart of the public had clearly been won by Ali, who had in the process also won a major victory for the anti-war movement in the country's ultimate court.

Although Ali lost no iconic prestige whatsoever in the first Frazier fight, and although he may even have gained some symbolic stature, the individual athlete had lost, and he knew it. In fact, from here on in, the boxer Ali would be far less dominant in the ring. His three fights with Ken Norton (the first of which he lost) all went the distance, as did the second Frazier fight, and in the third, the "Thrilla in Manila," Frazier could not come out for the last round. Just before that third Frazier fight, however, Ali fought one more iconic match. Again, he represented the new individualistic culture; again his opponent, George Foreman, stood for a complacent and uncritical status quo.

But there was a difference. Until now, Ali had represented the democratic values he saw eroded in his country; the only thing left was to stand for *all* the people, and particularly perhaps for the disadvantaged and ignored, for what Westerners patronize as the Third World. When Ali went to Zaire it was as if the great statue in New York harbor had come itself to the tired and the poor, or like Mohammed going to the mountain. In his third great symbolic fight, Ali publicized, embraced, and became a part of the entire globe.

Even in Zaire, however, Ali was, as always, the same man he had always been. It was Ali who thought up the phrase "the rumble in the jungle," and he also had the idea, which was never carried out, of entering the ring carrying three flags, those of Zaire, the Organization of African Unity, and the U.N., which would have been an obvious comment on the American flag Foreman waved at the 1968 Olympics. Before the fight, Ali said, with the eloquent simplicity of the man of the whole world he had become, "I feel at home."

After Ali's great upset victory, the writers realized more than ever that they were in the presence of a hero in the old, Greek sense. Larry Merchant, saying he'd watched "a steak jump up at the butcher," called the fight sublime and gave Ali the ultimate quality of godhead, immortality; six years after losing the title, Merchant said, "Ali reseated himself forever more" on the heavyweight throne. After the knockout, as Ali drove the forty miles to his quarters, dawn was breaking, and he remarked a number of times that it seemed right to be coming out of darkness into light.

The Ali–Foreman fight established the myth of Muhammad Ali utterly. After the fight, he became, certainly, the greatest sports legend in American history and, possibly, in modern history itself. After the knockout, Pete Bonvente of *Newsweek* went in search of the most recognizable face on the planet, the athlete of the century and man of the epoch, and, forty miles later, he found him in the most fervent and significant of all his incarnations, the man of the people:

> It was five in the morning, and Ken Regan [a photographer] said, "Let's drive out to N'Sele." Two hours after we started, we got to N'Sele. There was no press. The entourage was gone. We went over to Ali's cottage, and three hours after the greatest victory of his life, Muhammad Ali was sitting on a stoop, showing a magic trick to a group of black children. It was a rope trick, where the rope is cut in half and then it's suddenly back together again. And it was hard to tell who was having a better time, Ali or the children. All I could think was, I don't care what anyone says, there'll never be anyone like him again. (Hauser 280)

In the eleven years before he kayoed Foreman, Ali had fought out of country ten times (Toronto, Frankfurt, Zurich, Tokyo, Vancouver, Dublin, Djakarta, and three fights in London); for the seven years after and including the Foreman fight, and as if to reinforce his growing image as an international icon, he fought away from home six more times (Kinshaha, Kuala Lumpur, Quezon City, Puerto Rico, Munich, and Nassau). There was evidence, however, that the enormous success of the mythical idol may have convinced the fighter who had been so successful for nearly two decades that he needn't take his opponents all that seriously. That evidence became compelling when in 1978, just after turning 36, he lost his title to Leon Spinks.

All the athlete's loss did, however—and by then we were all tempted to say "of course"—was set up another comeback for the icon. In New Orleans, six months later, Ali won an easy decision over Spinks. Although there was none of the powerful social symbolism associated with Clay–Liston, Frazier–Ali, or Ali–Foreman, it won't stretch a point to say that this fight also had extra-pugilistic significance, if on a less important level. Spinks, whose success in dethroning "The Greatest" had certainly gone to his head, spent a plural number of nights away from his training camp, evidently trysting, and when he was in town he was driven around in a white stretch limo playing rap at top volume, protected by his bodyguard, the as yet little-known Mr. T. Conversely Ali, who never partied and who knew he had to get serious, trained hard, and the fight ended up an illustration of the failure of excess when confronted by a solid work ethic.

The story should end right there, in perfect symmetry, but we all know it doesn't, at least not as involves Ali the individual, the human, the actor in the drama who made the sad mistake of thinking he was closer to his indomitable image than he actually was. Ali fought twice more, once with Larry Holmes and once with Trevor Berbick, when he was so badly pummelled that—many think—it caused the Parkinson's Syndrome which afflicts him now. But neither does the saga of the mythical Ali end here. If we want to consider the fitting finale for Ali the icon—and this is undoubtedly unsafe, because he may have many acts left to perform—it must be the moment, fifteen years after those sad last fights, when, holding a torch in a visibly trembling right hand, he appeared at the top of the Atlanta stadium, like the god out of the machine, and lit that Olympic flame.

WORKS CITED AND RECOMMENDED

Ali, Muhammad, with Richard Durham. *The Greatest*. New York: Ballantine, 1975.
Bromberg, Lester. *New York World-Telegram & Sun* 29 Feb. 1964.
Hauser, Thomas. *Muhammad Ali*. New York: Simon and Schuster, 1991.
Merchant, Larry. *New York Post* 30 Oct. 1974.
Schecter, Leonard. *New York Post* 25 Feb. 1964.

Amish

David L. Weaver-Zercher

In 1989, President George H. W. Bush traveled to Lancaster County, Pennsylvania, to publicize his administration's "war on drugs." Accompanied by Attorney General Richard Thornburgh and drug czar William Bennett, the president first delivered an anti-drug speech to a suburban Lancaster high school, then ventured deeper into the countryside, where he and his entourage met with a dozen Old Order Amish and Mennonite church leaders. The meeting, according to Bush, was aimed at learning from these Old Order leaders "how your community manages to stave off the scourge of drugs." Transcripts from the meeting reveal that Bush administration officials did most of the talking and, correspondingly, probably learned little about Old Order Amish socialization practices. They did, however, succeed at making image points. The next morning, newspapers across the country carried an Associated Press photograph of a stately President Bush striding past a horse and buggy tied to a hitching post—a hitching post that, at the request of the president's staff, had been moved to a prominent, photogenic location, replete with rolling farmland in the background.

That a sitting American president would make a pilgrimage to Lancaster County to sit at the feet of Amish gurus—and, in a calculated way, capture the image on film—reveals the iconic nature of the Old Order Amish. So too does the media frenzy that exploded in the summer of 1998, when two Amish men were arrested for possessing cocaine with the intent to sell it to their Amish friends. In a matter of days, the story of their arrests had traveled around the world. As evidence of its cultural cachet, the story quickly became fodder for jokes on the nation's late-night talk shows (among his "Top Ten Signs Your Amish Teen is in Trouble," David Letterman included, "Sometimes he stays in bed 'til after 6 A.M."). As the story made its rounds, some observers complained that it was unfair to make such a fuss over the arrest of two 20-year-olds selling cocaine. The arrests would hardly have been noticed, they said, had the drug dealers been Presbyterians, Roman Catholics, or atheists. These critics were right: the newsworthiness of the story had little to do with the gravity of the crime, and everything to do with the fact that it was committed by members of a religious community that, in many Americans' minds, successfully avoided the indiscretions of modern American life. In that sense, President Bush's politicized employment of the Amish was the flipside—and perhaps even a contributor—to the media coverage surrounding the 1998 Amish drug bust. Few things make for better news stories than the sordid activities of a venerated icon.

It is ironic that the Old Order Amish, a religious community that shuns publicity (and actively discourages its members from seeking it), has become a renowned American icon, one that can be used both to depict the integrity of close-knit, rural communities and to illustrate their pitfalls. Historically speaking, this iconic status is a relatively recent phenomenon; despite a history that reaches back 300 years, the Amish have been renowned cultural icons only since the mid-twentieth century. The process by which the Amish achieved their iconic status as hardworking, morally virtuous, frontier-like farmers—in sum, hearty Americans—tells us some things about the Amish. It tells us even more about the trajectory of American culture in the late nineteenth and twentieth centuries.

The term "Amish" refers to a variety of small, sectarian Christian groups that trace their origins to Jacob Amman, a late-seventeenth-century Swiss-Alsatian Anabaptist. By that time, the Anabaptist movement was over 150 years old, first emerging in the 1520s during the Protestant Reformation. The Anabaptists, whose designation "ana-baptist" refers to their practice of "rebaptizing" one another as adult believers, sought to push other Protestant reformers to make more radical reforms to the sixteenth-century church. The prototypical example of this push came in Zurich, Switzerland, where youthful followers of reformer Ulrich Zwingli encouraged their mentor to abandon the church's tradition of baptizing infants. When Zwingli refused their demand, his disaffected followers moved ahead, rebaptizing one another to symbolize their break with the Protestant mainstream.

This act of adult baptism, performed in 1525, was met with stiff opposition, not only by church leaders like Zwingli, but also by government officials who sought to maintain a cohesive Christian society. The Anabaptists were quickly branded heretics and, in many regions of Europe, were forced to recant their views or face imprisonment, torture, and even death.

A poster of the Amish to promote Pennsylvania, ca. 1940. Courtesy of the Library of Congress.

Eventually thousands of Anabaptists were martyred, but many who survived continued to pursue their radical form of Christianity. Most Anabaptists came to see their powerlessness as a virtue, citing Jesus Christ as their model for responding to persecution nonviolently. Three centuries later, contemporary Anabaptists—who now carry the names "Mennonite" (for sixteenth-century leader Menno Simons), "Amish" (for seventeenth-century leader Jacob Amman), or "Brethren"—continue to espouse adult baptism and nonviolence, beliefs they sustain by pointing to Jesus' example.

The Amish, then, comprise one particular strand of Anabaptist Christianity. But what sets them apart from other Anabaptists? Here it is instructive to consider the concerns Jacob Amman first voiced in the 1690s. According to Amman, too many Swiss Anabaptists had become lax in their practice of the Christian faith. Church leaders in particular, he said, had lost the will to enact appropriate discipline within their flocks. Invoking earlier Anabaptist precedents for shunning wayward church members—that is, excommunicating unrepentant sinners and limiting social interactions with them—Amman and his followers demanded that these leaders reinvigorate "the ban." When Swiss Anabaptist leaders rejected the Ammanists' demand, in 1693, the Amish church was born.

Over the centuries, this thoroughgoing commitment to church discipline has continued to set the Amish apart from other Christian groups, including most other Anabaptist groups. Moreover, Amish communities have tended to produce longer, more determinate lists of lifestyle expectations than have other Christian churches. These lifestyle expectations, ranging from dress and grooming requirements (e.g., beards sans moustaches for married men) to technological constraint (e.g., refusal to hook into electric power lines) to various sorts of cultural resistance (e.g., retention of their Pennsylvania German dialect), when combined with an ardent commitment to church discipline, have given rise to distinctive religious communities that manifest a high degree of uniformity in belief and practice.

More than being *uniform*, however, many of these Amish practices became strikingly *visible* on the North American cultural landscape. Generally speaking, the visible eccentricity of Amish communities is a relatively late development, the roots of which can be traced to two contrasting but interrelated developments in late nineteenth-century America. On the one hand, ever larger segments of American society partook of the fruits of progress, many of which were technological. On the other hand, some Anabaptist communities, including many Amish communities, chose to reject those fruits. Over time, a significant lifestyle chasm developed between "Old Order" Anabaptist groups and their more progressive neighbors, including progressive Anabaptist groups. For even as other residents of rural America embraced motorized cars and tractors, the Old Orders continued to drive horse-drawn buggies and plows. Similarly, even as most rural Americans plugged into the electric power grid and public telephone service, the Old Orders opted for less technologically sophisticated ways of life. Not least, the

Old Order Amish remained overwhelmingly rural, forgoing the allurements of America's middle class, including suburban living. In response, popular fascination with the Old Order Amish grew, as did the list of newspaper and magazine articles describing the Amish and their "queer" ways.

Some onlookers interpreted Amish cultural resistance to progress as the last gasp of a dying religious culture. In 1937, for instance, the *New York Times* ran a piece entitled "Amishmen Battle to Keep Drab Life." This article, which appeared during an attempt by Lancaster County Amish leaders to resist school consolidation in favor of one-room schooling, was followed by an editorial predicting that the Amish children who attended these homey, one-room schools would soon be "big industrialists" themselves. In other words, the *Times*'s cultural prognosticators recognized the Amish were fighting to sustain their traditional way of life, but they forecast a quick surrender to progress's cultural authority. The Old Order Amish not only proved these prognosticators wrong, but they shattered their predictions with a degree of cultural vitality and numerical growth that, even now, shows no signs of abating.

Still, as impressive as Old Order numerical growth has been, it pales in comparison to the growth of their renown. Indeed, it is arguable that the Amish are one of the most recognizable religious groups in contemporary America. The 1985 movie *Witness*, in which Harrison Ford plays a Philadelphia policeman forced to go undercover on an Amish farm, contributed heavily to this renown. Decades before *Witness* hit the big screen, however, the Amish's transformation from a little known religious sect to an American

A typical Amish buggy in Ohio. Courtesy of Shutterstock.

icon was well underway. In the 1950s, for instance, Amish-themed tourism became a prominent business in Lancaster County, Pennsylvania, an enterprise that has continued to grow in Lancaster County and has since spread to other Amish-populated regions of the United States. In 1955, Amish characters made their debut in a Broadway musical, *Plain and Fancy*. More recently, Amish characters have appeared on network television shows, television commercials and print advertisements (many of which sell products Amish people are not allowed to own or use), romance novels, internet sites, and documentary films. In 2004, the Amish graduated to reality television: a series entitled "Amish in the City" featured six disaffected Amish youth living with six "city kids" in an ultra-hip house in the Hollywood Hills. The predictability of the show's premise—would these Amish youth return to their Amish communities, or would they choose instead the ways of the world—did little to stem its popularity.

The title of the reality show, "Amish in the City," provides some clues to the iconic nature of the Amish. In actuality, Amish people are not averse to spending time in cities, particularly those in proximity to their Amish settlements. At the same time, the Amish have been, and continue to be, rural people. Thus, the popular conception of the Amish, although sometimes overdrawn, is essentially correct: the Amish do not belong in the city. They are rural people, and they embody—in our imagination, if not always in reality—the best qualities of North American rural life. In fact, the employment of the Amish in popular discourse participates in a tradition that long predates North American rural life, a tradition that stretches back to the Roman poet Virgil, whose "pastoral" writings idealized rural settings as places of peace, tranquility, and moral virtue.

Cultural historians have effectively chronicled this longstanding affection for rural life, as well as the corresponding assumption that rural living successfully counters the ills of the city (e.g., Smith, Marx). Virgil is perhaps best known for fostering this pastoral ideal in which humans live in close harmony with nature, enjoy nature's bounties, and experience the tranquility and existential satisfaction that is supposedly absent from economically stratified, morally corrupt cities. Renaissance writers reiterated Virgil's concerns, as did eighteenth-century English advocates of "country ideology," which "set the country in opposition to the metropolis as the natural seat of all that was right and good" (Walbert). In eighteenth-century America, Thomas Jefferson became the most articulate advocate of this sort of thinking. America will remain virtuous, Jefferson wrote, only as long as it remains "chiefly agricultural," but when Americans "get piled upon one another in large cities, as in Europe, they will become corrupt as in Europe" (qtd. in Walbert).

Even as cultural historians have noted this strong affection for rural living, they have also observed its selective view of rural life. It is, in essence, a nostalgic vision, emerging most strongly when rural life is being overrun by urbanizing forces (Lasch). As with other expressions of nostalgia, longings for rural life rarely undertake a realistic assessment of rural existence, forgetting (or at least underemphasizing) the back-breaking toil required to produce crops, the stench of farm animals, and the general brutishness of nature. In addition, nostalgia for the country tends to forget that selfishness, economic oppression, and intense family squabbles are not restricted to the metropolis. Nevertheless, truths such as these are often obscured by the pastoral mythology, which tends to sell better in the marketplace of ideas. Indeed, the sale of nostalgic views of American rural life has long been a thriving enterprise in the United States, an enterprise that continues apace with Jeanette Oke prairie romances, "country" decorating themes, and ranching vacations for suburbanites.

America's continuing regard for the Amish—a regard that blossomed only in the twentieth century, as the family farm succumbed to big business—similarly reveals the potency of the pastoral ideal in contemporary America. Tourists who travel to Amish Country express a desire to witness life "as it was meant to be," which they find in the Amish as they work their small-scale farms. Some tourists endeavor to learn about the intricacies of Amish life, exploring the religious and sociological underpinnings of Amish culture. But in the final analysis, it is the pastoral ideal associated with the Amish that attracts most visitors to Amish regions of Pennsylvania, Ohio, and Indiana. That many Amish people now make their livings away from the farm (in Northern Indiana, many Amish men now work in factories) has done little to stem this consumer interest in the Amish. As long as *some* Amish people continue to tend their small, family farms, giving tourists a picturesque glimpse of the pastoral ideal, the Amish will maintain their iconic status in the American imagination.

At the same time, the high esteem in which the Amish are held will continue to provide a fertile context for demythologizers to do their work. In other words, as long as the Amish are employed to maintain the myth of the pastoral, those who wish to puncture that myth will be able to do so. The drug bust story of 1998, which revealed that the Amish had not successfully resisted "the scourge of drugs"; the 2002 documentary film *Devil's Playground*, which reiterated that same point with stunning footage from Amish barn parties; and *True Stories of the X-Amish*, a book that recounts the experiences of people who found their Amish communities harsh and oppressive—what these media offerings share in common is their myth-shattering content. If the Amish did not function as an icon for the pastoral ideal, these myth busters would have no story to tell—or, at the very least, would have far fewer consumers interested in hearing their stories.

An Amish father with his two children at a craft fair in Ohio. Courtesy of Shutterstock.

In sum, the Amish function in the American imagination as hearty, virtuous ruralists, representing what many Americans imagine to be the essence of the American past. They are in essence a saving remnant, possessing the qualities that, according to Thomas Jefferson, would make America great, qualities that (again, according to Jefferson) America forsakes at its peril (Weaver-Zercher). To be sure, even a little scratching beneath the surface reveals that the Amish are not very "American" at all. They look askance at the latest technologies, refuse to bow to Hollywood and Wall Street, and even refuse to participate in the military. Still, the rural existence they embody, often in striking ways, reminds many contemporary Americans, truthfully or not, of what most Americans used to be. That some who comprise this saving remnant would fall from grace not only makes for good newspaper stories, it also undergirds the widely held belief that the Amish *are* something other: a remnant of saints who occupy another realm, far above the sordidness of the modern metropolis.

WORKS CITED AND RECOMMENDED

Lasch, Christopher. *The True and Only Heaven: Progress and Its Critics*. New York: Norton, 1991.
Marx, Leo. *The Machine in the Garden: Technology and the Pastoral Ideal in America*. New York: Oxford UP, 1964.
Smith, Henry Nash. *Virgin Land: The American West as Symbol and Myth*. Cambridge, MA: Harvard UP, 1950.
Walbert, David. *Garden Spot: Lancaster County, the Old Order Amish, and the Selling of Rural America*. New York: Oxford UP, 2002.
Weaver-Zercher, David. *The Amish in the American Imagination*. Baltimore: Johns Hopkins UP, 2001.

Antiperspirant

Jimmy Dean Smith

You really do not *need* an antiperspirant. If you are clean and healthy and vary your diet so you are not constantly atomizing one overwhelming aroma, you will more than likely pass muster. No need for you to worry that you are being judged in the court of public opinion and found guilty. You understand that sweat, a substance most human beings create, is only natural. You know this. And yet, distrusting your brain, you probably still believe profoundly that you must not start your day without spraying or spritzing or smearing your underarms. The very thought of going out the door without using antiperspirant gives you the fantods. The whole world is watching (or, rather, sniffing) and judging, and you can use all the tricks applied chemistry offers to sneak past society's prying eyes (or nose).

A "deodorant," as the name suggests, works on a body's smells, while an "antiperspirant" works on its sweat. (The *Oxford English Dictionary*'s definition of *deodorant* is terrifying: "A substance or preparation that destroys the odour of fetid effluvia." About *antiperspirant* it remains silent.) The two substances are closely linked because sweat provides a fertile breeding area for smells, although sweat itself has no odor. That is, an otherwise clean person might perspire buckets and one would not know it except by looking: no smell would give away the person's sweatiness. All by themselves, the body's sweat-producing eccrine and apocrine glands should not be made to take the heat for the bad smells that some people exude.

Those people are troublesome not because they sweat but because the kinds of bacteria that grow on unwashed bodies smell very bad when millions and millions of them die. This is not a new discovery, and thus deodorants have been around for quite a while. Today's deodorants actually contain ingredients that attack and kill the bacteria before they have a chance to gain a foothold. In the beginning, deodorants worked (as best they could) by smelling stronger than the stench of decaying bacteria. The ancients of Egypt, Greece, and Rome, for instance, used perfume to outmuscle and defeat body reek.

Here is where sweat comes in. The body provides few climates more naturally conducive to bacterial fecundity than armpits. The heat of armpits makes them attractive to bacteria, but what really turns armpits into overgrown steamy jungles is the humidity: bacteria can't get enough sweat. Again, to reiterate: the sweat itself doesn't smell, and neither do the bacteria. But then they die, and decay, and sweat gets all the blame. Thus, antiperspirants treat a problem by attacking one of its causes rather than another (uncleanliness) or still another (new norms for polite behavior—see the paragraphs on advertising below).

The exact active ingredients that go into antiperspirants depend on how the antiperspirant is configured. A roll-on, for instance, might contain aluminum chlorhydrate. Sticks might contain aluminum zirconium tetrachlorohydrex GLY. In both cases, these aluminum salts help control the body's odor by reducing the amount of sweat it produces. Lacking a hospitable a climate to grow in, bacteria have no chance to thrive and die and stink. The way that these salts work gives medical professionals fits: they make the pores contract so sweat doesn't leak out of them. You don't even have to be an M.D. to understand why clogging your pores is probably an ill-advised idea. Even if you don't obsess over an obvious question (where does the bottled-up sweat go?), you will probably agree that contracted pores are a terrible, dehumanizing price to pay for a little dryness and a somewhat pleasanter smell.

Unless, that is, you happen ever to have watched television or read a commercial magazine. In that case, you have probably been just about convinced that having your sweat glands removed altogether is a remedy worth considering. Dehumanization seems all right compared with what advertising tells us is awaiting all who sweat and smell. Advertising has done such a complete job of making us aware of sweat—of making us fear and despise a substance our own bodies produce—that its wildly successful marketing of antiperspirants is really the iconic story. Of course, the ancients, among others, disliked the smell of a dirty human body; but turning that smell into a marker of class and creating a huge industry to treat a problem that other hygienic practices, like washing, would treat more healthily, inventing a paranoia that seizes at the soul of countless millions—that is the victory of advertising.

Imagine this: a man, Bill Brown, looking to all appearances utterly fastidious, stands before a mirror, knotting his tie, smiling as he confidently foretastes success in his day's every endeavor. His hair is cut and combed just so, his skin is clear and shining. Bill looks terrific. You're inclined to give him anything he wants: a job, your insurance account, your daughter's hand in marriage. And he seems to know that he cuts a fine figure: self-confidence rests lightly but surely on his broad shoulders. But suddenly a dark cloud passes over Bill's countenance. His sparkling eyes turn dull and his smile fades away. His lips tremble with—what is it? Fear? Disgust? Slowly his eyes move side to side. Slowly his arms rise—he looks as if he's imitating a very deliberate chicken—and his lips curl in agonized recognition. With a look of despair, Bill turns his nose to the side and down and, replaying a personal drama that is in its way as much an icon of the twentieth century as the Kennedy assassination

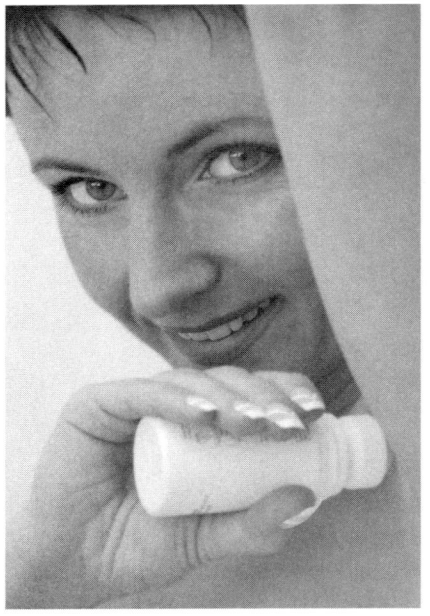

Advertisers want us to believe that only by using antiperspirant will we be truly attractive and acceptable to others. Courtesy of Shutterstock.

or the Beatles' triumphant appearance on *The Ed Sullivan Show*, sniffs his own offending armpit.

Or "underarm," as the advertisers would put it. Advertisers seem confused by the word *armpit* and so offer up a term that helps take one's mind off rotten, foul things suggested by "pits." Their marketing of antiperspirants and deodorants has always been an inspired mixture of delicacy and dread, as if Merchant-Ivory had hired George Romero to remake *Howards End* but with the suggestion that the late Mrs. Wilcox might return as a brain-eating zombie. *Armpit* would make us squirm in our easy chairs and wonder what's on the other channel; but, watching a television commercial that uses the word *underarm*, we feel secure, certain that somebody is watching out for our sensitivities and hopeful that we can repay their politeness in some small way.

Besides keeping us comfortably in the world of the commercial or print ad, such finicky language also makes advertisers' use of another word that much more devastatingly organic. No, in an antiperspirant commercial you will not suffer from *stink* or *reekiness* or *a general swamplike situation in the hot 'n' hairy places*. But you will suffer from "wetness." Bill Brown, who smelled his armpits, or underarms, before the mirror, will certainly worry that, as the day goes on, he will begin to show signs of "wetness." So complete is advertising's control of our vocabulary that we cannot imagine such a word used positively (cf. "One thing I love about Acapulco is its wetness"; "What makes the Colonel's chicken great is its wetness"). Instead, we can only think of it, both word and squeamishly euphemized substance, with dread. Thus, as another day progresses and despite the human body's annoying tendency to create a series of potentially impolite situations, everything seems to be going as well as can be expected until Bill Brown stands and stretches and—what is that? What is that dark stain creeping outward from his underarms, that ever expanding mark of his human frailty and thus of his shame? Is it—oh no, is it *wetness*?

In the collective nightmares called commercials, usually at this point Bill is asked to step into the boss's office, not for anything bad, but just because she needs to see him. Maybe she's giving Bill a raise. Maybe she's giving him her daughter in marriage. But he has *wetness*. He doesn't know how or why—this is a question for philosophers and theologians and space age scientists—but he has *wetness*. And it's coming out of his *underarms*. So he shuffles into her office and stands there while she tells him that he has indeed been given a raise and that she's thought it over and, welcome to the family, her daughter's hand is his. And the entire time, he's standing with arms clamped so hard to his sides that his elbows are making his lungs hurt.

(This posture, after the classic pit-sniff, is the second iconic gesture the antiperspirant industry has given us. The third is the frantic arm-flap. To do it, one holds one's arms loosely out to the sides, bent forward at the elbows and relaxed at the wrists, and flaps frantically, every joint floppy, perhaps with a look of sheer panic on one's face. He or she, unfortunately, has applied a roll-on antiperspirant that has not yet dried and thus will stain their clothes. What that person should have done, of course, is purchase and use a faster-drying roll-on or stick.)

Antiperspirants became a genuine icon when advertising started telling people what would happen to them if they didn't buy and use the product. A signal moment, then, took place in 1919 when Odo-Ro-No used the discrete, but terrifying, abbreviation "B.O." in its print ads. Suddenly body odor was not just something one should avoid but also something that one should not even speak of in polite society. An abbreviation would just have to do. People would whisper "He has B.O." in the same tones they'd whisper "He has V.D." and you'd hope they weren't whispering about you. Trading on just this combination of bourgeois niceness and desperate paranoia is, of course, one of advertising's specialties, and in few areas has it been so successful as with antiperspirants. In short, what advertising did was make the body's natural processes seem dirty, all the while avoiding some common sense measures (first, lighten up about how you smell, and, second, if you smell really bad, take a bath) that would, if taken to heart, obviate the need for antiperspirants and deodorants.

It is perfectly fine to sweat like a dockworker if you are actually working on a dock. Athletes are constantly sweating, slurping down gallons of "sports drink," and sweating away that stuff too, and no etiquette expert puts them in their place. As laborers, they are in their proper place—on the field, in the arena, in the ring. As it happens, for most people throughout human history the proper place was just about anywhere. People worked hard on farms and in mines and, naturally, they sweated. People lived without air conditioning and—why, of course—they perspired. For millennia there was another name for the working class: "just about everybody." And so sweat and stink were the natural order of things.

But if there are places where sweating is socially acceptable—in arenas, on construction sites, in the pre-air-conditioned past—there are other places—*nice* places—where one may not sweat: at a party, on a job interview, in a presidential debate with John F. Kennedy. To sweat out of bounds is to demonstrate that one is not middle class or following middle-class convention. An early stinker, Socrates, took it upon himself, as well as anybody who stood downwind, to go militantly unbathed and thus combat polite Athenian standards. Among its other uses, etiquette determines how the body may function—at least how it may *politely* function—and it says that what is natural under certain conditions is taboo in others. Smelling bad and sporting sweaty stains prove that one has not risen above the vulgarity of one's human origins; they are damning class signifiers. People have to stay "dry," to use the advertisers' term of art, and smell nice if they are going to make it in the rigidly polite society of middle-class America. If they sweat and stink, they reveal themselves to be just the vulgarians Americans are always rumored to be, although, of course, anti-sweat fetishism is more symptomatic of America than just about any place in the world, a sign that, no matter our promotion of freedom as one of our ideals, we are all rigidly Puritan at heart. (Residual cultural Puritanism explains why the other major kind of sweat besides that of workers also offends American sensibilities. Nervousness will also make a person sweat buckets; and nervousness, as good Puritans know, means that you have something to hide.)

Antiperspirants and their first cousins, deodorants, are American icons because they meet the needs of a class-anxious culture. Moreover, because they are not actually necessary (seriously: if you do sweat excessively or smell terrible, you need a physician, not an antiperspirant) but are marketed as if they are, antiperspirants are icons of advertising genius. That is, they meet the needs of the culture but only after advertising creates the needs.

The most class-conscious writer who ever lived, George Orwell, wrote that even politically progressive observers harbor an abiding suspicion about the working class: "They smell bad." Of all the horrors we can conjure up, smelling bad is, it would seem, or *should* seem, minor among them. Everyone sweats; everyone smells; and the solution to the problem, if it proves eye-wateringly great, is as simple as soap and water. But sweating and stinking are genuinely dreadful to many because they give away the game: that, no matter how much money we make or how nice our manners are, we are in many ways really no better than those foul-smelling lower classes. This is America, where we all started out with nothing (that's what the books say) and made something of ourselves. Along the way, we earned the right to forget about our lower-class origins—even, it seems, to deny our status as organisms. That's middle-class America, where all classes are equal and we'll clog our pores with aluminum salts before we'll be mistaken for our lessers.

WORKS RECOMMENDED

Angeloglou, Maggie. *A History of Make-up*. London: The Macmillan Company, 1970.

Boyd, Lydia. "A Brief History of Beauty and Hygiene Products." Ad* Access. 3 Jan. 2006 <http://scriptorium.lib.duke.edu/adaccess/cosmetics-history.html/>.

Butler, Hilda, ed. *Poucher's Perfumes, Cosmetics and Soaps*. 10th ed. Boston: Kluwer Academic Publishers, 2000.

Heil, Scott, and Terrance W. Peck, eds. *The Encyclopedia of American Industry*. 2nd ed. Detroit: Gale Research, 1998.

Laden, Karl, ed. *Antiperspirants and Deodorants*. 2nd ed. New York: Marcel Dekker, 1999.

Peiss, Kathy Lee. *Hope in a Jar: The Making of America's Beauty Culture*. New York: Metropolitan Books, 1998.

Robinson, Julian. *The Quest for Human Beauty: An Illustrated History*. New York: W. W. Norton and Co., 1998.

Art Fair

Mary Carothers and Sharon Scott

Climbing from garden club fundraisers to the elite heights of New York society, the art fair appears in multiple incarnations across the girth of the nation. Only recently validated by the authoritative establishments of art, the importance of the art fair has been felt by more humble American communities for decades. Vendors promoting each year's artistic achievements pop their tents in parks, streets, hotels, and convention halls to produce this event-driven exchange. The art fair presents an occasion full of options and competition for both buyer and seller. Possessing a temporary landscape, the art fair provides a place to see and to be seen—a stage for players and witnesses to converge.

There are as many art fairs as there are definitions of art. Each manifestation appeals to its buyers in relation to their aesthetic interests or social influences. It is a highly segregated phenomenon. One may encounter chainsaw art at the North Georgia Mountain Art Fair, but don't expect to find it at the Angola Prison Rodeo and Art Fair; the latter event, which shares its location with the recent Hollywood movie *Dead Man Walking*, features art from convicts on Death Row. The Body Art Fair in Costa Mesa, California, showcases live piercing and tattoo art. The Outsider Art Fair in New York City benefits the American Folk Art Museum. The ~scope contemporary art fair strikes seasonally around the world and at last it is possible to attend a virtual art fair without leaving home via www.internetartfair.com.

Of the features that identify the art fair, the consistent time and location seem to be the most imperative. Just as Persephone returns annually from Hades, the activity of the art fair bustles into town with the season. From teenage girls buying ceramic birdfeeders for Mother's Day to important curators purchasing for their collection, attending the art fair has become a ritual of American life.

Art fairs are efficient mechanisms of one-stop shopping. Virtually all of them employ committees to select exhibitors. The chosen applicants are charged rental fees for a square footage of the fair. Temporary displays in rows creating open corridors allow visitors to view many exhibits at once.

While the community art fair is free to the public, the high art fair charges shoppers admission. At the neighborhood art fair one finds an emphasis on home and fashion products. Items are crafty, affordable, and fun. (Stained glass versions of the magnetic "Support Our Troops" car ribbons are a current rage.) A shopper might purchase anything from welded nut and bolt creatures to refined Anagama pottery. Most shoppers are purchasing gifts. At the high art fair, on the other hand, money spent is considered an investment. The work in these fairs may be more intellectually challenging to traditional notions of beauty. The work ranges from multimillion-dollar Picasso paintings to Victorian wallpaper samples painted with the blood of an emerging artist who is struggling for recognition.

The American art fair is just turning fifty, yet it feels much older. Claiming lineage from the Victorian World's Fair and the regional state fair, this icon nestles itself securely in between the bosoms of Community and Progress. There are obvious links between the art fair and art exhibitions at the regional fairs. For one reason, state fairs have traditionally sacrificed the controversy of contemporary art exhibitions in favor of popular student art competitions. The Gaspirilla Fair in Florida, for instance, was born because depictions of nudes at the State Fair offended the livestock audience. The Gaspirilla Art Fair publicity materials say, "Controversy often attended the art exhibitions and some fair board members would like to have seen it dismantled altogether." For the most part, the art fair has always been an independent entity.

The idea of the community art fair was established by entrepreneurs seeking to revitalize downtown business districts affected by the suburban flight of the 1950s. The Metris Art Fair in Minnesota is one of these; in their publicity materials, Fair organizers describe the founders as entrepreneurial pioneers. The upscale contemporary art fairs were likewise established by innovative capitalists in the name of economic renewal. Currently one of the largest contemporary art fairs, the Armory Show: The International Fair of New Art, was organized by Manhattan dealers to jump-start the fledgling New York art market in the early 1990s. The contemporary art fair gains prominence as the New York gallery world declines.

Art fair attendees in Ann Arbor, Michigan. Courtesy of Shutterstock.

Connecting itself to history is imperative to the art fair's future. The Old Town Art Fair, the Old Country Art Fair, and the Old Capital Art Fair are but a few of the numerous fairs presenting themselves as living history. The only relation today's Armory show has with the influential Armory Show of 1913 is, however, New York City. Most art aficionados are aware of this but cannot deny the name solicits an automatically validating link. The art fair without tradition fails, even in the contemporary art world.

For publicity purposes and old time appeal, many contemporary art fairs claim to be the nation's oldest. Among these, the 57th Street Art Fair in Chicago's Hyde Park was established in 1948 by artist-gallerist Mary Louise Wormer as a means for artist networking. The Fair was open to all artists until 1963, when a group of critics, collectors, curators, and artists began selecting exhibitors. Today, the vast majority of the art fairs are similarly juried events in which the participants are selected by panels of art officials.

Despite obscure claims to be of benefit to struggling artists, virtually all of today's art fairs are business ventures whose purpose is raising capital for their organizers. While the fashionable artist unloads this year's inventory, the artist who is not commercially successful is losing money, confidence, and a place in next year's show. Rain or shine, the fair makes money on exhibitor entrance fees, sales commissions, and equipment rentals. Even Uncle Walt recognizes the money-making potential of organizing an art fair. On the Disney Family Fun Web pages there are simple instructions to gain capital by asking artists "to sell their work and donate the proceeds" (www.disney.com). A few nonprofit art fairs, including Womer's 57th Street Fair, are committed to serving the community with fair revenue. Most art fairs, however, cannot be considered philanthropic efforts.

In 2005, the Armory packed over 500 of the world's most exclusive contemporary art dealers inside two New York City convention halls. Selected galleries paid from $20,000 to $500,000 for a weekend's booth rental. The cost of the private preview party was $1,000 a head. Visitor admission was $20. The Armory Fair is annually sandwiched between commercial boat and ideal home shows. Come October, the Affordable Art Fair moves into the same hall. Its exhibitors rent booths for thousands less, the private preview party is a mere $100, and general admission is reduced to $12. The Affordable Art Fair is separate but available to shoppers of diverse economic backgrounds.

The Armory Fair has a closer relation in its origin to contemporary art fairs in hotels. The Armory Fair began when the contemporary art dealers Pat Hearn, Colin McLand, Paul Morris, and Matthew Marks invited select galleries to showcase work in the rooms of Gramercy Park Hotel. The success of this original incarnation of the Armory Fair co-mingles with the jewelry world's "trunk shows" to spawn the present generation of contemporary events such as -scope and DIVA: Digital and Video Art Fair. These cutting-edge art fairs transform swanky hotel rooms into makeshift galleries. Distant and perverse relations to the neighborhood art fair, these exclusive events strew emerging artists across crisp double beds where traveling collectors negotiate a price.

Back home in middle America, the Cherokee Triangle Art Fair in Louisville, Kentucky, is an outdoor event. Although it is only advertised in more affluent areas, it takes place on neighborhood streets and is ostensibly open to the public. The sun shines through the trees and it is a beautiful day at the fair. It is mostly a Caucasian crowd, yet there is a feeling that the entire community is participating. This relaxed and festive occasion is the celebration of a society shopping! Clowns and popcorn and kids: besides art, this fair offers music, games, regional foods, and the obligatory police on horses. There is an uncommon sense of well-being. Everyone is cheerful and swollen with community pride.

Whether they are elite New York events or popular street festivals, art fairs are obviously dealing in more than art. The art fair annually provides a hunt for something new within the security of the familiar. At each year's art fair, one never knows who or what will be discovered. Romance and mystery fill the air and everyone is on the prowl. It's interesting to note that writer Peter Hill has produced a novel called *The Art Fair Murders*. Twelve murders occur in twelve cities around the world. The novel, like the art fair itself, links international artists, gallery dealers, art critics, and collectors. In reality and fiction, the art fair is an island of treasure that provides the landscape between the searching predator and the hunted victim.

Since Paleolithic times, art has sistered the hunt. In a metaphorical relationship to the Altamira Caves in Spain, today's art fairs enact the ritual of hunters. It has been suggested that the paintings found within the caves served the ritual function of ensuring fertility and a good hunt. At the art fair, the hunt is on, but the danger has been eliminated. The panel of jurors may be intimidating to some artists and the event may be overwhelming, but the underlying intention of the event is to promote a fertile hunting ground that promises not to be threatening. Today's art fairs are carefully choreographed labyrinths of community shopping adventures taking place within the consumer comfort zone. The rummaging that takes place at every art fair confirms that the hunt for a new possession is accompanied by an excited frenzy not unlike the primal hunger for food.

The victors of the art fair are those who discover and claim the new. Here, everyone dreams of having the best taste, being the best shopper. The discovery of the "in" product is exciting. Smart shopping is rewarded heroically and remembered mythically. The buyer distinctly carries his purchase like a badge of some brave act. Participating in the ritual makes the individual proud. Conversely, refusing to participate in the art fair exchange is plagued by a sensation of guilt. Buying nothing at the art fair is not only rude towards the artist, selfish toward one's family, and disrespectful to the community, it is ultimately sacrilegious.

Recently in the Louisville *Courier-Journal*, Jerry Lyndrup, the co-chair of the Cherokee Triangle Art Fair, referred to visitors enacting "their rite of spring" (Hall B3). Similarly, *New York Times* arts reporter Carol Vogel reported "serious American collectors, dealers, auction house experts and museum curators attending an annual pilgrimage to Maastricht [art fair]" (B7). From local newspapers to quarterly art journals, the art fair is so idealized that it is spoken of in religious terms. Like football Sundays or fireworks on the Fourth of July, the days at the art fair provide the community with an occasion to hang memories upon.

This year's fair makes last year's purchases old and it is time to shop again. Americans understand that a new possession brings a certain satisfaction. They also expect this satisfaction will mutate into disappointment. Sooner or later the novel item works its way out of the art fair and namelessly rolls over onto the shelves of superstores and yard sales. Eventually the new becomes articulated so many times that it becomes old, and the demand for the art fair is regenerated. Americans look forward to the annual return of the art fair because it promises to bring them up-to-date.

It is this locomotive spirit of consumer lust that the contemporary art dealers have recently learned to appreciate. Although several high art fairs have existed in America for decades, their raging popularity began with the appearance of Art Miami in 2002. The most exclusive galleries in the world are now paying less attention to their physical homes and concentrating upon their presentation at the annual fairs. A gallerist may participate in as many as eleven shows annually. According to *New Criterion* editor James Panero, "Contemporary galleries now earn upwards of 50 percent of their sales from fairs where it once was 10" (42). Art fair–specific staff has been added to gallery payrolls, and artists are constantly pushed for trendy, portable work.

The immense popularity of the art fair within the contemporary art world raises obvious questions about the future of the gallery and eventually about the future of art. The cold, white gallery space may have dug its own grave via pretentious secretaries and stuffy parties, yet it consistently offered space for quiet aesthetic contemplation. The art fair is a boisterous, interactive event whose aim is to make art purchasing easy. Museums, on the other hand, are out to win respect of their viewing public by curating a masterful collection of art. In a museum, the same painting may cover the same piece of wall for months or even decades. The museum provides the work with the time and space to be seen. At an art fair, works must compete to be noticed. As a result, much of the work is flashy and shocking. One notable example was *Fuck Leg*, a lifelike gorilla leg severed with a meat cleaver that appeared on the floor of the 2005 Armory Show. In an art fair, an artwork is sold, removed, and replaced with a new piece. The most highly coveted artworks at the fair may not even reach the viewing walls, but be secretly traded many times back stage. Museum politics and art fair politics pit capitalism against aestheticism.

Most museum curators dislike art fairs, but visit them regardless. Many deals shake down and they too want to be part of the action. Dealers, on the other hand, are attending a sleep-away camp where like-minded camaraderie prevails. During the fair every gallery in town puts on its best show of the season and there may be 100 private viewings on the same night. There will be untold parties, private dinners, photo ops, and late night debauching.

ART FAIR

Sexiness, glamour, and randomness turn themselves into mini-marathons as the art fair ritual unfolds.

At the Los Angeles Art Fair, one painting by Pop artist Andy Warhol sold five times to five different galleries. The price went up each time it sold. In a culture that puts a premium on market value, the art fair proves itself to be a highly efficient exchange. These events become increasingly central to the financial and social mechanisms of the international art world and the local economies that harbor them.

The art fair places exhibitors back to back in aesthetic competition. Buyers can easily compare products and prices. At the fair, art patrons act more like mall shoppers rummaging through products, buying impulsively, and keeping up with the Joneses. Art at the fair must be dramatic and flashy enough to capture the overwhelmed eye. It must be "buzzy and fun," according to *New York Observer* reporter Choire Sicha (1). Limited by booth size, necessary portability, and continuous demand for supply, the art fair presently dictates the direction of contemporary American arts. The more popular the mobile art fair becomes, the more art representatives are pushing their artists to make compact, marketable art at an ever-increasing rate. The art fair is an experiential shopping event that may eventually take precedence over the artist's creative intention.

As the art fair gains prominence, it continues to raise questions about the buying and selling of art. How much are the demands of the fair determining the shape of contemporary art? Will the commercial world produce artists or will the artist create an intangible context? At this year's fairs, dealers have proven their business savvy by including such non-objective forms such as Performance Art, Installation Art, and Cyber Art within their inventories. If a work itself cannot be purchased, the artist's time can. The submission of art to the demands of the art fair means contemporary aesthetics are determined by supply and demand. When dealer and collector benefit from the convenience of shopping, the intentions of the creator are easily sacrificed. Inspiration, devotion, and expression are replaced by marketability.

Artist members of the American Association of Painters and Sculptors created and managed all aspects at the 1913 Armory Show. At the most recent Armory Show, very few artists were present. Many were discouraged from attending, as gallery representatives orchestrated the entire event. In one rare instance the artist was present but encased within a hollow wall. As a performance piece she revealed only her arm through a hole for buyers to see. A light bulb was clenched in her hand. At first glance, the arm appeared to be a cast object, at second glance, one began to realize that the arm was real. An American flag, colors inverted, was suspended just over the arm. One could assume this art act was a play on the Statue of Liberty and was questioning the idea of patriotism. Regardless of intention, this piece attested to the invisibility of artists at such a fair.

In contrast to the inaccessibility of the artists at the high art fair, creators at community art fairs are visibly managing their own displays. They are creating work at their booths and are openly interacting with the public. Excluded from this opportunity are creative artists who often feel dismissed by selection committees in favor of commercially driven craftsmen. As a response, recent years have seen the emergence of non-juried alternative events, such as The St. James Art UNFAIR in Louisville, Kentucky.

The art fair can adjust its tempo to the momentum of American culture and reinvent itself to suit all interests and economic groups; there are even art fairs for those who despise art fairs. Art fairs stand as community timekeepers: year after year Americans return to their ceremonial marketplace; they hunt fashion and like-mindedness as they participate in the consumer celebration. The wealth, time, and taste necessary to enjoy the fair attest to the prosperity of the nation. The art fair is an icon of social progress and individual achievement. Inside and outdoors, from high art to death row, in exclusive society or on the Internet, the art fair is a unifying ritual that perpetuates the survival of a capitalist culture.

WORKS CITED AND RECOMMENDED

The 57th Street Art Fair. 28 Apr. 2005 <http://www.57thstreetartfair.org/artfair.htm>.

Gasparilla Fesitival of the Arts. 30 Apr. 2005 <http://www.gasparilla-arts.com/history.htm>.

Hall, Gregory A. "Cherokee Triangle Fair Cool Dry and Artsy." *Courier-Journal* 1 May 2005: B2+.

Internetartfair.com. Liberal Arts and Crafts, Inc. 28 Apr. 2005 <http://www.internetartfair.com>.

Metris Uptown Art Fair. 30 Apr. 2005 <http://www.uptownminneapolis.com/art-fair/>.

Panero, James. "The New York Fairs." *The New Criterion* 23.8 (2005): 43–49.

Sicha, Choire. "Armory But Not Dangerous." *The New York Observer* 21 Mar. 2005: 1.

Vogel, Carol. "At the Fair Despite the Snow and Weak Dollar." *New York Times* 7 Mar. 2005: B1+.

Fred Astaire

Michael Dunne

Fred Astaire (1899–1987) was born Frederick Austerlitz in Omaha, Nebraska, but still went on to become an internationally acknowledged embodiment of romantic male sophistication. Tony Bennett, one of Fred's epigones, opines that Astaire ended up as "our national treasure" despite his Nebraskan origins. Whether dressed in top hat, white tie, and tails or in fashionable casual wear with a scarf serving as his belt, Fred Astaire always looked fabulous. Even while playing light romantic comedy roles in which he was usually called something like Jerry Travers, Fred Astaire epitomized whatever was cool at that time. According to Benny Green, "[Astaire] had an elegance that aligned itself with what I guess you'd call high society" (146). In the words of Howard Thompson, Astaire "gave to entertainment annals a champagne radiance that appealed to everybody on all levels, rich or poor" (9–10). No wonder Patrick Dennis's lead character—also called Patrick Dennis—admits in the novel *Auntie Mame* (1955):

> Our only god was Fred Astaire. He was everything we wanted to be: smooth, suave, debonair, dapper, intelligent, adult, witty, and wise. We saw his pictures over and over, played his records until they were gray and blurred, dressed as much like him as we dared. When any crises came into our young lives, we asked ourselves what Fred Astaire would do and we did likewise. (154)

As the history of American popular culture has attested, young Patrick was not alone in his hero worship in the 1950s, the 1930s—or much later on.

Even today, Americans can be expected to recognize the name Fred Astaire—at least in the judgment of E. D. Hirsch, Jr., in his 1987 *Cultural Literacy: What Every American Needs to Know* (157). Admittedly, today's Americans are likely to know about Fred Astaire through occasional revivals of his films on television or through the self-promotional MGM films *That's Entertainment* (1974), *That's Entertainment, Part II* (1976), and *That's Dancing* (1985). However, Benny Green asserts that "Astaire's uniqueness had long been apparent when the MGM retrospectives underlined

Fred Astaire, 1936. Courtesy of the Library of Congress.

the fact. People understood that there would never be anybody with whom to compare him, to duplicate the range of his achievement, least of all to replace him" (144). According to John Mueller, Astaire "is one of the greatest dancers and choreographers...one of the master artists of the century" (3). That is why Fred Astaire is truly an American icon. Unsurprisingly, he became an icon through the media of mass entertainment.

In the early days, Fred was successfully paired with his slightly older sister, Adele, first in vaudeville and then on the Broadway and London stages in musical comedies including *Funny Face, Lady, Be Good!*, and *The Band Wagon*. After Adele retired from show business in 1932 to marry the Duke of Devonshire, Fred starred on his own as a combination singer-dancer-light comedian in Cole Porter's *The Gay Divorcée*. Rather than continuing this comfortable pattern on Broadway or in London, however, Fred next went to Hollywood under contract to RKO. There, before he could begin filming *Flying Down to Rio* in which he was paired with Ginger Rogers, Fred was loaned to MGM to play himself as Joan Crawford's dancing partner in *Dancing Lady* (1933). The combination of these stars was unremarkable; if *Dancing Lady* is remembered at all today, it is mentioned merely as Fred Astaire's first Hollywood appearance. *Flying Down to Rio* was another story altogether. Released in the same year as *Dancing Lady* and starring Dolores del Rio and Gene Raymond, *Rio* was the first of ten films in which Astaire appeared opposite Rogers—nine for RKO, concluding with *The Story of Vernon and Irene Castle* (1939), and the last, *The Barkleys of Broadway* (1949), for MGM. As he and Ginger starred in a fabulously successful string of musical films including *The Gay Divorcée* (1934), *Roberta* (1935), *Top Hat* (1935), *Swing Time* (1936), and *Shall We Dance* (1937), it began to seem as if Fred had merely traded one female partner for another and would continue to be only one-half of a stellar show business team.

Then, in the period following the series of eagerly anticipated, annual RKO Fred-and-Ginger musicals, Fred began to dance with other partners at other studios. The first of these, Eleanor Powell (*Broadway Melody of 1940*), was perhaps the most talented female tap dancer of all time and a musical film star in her own right. However, when she danced with Fred, two masters were in full-out competition rather than in romantic union. Something along the same lines might be said of the much admired tap dancer Ann Miller (*Easter Parade* [1948]), although I have never cared much for her explosive dancing. Harriet Hoctor (*Shall We Dance* [1937]) was something of an acrobatic freak who could tap on point and also reach her foot up from behind to touch the back of her head. Arlene Croce is only one of many critics to find fault with Hoctor, writing that "Miss Hoctor can be taken for nothing human" (122). Lucille Bremer (*Yolanda and the Thief* [1945], *The Ziegfeld Follies* [1946]) was beautiful, graceful, and—by general consensus—entirely lacking in personality. Rita Hayworth (*You'll Never Get Rich* [1941], *You Were Never Lovelier* [1942]) was perhaps the most beautiful screen actress of all time, and a wonderful dancer too. Furthermore, these dancers were all of a suitable age to pass as Fred's romantic leads. With the magnificent Judy Garland, a new female generation emerged on the Astaire horizon in *Easter Parade*, and so Fred began to assume Pygmalion or fairy-godfather roles in films. Vera-Ellen (*Three Little Words* [1950], *The Belle of New York* [1952]) danced with Fred as well as she had done with Gene Kelley in *On the Town* (1949), but she seemed so much younger than Astaire that on-screen chemistry was lacking. This was perhaps even more the case with Leslie Caron (*Daddy Long Legs* [1955]), and Audrey Hepburn (*Funny Face* [1957]), although each costar was appealing in her own way. Age hardly mattered with the preternaturally beautiful and talented Cyd Charisse (*The Band Wagon* [1953], *Silk Stockings* [1957]). It is surely significant that, although his partners changed radically, Astaire continued to be Astaire. In the MGM clips film *That's Entertainment* (1974), Gene Kelly says about the number from *Royal Wedding* in which Astaire dances with a hatrack, "As usual, he made his partner look good." The same might be said about his on-screen pairings with these female costars of various ages and talents.

To some degree all of this success occurred because, as Howard Thompson writes, Astaire "had become known as one of the greatest perfectionists in the theatrical field, spending endless but regulated hours on sound stages working tirelessly on the dance tricks and routines that emerged with such seeming ease on the screen" (136). This is certainly the testimony of other dancers, including Bob Fosse, who proclaimed at the American Film Institute Lifetime Achievement Award ceremony for Astaire, "What always impressed me about Fred was his tremendous desire for perfection. I got a peek at him, rehearsing at M-G-M, even after he had mastered a movement, and he seemed to me to keep going over and over and over it again—until it became mechanical" (qtd. in Adler 177). On the same festive occasion, Mikhail Baryshnikov said about Astaire, "His perfection is an absurdity; it's hard to face" (qtd. in Adler 177). In specific terms, we might consider what Arlene Croce says about the number "Never Gonna Dance" from *Swing Time*: "[I]ts climax, a spine-chilling series of pirouettes by Rogers, took forty takes to accomplish, and in the middle of shooting, Rogers' feet began to bleed" (113). This is consistent with what Astaire told Howard Thompson: "My routines may look easy, but they are nothing you throw away while shaving.... It's always murder to get that easy effect" (136). And, it is not only Fred's partners who had to suffer in the cause of on-screen perfection. Alan Jay Lerner recalls Astaire's endless rehearsing and self-criticism in an anecdote that appears in Benny Green's book. All alone, after everyone else had left the MGM sound stage, Fred straggled out to greet a late-working Lerner with the self-doubting question of why anyone could even consider him a dancer. To Lerner, "[t]he tormented illogic of his question made any answer insipid" (148). After all, this was Fred Astaire, and he was still working on his dance numbers after all the other performers had quit for the day! In his autobiography *Steps in Time*, Astaire throws some light on all of this by writing that "[w]hat counts more than luck is determination and perseverance" (4). Whatever the cause, and whoever Fred's partner, all of his films contain truly memorable musical numbers, and these have consolidated his status as icon.

Eventually, of course, the American film musical seemed to have reached its natural point of exhaustion. As John Mueller explains in his *Astaire Dancing: The Musical Films*: "By the mid 1950s the era of the classic Hollywood musical as Astaire had experienced it—indeed, defined it—was coming to an end. Revenues were declining, costs were rising, the studio system was falling apart, competition with television was growing, popular music was moving into the age of rock and roll. Astaire and other products of the classic Hollywood musical, such as Freed and Kelly, were out of business as Hollywood created fewer and fewer musical films" (12–13). And so, Fred Astaire turned from Hollywood musicals to television, specifically to his Emmy-Award-winning song and dance spectaculars *An Evening with Fred Astaire* (1958), *Another Evening with Fred Astaire* (1959), and *Astaire Time* (1960)—all co-starring Barrie Chase. During this period, he also appeared in non-musical films, including *On the Beach* (1959) and *The Pleasure of His Company* (1961), as well as in the recurring role of a retired cat burglar on the television program *To Catch a Thief* (1968–1970), starring Robert Wagner. Fred also acted, sang, and danced in *Finian's Rainbow* (1968) opposite Petula Clark in an early—and not very successful—directorial effort by Francis Ford Coppola. Through it all, he exemplified what Patrick Dennis's character calls the "smooth, suave, debonair, dapper, intelligent, adult, witty, and wise" male icon.

As Arlene Croce writes about this musical comedy superstar, "His 'peerlessness' is a legend; it means, not that there were no other tap-dancers, but that there were no other Astaires" (6). Even so, Astaire's excellence as a dancer was undisputed. John Mueller, for instance, begins his book by noting that George Balanchine, Merce Cunningham, Rudolf Nureyev, and Mikhail Baryshnikov have all publicly testified in favor of Astaire's premiere terpsichorean genius (3). To quote Croce again: "When Fred dances alone, he's perfect. For as long as we have known him he has been simply Astaire, *the* dancing man self-defined. He is his own form of theater, and we ask nothing more" (6). As a singer, too, Astaire's exemplary status is noteworthy. The liner notes for *Nothing Thrilled Us Half as Much: Fred Astaire Sings and Dances His Greatest Hits* explain: "The Astaire voice has never been a serious threat to concert singers, but his singing has, if one defines singing as an artful blend of taste and intelligence and emotion. And for that reason, America's finest songwriters and lyricists have supplied him with some of their greatest songs." Howard Thompson agrees that Fred was "assuredly not the best singer" available (9), but he also points out that Irving Berlin, Jerome Kern, Cole Porter, Harold Arlen, and George and Ira Gershwin chose Fred Astaire to introduce some of their most memorable songs on stage and on the screen. In Benny Green's terms, in his own inimitable versions of these songs Fred "is saying, in effect, 'I may not be able to write songs as good as these, but at least let me draw your attention to the brilliance of those who can'" (22). Perhaps this recorded sophistication was owing to the fact, as Peter Gammond writes in *The Oxford Companion to Popular Music*, that Fred "contrived to be the perfect popular songster..., giving more meaning and strength to the songs than many with more impressive vocal chords could ever achieve" (24). So, even though we sometimes have to wonder whether Astaire is going to be able to hit a particular note in "The Way You Look Tonight" or "Cheek to Cheek," we are enchanted by his command of the song. In summary, we might consider Will Friedwald's comment in the liner notes for the *Fred Astaire at M-G-M* CD collection: "No composer, performer, producer, or writer so personified everything that was great about musical comedy—both on stage and screen—and Tin Pan Alley as did Astaire. He was the embodiment of all that was wonderful about the intertwined arts of song and dance." Friedwald's last sentence just about says it all!

WORKS CITED AND RECOMMENDED

Adler, Bill. *Fred Astaire: A Wonderful Life*. New York: Carroll & Graf, 1987.
Astaire, Fred. *Steps in Time*. New York: Harper, 1959.
Bennett, Tony. Liner notes to *Steppin' Out*. CD. Columbia, 1993.
Croce, Arlene. *The Fred Astaire & Ginger Rogers Book*. New York: Outerbridge & Lazard, 1972.
Dennis, Patrick. *Auntie Mame: An Irreverent Escapade*. New York: Vanguard P, 1955.
Friedwald, Will. Liner notes to *Fred Astaire at M-G-M*. CD. Rhino, 1997.
Gammond, Peter. *The Oxford Companion to Popular Music*. New York: Oxford UP, 1993.
Green, Benny. *Fred Astaire*. New York: Exeter, 1979.
Hirsch, E. D., Jr. *Cultural Literacy: What Every American Needs to Know*. Boston: Houghton Mifflin, 1987.
Mueller, John E. *Astaire Dancing: The Musical Films*. New York: Knopf, 1985.
Nothing Thrilled Us Half as Much: Fred Astaire Sings and Dances His Greatest Hits. LP. Epic, n.d.
That's Entertainment. Dir. Jack Haley, Jr. MGM, 1974.
Thompson, Howard. *Fred Astaire*. New York: Crescent, 1970.

Lucille Ball

Rhonda Wilcox

> Isn't it funny. I cannot for the life of me remember how the furniture was laid out in the living room of the house I grew up in, but I can remember where every stick of furniture was in the Ricardo house.
> ABC News Anchor Diane Sawyer, eulogizing Lucille Ball
> (Kanfer 301)

In the 1990 film *Pretty Woman*, which made Julia Roberts a star, the audience is given certain signals to show that the prostitute protagonist is worthy to be a Cinderella. She not only shows an untutored love of opera; she also demonstrates a gleeful, unfettered appreciation for *I Love Lucy*. Lucille Ball's is one of the most recognized faces on the planet. And when someone mentions the name "Lucy," very few anymore think of Wordsworth or even Bram Stoker. The recognition is instantaneous; but it is not as simple as it might at first seem. Lucy as an icon means different things to different people.

Lucy was enabled to become iconic because of a combination of talent, intelligence, hard work, and fortuitous historical timing. Lucille Ball had been a model, movie starlet, and radio performer; she and her husband, musical performer Desi Arnaz, Jr., wanted to be able to work together, so they took a gamble on television in its early days, knowing that if they failed, they might not be welcome back in the film world. Sponsors disliked the idea of the redhead and the Cuban as a married couple, but Lucy insisted; and Lucy and Desi invested their own money to help get the show off the ground. They did not want to move back to New York from California, so they filmed their shows before a live audience. To make this work, they initiated the use of the three-camera shooting style which became the standard for sitcoms, and which still structures our visual expectations. These two choices—the investment and the filming—meant that the couple ended up having behind-the-scenes power in the television business (they came to own the prolific Desilu Studios), and that while much early television work disappeared, Lucy, in her syndicated reruns, instead became immortal.

I Love Lucy ran from 1951 to 1961, stopping at approximately the same time as the couple's marriage. (*The Lucy Show*, without Desi, and later under the name *Here's Lucy*, ran for more than a decade after that.) Despite the sponsor's doubts, it quickly rose to number one in the ratings and stayed there for years. In a time period of few networks, Lucy drew as her audience approximately one-fifth of the population of America. When Dwight D. Eisenhower was inaugurated as President of the United States in 1953, 29 million watched; the night before, however, 44 million had tuned in to see Lucy Ricardo give birth to Little Ricky. But the show and the character were not just popular in their own time; those syndicated episodes have never stopped rerunning, and now people are buying VHS and DVD copies of the black-and-white redhead, too.

Lucy is the one so many of us love, but she emerged in a context. Redheaded zany Lucille McGillicuddy is married to handsome Cuban band leader and singer Ricky Ricardo; they live in a middle-class New York apartment rented from an older couple, stingy Fred and Lucy's sidekick Ethel Mertz. Ricky is the sensible husband (though Lucy's antics can drive him to comic loss of verbal control, vehemently expressed in his native Spanish), and Lucy is the wacky wife. In almost every episode, Lucy's facial expression would convey what the writers called the "light bulb" look of having an idea, conceiving an improbable scheme—sometimes, to get money; even more often, to get on Ricky's show. After twenty-some minutes of farcical deception and genuinely hilarious physical comedy (Lucy is seen as the inheritor of Charlie Chaplin), the world would right itself—as it always should in comedy. And in the 1950s, this meant that wife Lucy would be laughingly and lovingly put in her place. This world-order is something many find appealing even today. The shows are in some ways about a very traditional battle of the sexes, with Lucy and Ethel against Fred and Ricky (though the characters sometimes form different combinations). As Kathleen Brady writes, "it balanced temperaments in a way that harkened back to the 'humors' of the Elizabethan stage: patient Ethel, volatile Ricky, stolid Fred, and flighty, airy Lucy—couple against couple, boys against the girls" (194). And as Lucille Ball says, they agreed that "the humor could never be mean or unkind" (207).

Within this comfortingly controlled world, Lucy herself was on the loose, out of control—the unruly woman, as Kathleen Rowe terms it. In all sorts of ways she shows us the carnival wildness, the rule-breaking that Mikhail Bakhtin highlights in comedy. Her hair has to be red, vivid red—a color associated with high emotions—and wildly unusual, as is the character. The red hair helps us remember that she is also a bit ethnic: a McGillicuddy; and she definitely crossed an ethnic borderline by marrying her Cuban beloved—a step that meant more in the fifties, but that still means something today. Her scheming and deception make her something of a trickster figure; as Brer Rabbit, in some ways, represented blacks, Lucy represented many a woman who might feel that she had the right to some scheming because power was held by someone else. Though the Brer Rabbit stories were recorded by

Lucille Ball, 1960. Courtesy of the Library of Congress.

a white man, Joel Chandler Harris, they were told by blacks; as for Lucy, at least one of the series' three major writers was female—Madelyn Pugh.

When I was beginning to write this essay, I went looking for copies of *Lucy* episodes. A young black man who worked at the video store spoke up enthusiastically about his own enjoyment of the series. Asked about what he liked in the series, he replied, "Just the dumb stuff Lucy do." When Lucy has the chance to be in an Italian movie, she doesn't just look around to soak up the local color; she immerses herself in it quite literally. She sneaks into a group of women planning to work at a traditional winery, manages to be assigned to stomping duty, unintentionally gets in an all-out, falling-down brawl with another worker, and ends up grape-faced, stained purple, and unable to take the part when the movie's director shows up to offer it to her. The vineyard scene is quintessential Lucy. In an episode that cites sexy Italian stars such as Gina Lollabrigida, Lucy shows up at the vineyard in an off-the-shoulder blouse; but when she takes off her shoes to fit in with the other workers, her seductive posturing is disrupted by her hopping up and down on the hot paving stones. Her wild physical comedy is often predicated on the presentation of the body out of control. But the lack of control can have a childlike joy to it. When she is in the large vat, stomping the grapes, the woman she is paired with moves with a steady, sensible, businesslike rhythm. Lucy, once she gets past mugging her initial shock at the feeling of the grapes between her toes and up her legs, proceeds to happily fling herself into the experience, literally dancing rings around the other worker, arms enthusiastically akimbo. (Lucy's trademark way of crying, the "Waaah," wailing, is comparably childlike in its lack of control—as is her out-of-tune singing.) After an intervening scene with Ricky and Ethel, we return to see Lucy exhausted. When the other worker tries to pull her back to work, Lucy, in shaking her off, accidentally knocks her down into the grapes; and thus their tussle begins. It is important, in terms of the audience's emotional investment, that Lucy never intends harm—though once the fracas starts, she fights as enthusiastically as she has danced. She may be selfish, but she is never cruel.

Among the out-of-control elements, food and drink often play a part, and she is often immersed in the physical—in the grapes of the vat, for instance. Or consider the classic "Job Switching" episode, with the candy factory scene. Lucy and Ethel are switching roles with the men, who agree to temporarily take on the job as housekeepers. Ricky and Fred end up sliding about the kitchen floor under overflowing mounds of rice. Meanwhile, Lucy and Ethel stand by a conveyor belt. Having been told they'll be fired if they let a piece of candy get by unwrapped, they end up hiding the excess candy. Lucy swallows it, and stuffs it down her blouse, as she struggles, chocolate-mouthed, trying to keep up. (Years later, she stuffs eggs down her blouse in "Lucy Does the Tango"; of course the eggs will be crushed against her, sticky and dripping, in yet another Lucy dance.) The bit Lucy herself thought funniest involved drink, not food, and yet another unintentional rule-breaking: the Vitameatavegamin routine. Once again Lucy is trying to get into Ricky's show, if only in a commercial break for a health tonic. Though we in the audience know, she and the commercial director do not realize that the product (which she must repeatedly swallow as she rehearses) is 23 percent alcohol. So the very properly dressed representative of 1950s womanhood gets to end up flat drunk—with no moral guilt attached. Lucy starts out shuddering as she tries to deliver the line, "It's so tasty, too!" but she ends up making love to the bottle. And it is her seemingly out-of-control physical reaction—including her comically loving drunken approach to her husband as he performs in the show-within-a-show—that creates the humor.

These are the moments we remember—the moments that keep us coming back to Lucy. It is true that the status quo is always restored at the end; and many a critic has argued that Lucy's power (or woman's power) is thus denied. But there is a whole other level of meaning that many a viewer has enjoyed simultaneously. W.E.B. Du Bois talked about the "double consciousness" required of blacks who have had to think both in terms of white society and in terms of their own lives. There is a different kind of double consciousness about Lucy. The comedy gives a sense of power, and play, and delight in her being out of control; yet also conveys that behind the scenes, she *has* control. The audience knew that not only were the Ricardos married, but so also were Lucille Ball and Desi Arnaz. While other TV sitcom husbands had offstage, invisible work, Ricky (Desi) sang right in front of us. Lucy's real husband is *shown* being attractive and worth her desire; she has made a good choice, it seems. Because she had a cesarean section, Lucille Ball gave birth to her son on the same night that Lucy Ricardo gave birth to hers—a curious sort of control of the relationship between fiction and reality. It brought wild enthusiasm at the time, and even today, the line between character and actor is pleasurably blurred for many; a play with the edges of reality—despite what some know of the marriage's eventual break-up. And Lucy, who said "Yes, sir" and "No, sir," to her husband on camera, in the real world ended up buying him out of their company.

Another significant element of the play with lack of control is that former model and movie starlet Lucille Ball was a very beautiful woman. Like Carole Lombard and Ginger Rogers (whose mother was a mentor for Lucy), Lucy was not restrained by her beauty from taking comic roles. She did not have to mug and take pratfalls to compensate for homely features. Every pie in the face was a choice, and her audience knew it. Even the red hair was unreal, chosen—and the audience knew that, too, from repeated jokes in the series. Perhaps most important of all was the double consciousness of Lucy as entertainer. Ricky: "You cannot be in the show." Lucy: "Give me one good reason." Ricky: "You have no talent." Lucy: "Give me another good reason." Time after time this sort of interaction is reiterated. Time after time Lucy, like any good *id* character, goes after what she wants in spite of rational objections—with hilarious results. As Lucy herself said, she and Vivian Vance (Ethel) "both believe wholeheartedly in what we call 'an enchanted sense of play'" (Ball 208). But as with a virtuoso musician, the playfulness was earned. As Kathleen Brady points out, Lucy might rehearse for three hours with different sizes and weights of paper bags to get the best sound when she popped one (197). And as Susan Horowitz writes, "Ball's beauty, drive, willingness to learn, and comedic talent eventually led to fame and fortune, [while] Lucy Ricardo's hapless efforts lead only to laughs" (36). Many a viewer was conscious of the fact that Lucy Ricardo, who performed so badly, was entertaining precisely because Lucille Ball was a consummate performer.

When we laugh, we are out of control; for a moment, we share that freedom with Lucy. And while critics may point out that each episode ends with restrictive (or, depending on one's view, comforting) order restored, the fact that Lucy's humor comes on television means that there is another element to be considered. If she were bound down at the close of a movie, the weight of the ending would be heavier. But on episodic television, we know that she will play again another day. Not only in VHS and on DVD but still out on the airwaves, Lucy continues. Lucille Ball apparently wanted to be in the show just as much as Lucy did—and as so many of us do; and we love to know she got to. There is a sort of bravery of pleasure in Lucy's pursuit of her desire, in Lucy's being herself. That is something worth contemplating, something worth looking at again and again; that is why she is still an icon.

WORKS CITED AND RECOMMENDED

Ball, Lucille. *Love, Lucy.* New York: G. P. Putnam's Sons, 1996.
Brady, Kathleen. *Lucille: The Life of Lucille Ball.* New York: Hyperion, 1994.
Du Bois, W.E.B. "Of Our Spiritual Strivings." *The Souls of Black Folk: Essays and Sketches.* Greenwich, CT: Fawcett, 1961. 15–22.
Horowitz, Susan. *Queens of Comedy: Lucille Ball, Phyllis Diller, Carol Burnett, Joan Rivers, and the New Generation of Funny Women.* Amsterdam: Gordon and Breech, 1997.
Kanfer, Stefan. *Ball of Fire: The Tumultuous Life and Comic Art of Lucille Ball.* New York: Knopf, 2003.
Rowe, Kathleen. *The Unruly Woman: Gender and the Genres of Laughter.* Austin: U of Texas P, 1995.

Banjo

Jack Ashworth

The banjo, solidly associated with several types of musical Americana (bluegrass, old time, Dixieland, early jazz, vaudeville), is actually an African instrument. Originally made by cutting off the side of a gourd, affixing a skin over the opening, and attaching a wooden neck with strings made of animal or plant fibers, the instrument was described (though not named) as early as 1621, and manufactured commercially at least as early as the 1850s (Epstein 350, 357). Dena Epstein supplies a list of names used for the instrument from Africa, the West Indies, and North America between 1678 and 1851; most are recognizable cousins of today's *banjo* (e.g., *banjar*), although some are both more descriptive and more fun (e.g., *strum strum* and *merrywhang*, both Jamaican). The most typical American banjo is a five-string instrument with four strings of equal length and one shorter drone string, although two four-string versions of the instrument were popular, especially among Dixieland and jazz musicians, between about 1900 and 1930.

What world does the banjo conjure? Who owns the banjo, black America or white? Is it more likely to evoke romantic plantation scenes of the antebellum South, or rural poverty and ignorance? Is it a Southern thing, or an American thing?

Any such discussion must begin with Karen Linn's *That Half-Barbaric Twang: The Banjo in American Popular Culture*. Linn addresses many issues, presenting along the way a vast array of references from literature, drama, movies, and even cartoons, as well as multiple illustrations from both magazine advertising and the covers of sheet music; in doing so, she documents popular perceptions of the banjo in America from its early use in minstrel shows through the late twentieth century. Linn also demonstrates how the banjo has been a cultural player on several levels and in many contexts during the course of its American life. Considered from a cultural perspective, there have been a variety of banjos in the past 300 years, each with its own set of associations. Two of these, the nineteenth-century banjo of plantation blacks and the twentieth-century instrument of indigent mountain whites, have been at once consistent to themselves and different from each other, and meaning rings within their largely self-contained worlds. These two banjos lead to the contemporary icon.

To start with the black banjo, we begin with an instrument that came to the Western hemisphere with enslaved Africans, was taken up by whites, and by the 1840s had become a staple of the peculiar phenomenon known as the minstrel show, in which Northern white men blackened their faces with burnt cork and presented music and banter trading on the exoticism of the southern black man, while enjoying his lively music and a laugh at his expense. But while early minstrel musicians no doubt modeled their playing on what they heard from black banjo players to at least some extent, they were entertainers rather than reenactors and it is unlikely that an audience at a minstrel show would necessarily have heard the "authentic" sound of the plantation banjo, especially after the first few years of the fad (Linn 48).

About the same time there arose a body of sentimental popular culture woven around African Americans on the Old Plantation, starting at the time of Stephen Foster's songs (also 1840s) and extending through plays and movies as far as the 1930s, intended to evoke a romantic legend where the plantation black, carefree and happily ignorant, is frequently depicted with a banjo in his hand, or on his knee. This picture was heavily reinforced by the staging of the immensely popular *Uncle Tom's Cabin* shows which toured the country between 1852 and 1931, and in which blacks were portrayed as playing the banjo even though Harriet Beecher Stowe never once mentions the instrument in her book of the same name (Linn 58).

While whites were of course also playing the banjo as whites, and not just in blackface during the nineteenth century, it was not until approximately 1900 that the banjo begins to be found in popular culture as being connected with white players, and thus associated with whites as well as blacks by Americans far removed from the place where the banjo could actually be heard in its element. An early instance is the popular novel by John Fox, Jr., *The Little Shepherd of Kingdom Come* (1903), whose white protagonist Chad is discovered to be a fine banjo player—much to the surprise of those who hear him. Thus emerged a new stream of banjo consciousness, where the African instrument of the nineteenth century became the hillbilly instrument of the twentieth, an instrument that enjoyed a lengthy recording career starting in the mid-1920s with old time mountain string band musicians, and turned into the centerpiece of the standard bluegrass ensemble after Earl Scruggs transformed both the technique and the role of the banjo player some twenty years later. This white banjo took on one additional layer of meaning in the 1950s, when the folk revival movement, chiefly musicians from the North and East, began to identify the Southern white mountaineer as a true living remnant of pure Anglo-Saxon stock, Rousseau's Noble [English] Savage—albeit one whose nobility was slightly impaired in the popular imagination by a trifle too much moonshine and feudin'. The banjo was as much a part of his cultural kit as was his tumbledown shack.

BANJO

How is the banjo more than just a vehicle for musical accompaniment to a plantation frolic or a lonesome mountain song? For one nineteenth-century Massachusetts woman, it was important enough as a generator of cultural meaning that upon seeing some reference to Southern blacks neither knowing nor caring about the banjo, she felt compelled to write a letter to the editor: "I should be shocked to learn that the negroes of the South know nothing of the banjo. Somehow it has been a great comfort to me to associate them with that instrument" (Linn 40; the incident took place in 1883). We may owe at least some of this far-resounding resonance of the banjo's twang to Stephen Foster's popular songs romanticizing plantation life. The banjo shows up in many of these, most famously "Oh, Susannah!" The song is written in nonsense quatrains and so may only use the banjo incidentally as a handy two-syllable accessory to the Alabama-bound traveler. He's black (we know that from the dialect); he needs a two-syllable word: ah! *banjo!* (In terms of both scansion and sense it could as easily have been a "pumpkin" or a "shotgun" on his knee.)

Folk singer Pete Seeger playing banjo, 1948. Courtesy of the Library of Congress.

Foster's "Ring, Ring de Banjo!" is a song extolling the joys and stability of plantation life; in it, the freed slave comes hurrying back to the plantation. And as "massa" dies in verse four, it is none other than this freedman for whom the old man calls to softly waft his soul to the other side of the Swanee. The scene is completed by the banjo, yet it is an incongruous choice in that it is described as "dulcem"—right for the sickbed, but hardly an appropriate adjective for a properly-played banjo ("Early in de morning / Ob a lubly summer day, / My massa send me warning / He'd like to hear me play. / On de banjo tapping, / I come wid dulcem strain; / Massa fall a napping / He'll nebber wake again."). In verse one we had already learned that the singer could, in fact, play the piano if he wanted to, but he makes the conscious choice not to, unless it becomes necessary ("Den come again Susanna / By de gaslight ob de moon; / We'll tum de old Piano / When de banjo's out ob tune") (Foster 165–66). The fabricated world of the Old South is here both completed and authenticated by the banjo, a fact which Foster's consumers anticipated and, if they were like the woman from Massachusetts, required.

Jumping to the mid-twentieth century, we still find the banjo consciously used to evoke a fantasy world, although the exact locale of that world has not been as carefully worked out. The popular television show *Hee Haw* was a simplistic, cartoon-like succession of joke tableaux for which the show's writers and producers were clearly trying to evoke a country image. But just where is this "country"? With the idea that decisions made for the first episode might reflect the direction the show's creative team wanted it to take, we shall look at it in some detail.

In this episode (June 15, 1969), settings of jokes vary from a cowboy campfire to a barnyard to a cornfield to an outhouse to two different front porches, one serving as the residence of Mark Twain and the other populated by a whole passel of people and a dog. Except for the campfire (the Old West?) and Mark Twain's front porch (the banks of the Mississippi?), visual imagery does not suggest any one place, and certainly not the South—there are no plantation houses, for instance. But even so the viewer is still somehow sure that *Hee Haw*'s main (though not exclusive) cultural neighborhood is somewhere below the Mason-Dixon Line. This impression is partly due to the southern accents, but much of it also has to do with the banjo. And the way in which its use is specifically manipulated suggests that it is not just intended to provide a bit of local color.

The show opens over a driving bluegrass banjo number, but the context is strange: the other instruments heard are electric bass and, mostly, drums—sounds not associated with traditional bluegrass. Hosts Roy Clark and Buck Owens come on stage playing banjo and guitar, respectively. Owen's red, white, and blue-striped guitar grabs our visual attention, but all we hear is the banjo. The tune, written by Sheb Wooley (whose accomplishments include the fifties hit "The Purple People Eater"), includes a laughing segment to connect with the show's title, and the sense is that this is not so much a banjo number as it is a television theme song featuring a banjo. It is soon pulled down under the announcer's voice and the applause of the audience, but it has done its work: its presence authenticates the rest of the show for the viewer, whose upcoming vicarious experiences of being on that front porch and in that cornfield will now be subtly enhanced. It's a hook—an ear-con, if you will—reassurance that, yes, this is a country show all right, where "country" equals "Nashville" equals "South" as much as it equals "rural." Presumably, it could also mean that if you don't like the banjo, don't bother watching the show.

The banjo's next major appearance is in the cornfield scene, where various actors pop up and tell (what else?) corny jokes; their background music is (what else?) a banjo—which is heard, but not seen. A few jokes later we hear (but don't see) the banjo's friend the fiddle, whose music is background to the jokes told in front of the outhouse. Although cornfields and outhouses dot the whole American landscape, the sound of the banjo and fiddle anchor us in the South. They are a pair of aural overalls. And in one of this episode's musical interludes, Grandpa Jones, a well-known old-time banjo player and comedian, frails away happily on a bouncy tune which could almost (well, almost) be mistaken as something traditional except for its recurring chorus: "The banjo am the instrument for me." This is a faux grammatical blunder, and was certainly conceived to fill out and amplify the intended bumpkinicity of the banjo player.

It also deserves mention that one of the musical guests in this episode is Charlie Pride, an African American musician. Playing an electric guitar as he sings, he is backed by the "Nashville Sound" heard throughout the show—here consisting of a second electric guitar, pedal steel guitar and drums, with unseen piano and chorus added during the bridge. For once the banjo is not present, either visually or aurally: it is a richly ironic juxtaposition.

A highly popular film of approximately the same time also helped imprint the banjo into the contemporary American consciousness, though with a different range of associations. Bluegrass music is used in *Bonnie and Clyde* (1967), especially when the characters are speeding off in getaway cars. As Neil Rosenberg notes, "The music is connected to the exhilaration of lawlessness, escape, and travel, which from the outset have sexual connotations" (265). Bluegrass is also used under the scene where Bonnie finally succeeds in seducing Clyde. The fact that the first appearance of this sound, which came when Earl Scruggs joined Bill Monroe's band in 1945, postdates the year in which the movie is set (1933) by twelve years was not seen as an impediment to its use as background music by either the movie's producers or its audiences. Indeed, Flatt and Scruggs, whose "Foggy Mountain Breakdown" is the tune most associated with the movie, happily cashed in on its popularity by soon recording an album also called *Bonnie and Clyde*; they are pictured on the cover in gangster costumes. The resonance of this set of associations transcended even the facts of history, history which would have been actually lived through by many of those who saw the film and bought the album. Clyde Barrow could never possibly have heard a bluegrass band, and yet it is still somehow a convincing component of his world, not to mention the perfect back-up for a thrilling car chase. The banjo's exotic otherness no longer evokes just the southern plantation or mountain cabin, but also the American bad man folk hero and the entire romantic *monde noire* of early 1930s freewheeling lawlessness.

The Boston-based radio show *Car Talk*, from the very capital of Yankeedom, uses a banjo-centered bluegrass band for its theme music. Is it riding the "road music" imagery of *Bonnie and Clyde*? St. Paul-based *A Prairie Home Companion* also featured a banjo-laced bluegrass theme for several years, and bluegrass is still sometimes featured on the show. Are these merely transplanted examples of Southern rural white banjo music?

No: the banjo now rings with all its accumulated resonance. Through various adaptations, the African instrument has become an American idiom, and its sound evokes a visceral response that transcends any specific set of cultural associations: the banjo now conjures energy and good cheer, as much as anything. The Jamaicans had it right with their name, the *merrywhang*. As the *Peanuts* character Linus once said, "The way I see it, as soon as a baby is born he should be issued a banjo!" (Seeger 9). This would be neither an African plantation banjo nor a rural white banjo, but an American banjo.

sold in 144 countries worldwide (Weissman 88). According to *The Economist*, U.S. girls own an average of ten dolls apiece. There are Barbie computer and video games and even a work-out-video. Fans dedicate adoring websites to her and collectors attend conferences and conventions all over the country. Some fans even dress up as their favorite doll (*Barbie Nation*). Collectors can find out all sorts of Barbie-related trivia from the magazine *Barbie Bazaar*. Cindy Jackson made headlines in her attempts to restructure herself into Barbie's image through plastic surgery. The global sales figures and the activities of devoted fans point to the fact that Barbie is loved and revered throughout the world.

At the same time, Barbie has been banned by the Iranian government because of her corrupting influence on that country's traditional values (Coppen). She has been featured in numerous artistic parodies, many of which are based on the destruction and mutilation of the dolls. Barbie has been posed in a food blender, wrapped in tortillas and baked in an oven, and even been used as a dildo (Rand; Steiner). Artistic parodies of Barbie have included "Exorcist Barbie," "Sweatshop Barbie," "PMS Barbie," and "Teenage Pregnant Barbie," as well as "Suicide Bomber Barbie," a piece that was featured in a 2002 London art exhibit ("Life in Plastic"; Strohmeyer). Pop group Aqua's 1997 song "Barbie Girl" assures us that "Life in plastic / It's fantastic," while a popular bumper sticker reads "I want to be just like Barbie: That *Bitch* has Everything!"

These parodies make use of the fact that Barbie has been positioned by Mattel as an ubiquitous figure, fitting into any social role her wardrobe will allow. In fact, Barbie's creator, Ruth Handler, deliberately made Barbie's face as blank and bland as possible, in order to encourage children to "fill in" the blank with their own imagination and thus to open up as wide a range of potential imaginary identities for the doll as possible (Rand 40). Barbie's numerous careers over the years, ranging from a model to an astronaut, combine with this openness to make her a sort of "Everywoman."

Despite her seemingly "open" meaning, however, artistic parodies of the doll work because, Barbie, in fact, does have an identity to which we respond. The fact that Barbie, unlike most dolls, can be referred to by name and as "she" rather than an "it," points to her iconic status—"she" has a personality that has been carefully constructed by her Mattel parents. And most people "know" what this personality "means" or represents. Understanding Barbie as a corporate construction, Erica Rand argues, is essential to comprehending the ways in which Barbie comes to signify certain values and assumptions.

For example, the original brunette, brown-eyed Barbie was changed to a blonde-hair and blue-eyed model because her creators felt the original doll looked "too foreign." Although Mattel wanted to encourage children's fantasy, they apparently had little desire for children to fantasize about non-white identities (Rand 40). Thus, Erica Rand sees the language and imagery of "infinite possibility" used by Mattel "to camouflage what is actually being promoted: a very limited set of products, ideas, and actions" (28). Barbie models a normative vision of white, heterosexual affluence.

Yet it is perhaps her very normativity, and consumer awareness of it, that has forced the doll to change. As Rand notes, the difference between getting a consumer to buy a toy like an Etch-A-Sketch and a Barbie is that other toys, unlike Barbie, have never had to face criticism that the toy might compromise your little girl's self-esteem. Thus, Mattel has had to work to adopt (and adapt) various strategies over time to continue to win and re-win consumers at various points in the doll's history (29).

One such Mattel strategy has been systematically to attach Barbie to "culturally specific items and representations" which

Actress Millicent Roberts as "Barbie" poses with Mattel CEO Jill Barad and consumer advocate Francia Smith during a ceremony announcing the creation of a new stamp portraying the Barbie doll, 1999. AP/Wide World Photos.

work to assimilate the items into her own image (Weissman 85). Thus, although Barbie seemed relatively unaware of the feminist movement of the 1970s, in the 1980s there was a "Day-to Night" Barbie who dressed in a career outfit (albeit in pink), held occupations like "Business Executive" and "TV News Reporter," and owned a Barbie Home and Office playset (Dickey 27–29). Feminist criticisms of Barbie's unrealistic body proportions were addressed by Mattel in the late 1990s with the creation of a more "realistically" proportioned Barbie. The slogan "We Girls Can Do Anything" co-opted the language of feminism and suggested that Barbie was an empowered and empowering toy even though she remained a slave to fashion and consumption.

Similarly, in 1990 Mattel announced a new multicultural marketing strategy by launching ad campaigns for black and Hispanic versions of the doll. Mattel is clearly attempting to be (or appearing to be) more culturally sensitive and to appeal to a global market by featuring dolls of differing ethnicity, as well as, with dolls like Sign Language Barbie or Share A Smile Becky, representing the disabled community. However, this sensitivity is perhaps motivated more by concerns with penetrating a global audience than with concerns of social inclusion. Many have observed that the only difference between the traditional "white" all-American Barbie and the "ethnic" Barbie is the skin tone (Ducille; Hegde; Weissman). Ann Ducille writes that these dolls give us the "face of cultural diversity without the particulars of racial difference." Thus, she sees this move as a collapse into "easy pluralism that simply adds what it constructs as the Other without upsetting the fundamental precepts and paradigms of Western culture" (52–53). Radha Hegde likewise concludes that Barbie "survives as an icon of whiteness and femininity wherever she travels" (132).

These authors argue for the relative stability of Barbie's meaning: although she appropriates other discourses, she transforms their meanings into her own image and ultimately continues to signify hegemonic norms. However, it must be noted that even Barbie's "official" text—products marketed by Mattel—contain elements that can be understood in different ways. Rand notes the popularity of the Earring Magic Ken doll in the gay community and ties it to the "screaming gay subtext" of the promotional material for the doll. Skeptical that this imagery could be used unintentionally, she argues that it must be a sign of some intentional subversion on the part of workers within Mattel, if not by Mattel the corporation (88–89).

In the same way, although Barbie has been criticized by many feminists for representing unrealistic standards of passive femininity, she has simultaneously been seen as promoting a message of empowerment for girls. For example, Anita Brill has said that for girls of her generation, "Barbie was our liberator" (qtd. in Reid-Walsh and Mitchell 175). In contrast to the majority of toys aimed at girls that encourage girls to play games based upon the household tasks of adult women, Mattel never shows Barbie doing domestic labor. As Brill recalls, "Barbie's initial pre-feminist appearance signaled for us the universe of other possibilities. Gone from our agenda were the eternal rounds of playing mommy and daddy and baby doll, complete with baby carriages and strollers tailor-made for child-sized moms. With Barbie acting for us we could be exciting and interesting women in the world" (qtd. in Reid-Walsh and Mitchell 182). In the context in which she appeared, and for that audience of girls, Barbie signified freedom.

Furthermore, once a product has left its manufacturers, it leads its own life and can be appropriated by consumers for their own purposes (Jenkins). Consumers may choose to use and respond to Barbie variously. Often they do so in ways that are clearly not intended by her designers. These range from making clothes for the dolls to cross-dressing them to disfiguring them, actions that Rand calls a "queering" of Mattel's intentions. What does Barbie mean in the context of such actions?

Insofar as she represents an ideal, Barbie marks boundaries and sets limits. For example, she sets the standards of a slender, yet buxom, feminine beauty by which many women measure themselves. It is through our positioning against/in relation to these standards that we come to know ourselves as individuals—to acknowledge the ways we do or do not live up the ideal. The various uses to which Barbie is put may thus be seen as "acts of allegience to or rebellion against those to whom the doll refers or those who ascribe to its opposing values" (Rand 101). Barbie provides an embodied site where we can express our relationship to the dominant culture through the doll and engage with, or comment upon, or resist normative notions.

This opportunity perhaps supplies one reason why Barbie is frequently disfigured by the children who play with her. Tara Kuther and Erin McDonald note that Barbie play teaches girls about adult social roles and aids in the internalization of stereotypical feminine "scripts." They see the disfigurement of the doll as representing "girls' views about their developing feminine self.... The devaluation of Barbie dolls may symbolize girls' loss of voice and self, or their 'silencing'" (50). The disfigurement acts as a form of protest against norms of female behavior.

It's also important to note that destructive acts against the doll are assertions of a personal identity, a living subjective presence, that has the power to *be* critical of norms. What we do to or with Barbie is a form of expressing the self: we can define ourselves through play. For example, Reid-Walsh and Mitchell note the ways in which adult women's memories of, and attitudes toward Barbie, may be shaped by their own attitudes toward themselves. In their study, women tended to remember the ways they played with the doll as children as emblematic of the women they are today. In other words, women who saw themselves as conventional saw their present behavior reflected in the ways they had played with Barbie. At the same time, women who considered themselves unconventional saw their attitudes foreshadowed in the unconventional ways they had played with Barbie (186).

Insofar as Barbie is a representation of ourselves as Americans, it's useful to think of the ways she also functions to reflect those aspects of American culture we tend to repress. Every sign signifies its absent other. Barbie signals white, affluent heterosexuality, but in doing so, she also constantly reminds us of what she is *not*—she is not poor, not fat, not ethnic, not queer. Indeed, it is perhaps the ways in which Barbie signifies, through absence, those who are repressed in our culture that contributes to her popularity. A new layer of the Barbie mythology has arisen from within folk culture that clearly works to complicate her image.

As noted earlier, Barbie parodies abound on the Web and in ads for the Body Shop, as well as in art exhibits, bumper stickers, song lyrics, and even book titles. In most cases Mattel has not produced these images, and the company has launched numerous lawsuits to silence non-sanctioned uses of the Barbie image. Although not part of the official Barbie line of products, these renderings of Barbie are a form of folk culture that have become part of the larger culture by virtue of their mass circulation, and are by now an inseparable part of the meaning of the doll.

These appropriations of the Barbie image articulate consumers' ability to read and criticize the meanings of mass-produced culture. For example, "Sweatshop Barbie" by artist Sue Wandell most obviously highlights the uncomfortable reality of sweatshops that exploit the labor of thousands of women and children in nightmarish conditions, and Barbie's status as a beautiful, affluent consumer. Barbie might wear sweatshop-produced clothes—but would never work in a sweatshop herself. Texts like "Sweatshop Barbie" implicate the role of the consumer in the process of exploitation. The art piece functions by relying on our common understanding of what Barbie "means" (i.e., affluence, consumption, fashion), but also by highlighting the different ways that meaning can be evaluated. It speaks to the presence of a different subjectivity viewing the values of U.S. culture, the critical eye of the other turned against mainstream society's prevailing values and deeply held beliefs.

Barbie's iconic status—the very fixity of her image as an American ideal—gives us a shorthand way to communicate about certain values, attitudes, and assumptions in our culture. Ironically, however, such communications contribute to the ultimate destabilization of the Barbie image. Barbie floats because her meaning at this point is unstable: she is always both/and the other; it's virtually impossible for the modern consumer to think of Barbie without thinking of her detractors, or to think of the dream of American success she represents, and all the ways that dream has not been realized or has been found unworthy or flawed. Barbie the idealized American beauty is also always Barbie the oppressor. Yet despite our awareness of this, Barbie floats above the fray. She continues to flourish—floating about the globe, spreading the dream of a fabulous Malibu lifestyle where waists are small, breasts are high, and everyone's having a good time.

WORKS CITED AND RECOMMENDED

Barbie Nation: An Unauthorized Tour. Dir. Sarah Stern. New York: New Day Films, 1998.
Brill, Anita. "Barbie, My Liberator." *Revisioning Feminism Around the World*. New York: Feminist P, 1995.
Coppen, Luke. "Iran Bans Barbie." *The Times* 25 May 2002: 46.
Dickey, Susan J. "'We Girls Can Do Anything—Right Barbie!' A Survey of Barbie Doll Fashions." *Dress and Popular Culture*. Ed. Patricia Cunningham and Susan Vaso Lab. Bowling Green, OH: Bowling Green UP, 1991. 19–30.
DuCille, Ann. "Dyes and Dolls: Multicultural Barbie and the Merchandising of Difference." *Differences: A Journal of Feminist Cultural Studies* 6.1 (1994): 47–68.
Hegde, Rahda. "Global Makeovers and Maneuvers: Barbie's Presence in India." *Feminist Media Studies* 1.1 (2001): 129–33.
Jenkins, Henry. *Textual Poachers: Television Fans and Participatory Culture*. New York: Routledge, 1992.
Kuther, Tara, and Erin McDonald. "Early Adolescents' Experiences With, and View of, Barbie." *Adolescence* 39.153 (2004): 175–90.
"Life in Plastic." *The Economist* 21 Dec. 2002: 20–23.
Morgenson, Gretchen. "Saturation Barbie?" *Forbes Magazine* 20 Oct. 1997: 46–47.
Motz, Marilyn Ferris. "I Want to Be a Barbie Doll When I Grow Up: The Cultural Significance of the Barbie Doll." *The Popular Culture Reader*. Ed. Christopher Geist and Jack Nachbar. Bowling Green, OH: Bowling Green U Popular P, 1983.
———. "Seen Through Rose Tinted Glasses: The Barbie Doll in American Society." *Popular Culture: An Introductory Text*. Ed. Jack Nachbar and Kevin Lause. Bowling Green, OH: Bowling Green U Popular P, 1992. 211–34.
Rand, Erica. *Barbie's Queer Accessories*. Durham and London: Duke UP, 1995.
Reid-Walsh, Jacqueline, and Claudia Mitchell. "'Just a Doll?' 'Liberating' Accounts of Barbie Play." *Review of Education, Pedagogy and Cultural Studies* 22.2 (2000): 175–90.

Steiner, Christine. "Barbie Parody Tests Limits of Free Expression." *The Record* (Hackensack, NJ) 20 Jan. 2004: L11.

Strohmeyer, Sarah. *Barbie Unbound: A Parody of the Barbie Obsession*. Norwich, VT: New Victoria Publishers, 1997.

Weissman, Kristin Noelle. *Barbie: The Icon, the Image, the Ideal: An Analytical Interpretation of the Barbie Doll in Popular Culture*. [U.S.]: Universal Publishers/UPUBLISH.COM, 1999.

Bear

Richard Sanzenbacher

There have been few animals in our history that have sparked such imaginative fervor as the bear. Its indelible presence is everywhere: from the teddy bear and the cartoon characters of Yogi, Winnie the Pooh, Smokey the Bear, and others to the many animated films that feature the bear as the leading heroic figure, and the animal documentaries that overtly remind us of the dangers of this unpredictable creature, not to mention its use in advertisements and the cartoons of Gary Larson. And when considering holidays, what would Valentine's Day be without the bear, especially when we see the assorted array of stuffed animals, all of them attesting to a soft and romantic persona, a metaphorical construct that seems to assure us that everything will be all right? Plus, from a psychological perspective, the bear has been there to comfort and protect: we only need to visit a nursing home or a day care center to see how the stuffed bear works its magic, how it is clutched and caressed, given an important role in the lives of so many. Because of the many roles attributed to the bear, this majestic creature has become a powerful icon entrenched within the human consciousness.

Unequivocally, in Native American culture, the bear, its voice and presence, resonates in the tribal attitudes, customs, and rituals of the people. For them, the relationship between bear and human takes on a sacred and intimate quality, a kinship that embodies multiple dimensions. In David B. Rockwell's fine study *Giving Voice to Bear: North American Indian Myths, Rituals, and Images*, he observes that "Bears were often central to the most basic rites of many tribes: the initiation of youths into adulthood, the sacred practices of humanism, the healing of the sick and injured, the rites surrounding the hunt" (2). As he explores these rites in depth, he demonstrates the bear's presence in North American Indian myths and the proliferation of the bear's image in other areas of the Native American culture.

Beyond the totemic role of the bear in Native American tradition, on which much literature exists, the animal figures variously in popular culture. This entry focuses on ways the features of the bear, its physicality, and the contradictory messages associated with that physicality, images of cuddliness/

comfort versus ferocity/danger, play a definite function in the social and economic import of particular advertisements, and in the male gay community wherein a segment has built a tenuous identity around that physicality.

First, what is it about the bear in contradistinction to all other animals that would account for this fervor, this willingness to see some kind of connection to the other? Gary Brown, author of *The Great Bear Almanac*, provides a clue when he contends that of all the animals, the bear embodies several anatomical and behavioral features similar to the human. To begin with,

> bears stand bipedal and even occasionally walk in this manner;...lean back against objects to rest, and may even fold a leg across their other leg;...leave human-like footprints;...nurse and discipline their young, even spank; display moods and obvious affection during courting (petting); and are inquisitive, curious, and inflexible. (174)

Sharing similar traits, humans can imagine assimilation into the space of the bear, thus enabling them to traverse the boundary that exists between the human and the nonhuman.

It is not surprising, then, that people have constructed multiple perspectives from which to view this mysterious animal so that it has become a powerful, diverse icon. That is to say, the bear roams across many metaphorical boundaries: from images of power, renewal, healing, wildness, and primal fear to those of mystery, wisdom, playfulness, freedom, and spirituality. Whether it takes the image of a ferocious monster in the wilderness or of the endearing coziness in the teddy bear, the bear remains a fluid icon, shaped in the context in which it is imagined. More pointedly, whatever cultural lens we look through or whatever human constructs we build around this animal, the bear becomes a reality of our own making, a reality, of course, that does not necessarily reflect what the bear actually is. Yet, it is this anthropocentric imposition that accounts for the icon generated; therefore, it is important to keep this in mind when reflecting on the diverse nature of the bear as depicted in various images, if only to remind us that the bear out there in the wilderness and our idea of that same bear are two different things. The icon thus becomes our way of making sense of something that is essentially unknowable.

A poster advertising Smokey the Bear, 1970. Courtesy of the Library of Congress.

Arguably, the teddy bear phenomenon, begun by news reporters covering President Theodore Roosevelt's sportsmanship, reigns as one of the most salient illustrations of humankind's attempt to demystify the unknowable. Possibly as a way to control or strip the bear of its wild nature or as a way to coexist with an animal that instills unmitigated fear within the psyche, the teddy bear rose to its pervasive favor, becoming an icon that not only creates a comfort zone but one that embodies the Native American perception of the bear as Creator. Behavioral studies of the bear point to the fact that while in hibernation, the mother bear gives birth from one to three cubs. From this close relationship, in its perception by Native Americans, "the bear became a metaphor for the universal mother, the giver of all life." Furthermore, in "the Bear Mother creation story, the kinship of bear and human is established" (Ramsey 58–59). From one perspective, the teddy bear phenomenon may be seen as a response to the Bear Mother creation story in that this narrative foregrounds the maternal and caring nature of the bear (in addition to the fragile and vulnerable cubs), and de-emphasizes its ferocious and wild side.

The teddy bear is usually perceived from only one perspective: that of the fuzzy, cuddly bear cub that radiates a sense of coziness and comfort, an icon that manifests a space of safety, reassurance, and tranquility away from the world's problems. However, in several stores, the teddy bear cub is many times accompanied by the mother figure, a coupling that revitalizes and re-enacts the bear as Creator narrative. Accordingly, this intimate bond between the mother bear and its young replicates the human linkage between the human mother and her offspring, therefore establishing a familial connection. Seeing the teddy bear from this perspective opens up the multiple layers of this icon. On one level, the benign cuddly cuteness of the teddy bear symbolizes the ever-innocent state of the child and all the images associated with that time of life, while on another plateau it points towards universal issues of birth and nurturance. The ironic twist here is that something so fragile and vulnerable should take on such enduring cosmic significance.

A little girl playing doctor with a teddy bear. Courtesy of Shutterstock.

But while the dominant image of the bear for the last few decades has revolved around the teddy bear mystique, the world of advertisement has employed the image of the bear from diverse perspectives, going beyond and sometimes countering the cuddly persona. Some advertisements highlight the superior physical strength and prowess of the bear, while others emphasize the wild habitat in which they live and their humanlike postures. In some advertisements, the bear becomes a viable symbol for the natural world and purity. Possibly one of the most fascinating advertisements depicts a bear drinking a bottle of Valvert, pure mineral water, his paws surrounding the bottle, reminiscent of a human clutching a glass. The caption to the ad reads: "Somewhere in Belgium, there is a hidden and timeless spot pampered by Nature. On this virgin spot rises the Valvert water. The water taking its time. The water that after twenty years of percolating surfaces again tender and pure"("Animals in Advertising/Bears"). The physical and material presence of the bear becomes absorbed within the metaphor that the bear becomes. The paws enwrapped around the glass become our hands while the space that the bear occupies (standing in front of a blurry green backdrop) transports us to a pristine setting devoid of humans, pure and untainted. The overt emphasis on the natural becomes paramount here. Just as a bear would drink from a clear mountain spring, we, too, can do the same thing. The life force that water represents becomes intertwined with the life force of the bear. Put another way, if Valvert can sustain the survival of a creature in the wild, then its effect on the human can be transforming. The bear has become an icon of the wilderness, the pristine and the pure; the viewer wants to participate in that raw energy and refreshment. And how can this happen? Through the water, of course, which can be bought.

The connection of the bear to the wilderness and purity takes a different turn with an advertisement for Tryba, art-deco windows. The ad tells us that the polar bear is "king in the immense blue and whiteness of the arctic. He symbolizes for Tryba uncompromised power and serenity. In this world of pure air and water where everything stands for beauty and perfection, he is life itself"("Animals in Advertising/Bear"). Again, the bear represents the natural world and that life force, but this time the bear seems to take on a larger role than in the previous advertisement: it has been elevated to the stature of king, an image that delivers awesome power, yet a power tempered by a sense of serenity. The silence of the image seems to suggest an almost God-like presence, that ethereal voice lurking somewhere out there. This undetermined space is then further reiterated in the immense blue and whiteness of the arctic: immensity and whiteness implying spaces without boundaries. In some ways, the overly crafted image of the bear tends to wipe out the product of the advertisement, art-deco style windows. But from another perspective, we take on the kingship of the bear as we choose and control our gaze through these art glass windows, establishing our reign over the pristine land we want to imagine before us.

Although these advertisements respectfully glorify the immense power of the bear, other advertisements infuse this power with an element of danger, thus reaffirming the bear as an icon of the savage wilderness. Whereas in the water and window ads the natural world is depicted in almost mythical terms—an Eden-like setting in which the raw, violent energies of nature have been tempered or virtually erased—these advertisements circle back and zero in on the clear-cut ferociousness of this animal. One of the most telling ads depicts a close-up shot of a bear's face; however, the eyes, nose, and forehead of the bear are occluded by the open mouth and the killing teeth of this animal. This bear's face occupies at least three-fourths of the space of the ad, projecting unstoppable violence, precluding any sense of a maternal nature. In short, visions of an idyllic and tranquil wilderness implied in other ads are here unimaginable, indicating that within the icon of the bear as representative of the wilderness there are divisions, and turns of thought that tend to quarrel with each other. This ad's actual product, a network analyzer, appears in a small, side photo, with the caption, playing on the metaphor of a huge, horrible problem as "a bear": "Tame your datacomm problems easily—network analyzers." Beside the analyzer device in the photo sits a toy teddy bear, the artificial replacement for the huge, wild problem that threatens to engulf the would-be consumer.

Possibly the most intriguing use of the bear as an icon occurs within the gay male subculture. Although the beginnings of gay men's self-identifying themselves as bears is debatable, it is reported that by 1980 certain gay men in San Francisco, Toronto, Miami, New York, and elsewhere were placing a small teddy bear in their shirts or hip pockets. Supposedly, the teddy bear represented a man who was into cuddling and was a shared sign to other "bear" men. Eventually, a bear subculture emerged, its origin in San Francisco, along three lines: the underground press, private sex parties, and the newly formed medium of electronic communications. With this new venture into communication came *BEAR* magazine, a publication that became the home place and voice for this new movement. Almost overnight, the magazine became a huge sensation. More than a decade later, there were some 140 bear and bear-friendly clubs worldwide ("What Is a Bear"). These bear groups thus enabled some men to construct an authentic masculinity, a crucial outlet for those men who were contesting society's wrongheaded tendency to make being gay and being masculine mutually exclusive.

Les Wright, in *The Bear Book: Readings in the History and Evolution of a Gay Male Subculture*, offers further insight into this bear phenomenon as it relates to the gay male culture: "It may describe physical size, refer to male secondary sex characteristics, to alleged behaviors or personality traits of bears, or to metaphysical, supernatural, or other symbolic attributes of bears" (Wright, "A Concise History" 21). The most interesting aspect of this movement is why it occurred in the first place. For one thing, the bear community resisted and challenged the gay gender stereotype, that of an effeminate gay man, young in years, sporting a chiseled, slender body reminiscent of the typical *GQ* model. Identifying with the bear culture, the gay male was able to accept his own body type and be accepted by others in the same community. Essentially, according to a study of *BEAR* magazine by Joe Policarpo, the "general profile of a 'bear' includes at least some facial hair and some body hair..., a 'musky animality,' a blend of traditionally masculine aggressiveness and (feminine) desire to cuddle, muscles by Nautilus or physical labor, and a tendency to be older than the models found in most other gay male porn magazines" (qtd. in Wright, "A Concise History" 31). Yet, an overemphasis on the physicality of the typical gay male bear would disallow a significant aspect of the bear movement: the original impulse of the bears "to create a new way to express and find intimacy, emotional and sexual. Hence the emphasis on nurturing qualities, hence the idea of embraceable 'teddy bears,' hence the effort to create safe spaces" (Wright, "Introduction" 9).

The Bear movement of the 1980s also initiated a vital link with the coming of AIDS. Those infected with the disease could find a community that would not marginalize them or isolate them; instead, the movement enabled them to reconnect with life and with the social and sexual domains of gay life again. In all aspects, "The rise of a bear community is inseparable from the AIDS epidemic." It brought "the first broadly accepted sexualization of abundant body weight," something that was frowned upon and deeply contested in the traditional gay community (Wright, "Introduction" 15). But more important, the bear movement ushered in a certain mindset that encouraged authenticity, the importance of being oneself as opposed to being what one wasn't. Today, bear clubs are still active, but for "many bears, being a member of this group is not about much more than having fun and being social" (Zeffer). The nourishing aspect may still be there, but the surface, superficial qualities of good looks take precedence; appearance becomes paramount. As with any icon, the subject to which it refers is diminished in that the icon heightens only certain aspects of the bear to the exclusion of others; subsequently, the bear itself ends up being only an echo of itself, buried within the many layers of the icon.

In short, humankind's transactions with and reflections on the bear tend to imply a yearning we have for the Other, a deep need to transcend boundaries and be reunited with the natural world, to recapture that kinship between human and nonhuman that is missing from our lives. Just the fact that we construct these symbol-laden scenarios around the bear reaffirms more our endeavor to understand the mystery of bear, to situate ourselves within its proximity. Certainly, anytime we transform the nonhuman into something else, we remove ourselves that much more from the actual subject. But by creating tidy summations of the bear as reflected in the diverse icons surrounding this animal, we also open up further inquiries into the ambiguities and mysteries surrounding this wilderness wonder, thus assuring that this entity known as bear remains tentative, unfinished, yet to be envisioned in new ways, even though these ways of knowing will always fall short of completing what bear is.

WORKS CITED AND RECOMMENDED

"Animals in Advertising/Bears." 28 June 2004 <http://elve.net/panim/en/bear.htm>.

Brown, Gary. *The Great Bear Almanac*. New York: Lyons & Burford, 1993.

Ramsey, Michael S. "The Bear Clan: North American Totemic Mythology, Belief, and Legend." *The Bear Book: Readings in the History and Evolution of a Gay Male Subculture*. Ed. Les K. Wright. New York: Harrington Park P, 1997. 51–64.

Rockwell, David B. *Giving Voice to Bear: North American Indian Rituals, Myths, and Images of the Bear.* Niwot, CO: Roberts Rinehart Publishers, 1991.

"What Is a Bear." Nashoba Institute for Non-Hegemonic Masculine Identities, Culture and Communities. 28 Jan. 2004 <http://bearhistory.com/projects/.htm>.

Wright, Les K. "A Concise History of Self-Identifying Bears." *The Bear Book* 21–39.

———. "Introduction: Theoretical Bears." *The Bear Book* 1–17.

Zeffer, Andy. "The Bear Essentials." 23 Apr. 2004 <www.expresswaygaynews.com/2004/4-23/arts/feature/bear.cfm>.

Beats

Jason R. Kirby

Charlie Parker's musical expositions in cabarets made an indelible impact on white hipsters who came to be called the "Beats." They were intrigued by his ability to create melodies that reinforced their alienation from the prevailing cultural paradigm in America. Parker's music reigned in their psyches. As biographer Ross Russell notes, Bird's playing brought them in touch with a culture they could sympathize with, but could never quite wholly experience: "His playing, [and] his toughness and resilience, were expressive of the Afro-American ethos that has become the archetype of the loneliness and alienation of modern man" (367).

This entry focuses on the psychological effects Parker's musical improvisation created in the minds of white aficionados, concentrating on Jack Kerouac's impressions of Parker, because Kerouac is the most notable character of the white counterculture during the 1940s and 1950s. Parker's music created a sensation of euphoria that directly reinforced hipster contempt for rationality. Parker's improvisations allowed the "instinctive" passions to thrive in the mindsets of white hipsters. Parker was a "primitive" knight to hipsters not only for his musicianship and "blackness," but also because he represented the inexplicable "otherness" they extolled. There were discrepancies, however, between the characterizations hipsters attributed to Parker's music and life, and the realities of his musicianship and life. In short, white hipsters in their attempt to escape "whiteness" could never quite understand "blackness" in its entirety.

Charlie Parker's life and music were unconventional. Remarkably, many view him as the greatest saxophone player who ever lived, yet most of his extraordinary talent developed and evolved through self instruction (Gridley 143). After dropping out of high school, Parker commonly spent eleven to fifteen hours a day practicing his musical craft (Woideck 6). As his abilities flourished, he became instrumental in the birth of bebop, which challenged swing music, the dominant genre in jazz at the time. Contrary to swing, bebop (or bop) was distinctive for its individual instrumentation. Bebop bands typically consisted of three or four members, significantly fewer than those of swing bands; and the music gained a reputation for its faster tempo. This style provided artists, such as Charlie Parker and Dizzy Gillespie, much room to maneuver musically, whereas swing bands typically performed in a more structured arrangement. Even though swing bands were more "rational" in this regard, bebop music required more complexity and skill to play (Gridley 165; Lott 600).

From 1947 to 1950, Parker became the most celebrated figure of the bebop era. Parker's saxophone solos became legendary to those who witnessed his stage performances. Like fellow beboppers, he often performed into the early morning hours. While on stage, frequently juiced on heroin or some other intoxicant, Parker stood stationary as the notes poured out of his saxophone. Art Taylor, a former band member, describes Parker's distinctive stage demeanor: "He just stood there almost still as a statue, and when he finished, there was a pool of water at his feet" (Crouch 253–54). Other jazz musicians commonly tried to mimic Parker's virtuosity. Much to Parker's chagrin, some even began using heroin because they believed it could enhance their musicianship, because they surmised this drug had heightened Parker's creativity on stage (Davis 175).

Parker lived at the edge. Aside from his heroin addiction, Parker used marijuana and Benzedrine, was a womanizer, frequently went on eating binges, drank heavily, and smoked cigarettes. Whenever he tried to kick his heroin addiction the withdrawal symptoms became so excruciating that he generally drank himself into a stupor to alleviate the pain, which thereby reinforced his addiction to alcohol (Russell 263). Not surprisingly, on each attempt he made to quit, he only overcame his heroin habit for a short period before reverting back to the drug. The consequences of his addictions were many. For one example, aside from the debilitating health effects, he habitually showed up tardy for gigs, and on some occasions, he even missed scheduled events altogether (Bennett 73).

Jazz greats Charlie Parker, left, and Russell "Big Chief" Moore perform on the opening day of the International Jazz Festival in Paris, 1949. AP/Wide World Photos.

The de facto racism Parker experienced exacerbated both his excesses as well as his feelings of insecurity as an artist. Lerone Bennett, Jr., captures the dual alienation Parker felt: "He never believed in himself, and according to his friends, he embraced 'the needle' and the bottle to blot out the harsh reality of everyday life" (71). Following a 1950 tour in the South, even though his band fared well financially, Parker "vowed never again to set foot below the Mason-Dixon line" (Russell 291). Moreover, enacting an assault on the white establishment, Parker often slept with white women (Russell 257; Davis 171). Parker's music also represented rebellion against systematic racial injustice. As Lorenzo Thomas states while discussing the work of the famous black poet and beatnik Bob Kaufman, "Jazz music spoke a truth about existence that words were hard put to express" (Thomas 294). The use of jazz slang also challenged white oppression; as Neil Leonard explains, "Words like... 'sweet,' 'pretty,' 'square,' and 'straight' were pejorative" (152).

In 1955, Parker's indulgences finally caught up with him and contributed to his death at the young age of thirty-four.

The Beats enthusiastically embraced Parker for what they perceived as his "primitive" genius, despite the fact they misunderstood his life and the intricacies of his music (Nisenson 119). From their perspective, Parker's music represented inexplicable art. When the Beats witnessed Parker sounding off his musical motifs on stage, they yearned for the instinctive passions he represented in their minds. Parker's music symbolized for them the alienation they felt toward the world around them. Their psychological affinity with Parker, albeit often irrational, is crucial to understanding the various ideologies white hipsters favored.

To this white subculture, mainstream America offered little for the soul. While conventional white Americans embraced prosperity and conformity, white hipsters dreaded the trap of organizing their lives around the forces of the market. "Squares" (in the favored label for the white middle-class among hipsters) organized their lives efficiently, attended church regularly, refrained from indulging the senses, typically were politically conservative, engaged in materialistic acquisition, were either indifferent to or took part in racist activity, and generally considered themselves patriotic. Hipsters, contrarily, lived for the moment, scoffed at organized religion, embraced the senses, were politically liberal or apolitical, favored the instinctive over the rational, found racism repugnant, and took a fatalistic view of the world. Norman Mailer, a steadfast proponent of hipster culture, reveals this chasm in sharp terms in his landmark essay "The White Negro":

> One is Hip or one is Square...one is a rebel or one conforms, one is a frontiersman in the Wild West of American night life, or else a Square cell, trapped in the totalitarian tissues of American society, doomed willy-nilly to conform if one is to succeed. (339)

Hipsters found sanctuary in black culture. Jack Kerouac, for instance, through the lens of his narrator, Sal, in *On the Road*, clarifies the sentiments he felt toward his race: "[I wish] I were a Negro, feeling that the best the white world had offered was not enough ecstasy for me, not enough life, joy, kicks, darkness, music, not enough night" (180). To him, black culture exemplified an authenticity white culture lacked.

For hipsters, bebop concerts loosened inhibitions and offered a sanctuary from the Cold War reality nuclear weapons posed. To them, civilization seemed as though on a direct path to complete annihilation following the development of atomic weaponry, with Revelation and Christ's Second Coming playing no part in what appeared to be an impending apocalypse. As Norman Mailer contended in the "The White Negro," the profound devastation of World War II largely bolstered hipsters' sense of fatalism: "The Second World War presented a mirror to the human condition which blinded anyone who looked into it" (338). In such thinking, the next war involving America could only magnify in its destructive power, because the mere push of a button would propel the world into a nuclear holocaust. Mailer breaks down the impulses of hipsters in bearing Cold-War threats like an albatross wrapped around their necks:

> It is on this bleak scene that a phenomenon has appeared: the American existentialist—the hipster, the man who knows that if our collective condition is to live with instant death by atomic war...or with a slow death by conformity with every creative and rebellious instinct stifled..., why then the only life-giving answer is to accept the terms of death...[and] to divorce oneself from society, to exist without roots, to set out on that uncharted journey into the rebellious imperatives of the self. (339)

Charlie Parker's improvisations represented the medicine their souls required in a universe ostensibly doomed. Although they could not fully grasp the pain exuded through Parker's saxophone, hipsters knew it represented something arcane, and that the music transported their minds some place other than reality.

Jack Kerouac knew little about jazz or Parker's life, but he personified the various psychological sensations and effects Parker's music brought to the hipster generations of the late 1940s and 1950s. Kerouac became the rare white author who wanted to assimilate into the black community, for as John Ridener points out, "Until this point, most movements by and large had been to assimilate people of color into white society, creating the melting-pot ideology" (60). Parker's apparent spontaneity on stage forever changed Kerouac's writing style and approach to life. As late as 1968, Kerouac made his praise for Parker conspicuous, as he reportedly told one friend, "I got every record Charlie Parker ever made" (Amburn 48). Although Parker's riffs on stage required hours of arduous practice, Kerouac emulated his seemingly freewheeling musicianship in his writing, as he pursued spontaneous prose and seldom made revisions after his first book, *The Town and the City*. He felt writing was more genuine if it lacked "bookishness and what he referred to as 'tedious intellectualism' " (Foster 93).

Parker's music posed an alternative set forth in a standard critical work of the time, in the Apollonian and Dionysian dichotomy of Friedrich Nietzsche's *The Birth of Tragedy*. The Apollonian urge (named for the deity of civilization) emphasizes the rational faculties of human disposition, while the Dionysian (for the god of wine) celebrates the passions, the senses, the libido, and the irrational. Nietzsche claimed that in order to maintain emotional equilibrium, one had to have a balance between these two conflicting tendencies in the psyche; at either extreme, catastrophe befell. So Parker's indulgences and his eventual self-destruction modeled a Dionysian tragedy. The Beat Generation embraced their Dionysian desires. They frequently used drugs to expand their consciousness, indulged in sexual escapades, and often celebrated with alcohol. Norman Mailer romanticizes the reasons why the hipster performs such rituals in his essay "Hipster and Beatnik":

Jack Kerouac, 1967. AP/Wide World Photos.

> [H]e takes on the dissipation of drugs in order to dig more life for himself, he is wrestling with the destiny of his nervous system, he is Faustian.... He wants to get out of reality more than he wants to change it.... (374)

The Beat Generation sought Parker's music for religious enlightenment. He represented another element in their quest for hedonistic ecstasy, and as Lee Bartlett explains, "Ecstasy is...the central factor in the Dionysian vision" (120). Parker's music was godlike to Kerouac. In *Mexico City Blues*, Kerouac eulogized Parker after his untimely death, and tailored the text in his prototypical desultory fashion so it would epitomize a Parker solo on stage.

Other hipsters, like Kerouac, deified Parker and, according to Francis Davis, "swore that Parker once walked on water" (174). The Beats thought Parker's music represented the inexplicable "holy." His music embodied a religious experience, something greater than the here and now. His tunes symbolized everything hipsters lived for and worshiped. His riffs represented the indefinable "IT." "IT" in beatnik vernacular meant spiritual enlightenment and the supernatural unknown. "IT" described the nonmaterial and metaphysical aspects in mental associations that somehow transcended and surpassed the earthly void that frequented the minds of hipsters. Regina Weinreich explains "IT," stating what Kerouac means by his use of the expression in *On the Road*: "'It' is a form of instant gratification, a thrill, an epiphany, more significant to Sal [Kerouac] than the pursuit of more conventional values such as permanence and the ultimate security—the delusion of the hearth" (151).

As Mailer states in the "The White Negro," "IT" represented the God of the senses and the antithesis of Apollo: "... 'It'; God; not the God of the churches but the unachievable whisper of mystery within the sex, the paradise of limitless energy and perception just beyond the next wave of the next orgasm" (351).

Kerouac and other hipsters visited jazz clubs habitually for the spiritual medicine these venues provided. Parker became the ultimate messiah for exuding "IT." His riffs are orgasmic to Sal in *On the Road*, as he describes the emotional euphoria his protagonist Dean Moriarty experiences at a Parker-like gig, clearly expressing his belief in the superiority of "blackness":

> Out we jumped in the warm, mad night, hearing a wild tenorman [*sic*] bawling his horn across the way, going "EE-YAH! EE-YAH! EE-YAH!" and hands clapping to the beat and folks yelling, "Go go, go!" Dean was already racing across the street with his thumb in the air, yelling, "Blow, man, blow!" A bunch of colored men in Saturday-night suits were whooping it up in front.... [The] tenorman was blowing at the peak of a wonderfully satisfactory free idea, a rising and falling riff that went from "EE-yah!" to a crazier "EE-de-lee-yah!" and blasted along to the rolling crash of butt-scarred drums hammered by a big brutal Negro with a bullneck who didn't give a damn about anything but punishing his busted tubs, crash, rattle-ti-boom, crash. Uproars of music and the tenorman *had it* and everybody knew he had it.... Groups of colored guys stumbled in from the street, falling over one another to get there. "Stay with it, man!" roared a man with a foghorn voice.... Dean was in a trance. The tenorman's eyes were fixed straight on him; he had a madman who not only understood but cared and wanted to understand more and much more than there was, and they began dueling for this; everything came out of the horn.... and everybody pushed around and yelled, "Yes! Yes! He blowed that one!" Dean wiped himself with his handkerchief. (196–98)

In their hedonistic quests for euphoria, the Beats transformed Parker's improvisations into mental constructions that represented their values. They used Parker's music to reinforce the alienation they felt toward a society that appeared cold and repressive. Even though this relationship speaks volumes about their subculture, it does not do justice to Parker as an artist. White hipsters seemingly viewed Parker's death as an example that reinforced their predilection to fatalism. From their perspective, Parker represented a paragon of someone who lived to extremes in order not to "die" of conformity. In truth, Parker had a severe drug addition to heroin which he had attempted to break on a number of occasions in order to continue his life. Because heroin is the most addictive drug, especially as a result of its excruciating withdrawal symptoms, he remained trapped in the cycle of addiction. Additionally, the club scene did not provide a milieu conducive to sobriety.

Parker's music did induce a levitating effect on the psyche, but his improvisations were framed on years of meticulous practice rather than spontaneous whims on stage. Eric Lott, setting bebop in its original context of African-American society, discounts the white hipster version:

> White-Negro revisionists Kerouac and Mailer to the contrary, bebop was no screaming surge of existential abandon, its makers far from lost. And while bebop said there was a riot going on, it was hardly protest music.... Bebop was about making disciplined imagination alive and answerable to the social change of its time. (597)

The music of Parker and others grew out of African-American resistance to and protest of racial injustice in World War II, and migrations in which ethnic awareness as well as musical styles coalesced, in Harlem. The resultant ferment of creativity in bebop responded in "a politics of style beyond protest, focusing the struggles of its moment in a live and irreverent art" (Lott 599, 603). Moreover, as Amiri Baraka (formerly the black beatnik LeRoi Jones) explains, black musicians of the period, unlike their white counterparts, were already outside the mainstream: "The young Negro musician of the forties began to realize that merely by being a Negro in America, one *was* a nonconformist" (Jones 188). In addition, Parker's own life and music were very complex, and even biographers find it arduous, and in some cases impossible, to define Parker (Nisenson 118).

Charlie Parker's artistic ingenuity made him a hero to white hipsters. His music reinforced their estrangement from mainstream American values. He gave them Dionysus through his saxophone, and metaphorically attacked Apollonian values in the process. Parker's musical genius allowed for a vast range of emotional responses among white listeners; and for the white community, his solos became in figurative terms a litmus test for whether one was hip or whether one was square.

WORKS CITED AND RECOMMENDED

Amburn, Ellis. *Subterranean Kerouac: The Hidden Life of Jack Kerouac*. New York: St.Martin's, 1998.
Bartlett, Lee. "The Dionysian Vision of Jack Kerouac." *The Beats: Essays in Criticism*. Ed. Lee Bartlett. London: McFarland, 1981. 115–26.
Bennett, Lerone, Jr. "Charlie (Bird) Parker—Madman or Genius?" *Negro Digest* 10 (Sept. 1961): 70–75.
Crouch, Stanley. "Bird Land: Charlie Parker, Clint Eastwood, and America." *The Charlie Parker Companion*. Ed. Carl Woideck. New York: Schirmer Books, 1998. 251–62.
Davis, Francis. "Bebop and Nothingness." *The Charlie Parker Companion*. 174–78.
Foster, Edward Halsey. *Understanding the Beats*. Columbia: U of South Carolina P, 1992.

Gridley, Mark. *Jazz Styles: History and Analysis*. Englewood Cliffs, NJ: Prentice Hall, 1994.

Jones, LeRoi. *Blues People: Negro Music in White America*. New York: William Morrow and Company, 1963.

Kerouac, Jack. *Mexico City Blues*. New York: Grove P, 1959.

———. *On the Road*. New York: Penguin Books, 1957.

Leonard, Neil. "The Jazzman's Verbal Usage." *Black American Literature Forum* 20 (Spring–Summer 1986): 151–60.

Lott, Eric. "Double V, Double-Time: Bebop's Politics of Style." *Callaloo* 11.36 (1988): 597–605.

Mailer, Norman. *Advertisements for Myself*. New York: G. P. Putman's Sons, 1959.

Nietzsche, Friedrich. *The Birth of Tragedy*. New York: Vintage Books, 1967.

Nisenson, Eric. *Blue: The Murder of Jazz*. New York: Da Capo P, 1997.

Ridener, John. "Charlie Parker Looked Like Buddha: the American Road and its Literature." Ph.D. Diss., Division III Project, Volume 1, Hampshire College, 1998.

Russell, Ross. *Bird Lives! The High Life and Hard Times of Charlie (Yardbird) Parker*. New York: Da Capo P, 1973.

Thomas, Lorenzo. "Communicating by Horns: Jazz and Redemption in the Poetry of the Beats and the Blacks Arts Movement." *African American Review* 26.2 (1992): 291–98.

Weinreich, Regina. "The Divine Comedy of the Bebop Buddha: Kerouac, Jazz, and 'It'." *Beat Culture: The 1950s and Beyond*. Ed. Cornelis A. van Minnen, Jaap van der Bent, and Mel van Elteren. Amsterdam: VU UP, 1999. 149–57.

Woideck, Carl. *Charlie Parker: His Music and Life*. Ann Arbor: U of Michigan P, 2001.

Betty Crocker

Pauline Adema

Betty Crocker, one of the most widely recognized names in the food industry, was never a real person: she was the creative brain child of the Washburn-Crosby Company. It is difficult to overestimate the impact this domestic icon has had on corporate advertising strategies, American domestic cookery, and perhaps most importantly, on eating. Her near-century long influence is attributable to her dynamic and malleable persona—or, rather, the creative manipulation of her by her corporate guardians. Betty Crocker–branded books and products continue to address changing notions of what it means to be a homemaker as well as changing attitudes toward cooking and eating.

By the end of the nineteenth century, food companies faced increasing competition and a burgeoning national market. To distinguish their products many corporations created fictitious personas that consumers could associate with their foodstuffs. One of the oldest and most familiar commercial icons is Aunt Jemima, whose image appeared as early as 1893. Second to Aunt Jemima and nearly thirty years her junior is Betty Crocker. Since her creation in 1921 Betty Crocker has won the admiration of generations of American homemakers.

In response to a magazine advertising contest promotion, the Washburn-Crosby Company, which became General Mills in 1928, received not only contest entries but also letters from homemakers across the country asking for baking advice. For a short time the company's team of nearly fifty home economists answered the thousands of letters and a male executive signed each letter. Realizing that a woman would be a more appropriate authority to dispense baking advice, Washburn-Crosby created home economist and cooking expert Betty Crocker. The name "Betty" was chosen for its all-American friendly sound; the surname "Crocker" honored a retired director of the company. Betty Crocker quickly established a reputation for accessible, reliable recipes and sound domestic advice.

Among the team of home economists working at Washburn-Crosby was Marjorie Child Husted. By the time Husted became the head of the Home Service Department in 1926, Betty Crocker was already a household name.

Under Husted's guidance, Betty Crocker's role expanded from signing letters and offering recipe pamphlets to hosting radio and, subsequently, television shows on which she presented recipes and provided cooking advice to eager audiences of homemakers.

Betty Crocker endowed a male-dominated corporation with a feminine identity. In promoting its products, she instructed housewives across the country how to use a rapidly expanding array of packaged foods and modern kitchen appliances. Through her advice she affirmed the value of woman's role as caretaker and provider for her family's health and emotional well-being. Inspired by Betty Crocker's success, several other companies created fictitious spokeswomen. Among the most notable were Ann Pillsbury for Pillsbury Flour, Kay Kellogg for Kellogg's cereal, Martha Logan for Swift Meats, and Anne Marshal for Campbell Soup, all part of a burgeoning field of real and fictitious female experts who personalized otherwise impersonal corporate consumer culture.

"AMERICA'S FIRST LADY OF FOOD" ON THE RADIO

"The Betty Crocker Cooking School of the Air," inaugurated in 1924, introduced a disembodied Betty Crocker to a rapidly-growing radio audience. Like other radio homemakers of the 1920s, the voices that portrayed Betty Crocker radiated confidence, enthusiasm, and concern. Radio programs provided isolated, especially rural, women with a friendly female voice that offered them companionship and advice. But it was not only radio listeners who benefited from Betty Crocker's wisdom. Newspaper and magazine advertisements increased her audience. The more people read or heard her, the more letters she received asking for advice and requesting recipe booklets. "The Betty Crocker Cooking School of the Air," which began on the Washburn-Crosby owned radio station WCCO, was so successful that it had expanded to thirteen regional stations by 1925. Thirteen different women across the country trained to be the voices of Betty Crocker. Playing the role of Betty Crocker, they broadcast food and cooking tips for the nation's first-ever radio cooking program. The program joined the roster of NBC, then a nascent national radio network, in 1927. In 1936, thanks to developments in radio technology, listeners heard a single voice as Betty Crocker.

Introduced as "America's First Lady of Food," Betty Crocker's radio career grew throughout the 1930s and into the 1940s. She offered help and support to her listeners while promoting food products and domestic ideology. Housewives wrote letters to Betty Crocker asking cooking questions. She answered their questions on the air and always recommended General Mills products. Her written and spoken advice blurred the line between recipes and corporate endorsement. Through Betty Crocker, General Mills had a direct link to domestic consumers and developed a loyal customer base. Once again other food companies followed in Betty Crocker's successful footsteps.

BETTY CROCKER

General Foods, for example, created the "General Foods Cooking School of the Air" early in the 1930s, employing their version of Betty Crocker, Frances Lee Barton.

During World War II Betty Crocker did her patriotic duty by advising readers and listeners how to make the most of the foods available while dealing with food shortages. Her wartime radio program, "Our Nation's Rations," was produced by General Mills under commission from the War Food Administration. Her widely distributed wartime recipe pamphlet, "Your Share," further reinforced her reputation as a cookery expert. Betty Crocker also was featured in wartime film strips and booklets about low-cost menus. By 1945, 91 percent of American housewives knew Betty Crocker's name. More than 50 percent of respondents correctly associated her with General Mills. That same year, Betty Crocker was named the second-most-admired woman in America, second only to Eleanor Roosevelt.

After the war Betty Crocker, a well known "live trademark" as such corporate icons were called, maintained her role as radio homemaker. Husted continued to create and script her shows, as well as other promotions and contests. She developed two new radio programs after the war, "The Betty Crocker Magazine of the Air" and a five-minute show called "Time for Betty Crocker." Thanks to Husted, the Betty Crocker persona was that of a strong woman who took very seriously her role as advisor, asserting the value of women's work in the home and her role as caretaker of the family. Each woman put forth a professional image, affirming Betty Crocker's role as the nation's leading (though fictitious) home economist.

By the late 1940s, home audiences spent less time listening to the radio than watching television, bringing a new medium through which companies could promote their products. Following successful early cooking TV shows like James Beard's *I Love to Eat*, *The Betty Crocker Show* premiered on CBS in 1950. Following the custom of the day to incorporate commercial products into company-produced programs, Betty Crocker's show was a scripted advertisement for General Mills baking products. The show failed, however, because of its incongruous images of Betty Crocker as well as its "stodgy writing and leaden patriotism" (Shapiro). After one more unsuccessful attempt at a television program, General Mills relegated Betty Crocker to an advisor and recipe-giver primarily through radio, letters, and printed media, with a presence in short TV commercials.

PICTURING THE IDEAL

The first visual image of Betty Crocker was created in 1936. Since then, her likeness has been updated seven times (1955, 1965, 1968, 1972, 1980, 1986, and 1996) to keep up with changing societal moods and evolving conceptions of the "ideal" woman. The changing faces of Betty Crocker are a barometer of shifting concepts of domesticity and women's role as homemaker in the

The different versions of Betty Crocker throughout the twentieth century. AP/Wide World Photos.

twentieth-century United States. When she first appeared in picture form, Betty Crocker was a stern grey-haired matriarch. To balance the nurturing softness associated with a maternal image, she appeared in a crisp red jacket and unruffled blouse. She exuded confidence. She looked like an authoritative woman who would deliver opinions with a gentle but firm touch.

Betty Crocker's portraits always present her in red and white, the colors of the easily recognized Betty Crocker logo of a red teaspoon bearing her signature, and she always has dark hair and eyes. The most recent portrait, prepared in honor of her seventy-fifth birthday, is an amalgamation of seventy-five images submitted by consumers who were asked to create their "ideal Betty." She is shown in her trademark red jacket over a white shirt. She sports neatly styled but not fussy short, dark hair and subtle jewelry. A distinguishing feature of the contemporary Betty Crocker is her broad smile. The 1955 portrait is the only other one in which Betty Crocker's smile is expansive enough to expose her teeth, which are perfectly straight and white—much like Betty Crocker was conceived to be. The most recent portrait presents Betty Crocker with dark yet nonspecific features. Her modern incarnation suggests that she is not so purely Anglo-American as she used to be, reflecting the reality that neither her target consumer population, nor the American domestic ideal, is as predominantly white as in the past.

"BIG RED" AND BETTY CROCKER'S COOKBOOK LEGACY

Between 1930 and 1950, General Mills published several Betty Crocker recipe pamphlets that were widely distributed to homemakers. A 1933 pamphlet "Betty Crocker's 101 Delicious Bisquick Creations as Made and Served by Well-Known Gracious Hostesses" promoted the relatively new General Mills product Bisquick, introduced two years before as the first pre-mixed baking mix. Consumers had to learn to make biscuits and other baked goods from a mix, helped by directions. The popularity of Betty Crocker's recipe pamphlets anticipated the resounding success of her cookbooks.

By the time Marjorie Husted retired from General Mills in 1950, Betty Crocker's role was changing from that of a leading expert on domestic food to a corporate figurehead who gave less baking advice and more cooking demonstrations. This gradual transformation paralleled changes in the food industry which, in turn, facilitated and reflected changes in the American family as well as cooking patterns. Bisquick was part of a trend within the food industry to create shortcut food that required less cooking skill. It represented the future of the American food industry: convenience foods. Food and appliance technologies were transforming the ways Americans cooked, entertained, and ate. As the availability of packaged foods increased, so too did housewives' desire to learn to use them.

In addition to guidance on making cakes from scratch, Betty Crocker offered advice on using her cake mixes. Referring to the predictability of her cake mixes, in 1953 Betty Crocker introduced what became her famous tagline: "I guarantee a perfect cake, every time you bake—cake after cake after cake." That statement typifies the way the food industry promoted its products in much of popular culture; that is, food from a package is easy to prepare and will produce consistent results, time after time. The domestic ideal of the 1950s still placed a woman in the kitchen, but it had her taking full advantage of the conveniences afforded her by modern appliances and packaged foods. Recipes in the 1950s moved away from cookery that required skill toward providing directions for combining and heating packaged, canned, and frozen foods.

Embodying this shift in cooking patterns and an idealized white middle-class domesticity of mid-century America is *Betty Crocker's Picture Cook Book* (BCPCB), first published in 1950. It sold more copies than any other nonfiction book that year. By 1951, 1 million copies were in print. All nine editions up to 1998 were published in usable three-ring binder and spiral bound formats. It remains among the most popular cook books ever printed. BCPCB, affectionately called "Big Red" because of the first edition's red cover, quickly joined the ranks of other kitchen bibles such as Fanny Farmer's *Boston School Cook Book* (1896) and Irma Rombauer's *Joy of Cooking* (1931). Unlike those books, however, Big Red was the product of a committee. The General Mills home economists who contributed to it not only wrote and tested the recipes, they also cooked at home and knew the realities of being a busy homemaker. Their personal experiences woven into the book's extra-recipe text became part of its appeal for many other women. As with other popular mid-century cookbooks, Big Red offered readers ideological messages on how to administer housewives' roles as household managers, primary caregivers, and wives.

Big Red was geared toward young women who missed learning how to cook at home, for several possible reasons. Some young brides came from homes where domestic workers had done most of the cooking. As newlyweds on their own they were left to learn basic kitchen skills. Some young women missed learning how to cook because they, and possibly their mothers, worked during the war. Still others lacked cooking skills because they attended residential colleges that took them away from the kitchen classroom at home. For various reasons, many women in America's postwar emerging middle-class had to learn to cook.

Big Red was just the tool kitchen neophytes needed. Accompanying its straight-forward recipes and practical tips were 633 instructional black-and-white photographs. In addition to the ground-breaking photographic instructions were thirty-six color photographs. These glamour shots showed the housewife how the finished dishes should look when she presented them to her family and guests. They were a visual representation of the 1950s food ideal. Implicit in the ideal was the message that it was the responsibility of the woman of the house to attain it. Through its extra-recipe rhetoric and illustrations the book affirmed the importance of food as literal and symbolic sustenance for individual, familial, and social identity. It served as pedagogical tool on multiple levels, teaching not only how to cook but also how to plan meals that would please the family and impress guests. In this way the book had a socializing function, reinforcing women's place in the home.

The stereotype of a homemaker in a somnolent mid-century America belies the era's social and political tensions. Simmering alongside postwar national pride and prosperity was paranoia as Cold War fears dominated public discourse and shaped public policy. Jennifer Horner argues that *Betty Crocker's Picture Cook Book* was a gendered response to a post–World War II social crisis, part of a larger mass-media campaign of reintegration for returning veterans. Popular media such as magazines, television, and cookbooks presented women's domestic work as civilizing children and men, the latter especially important because 11 million United States service men reentered society after the war. Post–World War II emphasis on the domestic sphere and women's role in it was not without contention. Beneath the apparent placidity of the 1950s festered discontent that resulted in Betty Friedan's 1963 book *The Feminine Mystique*.

While Big Red promoted conformity to homemaking, it also advocated some adventure and diversity. By the 1950s, housewives were being encouraged to transform creatively packaged foods into chic (for the era) meals. Big

Red embodied the seeming paradox of creating "authentic" international dishes using American-made convenience foods, and invited domestic cooks to be adventurous within the safety of their kitchens and with familiar American products. Under "National Soups," for example, the cook found recipes for "Italian Minestrone," "Scotch Broth," "Potage de Fromage," "Borsch," and "Swedish Pea Soup." The book's inclusion of recipes from a variety of ethnic groups reflected a growing interest in international foods and presaged future Betty Crocker ethnicity-specific cook books. The incorporation of recipes representing different ethnic or cultural groups can also be interpreted as General Mills' attempt to recognize the diversity of America's population and the contributions such groups made to American foodways. Noticeable by its absence, however, is mention of African Americans, who comprised a substantial segment of the population. That omission typifies the cautious, indeed fearful, mid-century attitude about race in the Unites States.

Since the 1950s, Betty Crocker's name and signature-bearing teaspoon logo have appeared on more than 200 cookbooks. As Americans' interest in cooking ethnic foods blossomed and persisted, so too did her bibliography of specialty ethnic cookbooks. For example, the 1981 *Betty Crocker's Chinese Cookbook* was revised and updated with new recipes in 1991, resulting in the *Betty Crocker's New Chinese Cookbook*. In keeping with an increasingly health-conscious society, Betty Crocker added terms like "diet," "low fat" and "cholesterol" to her vocabulary. For body-conscious cooks and eaters she produced titles such as *Betty Crocker's Eat and Lose Weight* (1992, with several updated editions since then) and *Betty Crocker's Healthy New Choices* (1998). Yet, attesting to the ongoing popularity of her now-classic first book, a facsimile edition of the original *Betty Crocker's Picture Cook Book* appeared in 1998. From it contemporary cooks can prepare recipes such as "Canary Corn Sticks" and "Chocolate Chip Chiffon Cake," or read tips for "thrifty [meat] buying" just as preceding generations of home cooks have done.

Betty Crocker's cookbook legacy is not limited to printed media. She entered the electronic age by producing "Betty Crocker's Cookbook," a handheld, electronic cookbook. Betty Crocker entered the computer age by offering "Cook'n With Betty Crocker" recipe software. Not one to shun promotional opportunities or new media, Betty Crocker has a presence on the World Wide Web. At the Web site www.bettycrocker.com, visitors can "Take a peek at America's Most Trusted Kitchens where over 50,000 recipe tests are performed each year." And of course visitors to the site can access thousands of test-kitchen tested recipes that are "fun and easy to make."

FUN AND EASY TO MAKE: AN ENDURING LEGACY

The number and types of products bearing Betty Crocker's name and her familiar red spoon logo have grown exponentially since her letter-writing days. From Gold Medal Flour to small kitchen appliances to toys, the Betty Crocker brand is affixed to a wide assortment of consumer goods. Among the most enduring non-food items bearing Betty Crocker's seal of approval is the Easy-Bake Oven. Introduced in 1963 by Kenner Products, purchased by General Mills in 1968, the Easy-Bake Oven was a child-size version of the domestic oven. More than 500,000 of these working toy ovens sold in its first year on the market. With the Easy-Bake Oven young cooks—mostly girls, especially in its early years—could actually bake miniature cakes and cookies in a mini-oven "just like mom's!" As with other Betty Crocker items, the Easy-Bake Oven was fun and educational. It taught little girls baking basics while affirming traditional gender roles. The Easy-Bake Oven playfully taught little girls that their place was at the stove and that Betty Crocker products were integral to their baking experiences. The popularity of the Easy-Bake Oven inspired spin-off products including miniature versions of Betty Crocker cake mixes and miniature TV dinners. Renewed interest in Easy-Bake Ovens at the end of the twentieth century inspired cookbooks such as *The Official Easy-Bake Cookbook!* (1999) and *The EasyBake Oven Gourmet* (2003).

Betty Crocker remains relevant because she and her product lines adapt to shifting political, social, and economic currents. At the fore of the convenience food trend with her cake mixes, Betty Crocker anticipated the meal in a box trend when she launched Hamburger Helper in 1971. It was so successful that she followed it with Chicken Helper and Tuna Helper, also dry dinner kits to which consumers just add the meat or tuna. A more recent variation on one-dish casseroles is her new (2002) shelf-stable complete dinner kit, Complete Meals.

As a persona, Betty Crocker has endured through generations for whom, as Mary Drake McFeely comments, "like many good fictional characters she had assumed a convincingly real presence as an omniscient and reassuring domestic advisor." It is easy to forget that she is not a real person. Her tenacity in the American imagination—and in our kitchens—attests to her timelessness as a merged corporate and domestic icon.

WORKS CITED AND RECOMMENDED

Horner, Jennifer R. "*Betty Crocker's Picture Cookbook*: A Gendered Ritual Response to Social Crises of the Postwar Era." *Journal of Communication Inquiry* 24.3 (2000): 332–45.

Inness, Sherrie A. *Dinner Roles: American Women and Culinary Culture*. Iowa City: U of Iowa P, 2001.

Marling, Karal Ann. "*Betty Crocker's Picture Cook Book*: The Aesthetics of American Food in the 1950s." *Prospects* 17 (1992): 79–103.

McFeely, Mary Drake. *Can She Bake a Cherry Pie? American Women and the Kitchen in the Twentieth Century*. Amherst: U of Massachusetts P, 2000.

Mendelson, Anne. *Stand Facing the Stove: The Story of the Women Who Gave America the Joy of Cooking*. New York: Henry Holt, 1996.

Neuhaus, Jessamyn. *Manly Meals and Mom's Home Cooking: Cookbooks and Gender in Modern America*. Baltimore: Johns Hopkins UP, 2003.

Shapiro, Laura. *Something from the Oven: Reinventing Dinner in 1950s America*. New York: Viking, 2004.

Bomb

Margot A. Henriksen

The atomic bomb's attainment of iconic status is seemingly frozen at a very specific point and place in time. At 8:15 A.M., on August 6, 1945, the United States dropped an atomic bomb on Hiroshima, Japan, simultaneously contributing to the end of World War II and the beginning of the atomic age and the Cold War. The atomic explosion that devastated Hiroshima continues, however, to reverberate into the present. Its enduring centrality to the history of the twentieth century found confirmation at the end of the century, when select journalists and scholars in 1999 voted the atomic bombing of Hiroshima the most important story of the last 100 years. Likewise does the significance of the atomic bomb itself continue to resonate, albeit as incorporated into broader and more inclusive designations such as nuclear weapons or weapons of mass destruction.

The iconic weapon of choice after Hiroshima and during the Cold War, the atomic bomb and its more potent successors did not disappear when that ideological conflict between the superpowers came to a conclusion upon the dissolution of the Soviet Union in 1991. In the post–Cold War "Second Nuclear Age," the atomic bomb retains its authority as an icon, as nuclear stockpiles and nuclear weapons development persist as major shaping forces in the exercise of American power. The potential and real proliferation of these weapons of mass destruction outside the American sphere has profoundly altered the practice of American foreign policy, most recently in the wake of the September 11, 2001, terrorist attacks on the United States. Saddam Hussein's presumed cache of weapons of mass destruction provided one rationale for President George W. Bush's 2003 preemptive strike against Iraq in his continuing war on terrorism; North Korea's nuclear program has landed that country squarely within Bush's "axis of evil"; and so-called "dirty bombs," small, portable nuclear weapons, comprise yet another possible terrorist threat. The atomic bomb possesses relevance as an evolving and ambivalent American icon, signifying both awesome American strength and apocalyptic American fear.

The U.S. government and military shrouded the birth of the atomic bomb as an iconic American weapon in secrecy. The Manhattan Project established in 1942 to develop the weapon operated as a top-secret endeavor and conducted its official Trinity test of the atomic bomb in the remote deserts of New Mexico on July 16, 1945. Even with the public, wartime atomic bombings of Hiroshima and Nagasaki on August 6 and 9, 1945, officials released very little information about this ultimate weapon and kept its human effects largely invisible. Iconic imagery of the atomic bomb appeared shadowy, often expressed in metaphoric fashion in ancillary atomic representations such as the majestic yet terrible mushroom cloud that towered into the sky after an atomic explosion. Technologically complex and capable of a vastness of destruction hitherto unknown, the atomic bomb proved intellectually and psychologically difficult to comprehend or to represent. The difficulties seemed greatest when attempting to envisage the human and material devastation beneath the mushroom cloud. Emerging from mystery and taking on various incarnations as nuclear weapons technology and public knowledge deepened, the atomic bomb developed into an unstable icon whose different meanings received a mixed reception in American society and culture. Rather than serving as a unifying American icon, the atomic bomb became a site of dispute, open to often radically divergent political and cultural representations. At the extreme ends of interpretation, the atomic bomb conjured either triumph or tragedy; peace and hope or death and despair; utopian promise or apocalyptic peril. The atomic bomb's divisive and ambivalent iconography arose from the ashen landscapes of Hiroshima and Nagasaki.

When President Harry S. Truman announced to the American public on August 6, 1945, that one bomb, an atomic bomb, had been dropped on the Japanese city of Hiroshima, he explained the revolutionary destructive power of the weapon as stemming from its harnessing of the basic power of the universe, akin to the forces powering the sun. The iconic significance of this stunning if abstruse weapon became more concrete to Americans as Truman's threatened "rain of ruin from the air" materialized next over Nagasaki, Japan, thereafter bringing about Japanese surrender and the end of World War II. Americans celebrated the atomic bombings of Hiroshima and Nagasaki for concluding a long and deadly global conflict, for assuring the unconditional surrender of Japanese forces, and, by doing so, for preventing a massive loss of American life in an anticipated invasion of Japan. The American soldiers scheduled to participate in that invasion hailed this new and awe-inspiring atomic bomb with especial fervor, often "thanking God" for its advent and application against the merciless Japanese enemy who had initiated hostilities at Pearl Harbor. The atomic bomb earned early iconic glory as a war-ending weapon that secured the triumph of the United States in World War II.

Enveloped in the narrative of World War II, "the good war," the atomic bomb came to represent from an American point-of-view a weapon of peace, a weapon that saved lives. Americans began to accustom themselves to the sometimes arcane and amazing iconic elements associated with these first atomic bombs dropped on Hiroshima and Nagasaki—designated "Little Boy" and "Fat Man"—explosions produced through fission and the energy-releasing splitting of atoms in a scientific endeavor of technical marvellousness, each capable of obliterating a city then left in smoldering ruins, its observers blinded by a flash of light brighter than the sun and then shadowed by the billowing mushroom cloud. At the same time, other more unsettling iconic imagery began to be associated with the atomic bomb. Uncomfortable atomic images arose in the American imagination from the time of these initial uses of the atomic bomb, becoming even more profoundly disturbing as further information and select photographic materials circulated in the public sphere. On the very day that President Truman revealed the existence of this secret weapon of victory that could vaporize an urban center, one radio commentator wondered whether the United States had created a Frankenstein. Monstrous images of death, charnel smells of burning flesh, and visions of apocalypse also attached to the new American icon. A nervousness that this American creation would turn on its creators pulsed in the United States.

The publication of John Hersey's *Hiroshima* in 1946 sealed the iconic association of Hiroshima and the atomic bomb, and familiarized anxious Americans with monstrously deadly and tragically threatening signifiers of the atomic bomb. Hersey released his journalistic account of six survivors one year after the bombing; his account reflected the increased knowledge of the atomic bomb and its effects that had accrued. More importantly, it switched the point of view on the atomic bomb to the Japanese. Although designated by American political and military leaders as a "military target," Hiroshima also served as home to thousands of civilians—a point stressed by Hersey in his choice to follow the stories of women, priests, and doctors. Along with the dead, these atomic survivors represented the first victims of the atomic bomb and provided a view from beneath the mushroom cloud. And it was a horrifying vision, replete with detail on the terror-inducing and stupefying physical consequences and aftereffects of an atomic bomb: thousands instantly incinerated by the scorching blast of the bomb, deformed by melting eyeballs and skin burned so badly it sloughed off in sheets, thousands more survivors, nearly impossible to distinguish from the dead given their wounded, singed flesh and their dazed, zombie-like confusion, all subject to strange atmospheric conditions—huge, radioactive raindrops, wild winds, and fires that took away any shelter in a city already largely reduced to rubble and ashes. Thousands who lived through the bombing nonetheless died in the following hours, days, and weeks, succumbing to the radiation sickness that was a by-product of the bomb's fallout. Such images entered a newly atomic apocalyptic imagination in America, and Americans visualized themselves along with the Japanese as potential victims of this iconic bearer of irradiated mass death.

Hiroshima and Nagasaki set the terms of iconic struggle regarding the atomic bomb, whereby the bomb belonged either to the victors or the victims,

Hiroshima atomic dome. Courtesy of Shutterstock.

and promised peace and security or betokened violence and annihilation. Expressions of atomic bomb guilt and fear, such as those fanned by Hersey's *Hiroshima*, surfaced and yet were countered by more confident assessments of atomic security and safety. As World War II bled into the cold war, United States leaders sanctified the atomic bomb as a means of preserving peace and security in a world now threatened by Soviet communist expansion. Intent on protecting the American monopoly on the atomic bomb and institutionalizing the system that had produced the weapons for Hiroshima and Nagasaki, the United States government enshrined the atomic bomb as a weapon of peace designed to allow the United States to prevail in the Cold War. The state also closely guarded the bomb's secrets—both in terms of its scientific and industrial production and in terms of its dangers.

One group of Americans, themselves atomic icons, did challenge the government's comfortable assumptions about atomic moral certitude and the feasibility of maintaining indefinitely a monopoly on the bomb. The physicists of the Manhattan Project, those "atomic scientists" credited with the invention of this scientific and military breakthrough, gave voice to remorse about the weapons they had created. They often advocated international control over atomic weapons, because they believed it was just a matter of time before Soviet scientists matched their feat. J. Robert Oppenheimer, the "father of the atomic bomb," famously stated that the physicists had "known sin" as a result of their work on the atomic bomb, addressing the guilt associated with Hiroshima and Nagasaki. Founding the *Bulletin of Atomic Scientists* in 1947, in part as a forum to discuss their views, atomic scientists included on the cover of each issue the "Doomsday Clock." The hands of the clock took position in relation to a dark midnight, symbolic of nuclear war and destruction and expressive of physicists' fears for the future of humans in the atomic age. In 1947, the hands of the clock read seven minutes to doomsday. The prospects for annihilation appeared even more likely once the Soviets tested their own atomic bomb in 1949 and once the United States launched plans to invent a "super bomb." A number of scientists, including Oppenheimer, argued against working on what would be a hydrogen bomb, a fusion device of thermonuclear proportions; its exponential increase in devastating power would make it a genocidal weapon, an instrument for the mass slaughter of civilians. The Atomic Energy Commission (AEC), which oversaw atomic developments, nonetheless approved the project. In 1952 and 1953, the United States and Soviet Union each tested workable H-bombs. The *Bulletin of Atomic Scientists'* Doomsday Clock moved within two minutes of midnight.

In the intense atmosphere of the Cold War and an atomic and hydrogen bomb arms race between the superpowers, the warnings of scientists had little effect on the government's embrace of atomic and hydrogen bombs as icons of Cold War–security and safety. That search for safety and security included ferreting out "atomic spies" who had presumably allowed the Soviet Union to attain atomic secrets. It enfolded other Americans deemed to be "subversives" or "security risks" because of their political affiliations with communism or because of their criticism of the American system and its atomic icon. Julius and Ethel Rosenberg were sent to the electric chair in 1953 as atomic traitors, and even J. Robert Oppenheimer lost his security clearance with the AEC in 1954, partly as a result of his political past but mostly as a result of having tainted iconic nuclear weapons with guilt, remorse, and moral opposition. The way was clear for the atomic bomb to remain at the sacred core of an evolving nuclear weapons arsenal aimed at deterring a Soviet attack or World War III. Atomic bombs, hydrogen bombs, and intercontinental ballistic missiles made viable American foreign and military policies of deterrence based on "massive retaliation," "brinksmanship," and mutually assured destruction—all of which entailed an American willingness to prepare for and wage nuclear war.

American officials coupled this preparation for war to a preparation for peace, threatening the Soviets with destruction while promising Americans a utopian peace made idyllic by atomic energy and nuclear deterrence. President Truman had described the atomic bomb as a "weapon of peace," and President Dwight D. Eisenhower promoted "Atoms for Peace" in 1953, even as news of successful hydrogen bomb tests arrived. The Air Force's Strategic Air Command, tasked with flying the aircraft that would deploy the bombs, adopted "Peace Is Our Profession" as its motto. Although wrapped in peaceful imagery, safe behind a veil of secrecy and security, the atomic bomb and its more powerful heirs nonetheless remained subject to iconic debate and exposure to more dangerous imagery that recalled Hiroshima and Nagasaki, as well as scientists' warnings about doomsday. American preparedness entailed the widespread testing of atomic and hydrogen weapons, tests stunningly visible to the public in newsreels, on television, and even in person on the outskirts of Las Vegas at the Nevada Proving Ground (later the Nevada Test Site). Preparedness also involved protecting Americans against possible Soviet attack, in the form of civil defense drills and the construction of bomb shelters. Bomb tests and bomb shelters offered surrogate atomic forums, and produced real and allusive iconic representations that at once corresponded to and conflicted with peaceful atomic notions.

The atmospheric testing of atomic and hydrogen bombs took place in the Pacific and in Nevada between 1946 and 1963, showcasing for Americans the power and presence of the weapons being marshaled in their defense. In the environs of 1950s Las Vegas, a bomb-test-watching craze developed, and suggested a patriotic acceptance of and acclaim for these nuclear icons. Residents and tourists gathered to observe that most recognizable of atomic icons, the mushroom cloud, which could be seen from rooftop bars, mountain picnic spots, or way stations like the Atomic View Motel. Las Vegas hotel-casinos hosted the Miss Atomic Bomb Contest, concocted atomic cocktails, and coiffed atomic hairdos. Clark County, Nevada, refashioned its governmental seal to feature the mushroom cloud, grateful for the prosperity spawned by the atomic bomb tests. Atomic giddiness coexisted, though, with a frightened gravity over the radioactive fallout spewed by these tests. Especially shocking were the hydrogen bomb tests in 1954 on Bikini atoll; more powerful than expected, the blasts contaminated a distant Japanese fishing boat named the *Lucky Dragon* and led to the death of a crew member.

Such fearful knowledge brought imagination of vaster horrors; science fiction films of the time crafted a perilous atomic iconography of creatures born from testing and fallout, creating atomic monsters to populate the American imagination. The fictional marauders awakened or mutated as a result of American bomb tests included a prehistoric sea serpent (*The Beast from 20,000 Fathoms*, 1953), gargantuan ants (*Them!*, 1954), and *Godzilla* (1954/1956). The real terrors for living human beings were not outstripped, however. The 1955 arrival in the United States of the Hiroshima Maidens—young women disfigured by the bomb and seeking corrective plastic surgery—simply underscored the monstrous capacities of the atomic bomb. Organized anti-nuclear groups coalesced against the dangers posed by fallout, and also represented opposition to the claims of patriotic civil defense. For example, the Committee for a Sane Nuclear Policy (SANE), founded in 1957, contrasted sharply with the government and its evolving policy of deterrence through MAD.

Civil defense drills and fallout shelters promoted survival in the atomic age, but proponents of civilian preparedness had to stress the iconic deadliness and devastation of the bomb in order to arouse public awareness and interest. In educational civil defense films, "Bert the Turtle" urged American youths to "duck and cover," to mimic his head tucking into his shell. Images of children cowering under school desks or adults digging underground shelters for their homes called into question a triumphal American Cold War vision of life. The Berlin crisis in 1961 threatened a thermonuclear confrontation, and prompted President John F. Kennedy to urge on television that all Americans busy themselves building shelters. A panicked dedication to survivalism and shelter-building ensued, but so too did a more reasoned understanding of the essential immorality of shelters: they made nuclear war thinkable and human extinction more likely. Emerging from concerns about fallout and shelters in the late 1950s and early 1960s, the "Armageddon attitude" filtered into iconic associations with the atomic bomb: the atomic bomb meant death and human annihilation, and the Cold War nuclear system was therefore irrational and in need of control or abolition. Poetically expressed in Nevil Shute's novel *On the Beach* (1957) and raucously satirized in the black humor film *Dr. Strangelove or: How I Learned to Stop Worrying and Love the Bomb* (1964), the bomb came to stand as an icon for military madness and the end of human life.

In *Dr. Strangelove*, Major King Kong exuberantly rides an H-bomb falling to earth like a bucking bronco; his irreverent atomic age persona symbolized a new courage in openly addressing the perils of the atomic bomb and the pitfalls of the Cold War system. The shelter craze died and bomb tests moved underground after 1963, a result of the Soviet-American Limited Test Ban Treaty, itself a signal of official recognition of human susceptibility to atmospheric fallout and atomic annihilation after the 1962 Cuban missile crisis. Still, the atomic bomb had become a visible and recognized icon for often-conflicting understandings of American life and cold war policy.

The iconic battle between triumph and tragedy, peace and peril, persisted through the Vietnam era to the end of the Cold War. To those in the antiwar movement, the bomb served as a symbol for deadly Cold War militarism along with the Vietnam War; to government and military officials, the bomb stood as a symbol of their restraint in the Cold War because they did not resort to using this ultimate weapon in Vietnam. When Cold War tensions intensified in the 1980s under President Ronald W. Reagan, his atomic enthusiasm faced dampening atomic opposition in anti-nuclear activism that proposed a "nuclear freeze" and presaged a "nuclear winter," devastating climatic changes that would extinguish all life on earth after a massive nuclear exchange. At the end of the Cold War, many Americans again hailed the atomic bomb and its nuclear descendants for proving the sanity of MAD and for allowing the United States to win the war. Others pushed to abolish an arsenal that included thousands of nuclear warheads, now that a new era had presumably rendered the atomic icon irrelevant, a historic relic.

Suggestion of a sort of circularity in the atomic age, as well as the continued potency of the atomic bomb as a contested American icon in post–Cold War America, arrived in the commemoration of the fiftieth anniversary of the bombings of Hiroshima and Nagasaki. The Smithsonian's National Air and Space Museum proposed an exhibit based around the *Enola Gay*, the B-29 that had dropped the bomb on Hiroshima. Organizers intended to incorporate critical historical perspectives on the atomic bombing, as well as visual and material evidence of the bomb's devastation in Hiroshima. World War II veterans, members of Congress, and others raised a storm of protest, particularly about the photographs and artifacts from under Hiroshima's mushroom cloud: pictorials of the seared human victims of the bomb, a Japanese school girl's burnt lunch box. Only a drastically scaled-back exhibit focusing on the *Enola Gay* itself survived the furor, leading Japanese observers to note how the bomb remained a "holy relic," a national hero for the United States.

The rehabilitation of the heroic status of the atomic bomb continued, from the halls of government to popular culture. Talks on the issues of nuclear non-proliferation and arms reduction stalled, securing a place for the bomb among post–Cold War weapons. Films like *Independence Day* (1996), *Armageddon* (1998), and *Deep Impact* (1998) employed nuclear weapons to save earth and prevent the extinction of human life by aliens, asteroids, and comets, contesting competing visions of nuclear-borne annihilation.

Ambivalent iconography of the atomic bomb has persisted from 1945 to the present, maintaining a precarious balance between hope and despair, subsumed, as the icon has long been, within images of triumph and tragedy, salvation and extinction. It should come as no surprise that the Doomsday Clock on the 2005 cover of the *Bulletin of Atomic Scientists* is set at exactly seven minutes to midnight, just where it began.

WORKS CITED AND RECOMMENDED

Boyer, Paul. *By the Bomb's Early Light: American Thought and Culture at the Dawn of the Atomic Age*. New York: Pantheon Books, 1985.

———. *Fallout: A Historian Reflects on America's Half-Century Encounter with Nuclear Weapons*. Columbus: Ohio State UP, 1998.

Gusterson, Hugh. *People of the Bomb: Portraits of America's Nuclear Complex*. Minneapolis: U of Minnesota P, 2004.

Henriksen, Margot A. *Dr. Strangelove's America: Society and Culture in the Atomic Age*. Berkeley: U of California P, 1997.

Hersey, John. *Hiroshima*. 1946. New York: Bantam Books, 1985.

Lifton, Robert J., and Greg Mitchell. *Hiroshima: Fifty Years of Denial*. New York: G. P. Putnam, 1995.

Rhodes, Richard. *The Making of the Atomic Bomb*. New York: Touchstone, 1986.

Titus, A. Costandina. *Bombs in the Backyard: Atomic Testing and American Politics*. 2nd ed. Reno: U of Nevada P, 2001.

Winkler, Allan. *Life under a Cloud: American Anxiety about the Atom*. New York: Oxford UP, 1993.

Daniel Boone

Richard Taylor

As Franklin, Jefferson, and Washington were enshrined as founders of the American Republic and exemplars of man in civil society, their contemporary Daniel Boone won fame at the beginning of the Westward Movement as man in a state of nature, a son of the wilderness guided by virtue and natural wisdom. An enduring American icon, Daniel Boone (1734–1820) is the wearer of many hats, including the coonskin cap depicted in Enid Yandel's popular sculpture of the frontier hero at the entrance to Cherokee park in Louisville, Kentucky, one that in life he never wore. Like Walt Whitman's persona in "Leaves of Grass," Boone "contains multitudes," some of them creating inconsistencies and contradictions—an indication of the multiple roles the iconic Boone plays in American culture.

At root, Boone the pioneer should be viewed as a variant of Jean-Jacques Rousseau's eighteenth-century natural man, a Noble Savage, an idealization of an uncivilized man, an emblem of the innate goodness of men freed from the corrupting influences of civilization. This Boone of the wilds is fictionalized in James Fenimore Cooper's Natty Bumppo, a figure similarly unsullied by civilization and its corrupting tendencies. In the five Leather-Stocking novels written between 1823 and 1841, Bumppo, a Boone-like son of the wilderness, moves through incarnations of Deerslayer and Pathfinder to full-fledged Pioneer. These novels of search and rescue are the first of the popular genre of westerns. Though their locus moves west, as did Boone's, they might more accurately be called eastern westerns, and to some degree they prescribe the conventions of the modern genre of westerns—the laconic and lone hero who is a Euro-American knight of the prairie, overcoming adversity in many forms, never really falling for the allure of material riches or domesticity. Throughout the nineteenth and early twentieth centuries lesser writers churned out pale imitations of wilderness archetypes—of Davy Crockett, Kit Carson, and Simon Kenton, and of Boone himself in books whose primary audience was young readers.

The popular image of Daniel Boone has been appropriated as a model for American youth, especially through the outdoors movement whose publicist was Dan Beard (1850–1941), a surveyor, writer, and illustrator who founded the Sons of Daniel Boone (1905), the earliest precursor of the Boy Scouts of America. Beard, who grew up in Covington, Kentucky, on the banks of the Ohio, eventually moved to New York and wrote more than a dozen handicraft books for boys "to encourage conservation, love of the outdoors, and the pioneer spirit" ("Beard"). He went on to found the Boy Pioneers of America, an organization that influenced the formation of the boy scout movements in England and America. His books mirrored the times, compatible with Theodore Roosevelt's popularization of fitness, the robust outdoor life as a means to develop character, and the dedication of national parks to preserve the last wilderness lands of America. In his *Winning of the West* books Roosevelt himself idolized Boone as an embodiment of the pioneer spirit. He recognized in Boone an exemplar of the rugged individual able to survive the frontier's harsh environment and draw moral nourishment from it, an individual schooled in the ways of nature, possessing the values of self-reliance and stewardship that nature came to represent for those who challenged its despoilment during the high tide of American industrialization.

These forces and a revival of nationalism in American culture spawned dozens of Boone biographies and popular adventure books for boys, including *Scouting with Daniel Boone* (1914) by Everett Tomlinson, a fictional, character-building book that was part of the Every Boy's Library Series authorized by the Boy Scouts of America. Other fictional renderings of Boone's life followed, including Stewart Edward White's *Daniel Boone: Wilderness Scout* (1922), with stunning color illustrations by James Daughtery, who would later produce his own Boone book. In his introductory chapter White outlines the connections between Boone and scouting:

> If the Boy Scouts would know a man who in his attitude toward the life to which he was called most nearly embodied the precepts of their laws let them look on Daniel Boone. Gentle, kind, modest, peace-loving, absolutely fearless, a master of Indian warfare, a mighty hunter, strong as a bear and active as the panther, his life was lived in daily danger, almost perpetual hardship and exposure; yet he died in his bed at nearly ninety years of age. (3)

More concerned with shaping an image than probing the complexities of Boone's character, White unquestioningly accepts the paradox of the peace-lover who excels in violence, the gentle man hardened by necessity, the refined man whose physical attributes are comparable to those of beasts. A slightly different take on Boone is found in Daniel Henderson's *Boone of the Wilderness: A Tale of Pioneer Adventure and Achievement in "The Dark and Bloody Ground"* (1921). Adopting the view of Boone as a bold bearer of civilization rather than an escapee from it like Natty Bumppo, Henderson introduces his book with a poem that accents Boone's heroic mission to tame the wilds:

> "You dare not cross the Cumberlands!" the voices said to him;
> You may not tread the azure grass beyond the mountain's rim!

> No white man's foot may follow the deer and buffalo—
> The red men guard the ranges!" but Boone replied, "I go!" (viii)

James Daughtery's *Daniel Boone* (1939), whose bold and swirling lithographs of Boone brought the Kentucky frontier alive for me in the public library, addresses Boone in the invocation that begins his children's biography as "a living flame, ever young in the heart and bright dream of America marching on" (7). Depicting Boone as a foot soldier in the march of Progress, Nationalism, and Democracy, he called for transferring the spirit of the frontier to a new generation of youth, "That you may have the enduring courage to cut a clean straight path for a free people through the wilderness against oppression and aggression" (7). Written as clouds of impending war were darkening Europe, Daughtery's bravado today would spark the objections of revisionists who would describe Boone less as a pioneer taking a first step in the movement west than an accessory to those who participated in the aggressive thrust of Manifest Destiny and the decimation of America's native peoples. Edna McGuire in her fictionalized biography *Daniel Boone* (1945) in The American Adventure Series reaffirmed this view of Boone as a foot-soldier in the advance column of democracy, describing him as a "freedom-loving" and "home-seeking" pioneer who fought bravely in defense of his home and faced the hardships of the frontier with "high courage" (prefatory note). My own favorite early portrayal of Boone was Louisville-native John Mason Brown's *Daniel Boone: The Opening of the Wilderness* (1952) in the popular Landmark series of American history, a series that fueled among many of my generation a love of history.

Many books cast in this mold were written for adoption in the classroom, as, for example, Frances M. Perry and Katherine Beebe's *Four American Pioneers: A Book for Young Americans* (1900), which also contained selective biographies of George Rogers Clark, David Crockett, and Kit Carson, fellow travelers in the frontier caravan. Their presence in the public schools accounts for the pervasiveness in American culture of Boone as an all-purpose utility for American values.

Though the proliferation of such books began early in the twentieth century, their predecessors appeared before the Civil War in Timothy Flint's *Biographical Memoir of Daniel Boone, the First Settler of Kentucky* (1833), in which he was portrayed, in the words of Boone biographer John Mack Faragher, as a "providential pathfinder for civilization" (322); in W. H. Bogart's *Daniel Boone and the Hunters of Kentucky* (1854); in George Canning Hill's *Daniel Boone, the Pioneer of Kentucky* (1860); and John Peck's *Daniel Boone* (1847) in the Library of American Biography. Such nineteenth-century biographies created an appetite for the Boone adventure books in the early twentieth, a growth industry that a century later shows few signs of waning.

There are two central archetypes that these depictions of Boone seem to reinforce. One focuses on place, an Adamic figure's longed-for return to

DANIEL BOONE

Eden, an unspoiled reserve where nature predominates and man can recover his lost innocence. The world he is redeemed from is not only the established civilization of the Eastern colonies but the Old World itself. A new man supplants the guilt and moral jadedness of eighteenth century Europe, what R.W.B. Lewis describes as an "American Adam." The other, almost its opposite, is an archetypal image of the Man Who Copes—Boone as a kind of North-American Robinson Crusoe, bold, self-reliant, resourceful, more than equal to the hardships posed by wilderness and the red man who inhabits it. Reflecting conventional sentiment of the time, this model finds fault with the Native American's stubborn defense of his homeland, identifying him as a Manichean counterpart of the bringers of light and civilization, a devil.

An undated lithograph of Daniel Boone. Courtesy of the Library of Congress.

To place Boone more accurately, he occupies a kind of no-man's-land between the wilderness that is and the settlement that will be, neither a builder nor a farmer but a hunter, a Nimrod providentially equipped to explore the vast cipher of the continent and mark a trail for others. This image of Boone is embodied in George Caleb Bingham's "Daniel Boone Escorting Settlers through the Cumberland Gap" (1851–1852), a painting that depicts Moses-like Boone with confident stride leading pioneer families through Cumberland Gap to the Promised Land. He is also the image of Jefferson's sturdy yeoman whose legions will transform the wilderness into farms and market towns. Boone was, in fact, by profession a surveyor, a good one, who platted thousands of acres for those who would become the yeoman farmers that Jefferson envisioned populating the West. He was also a legislator and would-be government contractor. For a time he also kept a tavern and trading post at Limestone (Maysville, Kentucky), one of the primary points of debarkation on the Ohio. Behind this romanticized leader is the provider, a man with a family who increasingly felt the economic press of mouths to feed. An inventory of Boone's résumé should refer to these livelihoods in addition to his popular pastimes as explorer and Indian fighter.

John Filson's *The Discovery, Settlement, and Present State of Kentucke* (1784), later published in French and German editions, is the first, perhaps least accurate, and most memorable of these glorifications of the frontiersman's life. John Filson (1753–1788), biographer, historian, cartographer, explorer, was born in Pennsylvania, educated in Maryland, taught school in

Pennsylvania during the Revolution, then in 1783 immigrated to Kentucky where he practiced surveying, interviewed settlers, and began making the first creditable map of Kentucky country. His *Discovery, Settlement, and Present State of Kentucke*, the book he published in Delaware in 1784, had an appendix entitled "The Adventures of Colonel Daniel Boone." He drafted the manuscript, at least in part, to promote his speculation in land, and though he surveyed a road from Lexington in central Kentucky to the mouth of the Licking River and helped found Losantiville (the "city opposite the mouth of the Licking River" that later became Cincinnati), his reach exceeded his luck, for he disappeared while exploring the site and was believed to have been killed by Indians. The Boone narrative, though written with ornate language and elaborate locution alien to Boone himself, represents the birth of Daniel Boone in the public consciousness, the first in a long list of books that have had a perennial market in America and beyond.

Boone's own narrative history of his life, started in old age after he had emigrated to Missouri, was lost in a move when a canoe carrying his goods capsized. Had it survived, some of the mythic scale of his life might have been trimmed more modestly to size, the record set straight. Hyperbole was simply not congruent with his character. What may have been the other great corrective to the Boone myth, the book projected by Lyman S. Draper (1815–1891), who faithfully collected Boone material for most of a lifetime, was still unwritten at the time of the collector's death. Because little that Boone said or wrote has come down to us intact, much of the well we draw from is tainted by hearsay, some of it well-intentioned apocrypha, some of it outright lies. Compared to others who have been elevated to mythic status, Boone, the most authoritative source of matters relating to his life, is virtually silent—maybe in part achieving his mythic status because of that silence. Others stepped in to fill the void. To this day, the name Boone guarantees robust sales, a testimony to Boone's place in the American pantheon. The cottage industry of books in print about Boone at the time of this writing exceeds 100; who knows how many have been superseded and are out of print?

It is not so much the particulars of Daniel Boone's life that raised him to the rank of America's quintessential pioneer as it is the larger-than-life image that others have created in children's histories, biographies, statues, painting, engraving, movies, television serials, and the wholesale hagiography accorded to those associated with the Westward Movement. After all, the lives of James Harrod, founder of Kentucky's first permanent settlement, and Simon Kenton both equal Boone's adventures and exploits and even surpass Boone's in terms of lasting accomplishments. Both of the settlements they founded, Harrodsburg and Maysville, Kentucky, survive as modern-day communities, unlike Boonesborough which is now a state park with a replica of the original fort. General George Rogers Clark, founder of Louisville and conqueror of the Northwest Territory during the Revolution, easily has cut a much wider mark in American History. Other less well-known figures, including John

Floyd, Benjamin Logan, even Boone's own brother Squire Boone (1744–1815), in many ways match or surpass Boone in their actual contributions.

Though I heard stories about the frontier hero from a time beyond memory, my first printed encounter with Daniel Boone was in my fourth-grade reader, *Adventures in Pioneering* by Mary Browning. Written to introduce children to Kentucky history, Browning's narrative presents the frontier through "Grandma," one of the first generation of pioneers who describes the exploits of James Harrod and Daniel Boone to Jimmy Fisher and his sister Sally, her grandchildren. Under the old oak tree she tells the "story" of Boone's capture at Blue Licks where he went with a party from Boonesborough to boil the brackish water for salt. Captured alone during a snowstorm, he asks his captors to adopt him. He then persuades the outnumbered saltmakers to surrender in return for a promise of good treatment. After winning the Shawnees' confidence and learning of a plan to attack Boonesborough, he escapes and brings the news back to the settlement. The children conclude that he is the "bravest man in the world," brave and clever.

Grandma later resumes her story of Boone, recounting the siege of Boonesborough in August of 1778 when Boone and his comrades withstood an attack of 400 Indians. As might be expected, these accounts were sanitized, sensitive to depictions of violence, and silent on the issues of empire and Indian rights. Boone was portrayed as a peaceable man forced to defend himself and his neighbors to make Kentucky safe for settlement. If he is not the bringer of culture to the wilderness in the popular depictions, he is the safekeeper of settlement, both the point man and bodyguard, so to speak, of civilization.

In the popular imagination, the bundle of virtues he possessed included valor, foresight, resourcefulness, pureness of spirit, benevolence in peace, ferocity in war—qualities that do not differ substantially from America's most hopeful assessment of itself. To a great degree, Boone is presented as a kind of wilderness saint, a St. Francis with a flintlock, whose virtues are highlighted in a series of parables and homilies, all sweetness and light, as he carves a pathway to Paradise. This heroic view of Boone is reflected in William Ranney's painting "Boone's First View of Kentucky" (1849). It depicts Boone and five companions in 1769, standing atop an eminence thereafter known as Pilot Knob, gazing out at the "beautiful level of Kentucky." An adaptation of this critical moment, with its threshold of promise and unanticipated suffering, is the subject of Gilbert White's large lunette in the Kentucky statehouse. The four panels on the monument at his gravesite above the Kentucky River are an abbreviated and over-simplified synopsis of his life. In milky marble they depict Boone grappling with a tomahawk-wielding Indian, Boone resting beside a downed buck, Boone, his rifle at rest, instructing a behatted slave whose eyes are respectfully downcast, and a woman (presumably Rebecca) milking a cow. In this scene of home, Boone, as was so often the case, is absent.

The darker side of this bright vision of the opening of the West so embedded in the folk imagination is personified by Simon Girty (1741–1818).

What Boone is to the bright aspect of America's playing out of Manifest Destiny, Girty is to its dark side, the acknowledgement of the shadowy subtext of America's conquest, for Girty is portrayed as a betrayer of his race. This so-called "White Savage" is perceived as delighting in the torture and annihilation of his white brothers. Allying himself with the British and Indians during the Revolution, "The Great Renegade" operated over thirty years as a kind of scout and provocateur in the Ohio River Valley. Son of an Irish immigrant living on the Pennsylvania frontier, Girty was captured by Indians as a teenager, learned several native languages, and through a complex series of swervings in loyalty finally committed himself to resisting settlement in the Kentucky country. He was active during the siege of Bryan's Station as well as the Battle of Blue Licks (1782), St. Clair's Defeat (1791), and Fallen Timbers (1794). If his path and Boone's crossed, it was never closer than shooting distance—both were at Blue Licks, the greatest defeat of Kentuckians during the Indian Wars. Though history does not record a meeting between them, each was keenly aware of the other's existence. Like Boone, Girty was a man more complex than history has remembered him, on occasion acting mercifully to secure the release of white captives, including his old comrade Simon Kenton, whose life he saved twice (as Kenton later saved Boone's).

What earned Girty his badge of infamy was the burning at the stake of William Crawford after the colonel's capture near Sandusky Plains in Ohio, following the defeat of Crawford's forces during a punitive expedition against the Ohio tribes. Another captive, Dr. John Knight, reported, probably with some fabrication, that Girty took pleasure in the burning of his former acquaintance and refused all aid to him, even a request to shoot him as relief from his agony. Escaping, Knight lived to write an account of his captivity, including damning remarks about Girty later confuted by other witnesses. As a consequence of Knight's accusations, Girty was regarded as a *bête noire* during the nineteenth century, perhaps the most detested man in American history. He entered American folklore and literature as a dark demon of the wilderness, whose name mothers invoked to terrorize their disobedient children. He was the subject of popular romances such as *Simon Girty, the Outlaw* by Uriah Jones (1846), and mentioned in Stephen Vincent Benét's frequently anthologized short story, "The Devil and Daniel Webster," in which he is recruited as a member of the Devil's jury:

> ...and there was Simon Girty, the renegade, who saw white men burned at the stake and whooped with the Indians to see them burn. His eyes were green like a catamount's, and the stains on his hunting shirt did not come from the blood of deer. (594)

In broad profile, Boone and Girty represent two sides of the American psyche as described in an evolving mythos of light and dark, good and evil, courage and cowardice.

Any deeper probing of either Boone or Girty reveals that they were more ambiguous and complex than textbooks or the popular imagination portrays them. For example, Boone the Quaker pacifist was also touted as a great Indian-fighter. During his long life Boone was in fact certain of killing only two Indians. One was at Blue Licks shortly before his son Israel was killed. The other killing he acknowledged was less justifiable, less often mentioned, bordering on gratuitous homicide. According to his son Nathan in Draper's interviews, Boone, in the summer of 1770 near what would become Frankfort, shot a lone Indian who was fishing from a fallen tree by the Kentucky River. Though Boone did not confess outright that he murdered him and there may have been mitigating considerations of safety that justified his doing so, in his later years he simply told his son Nathan that "While I was looking at him he tumbled into the river and I saw no more of him" (Hammon 111). About the same time, on the other hand, he met an aged Indian who had been left to die by his comrades. Boone charitably killed a deer, took only a small portion of it for himself, and presented the remainder to the old Indian. In his *In the American Grain* (1925), William Carlos Williams regards Boone not as the Indian's nemesis but as his model: "To Boone the Indian was his greatest master. Not for himself surely to be an Indian, though they eagerly sought to adopt him into their tribes, but the reverse: to be *himself* in a new world, Indianlike" (137).

Most of us interpret Boone according to our own predilections. Some remember him as Boone the Rescuer, referring to his pursuit of the band of Shawnees that kidnapped his daughter Jemima and two other girls as they dangled their feet from a canoe on the Kentucky River near Boonesborough one Sunday afternoon in 1776. When the alarm was sounded, Boone was in such haste to begin the pursuit that he left without moccasins on his feet. By second-guessing the kidnappers' route north and exercising extreme caution, he succeeded in rescuing the girls. Others cite his deliverance of Boonesborough with his timely warning and heroic defense during the siege.

Still others are taken by his stoical acceptance of conditions over which he had no control, as in his capture at Blue Licks in February of 1778, giving in when resistance was senseless and then persuading the party of men that accompanied him to surrender without a fight when it was clear that the odds were against them. After gaining the confidence of Blackfish, the Shawnee chief who adopted him as son and renamed him Shel-Tow-Y ("Big Turtle," said to be a reference to his broadening girth during middle age), Boone lived quite contentedly with his captors until he learned they were preparing to attack Boonesborough, at which time he planned and cleverly executed his escape.

Skeptics cite inconsistencies in the stereotype of Boone as an unlettered son of the wilderness—for example, his drawing on Jonathan's Swift's *Gulliver's Travels* to name an obscure creek Lulbegrud, a misspelling of Lorbrulgrud, the capital of the Brobdingnags in a book that he had fetched to the wilderness and read aloud to his comrades during evenings by firelight. My own favorite is the story told by a party of Long Hunters in the years before

Roosevelt, Theodore. *The Winning of the West*. 4 vols. New York: G. P. Putnam's Sons, 1889–1896.

Tomlinson, Everett. *Scouting with Daniel Boone*. New York: Doubleday Doran & Co., 1914.

White, Stewart Edward. *Daniel Boone: Wilderness Scout*. Garden City, NY: Garden City Publishing Co., 1922.

Williams, William Carlos. *In the American Grain*. Norfolk, CT: New Directions, 1925.

Boy Scout Knife

R. H. Miller

> Boy Scout knife, like ladies' hairpin, have many uses.
> *Charlie Chan's Secret* (1936)

In 1997, when the critic John Lahr interviewed the playwright David Mamet, at the outset of their meeting Mamet presented him with a Boy Scout knife. It must have been one of the very rare older models issued by the New York Knife Company, as it carried only the motto "Be prepared" on one side (Lahr 70; "BSA Scout Knives"). In his account of that interview in *The New Yorker* Lahr surmises presciently that the motto seems to have a double meaning, signifying both "prowess and paranoia" (70). In the course of the interview Lahr tried to puzzle out the meaning of the gift and finally concluded that in some way it was connected to Mamet's play *The Cryptogram*:

> As I attempted to ask him unwelcome questions about his childhood, the presence of the Boy Scout knife on the table reminded me of the knife that the distraught ten-year-old boy John flashes in Mamet's autobiographical masterpiece *The Cryptogram*—a play about the betrayal of the boy by his parents. He is on the stairway looking down at the living room, where his mother, abandoned by his father and unable to meet his emotional needs, sits in the tortured last beat of the play. At whom, exactly, is the boy's murderous energy aimed, himself or others? His gesture foreshadows the life of the playwright, who learned to turn aggression into art: the knife became a pen. (72)

Mamet's (and Lahr's) sensitivity to the layered meanings bound up in this seemingly innocuous object is not unusual at all. Perhaps no other icon of white middle-class male culture carries the talismanic significance of the Boy Scout knife. It is a frequently recurring figure in our imaginative literature, in fictional accounts, stories taken from real life, in stories from film and TV. For the more than 100 million boys who have been in the scouting ranks since its founding, the Boy Scout knife has served both as a useful tool and a powerful symbol.

The appearance of the Boy Scout knife follows close on the founding of the organization itself. The Boy Scouts of America was established in 1910, only a year after Lord Baden-Powell formed its parent organization, the British Boy Scouts. The earliest Boy Scout knives came on the market in 1911, manufactured by the New York Knife Company, which continued to produce the knives until 1931. The knives were also issued by Imperial; Universal/Landers, Ferry & Clark; Remington/PAL; Schrade; and Ulster, among others, and beginning in 1946 by the Camillus Cutlery Company of Camillus, New York, which is now the major purveyor of the product. Since 1911 many variations of the knife have been manufactured—a Norman Rockwell knife, a whittler, a woodsman, a two-blade, a three-blade, a four-blade, a deluxe five-blade, and special knives for various special uses—but it is still the Camillus four-bladed knife with its stainless steel blades, brown delrin plastic body, Scout insignia, and key chain ring that remains the standard Boy Scout knife. For the more patriotically minded, the Norman Rockwell version is still available, with Rockwell's various full-color portrayals of young Scouts permanently preserved beneath a plastic overlay on its handle.

In due time the Girl Scouts of America issued the Girl Scout knife, a green plastic-bodied version of the Boy Scout knife; but, with all due respect, it has not woven itself into the fabric of American life and culture as has the Boy Scout knife. The fact points out all the more directly that the knife is a carrier of deep, psychic male signification. Today the difference between the significance of the Boy Scout knife and the Girl Scout knife is instructive. On the Internet search engine Google there are almost three times as many Web sites noted for the Boy Scout knife as there are for the Girl Scout knife (about 1500 versus 500). The original Kutmaster Girl Scout knife was a worthy rival to the Boy Scout knife, but today it has been replaced by a cheap-looking three-blade utensil priced at $18.95 (compared to the robust Camillus Boy Scout camp knife at $27.95). Clearly, for the young woman—the Brownie becoming a Girl Scout, the knife has been of little significance, other than as a utilitarian object. Not surprisingly, about 30 percent of the "hits" for the term "Girl Scout knife" direct the searcher to pornographic Web sites. On the Web the Boy Scout has retained his image as the boy-man, while the Girl Scout has been appropriated as another sex object alongside the *gamine*, cheerleader, and dental hygienist. The Girl Scout knife continues to be little more than a practical tool, while the Boy Scout knife remains a powerful icon of our culture.

On the other hand, the literature issued by the BSA about the knife is careful to deal exclusively with its utility. *Boy's Life*, the scouting magazine, contains numerous stories and first-person accounts in which the knife figures as a handy, indeed essen-

Boy Scout knife. Courtesy of Shutterstock.

tial scouting tool (Butterworth). Yet nowhere is it even suggested that the knife might be used for some other purpose, let alone be a cultural signifier.

A boy's acquisition of a weapon is a male rite of passage, highly charged with cultural significance; and in the context of the urban-suburban world that constitutes the social base of the Boy Scouts, a boy's acquisition of such a knife became a potent sign of the taking on of manhood. In rural America such weapon bestowing usually occurs very early in a boy's life and typically involves not only the acquisition of a knife, but eventually a firearm, most often a .22 caliber rifle, or at an earlier stage, a BB gun, preferably the Red Ryder. Where urban parents cautiously bestow the BB gun on their boys ("You'll shoot your eye out!"), they treat the Boy Scout knife as a more acceptable weapon, because it is associated with an organization that takes upon itself the duty to teach knife safety and also to promote the moral and spiritual initiation of young boys from age 11 upward (and now even younger) into the Judeo-Christian masculine world. And, of course, the Boy Scout knife's potential as a weapon can be mitigated by its many utilitarian purposes, although I have often wondered how many Scouts actually find those other three blades useful.

Of some of the practical uses of the knife we have many accounts. Soldiers in World War I and II were issued pocket knives made by the Camillus Cutlery Company of New York, which were modeled on the traditional four-bladed Boy Scout knife, but many soldiers also secretly carried with them into battle their revered boyhood talisman, which served duty as a defensive weapon, as a tool for cutting yourself loose from your tangled parachute straps, for example, or for removing some souvenir of war that you decided to carry home with you. Stories abound of rescues and clever uses inspired by trusty Boy Scout knives. As evidence of its utility, in J. D. Salinger's novella *Franny and Zooey*, Mrs. Seymour Glass, the mother, wears a kimono around the house, which has a pocket full of useful tools, one of which is a Boy Scout knife that was a castoff of one of her sons. As testimonial to the object's potency as a symbol of patriotic fervor and manly achievement, what can be more telling than the astronaut John Glenn's carrying his son's Boy Scout knife with him on his first mission in space?

Like William Blake's sick rose, the knife has its potent, evil side as well. The Beat generation figures William Burroughs, Allen Ginsberg, and their friend Lucien Carr were involved in a murderous episode that took place in New York City, in Riverside Park, in 1944. In the late summer, the trio were involved in a knifing, in which Carr stabbed to death one David Kammerer, a college teacher, in order to stave off his homosexual advances. The weapon in question was of course a Boy Scout knife. The crime seems to cry out for semiotic analysis. What could be more signifying in the murder of a gay man than to use a talisman of an organization that has since its inception been devoted to the cultivation of muscular Christianity, to the values of the heterosexual male, that has spent millions of dollars in legal costs to prevent gays from participating in scouting? Carr was not charged because of his claim of self-defense.

In a similar manner, the notorious boxer Rubin "Hurricane" Carter, at the age of twelve, was arrested and incarcerated in the Jamesburg (New Jersey) State Home for Boys for stabbing a man with a Boy Scout knife. Carter claimed the man was a pedophile and was attempting to molest one of his companions. Before his six-year sentence was up, he managed to escape from the home. He joined the Army in 1954 and was never caught until his release two years later, at which time he was returned to prison to serve the remaining ten months of his sentence. Carter figured as the subject of the film *The Hurricane* (1999), starring Denzel Washington. The movie does not stint in its portrayal of this episode, but the knife young Carter uses is a switchblade, not a Boy Scout knife. Was the director, or someone else, loath to sully the image of the Boy Scout knife, to violate its cultural sanctity? And further, although the event is not particularly notable, the appearance of a Boy Scout knife in the hands of a young black surely must signify an unusual crossover in cultural identity, for here we have a young black street urchin using a "white boy's" weapon. Perhaps on both counts the director, or the powers that be, thought it dangerous to wade into those perilous cultural waters.

In another episode, we have the eerie account of a 14-year-old Scout by the name of Thomas Sullivan, Jr., who strayed from the path of scouting and delved into studying books on the occult and on Satanic practices. At least that is the story the Jefferson County, New Jersey, county prosecutor published to the world.

In 1988, on January 11, young Sullivan, in a murderous rage, stabbed his mother twenty-seven times with his Boy Scout knife, and then tried to kill the rest of his family by setting the family home on fire. When that stratagem failed, he took his knife and committed suicide by cutting his wrists and slashing his throat. Under ordinary circumstances the case would have drawn little notice, but because of the involvement of the Boy Scout knife, it has taken on mythic proportions, particularly because Sullivan was apparently the epitome of the Good Boy Scout, a bright student and outstanding athlete. The event represents an almost perfect inversion of the iconic import of the knife. The son takes upon himself an Orestes-burdened revenge against the mother, with a weapon that was most likely a gift from the father or both parents to him, and all that is good and pure in it is converted into the Satanic, the vengeful, the destructive.

Perhaps most revealing of the hidden sexual potency of this icon is a "Boy Scout" modern variation of the old medieval tale of the loathly hag, which figures prominently in Chaucer's "Wife of Bath's Tale." The story goes that a young man, in an attempt to secure the sexual favors of an attractive young woman, promises her anything she wants if she will have sex with him. In turn, she asks for a solid gold Boy Scout knife. The exchange is effected, and during their postcoital conversation, the lad happens to notice her slip the knife into a chest, which is filled almost to the brim with solid gold Boy Scout knives. When the man asks her why she is collecting the knives, she replies, in these words or similar, "Right now I'm young and desirable, but some day I'll be an old ugly crone. And I'll have these knives, and you know a Boy Scout will do anything for a solid gold Boy Scout knife!" This phallic exchange that the future crone delineates goes to the deeper signification of the knife as a penis form become phallus, a body part that comes to signify sexual prowess, in the most perfect male shape, an idealized penis, made of the most perfect element, gold, whose symbolic meanings are unlimited. It is a tool, and it is also "a tool."

One of the most intriguing uses of the iconic significance of the Boy Scout knife in a literary setting occurs in Philip Roth's 1971 political satire *Our Gang*. President Trick E. Dixon, or "Tricky," as he is styled, gives an address to the nation in which he characterizes the Scouts as the unwitting dupes of Curt Flood, the baseball player who challenged the reserve clause and paved the way for a free-agent system, in an attempt to arouse public feelings against the president. In a further stretch of the imagination, Tricky goes on to characterize the Boy Scout knife as a weapon even more dangerous than the Italian surplus military rifle used to assassinate the late President John Charisma (read "Kennedy"). What Tricky must have failed to realize is that the Boy Scout knife is often viewed in the law as a benign instrument, not necessarily a weapon. In fact, some lawyers advise that if you are planning to arm yourself, carry a Boy Scout knife, because many judges treat it as a utilitarian instrument, not as a concealed weapon.

Included in Tricky's diatribe are specific data on the knife, its dimensions, its materials, and the particular diabolical uses to which each of the four blades might be put. On the can-opener blade he thunders,

> You will observe that it is hook-shaped at the end, and measures one inch and one-eighth. It is employed during the interrogation of prisoners primarily to gouge out one or both of the eyes. It is also used on the soles of the feet, which are sliced open, like so, with the point of the hook. Last, but not least, it is sometimes inserted into the mouth of a prisoner who will not talk, in order to slit the flesh at the upper part of the larynx, between the vocal cords. That opening up there is called the glottis, and "bottle opener" is derived from "glottal opener," the pet name originally attached to the blade by its most cold-blooded practitioners. (112)

Suffice it to say that the blade is known officially as the "can opener" and that Tricky's fanciful description is so absurd as to beggar the imagination. Roth continues on to show the sharpness of the knife blade by using it to shred a page of the Preamble to the American Constitution and the Bill of Rights (114).

In fact, the absurdity of Tricky's revelation is quite the point of Roth's satirical strategy, which is to take one of America's most precious icons and, by a stentorian exaggeration, attempt to turn it into its "bizarro" opposite. In Tricky's opinion, it is precisely because the Boy Scout knife is such a symbol of honorable American masculinity that it can be seen to be in fact the whited sepulcher of American iconology, and in a twist of its meaning, can be turned into a terrorist weapon that exposes the machinations of this seemingly patriotic group of youngsters. Roth's ultimate satirical ploy is to expose Tricky for the duplicitous person he is through his ridiculous suspicions, just as the McCarthyites in their paranoid ranting tried to portray loyal Americans as Communist dupes.

I remember "the knife" as an item both to be feared and revered, because of its potency as a weapon and its power as an artifact of my culture. I think my first scouting possession was indeed a Boy Scout knife, and it was given to me at great expense because at the time my dad was out of work, and our family was struggling to survive after WWII in a small apartment in Toledo, Ohio. I was a member of a troop at Ashland Avenue Baptist Church, at the corner of Woodruff and Ashland Avenues. Because I had three younger brothers I was never allowed to open it at home (although I did, many times). As my fortunes turned out, my knife got stolen at Scout camp. Later, during a run of good times, when Dad was working, he replaced it. Then Dad hit another dry spell. I left the troop under a cloud, because my parents couldn't afford the Scout uniform, and I was tired of being badgered by my troop leader for not having one. But I had that knife, and I took it with me when we moved back to the farm and the life I describe in my memoir, *Deaf Hearing Boy*. Out in the wilderness of rural Ohio, however, I was forced to grow up fast, and soon a rifle, and a shotgun, and a sheath knife replaced the pocketknife. What happened to my Boy Scout knife, I do not know. I suspect my grandmother lifted it and added it to her hoard of my abandoned toys she kept as a kind of secret trove, which we discovered after she died (Miller 142). In that hodgepodge of rusty toy farm implements, whistles, and plastic cars, though, the knife was nowhere to be found.

Practical tool, defensive weapon, exemplar of a utilitarian yet aesthetic design, murder weapon—on a non-symbolic level the Boy Scout knife is an artifact of great importance. As an American icon of middle-class male acceptance, of patriotism and all that it signifies, of passage into male adulthood and as a marker of masculinity, of Judeo-Christian male do-goodism, patriotism, as a symbol of sexual coming of age and sexual power, of the potential to signify the essence of aggression and rage in any red-blooded American male, the Boy Scout knife is almost unrivaled in its ability to contain within itself layer upon layer of signification.

WORKS CITED AND RECOMMENDED

"BSA Scout Knives." <http://www.scoutersattic.com/knifes.htm>.
Butterworth, W. E., IV. "Tool Time." *Boy's Life* June 1996: 26+.
Lahr, John. "Fortress Mamet." *New Yorker* 17 Nov. 1997: 70+.
Miller, R. H. *Deaf Hearing Boy: A Memoir*. Washington, DC: Gallaudet UP, 2004.
Roth, Philip. *Our Gang*. New York: Random House, 1971.
Salinger, J. D. *Franny and Zooey*. Boston: Little, Brown, 1961.

Capitol

Karelisa V. Hartigan

The Capitol, as most commonly seen, is $50. As the building imprinted on the fifty dollar bill, it appears to be worth more than the White House, which adorns the back of the twenty, the Treasury building on the ten, or the Lincoln Memorial on the five, but less valuable, somehow, than the ineffable Independence Hall in Philadelphia, which graces the hundred dollar note. But as American cultural capital, this immediately recognizable sign of the American government has accrued immense value, rich in associations and resonance that inspire responses ranging from the unthinkingly emotional to the acutely rational. References to "The Capitol" in Washington, D.C., are ubiquitous in American culture, and they contribute meaning to texts ranging from poems and novels, to plays, to movies, to advertising, to corporate logos, to tourist souvenirs, to political campaign literature, to bumper stickers, and to a host of other ephemera.

The towering dome of the United States Capitol has come to symbolize American values: freedom, whose statue stands atop it, democracy, and the American way of life. The Capitol, and its interior and exterior decoration, reflect Americans' view of themselves. The U.S. Capitol was designed to promote a visual memory of the political actions that led to America's creation. By consciously echoing the art and architecture of classical Rome, the Capitol's shape and art elevated the story of the America's birth to a level of new American myth.

"Capitol" comes from *Capitolium*, the ancient temple of Jupiter and its hill overlooking the Roman Forum, the first of many terms and ideas borrowed from classical Rome as the new American nation began to develop signs of its authority. As the name Capitol came from ancient Rome, so did the idea for its dome. Once Washington had been laid out as the site of the new nation's capital, architects and plans were solicited for the buildings of its government. George Washington was interested in the design of the city; but Thomas Jefferson was concerned with the design for the new Capitol, a building to provide accommodation for the nation's new bicameral legislature and to offer an accessible public space. He favored the plan of William Thornton, one based on the Pantheon in Rome, and selected its architect, Benjamin H. Latrobe. The Jefferson-Thornton-Latrobe building was completed in 1811.

In August 1814 the British attacked Washington and burned the new Capitol. Rebuilding began the following year, but more than five decades would pass before the Capitol achieved the form seared into the visual memory of virtually all Americans and many throughout the rest of the world. When Latrobe resigned from the rebuilding in 1817, Charles Bulfinch took over his work and retained, more or less, the design of the original Capitol. Although hailed as an architectural wonder, the Capitol's space was soon discovered to be inadequate for its purposes. Redesign of the interior soon began, and with the reconstruction Thomas Walter created a more impressive dome. Completed in 1858, his cast iron creation towers above the Capitol building we know today. Walter transformed the shape of Capitol dome from that of the Pantheon to that of St. Peter's. Thus America's building that perhaps best represents the separation of church and state traces its origin to both pagan and Christian religion.

The dome of the United States Capitol has come to represent American democracy. Steeped in classical tradition, America's founding fathers looked to the ancient world for inspiration. They found in Greek and Roman statuary and architecture the ideas they wished to promote for their new nation. The Pantheon, commissioned by the Roman emperor Hadrian as part of his political statement about Rome's position in the Mediterranean world, re-

The Capitol building. Courtesy of Shutterstock.

mained intact and was widely admired. For political and aesthetic reasons, it was the logical choice upon which to model the new nation's most important government building. America could acquire from the Pantheon an immediate veneer of culture.

Domed structures have a long history as places of significance. The word dome comes from both Greek and Latin, *domus*, house, a covered important space. A dome covers a circular building, and the circle also has meaning: it is inclusive, promoting a sense of equality among those gathered within it. The covering dome is said to represent the sky above, the whole then being an earthly pattern of the cosmos itself. A domed religious building was considered a *Domus Dei*, a House of God; the word survives into modern languages in terms for a cathedral.

Circular structures were first used in the Greco-Roman world as tombs, the last resting place of revered ancestors. The earliest Greeks buried their dead in circular, or *tholos*, tombs; the Romans often emulated the shape for imperial tombs. When the Capitol rotunda was first designed, the popular intent was to bury Washington within it, and a crypt extends beneath its floor. Horatio Greenough's statue of Washington, modeled upon the statue of Zeus at Olympia, one of the Wonders of the Ancient World, was commissioned to stand above the tomb. But the statue sat within the Rotunda only two years before being moved outside, and Washington remains buried at Mt. Vernon.

In the Athenian agora, the central place of Athenian democracy, annually elected state officials met in a round building just below the area's single hill. But the agora tholos did not have a domed roof, so while the circular building can be connected with early democracy, the idea of the dome derives directly from the Romans. It was they who perfected the means to create the vault, and how to admit light into it: an opening, the *oculus* or eye, at the center of the Pantheon's dome, admits light into the interior. When Thomas Walter redesigned the Latrobe/Bulfinch dome, he did not keep the open oculus but did maintain its concept. The dome's cupola is really an enclosed eye, and Constantino Brumidi's encircling paintings emphasize the design.

The Capitol and its dome have come to represent democracy, and the sculpture on the building and the art within it contribute to this representation. The paintings made for the Capitol and the sculptures commissioned for it reflect the values of both politicians and citizens of the period 1815–1865. This art sought to unify emerging beliefs into a single state-supported ideology, to underscore the ideas that formed the states into a union, to create in the Capitol a physical reflection of the new nation's values and principles.

At first, the recently ended Revolutionary War provided the symbols for such concepts as liberty, justice, and unity. John Trumbull's paintings, commissioned to hang within the Capitol's Rotunda, are scenes from the Revolution. Trumbull portrayed British and American generals at their moments of victory or defeat. Military art at that time focused upon the general, not the common soldier; the idea that the true hero lay in the trenches did not become popular until after World War II. Thus the four paintings displayed in the Capitol show the generals, and not those who died for them. Trumbull portrayed noble men embarking upon noble venture in signing the Declaration of Independence, facing defeat or accepting victory honorably in the battles at Saratoga and Yorktown, and stepping aside with dignity in Washington's resigning rather than becoming king. These vast canvases, representing the new nation's freedom and political originality, are also projections of how America wanted to be viewed. The subjects were native and did not try to achieve greatness through association with classical Rome. Trumbull's paintings—works on canvas, not in stone, it should be noted—were to hang in the classically inspired Rotunda, but they initiated themes that would continue to guide the creation of the Capitol and its decoration: art and architecture blended old themes with new.

The Rotunda frieze, designed by Constantino Brumidi and painted by three artists, consists of nineteen separate scenes, each representing a moment in American history. Brumidi lived to paint the first eight of a planned sixteen scenes, from "America and History" to "William Penn and the Indians." Filippo Costaggini took up the work and completed the designs for the remaining eight, a series ending with the "Discovery of Gold in California." These paintings did not fill the space, however, and a gap of over thirty feet remained for nearly fifty years. Finally in 1951 Allyn Cox was commissioned to paint three more panels, tracing American history from the Civil War to the invention of the airplane. In the scenes' final form, from the landing of Columbus to the flight at Kitty Hawk, in 300 feet of fresco painted to resemble sculpture, the main emphasis is on the Revolutionary War and the conquest of the Indians, events which dominated American ideas at the time of the original designs. Only in the last scene do we see a reference to the nation's advances in technology. We must turn to the sculpture of the Capitol for representation of America's contributions to a better life.

When the legislative wings were built, appropriate pediment sculpture was commissioned. Here again classical style blends with American themes and ideology. Paul Wayland Bartlett's *The Apotheosis of Democracy* on the House wing reflects directly the sculpture on the temple of Zeus at Olympia and that on the Madeleine in Paris. While pediment shape demands a central figure surrounded by others who must gradually bend to the raked corners, here subject matter clearly replicates ancient themes. The Zeus temple at Olympia celebrates Apollo, deity of civilization, triumphant over the barbarous centaurs. The Madeleine pediment shows Christ giving pardon at the Last Judgment. Bartlett's *Apotheosis* personifies American democracy as a goddess of peace. She is attired as the Roman Minerva, but has laid aside her implements of war. The olive tree of Athena stands behind her, now the olive of peace. Beneath her outstretched hand the child genius, free to develop, cradles the torch of immortality. Flanking this democracy/peace personification are figures representing sources of American wealth: iron and textile industries fill the left frame; agriculture and animal husbandry stand on the right.

The pediment sculpture of the Senate wing portrays *Progress of Civilization*. Thomas Crawford's work presents a program similar to Bartlett's. America, again as a woman, stands at the center, with an eagle beside her, the sun behind. The early days of American civilization are represented on the right by a Native American chief, woman, child, and a grave. The diversity of progress fills the left, including a soldier, merchant, and mechanic. No tomb appears with the industrious citizens gathered to represent American progress: white American civilization triumphs over that of the Native American.

A simple design adorns the pediment of the Capitol's east entrance. Luigi Persico's *Genius of America* comprises but three figures: America herself, in the center, points to Justice with her scales on her right. Flanking America on her left are an eagle and the figure of Hope. Three inscriptions augment the trilogy: "USA" on America's shield, "July 4, 1776" on her altar, and "Constitution, 17 September 1787" marked on Justice's scroll. Hope lacks a date: she looks to the future.

American political art created for the Capitol expresses a continual dichotomy between the classical tradition and a desire to be new. The tension between antiquity and modernity is often not truly resolved but merely juxtaposed, at times becoming an uneasy replica of the Etruscan chimera: a blending of many elements into something new and strange. Brumidi's frescoes for the Rotunda ceiling, those encircling the dome's eye, might be called chimerical.

The Apotheosis of George Washington unites the deities of ancient Rome with the founders of the United States. The title of the frieze suggests a deification of a mortal, an idea borrowed from imperial Rome, where each emperor was thought to become a god after his death—some believed in their divinity while on earth. Washington, flanked by Liberty and Victory, is portrayed as he was in Greenough's statue: he sits enthroned like the Zeus at Olympia, but here wears attire of his own period. Each scene has its guiding classical deity. Minerva protects "Arts and Sciences" as Franklin, Morse, and Fulton look up at her. In "Agriculture," Ceres with a cornucopia sits upon a McCormick Reaper. Vulcan takes the central position in "Mechanics," Mercury guides "Commerce," while Neptune overlooks the "Marine" scene. Brumidi's blatant association of the classical world with the new nation was hailed by all as a triumphant illustration of American values.

Atop the Capitol's dome stands the Statue of Freedom. Also the work of Thomas Crawford, this bronze statue blends classical with Native American images. Freedom, a woman, attired in Roman garb, holds or wears a variety of symbolic items. The laurel victory wreath in her left hand recalls Apollo. As Minerva held a shield, so Freedom grips one adorned with thirteen stripes. Her Roman helmet, also borrowed from Minerva, features a crest of eagle feathers, a reference to the Native American headdress.

The Capitol and its bicameral wings signify the ideals the American nation wished to claim as its own. The classical influences in design and sculpture offered instant culture to the new nation; the figures represented every man and woman who brought European civilization to the land. In form and art the Capitol stands as a central icon for the United States.

The Capitol's dome has been replicated across the country: a majority of state capitols echo its form. While each reflects regional interests, almost all include a dome. Most state capitol buildings had a dome in their original design, but often had to wait until finances permitted construction; Oklahoma's capitol rotunda had to wait until 2001 for its grand dome.

The few capitols without the iconic dome emulate the rotunda in shape or concept. Santa Fe, New Mexico, boasts a magnificent round structure resembling a Roman amphitheater with walls of native adobe. Hawaii's capitol, reflective of the island's geography and its history, is a square open to the elements at the center, an echo of the Pantheon's oculus or a Roman atrium. The skyscraper inspired only three capitol buildings. Nebraska, North Dakota, and in recent years, Louisiana, built their government buildings high into the sky. Nebraska was the first to abandon the familiar dome, although its architect capped the skyscraper with a domed roof. Louisiana recently replaced its government castle with the nation's highest capitol tower, but, again, topped with a dome. Only North Dakota rejected the dome entirely. Its vertical mass towers above Bismark as a symbol of its efficient government. Virginia's Capitol also lacks a dome, but is a replica of the Maison Carrée, the Roman temple of Augustus and Livia in Nimes.

Americans love to take well-known, easily recognizable images and reproduce them on souvenirs or use them in advertisements. The Capitol's dome adorns everything from candles to tote bags. One can buy replicas of the building or just its dome at tourist shops in Washington or on the Web. Numerous products, from crackers to comedy groups, from biscuits to wall paper, have used the towering dome as their logo. Although there are other monuments on the Washington Mall, it is the Capitol that most frequently appears to identify the place in films or TV shows set in the city and newscasts from it. The Washington Monument, a replica of an ancient obelisk, stands taller, but the Capitol has become the logo of the city, and hence the nation.

The buildings of the Washington Mall collectively commemorate both America's tripartite government structure and many, but not all, of its wars. It is also the place where democracy is celebrated and practiced. The iconography of the Mall reflects American values; its monuments remind, and instruct, both visitors and workers about these values. The Capitol, anchoring the east end of the Mall, leads the way in proclaiming America's history and the nature of its people: from its dome and its sculpture the nation's self-image is asserted. From ground level one cannot read the inscription on Freedom's base atop the Capitol, *e pluribus unum*, but every American knows the Latin phrase symbolizes the nation's unity. The towering circle of the Capitol dome expresses that idea in its form; it is the nation's most perfect *domus*, its most splendid house.

WORKS RECOMMENDED

Fryd, Vivien Green. *Art and Empire: The Politics of Ethnicity in the United States Capitol, 1815–1860*. New Haven, CT: Yale UP, 1992.

Griswold, Charles. "The Vietnam Veterans Memorial and the Washington Mall: Philosophical Thoughts on Political Iconography." *Critical Inquiry* 12 (1986): 689–719.

Kennon, Donald R., and Thomas P. Somma. *American Pantheon: Sculptural and Artistic Decoration of the United States Capitol*. Athens, OH: U.S. Capitol Historical Society–Ohio UP, 2004.

Scott, Pamela. *Temple of Liberty: Building the Capitol for a New Nation*. New York: Oxford UP, 1995.

Smith, E. Baldwin. *The Dome, a Study in the History of Ideas*. Princeton, NJ: Princeton UP, 1978.

Somma, Thomas P. *Apotheosis of Democracy, 1908–1916: The Pediment for the House Wing of the U.S. Capitol*. Newark: U of Delaware P, 1995.

Taylor, Joshua C. *America as Art*. Washington, DC: National Collection of Fine Arts–Smithsonian Institution P, 1976.

Johnny Carson

David Lavery

> By defying the TV reductionism that renders all things knowable and ultimately trivial, Carson made himself into one of the medium's only characters worth watching, night after night.... [W]e knew Johnny Carson like we knew ourselves. Which is to say we hardly knew him at all.
> Steven D. Stark, *Glued to the Set*

In the early 1990s, in a series of *Saturday Night Live* skits, Dana Carvey and Phil Hartman parodied their fellow NBC late night program, the long-running *Tonight Show* (1954–). As Johnny Carson, the show's host from 1963 to 1993, Carvey reduced the talk show legend to a series of familiar ticks and the constantly repeated, applicable to everything, exclamation "That's wild stuff"; mimicking sidekick-announcer Ed McMahon, Hartman was all boisterous laughs and endlessly repeated "Heigh-o's." For critic Ken Tucker, the parodies, "at once mean and respectfully accurate," spelled cultural doom for the King of Late Night: "Carvey was pointing out the way Carson had become increasingly out of it, seemingly unaware of the pop culture around him" ("Still Crazy After All These Years").

In a May 1991 installment of the recurring sketch, Carvey answered Ed's "Here's Johnny" summons and emerged from behind the curtain not in his usual dapper sport coat and slacks, not with short, graying hair, not to perform his usual golf-swing-punctuated monologue and announce "We'll be right back," but as "Carsenio," a bleached-blonde, flat-topped, Caucasian-version of African-American comedian Arsenio Hall, the late night syndicated host whose fist-pumping, hipper humor and more contemporary guests had begun to woo away the younger end of Carson's demographic.

The sight of the Carvey version of the King of Late Night stooping to emulate his distant rival could only provoke sadness, not laughter, in the longtime *Tonight Show* watcher. The spectacle of Carson trying to be the "terminally charmless" Jay Leno, his successor as *Tonight Show* host (Shales), or Carson-as-Letterman, the loser in the "network battle for the night" that erupted after Johnny's retirement (Carter), would be just as distressing. The

JOHNNY CARSON

Johnny Carson who had become an American icon, "NBC's answer to foreplay" (Tynan 315), "history's most effective contraceptive" ("Johnny Carson"), and "the greeter and spokesman for the United States" (Letterman, quoted by Zehme), while remaining an essentially private, reclusive individual—"the Garbo of Comedy, the Salinger of Television" (Zehme)—that Carson never really changed. "The idea that one man, basically unscripted, could last on TV for 30 years," a former NBC executive would maintain, "it's a freak of television" (quoted in Zoglin).

When Shakespeare left the theater for good, he put the London stage behind him completely and remained content to be a retired impresario back home in Stratford; when Carson, the most watched performer in the history of entertainment, his show the biggest money-maker the medium had ever known, left television after his 4,530th show, he returned home to Malibu pretty much never to be seen again. "Like sun and moon and oxygen," Bill Zehme, contemplating his disappearance, would write movingly in 2002, "he was always there, reliable and dependable, for thirty years. Then he wasn't anymore. And he didn't just simply leave: he vanished completely; he evaporated into cathode snow; he took the powder of all powders." In January 2005 the news broke that Carson, who had spent almost his entire career on NBC, was occasionally providing jokes for David Letterman's *Late Show* monologue on rival CBS. Soon after, on January 23, 2005, came the shocking news that Johnny Carson was dead from emphysema, having passed away while these pages were being written. Judging by some of the hagiographies that appeared in the media after his death, critic David Edelstein would justifiably complain, "You'd think that Carson was some sort of egoless saint of television."

More than just a celebrity (defined by Boorstin as someone merely "known for his well-knownness" [57]), the "Greatest Generation" Carson (Shales) once represented something distinctly American. "More people look at Johnny," an NBC press agent once bragged about its prize commodity, "than look at the moon" ("Johnny"). But what did they see? As television scholar Jimmie Reeves once observed, Carson was never a simple star in the firmament: "It's [Carson's] elusivity that keeps him fresh.... We can put ourselves into him. He's familiar enough to be recognizable, yet unique enough to be interesting. There's more to Johnny Carson than meets the eye" (quoted in Stark 184).

In private, Johnny Carson was, by all reports, a loner, uncomfortable in social situations, seemingly ill-suited to the life of celebrity. The screenwriter George Axelrod once observed that "Socially, [Carson] doesn't exist. The reason is that there are no television cameras in living rooms. If human beings had little red lights in the middle of their foreheads, Carson would be the greatest conversationalist on earth" (quoted in Tynan 312). (The camera, Tynan quipped, "act[ed] on him like an addictive and galvanic drug" [311].)

Critics like Richard Poirier have documented the pronounced tendency of key figures in American literature, culture, and politics to create imaginary public personas often at odds with their private selves. Though Carson's longtime producer Fred de Cordova once insisted that while "George Burns and

Johnny Carson, 1965. Courtesy of the Library of Congress.

Jack Benny assumed a façade," his star was himself, "not a character named Johnny Carson" (quoted by Stark 185); was it not in fact his "negative capability" that enabled him to become not only Carnac the Magnificent and Aunt Blabby, Art Fern and Floyd R. Turbo, but also his greatest creation: Carson the congenial conversationalist?

A year after Carsenio made his *Saturday Night Live* appearance, Carson ended his run just short of three decades behind the desk. His final two shows, cultural spectacles comparable to the series finales of *M*A*S*H*, *Seinfeld*, and *Friends*, drew huge audiences (50 million watched the last one, a guestless retrospective clip show, on May 21, 1992), but it was the penultimate one, in which Bette Midler crooned "One More for My Baby (and One More for the Road)" to an obviously moved Carson, that everyone remembers, producing as it did what David Bianculli called "a perfect moment of television, a guaranteed tearjerker, and a fitting finale (even if it was a day early) to one of the most durable and impressive careers in show business" (342). Television scholar David Marc would see in Carson's retirement the end of an era: "For 30 years, prime time was bracketed by two men: Walter Cronkite, who gave the news in his daily report, and Johnny Carson, who reviewed the news in his daily monologue.... Johnny, like Walter, is part of the lost world of three-channel culture" (quoted in Tucker, "Johnny's Last Laugh").

Though he came to be a Hollywood gatekeeper with the power to make or break careers—scores of comics, from Roseanne Barr to Jerry Seinfeld credited him with their first big break—Carson never shed his image as a Midwestern boy (born in Iowa, he grew up in Nebraska). Watch *Johnny Goes Home* on *The Ultimate Collection* DVDs, narrated by and starring Carson as he wanders about Norfolk, Nebraska, even sitting down for a refresher penmanship lesson by his then-elderly grade-school teacher, and it becomes apparent that Johnny had not succeeded, nor perhaps even attempted, to take the farm out of the boy. If fellow Nebraskan talk show host Dick Cavett would discern in his one-time boss and later rival "that wonderful naughty-fraternity-boy quality...he never outgrows" (quoted in Zoglin), Carson's impish taste for the risqué, his adeptness at double-entendre, were equally apparent to any alert viewer.

Carson's distinct style emerges in Edelstein's discerning obituary of him:

> When Carson succeeded Steve Allen and Jack Paar as host of...the *Tonight Show*, the shift in tone was radical. Although Allen was underappreciated as a satirist, he had a fundamentally earnest presence, and Paar was, if anything, overearnest (to the point of bathos). But Carson was cutting: there was always a chill behind the twinkle. If he cultivated the look of a boyish Midwesterner..., he could turn into a bad boy (or a smutty-minded boy) in an instant.

Although no one seems able to confirm (and Carson himself denied it) that he once responded to a Persian-cat-toting Zsa Zsa Gabor's invitation "to pet my pussy?" with "Sure, if you move that damn cat out of the way!" (Cox 77), he very definitely did tell the voluptuous Dolly Parton that he would "give about a year's pay to take a peek under there" (Cox 84). Who can forget his wide-eyed response, captured in close-up, when the late Madeline Kahn responded to his inquiry about her phobias with "I do not like balls coming toward me." Carson's use of "the camera as a silent conspirator," Kenneth Tynan once observed, was his "most original contribution to TV technique." But it was not his only one.

Writing in *USA Today*, Wes Gehring would offer an astute analysis of Carson's comic style:

> [B]ecause Carson was such a student of laughter, he often existed as a pluralist comedian, gifting audiences periodically with such signature expressions as Oliver Hardy's embarrassed tie-fiddling look, Stan Laurel's teary elongated face, Benny's direct address (staring at the camera) deadpan, and a Groucho Marx eyebrow twitch after a mildly suggestive double entendre. What made these and other assorted funny footnotes all Carson was the ease with which he segued through such shtick. It was a tour de silly each night of the week. (68)

He was a superb physical comedian, as good at pratfalls as a Chevy Chase, willing to get down on all fours, pretending to be a dog gobbling the Alpo a real dog had rejected, saving Ed McMahon's live ad. Wonderfully uneasy with the parade of animals the San Diego Zoo brought to the show, he could secure uproarious laughter from a face-off with an orangutan, a marmoset urinating on his head, a boa constrictor's tail surprisingly emerging between his legs.

Virtually every recognizable figure from entertainment and politics, both fellow icons and lesser lights, from Martin Luther King, Jr., to Dean Martin, Richard Nixon to Bob Hope, Shelley Winters to Carl Sagan, Bill Clinton to Tiny Tim, sat down beside him. "It is still the most exciting moment in show business to walk out from that curtain and sit in this chair," Tom Hanks has confessed (Zoglin). He was absolutely wonderful with children and the elderly; and with ordinary Americans (deemed "civilians" by the show's staff), he could be the perfect host, hardly ever condescending, though often playful (that time, for example, when he pretended to eat one of the prized potato chips in which a woman had found a variety of animal and human faces).

With *Dragnet*'s Jack Webb, he could do tongue-twisting verbal humor about copper clappers and kleptomaniacs, or, portraying President Reagan, revisit Abbott and Costello's "Who's On First" routine with Hu, Watt, and Yasser Arafat replacing Who, What, and friends. The *Ultimate Collection* Carson DVDs are full of such moments of clever, imaginative, often literate comedy. In one particularly memorable skit, Carson, dressed in Renaissance garb, plays Hamlet, reciting, or so it seems, the famous "To be or not to be" and "Alas, Poor Yorick" soliloquies; but Shakespeare's powerful words turn out to be mere product placement for a shameless series of commercials: "sleep no more" inspires a plug for Sominex; "The heartache, and the thousand natural *shocks* / That flesh is heir to" (emphasis added) leads to an ad for Aamco; "ay, there's the rub," turns out to be, of course, a set-up for promotion of Mentholatum Deep Heat Rub. Yorick, in turn, is warned not to leave Denmark without his American Express Card.

But it was, of course, Carson's monologues that were his comic signature. Whether his one-liners produced laughs or bombed (he was a master at transforming even his failures into hilarity), his opening litany of jokes, almost certain to include gags about Ed's drinking, bandleader Doc Severinsen's wardrobe (or substitute Tommy Newsom's drabness), and his own former wives, was often the highlight of the show and sometimes the only part of the show for which sleepy Americans could stay conscious. Carson "dealt with topical events as reliably as Walter Cronkite," Bianculli has observed, "and the impact of his monologue made Carson the TV equivalent of Will Rogers: one joke could make all the difference in indicating whether someone (or something) was up or down, in or out" (341). It should not surprise us that Carson's monologue came to possess such influence, for, as Stark notes, "like an anchorman (or a president), Carson was one of the few performers whom TV etiquette allowed to address the camera directly—the culture's ultimate sign of respect and authority" (183).

In perhaps the most discerning piece ever written on Carson, Kenneth Tynan articulates the dilemma that faced Carson both the performer and the icon:

> Singers, actors, and dancers all have multiple choices: they can exercise their talents in the theatre, on TV, or in the movies. But a talk-show host can only become a more successful talk-show host. There is no place in the other media for the gifts that distinguish him—most specifically, for the gift of re-inventing himself, night after night, without rehearsal or repetition. Carson, in other words, is a grand master of the one show-business art that leads nowhere. He has painted himself not into a corner but onto the top of a mountain. (353–54)

If television had a Mount Rushmore, Johnny would be on it.

WORKS CITED AND RECOMMENDED

Bianculli, David. *Dictionary of Teleliteracy*. New York: Continuum, 1996.

Boorstin, Daniel. *The Image: A Guide to Pseudo-Events in America*. New York: Atheneum, 1961.

Carter, Bill. "O'Brien to Succeed Leno on 'Tonight Show'." *New York Times* 28 Sept. 2004, E1 Op. 1c.

Cox, Stephen. *Here's Johnny: Thirty Years of America's Favorite Late-Night Entertainer*. Nashville: Cumberland House, 2002.

Edelstein, David. "Johnny Carson: The Naughty Genius of Late Night." *Slate* 24 Jan. 2005 <http://slate.com/id/2112604/>.

Gehring, Wes D. "'Heeeere's Johnny!' Forty Years Ago, Johnny Carson Moved into America's Living Rooms and Bedrooms as the Host of NBC's *The Tonight Show*." *USA Today Magazine* July 2002: 66–69.

"Johnny Carson." *Television's Top 25 Stars*. *People Weekly* Special Issue 20 (Summer 1989): 20–21.

Poirier, Richard. *A World Elsewhere: The Place of Style in American Literature*. New York: Oxford UP, 1966.

Shales, Tom. "Missing the Inimitable Johnny." *Electronic Media* 6 May 2002: 47.

Stark, Steven D. *Glued to the Set: The 60 Television Shows and Events That Made Us Who We Are Today*. New York: Free P, 1997.

Tucker, Ken. "Johnny's Last Laugh: Eight Years Ago, Johnny Carson Bid Adieu to Late Night When He Broadcast His Final Tonight Show." *Entertainment Weekly* 26 May 2000: 80.

———. "Still Crazy After All These Years." *Entertainment Weekly* 15 May 1992: 51.

Tynan, Kenneth. "Fifteen Years of the Salto Mortale." *Life Stories: Profiles from* The New Yorker. Ed. David Remnick. New York: Random House, 2000. 310–54.

Zehme, Bill. "The Man Who Retired; Ten Years Ago, the King of Late Night Went Away for Good, Vanished. The Garbo of American Comedy. But Now, Just One Last Time, Here's Johnny." *Esquire* June 2002: 88–99.

Zoglin, Richard. "And What a Reign It Was: In His 30 Years, Carson Was the Best." *Time* 16 Mar. 1992: 62–64.

Johnny Cash

Don Cusic

During his lifetime, Johnny Cash did just about everything he could to destroy his career. He became wasted on drugs, unreliable, surly, and diffident. And yet, when he died in September 2003, he was widely considered one of the most important—if not *the* most important—artist in the history of country music.

Johnny Cash came to symbolize country music, or at least country as those both inside and outside the world of country music see the genre. He grew up poor and rural—an essential element in creating a country music icon. He was deeply religious, fell into an addiction to drugs, then was redeemed by a "good woman," and along the way recorded hit songs and concept albums. In some of his hit songs and concept albums he aligned himself with the cowboy and American West—which has long been part of the image of country music. Cash starred in his own network TV show, appeared in several movies, sang on some soundtracks, and in his later years became "cool" to young people by being produced by a rap and alternative record producer.

Johnny Cash was a man who conveyed deep thoughts in a deep voice; he wrote anthems for youth when country music and the youth culture were at odds. He was a patriot and veteran who dared question the Vietnam War, and he spoke up for the downtrodden—Native Americans and prisoners—during the 1960s. It's a classic rags to riches tale, the story of somebody growing up a poor nobody and dying an important figure in country music and popular culture. Is it any wonder that Johnny Cash is not just a person but an icon in country music?

J. R. Cash (he did not become "John" until he entered the military, and became "Johnny" when Sam Phillips released his first record on Sun) was born during the Great Depression (February 26, 1932) and grew up in the northeast corner of Arkansas where his parents, Ray and Carrie Cash, were tenant farmers. Every evening young J. R. Cash sat at the kitchen and listened to the radio, but that radio wasn't just music for idle time; it gave him inspiration and relief from the daily grind of farming, a dream and vision he would pursue.

After graduating from high school in 1950, Cash made the trek that so many southern boys made—to the car manufacturing plants in Michigan—and obtained a job at the Fisher Body factory in Pontiac. He worked there for two weeks, then went back home and enlisted in the Air Force. Cash was sent to Landsberg, Germany, where he was a radio operator. But, more importantly, there Johnny Cash bought a guitar, learned how to play it, and made his first steps towards being a performer. In the summer of 1954, Cash was discharged from the Air Force; he returned to Arkansas and married a young lady he had met during basic training in Texas.

During the first twenty-two years of Johnny Cash's life, he was shaped by several factors. First, his rural upbringing in Arkansas on a cotton farm had given him the kind of background that served as a common thread for country boys in the Depression. The radio brought him country music and allowed him to hear songs and singers he wouldn't have been able to hear before, and so shaped his musical tastes. His family was very religious and the early exposure to church gave him a deep, abiding faith that was always a part of him. And the personal tragedy of his brother's death left a huge emotional gap in his life.

Jack Cash, two years older than John, was fourteen when he was pulled into a table saw while cutting fence posts at a sawmill. Cash said that the memory of his brother was always with him during his entire life.

Living in Memphis, Cash met Luther Perkins and Marshall Grant, two mechanics who worked at a Chevrolet dealership. The three young men, all acoustic guitar players, began practicing together. One night Cash suggested Perkins and Grant each play different instruments; Perkins began to play lead guitar and Grant picked up the bass. Thus, Cash's original back-up group the Tennessee Two was born.

John Cash was aware of Sun Records in Memphis; by this time Elvis's first recordings had been released and there were articles in the paper about the label. Cash began to stop by Sun Records in hopes of meeting Sam Phillips. After a number of times when Phillips wasn't in or was in a meeting or otherwise occupied, Cash finally saw him, introduced himself, and asked for an audition. Phillips invited him in and Cash sang a number of songs for Phillips. Probably during this meeting, in late 1954, Phillips recorded two songs with just Cash and his guitar. Later, Cash came back with Luther Perkins and Marshall Grant and they auditioned. At this point the group viewed itself as a gospel group and Cash wanted to do gospel material, but Phillips was reluctant to record gospel because Sun couldn't sell it; the future for the record company was in what became known as rockabilly. Cash quickly realized this, and during this audition, probably in early 1955, Sam Phillips recorded them doing several songs, including "Folsom Prison Blues" and "Hey Porter." In February 1955, Cash, Grant and Perkins went into the studio and recorded "Wide Open Road," "Cry, Cry, Cry" (which he had written since the last session), and "Hey Porter"; the last two would be his first single release from Sun with "Cry, Cry, Cry" entering the *Billboard* country chart.

and Tears. Cash did not write any of these songs except "Legend of John Henry's Hammer," where he took the basic folk song of "John Henry" and turned it into a dramatic eight-minute masterpiece.

In 1963 Johnny Cash began a string of top single hits for Columbia, beginning with "Ring of Fire," written by June Carter and Merle Kilgore, and "The Matador," written by Cash and June Carter, both that year; "Understand Your Man," "The Ballad of Ira Hayes" and "Bad News" in 1964; "Orange Blossom Special," "The Sons of Katie Elder" (the title track from the movie of the same name), and "Happy To Be With You" in 1965; and "The One On the Right Is On the Left" in 1966. His album *Ring of Fire* was a huge success, and it contained songs such as the TV theme song "The Rebel—Johnny Yuma" and the title track (neither of which he wrote) in addition to the self-penned "I'd Still Be There" (written with Johnny Horton), "What Do I Care," "I Still Miss Someone," "Forty Shades of Green," "The Big Battle" and "Tennessee Flat-top Box." This was his strongest album so far and Cash was a commercial as well as critical success; this album was Cash's first to go "gold" (sales of half a million units).

The widespread interest in cowboys may have spurred Cash's interest in Indians. He was part Cherokee, so there was a natural interest; but the 1950s and 1960s also saw Indians and the Old West reexamined through a number of movies. Johnny Cash had written "Old Apache Squaw" and it was released on the album *Songs of Our Soil*. But Cash's interest in Indians was spurred further when he heard Indian songwriter Peter LaFarge performing in 1963 in Greenwich Village at the Gaslight Club. On this same evening, Cash first met Bob Dylan.

"The Ballad of Ira Hayes" tells the story of an Arizona Pima Indian who was one of those who raised the flag at Iwo Jima, immortalized in a photograph and a monument at Arlington National Cemetery. But when Hayes returned home he faced discrimination, humiliation, and poverty. An alcoholic, Hayes died a tragic death, drowned in a ditch. Cash recorded "The Ballad of Ira Hayes," a protest song in the era of protests. After this single, Cash recorded the album that would become *Bitter Tears*.

Cash's reasons for recording a concept album about Indians—indeed, it was an angry album as much about civil rights and protest as about Indians per se—were artistic as well as commercial.

Johnny Cash's interest in the West and cowboys, which he originally expressed in songs like "Give My Love to Rose" and "Don't Take Your Guns to Town" led to a double album of cowboy songs, *Johnny Cash Sings the Ballads of the True West* that was recorded in March 1965. This album includes a number of old cowboy classics, such as "The Streets of Laredo," "I Ride an Old Paint," "Bury Me Not on the Lone Prairie," and "Green Grow the Lilacs" as well as some original songs. Cash adds some narration on the album in addition to the songs, further showing the diversity of the West.

After Columbia released the double album of *True West* they edited the album down to a single album entitled *Mean As Hell* and released that as well. And so 1965 ended with Johnny Cash's image firmly established as a folk singer of the mythical West.

Many people saw Johnny Cash as larger than life; he probably saw himself the same way. In his songs, albums, and life he always projected a sense of vision, a sense of "calling" and a higher purpose to his life and work. He had never been just another artist looking for the next hit or a singer just trying to get to the next gig. If Johnny Cash achieved the status of a great man it was because he aspired to become a great man. He set high standards for himself—in his life and his work—and worked hard to fulfill them. Although he may have fallen short of greatness at times in his life and work, his vision was always there and he was able to continue his journey having learned his lessons. Few people carry the ambition and resolve to become a great man in their lives; Johnny Cash was one of them.

On June 7, 1969, *The Johnny Cash Show* became a weekly TV show on ABC-TV. The hour-long show was originally a summer series, broadcast on Saturday nights. In the fall of 1969 the show was moved to Wednesday evenings, where it continued its run until May 1971. This popular television program brought Johnny Cash into American homes each week and multiplied his fame. Again, he used this platform to do more than entertain; he had a "Ride This Train" segment which combined history and geography, he featured gospel music, and he featured performers such as Bob Dylan and Kris Kristofferson. With this TV show, Johnny Cash went from being a superstar in country music to an American icon and a figure in country music of almost mythic proportions.

In addition to his TV show Cash made other notable appearances; in 1969 he toured Vietnam, singing for the troops, and in 1970 he performed at the White House for President Richard Nixon. It was a busy time for Cash, who spent these two years in heavy public demand. This high-profile time yielded great rewards in terms of personal bookings and also fueled his creative juices. Cash always thrived on activity and seemed to be at his most creative when he was busiest and shouldering major responsibilities.

In March 1970 Cash recorded "What Is Truth," which connected him to the youth of the nation and once again made him a spokesman for the outcast—in this case, the long-haired youth of the day who represented a cultural gap and great division between the generations. But although this was a hit single, it would not be released on an album.

The fame from the TV show seemed to increase Cash's self-confidence and awareness of himself. In February 1971 he recorded "Man in Black" which stated, in essence, that he was on the side of the downtrodden. In this song he states he wears black for the poor, hopeless, prisoners, and those who have never heard the message of Jesus, concluding that he'd love to wear bright colors but "I'll try to carry off a little darkness on my back," and so he'll be a man who wears black.

After his TV show ended in March 1971, Cash embarked on a project that had deep significance for him, the movie *Gospel Road*, which he financed himself. *Gospel Road* consumed a great deal of Cash's time and energy and strengthened his marriage and working relationship with June Carter.

Johnny Cash wrote all of the songs on his album *Ragged Old Flag*, which came out in 1974. The album came at a time when America was getting out of Vietnam, only to become embroiled in the Watergate scandal of President Richard Nixon. So when Johnny Cash recorded "Ragged Old Flag," he confronted that sense of shame and countered with an unabashedly patriotic song.

Creatively, the 1980s were a long dry spell for Johnny Cash. Although he collected honors and awards and was seen as a "senior spokesman" for country music, he didn't seem to have a spot in the contemporary country music world. The excitement of new audiences and big sales left some of the old timers in the dust; for someone like Johnny Cash it was a frustrating, disappointing period.

Then, in 1994 he released an album *Cash: American Recordings* on the new American Recordings label produced by alternative producer Rick Rubin. The album was done with just Cash and his guitar and summed up Cash's career pretty well. There were folk songs ("Tennessee Stud" and "Delia's Gone"), a humorous song ("The Man Who Couldn't Cry"), a cowboy song ("Oh Bury Me Not"), a gospel song ("Why Me, Lord"), songs with a haunting personal vision ("The Beast In Me" and "Bird on a Wire"), and four songs he wrote. The self-penned songs tell stories and encompass Cash's spiritual vision. There was nothing new on this album except the audience; young people suddenly discovered Johnny Cash and found him both profound and "cool." It was a surprising rebirth for a man whose audiences and fans now included people younger than some of his grandchildren.

The *American* Recordings album validated Cash's status and stature as an American icon and gained him a new, young audience. After the first album, three others followed.

In May 2003, June Carter Cash went into the hospital for heart surgery and fell into a coma; she died on May 15. During the four months between her death and his, Cash recorded about fifty songs. In September he was set to fly to Los Angeles to record some more songs with Rick Rubin, but failing health forced him to enter the hospital, where he died on September 12.

It took a long hard life to write the songs that Johnny Cash wrote, and a good, sweet life to sing them. Johnny Cash lived both. The songs he wrote reflect both the hardness and the sweetness of his life, the sinner and the saint, the success and the failures, the strengths and weaknesses, all wrapped up in the greatness that called itself Johnny Cash.

WORKS RECOMMENDED

Brooks, Tim, and Earle Marsh. *The Complete Directory to Prime Time Network TV Shows 1946–Present*. New York: Ballantine Books, 1988.

Cash, Johnny. *Man in Black*. Grand Rapids, MI: Zondervan, 1975.

Cash, Johnny, with Patrick Carr. *Cash: The Autobiography*. New York: HarperSanFrancisco, 1997.

Smith, John L. *The Johnny Cash Discography*. Westport, CT: Greenwood, 1985.

Whitburn, Joel. *Top Country Singles 1944–1988*. Menomonee Falls, WI: Record Research, 1989.

Wren, Christopher S. *Winners Got Scars Too: The Life and Legend of Johnny Cash*. New York: The Dial P, 1971.

Cell Phone

John P. Ferré

At the start of the twentieth century, when Guglielmo Marconi was refining his wireless telegraph for ship-to-ship and ship-to-shore communication, the English engineer William Ayrton prophesied an entirely different use of the new medium. He envisioned private conversations conveyed electronically across the world:

> If a person wanted to call a friend he knew not where, he would call in a loud, electro-magnetic voice, heard by him who had the electro-magnetic ear, silent to him who had it not. "Where are you?" he would say. A small reply would come, "I am at the bottom of a coal mine, or crossing the Andes, or in the middle of the Pacific." Let them think of what that meant, of the calling which went on every day from room to room of a house, and then think of that calling extending from pole to pole; not a noisy babble, but a call audible to him who wanted to hear and absolutely silent to him who did not. (quoted in Czitrom 67)

The mobile telephones Ayrton foresaw were reliable, secure, and useful, very much like the cell phones we have today.

Cell phones became commercially viable in 1983 when Motorola introduced the DynaTAC, but mobility had long before been a goal for wireless communications. Although radio had always been mobile at sea, the first mobile land use for radio began in 1921, when the Detroit Police Department instituted a one-way radio messaging service. Twenty years later, Motorola installed the first two-way radio in a police cruiser. The development of the cell phone finally liberated Americans from phones tethered to walls at work and home. The desire for cell phones was so great that twenty years after Motorola introduced them to American consumers, 60 percent of Americans had one.

But however quickly Americans incorporated cell phones into their lives, they did so with mixed emotions. The cell phone quickly came to represent disparate values. Advocates recognized in the cell phone safety and connectedness; detractors, by contrast, saw physical dangers and the erosion of considerateness. Whether the cell phone represented social advancement or nuisance depended upon who was asked. An icon of mobility, the cell phone was also a Rorschach Test for attitudes toward social life at the turn of the twenty-first century.

ADVOCATES

Safety is the primary reason that people buy cell phones. People want instantaneous communication in an emergency both for themselves and their families. Indeed, having peace of mind and keeping track of their children motivates many parents to give cell phones to their children. More than half of children from 11 to 17 years old have a cell phone, and nearly half of children from 8 to 10 years old have one. To encourage even more parents to buy cell phones for their children, companies have devised family plans that include free calls between family members.

While emergencies account for a small percentage of the cell phone calls that are actually made, the Cellular Telecommunications & Internet Association reports that 200,000 calls for help are made on cell phones every day. These calls can be as mundane as a call for a tow truck or a ride, or they can be for police, firefighters, or EMS. Some cell phone calls have been so dramatic that they have made the news, as was the case of a hunter lost in a northern Minnesota forest in freezing temperatures who was rescued by sheriff's deputies after he called 911 on his cell phone, or the rescue of a mountain climber who managed to call 911 after being snowbound for three nights on Mount Shasta in northern California. Safety is such an important dimension of cell phones that the Federal Communications Commission mandated that by 2006 emergency dispatchers be able to use the global positioning chips in cell phones to pinpoint the location of almost any 911 call. Cell phones can also be set up in an emergency message network to receive instant messages about emergencies and response plans, an arrangement used mostly by government agencies, schools, and transport companies.

Of course, cell phones mean much more than safety. Surveys of cell phone buyers suggest that, after safety, socializing, convenience, and business are the most important reasons for having a cell phone. Cell phones, in other words, signify easy accessibility to friends, family, and business associates. Those who have not bought cell phones tend not only to be unable to afford the payments, but they also tend to be much older than cell phone users, leading one researcher to observe that non-use of cell phones amounts to "a process of social exclusion" (Wei 715). The irony here is that unlike traditional land telephone service, which includes a listing in a telephone directory, cell phones, which signify accessibility, are not listed; and cell phone users are often reluctant to share their numbers with very many people.

The ultimate confluence between personal connectedness and emergency use occurred on September 11, 2001, in a flurry of highly publicized cell phone calls during the terrorist attacks of that day. Some of the calls occurred between the terrorists, as they coordinated their attack from aboard the

Camera phone with picture of a camera phone. Courtesy of Shutterstock.

planes they would soon hijack. After the planes were hijacked, some passengers on each of the four hijacked planes managed to phone home to report what was going on and to say goodbye to their loved ones. The call that became iconic was made on United Airlines Flight 93 by Todd Beamer, who used an air phone to provide an operator with information about the hijacking. After saying the Lord's Prayer with her, he kept the connection open while he and other passengers prepared to attack the hijackers. "Are you ready guys?" Beamer asked. "Let's roll" (Dutton 237–45).

The phrase "Let's roll" immediately came to represent the bravery of Americans who would fight to the end to protect Americans from terrorists. The phrase quickly appeared on a variety of patriotic consumer items. There were "Let's Roll Flight 93" lapel pins, "Let's Roll" ball caps, and "Let's Roll" bumper stickers. Rock musician Neil Young wrote a song called "Let's Roll," and Beamer's wife Lisa later wrote a book entitled *Let's Roll! Ordinary People, Extraordinary Courage*, which she also narrated as an audio CD.

Cell phones were again in the news after the 9/11 attacks when the *Washington Post* reported that Americans had nearly captured the Al Qaeda mastermind, Osama bin Laden. In late 2001, U.S. intelligence agencies were following bin Laden's satellite phone signal in the Tora Bora mountains of Afghanistan, but before U.S. forces could close in on him, bin Laden gave his phone to a bodyguard, who led the American pursuers away from him.

DETRACTORS

In every generation since electricity was first harnessed, there have been people who feared exposure to it would cause physical harm. As telegraph wires were strung between poles throughout the country in the nineteenth century, some people would walk well out of their way to avoid getting too near to them. In *My Life and Hard Times*, James Thurber told of his grandmother who feared that electricity was leaking throughout the house from empty sockets in rooms where the wall switch had been left on. Mothers warned their children in the 1960s not to sit too close to the television.

Cell phones are the most recent in a line of electronic technologies that have been seen as potentially dangerous. Some people have worried that holding a device that emits radio-frequency radiation to one's ear could, over time, be as dangerous as prolonged exposure to the ionizing radiation produced by x-ray machines and radioactive materials. This was the claim of

CELL PHONE

David Reynard of Madeira Beach, Florida, who sued NEC Corporation in 1993 after his 33-year-old wife died from a brain tumor. After Reynard appeared on CNN's *Larry King Live*, where he recalled that "she held it against her head, and she talked on it all the time," fears that cell phones could cause brain cancer proliferated. Reynard repeated his story for various news media, including ABC's *20/20*, even after his lawsuit was dismissed for lack of evidence. Despite Reynard's lack of success in court, Christopher Newman, a 41-year-old neurologist from Baltimore, Maryland, sued seven cell phone companies, including Motorola, in 2000, claiming that six years of cell phone use had produced his malignant brain tumor. A federal judge dismissed Newman's $800 million lawsuit due to lack of evidence. She also dismissed five class-action lawsuits that claimed cell phone manufacturers were negligent because they did not provide headsets to protect users from cell phone radiation (Parascandola 338).

Advertisements show people using cell phones at home, outside, and in stores, but never behind the wheel of a car. That's because of a persistent suspicion that talking on the phone while driving causes accidents. This suspicion is supported by some anecdotal and scientific evidence. A court in Hawaii ordered a teacher who struck a pedestrian as she finished a cell phone conversation to pay $7.5 million in damages. An Arkansas lumber company settled a case for $16.2 million after a company salesman who was making a sales call struck a woman, who was left disabled from the accident. A widely cited 1997 article in the *New England Journal of Medicine* reported that drivers are four times more likely to have a collision when using a cell phone (Glazer 203–11).

In light of such evidence, every state in the country has considered cell phone legislation, and some have gone so far as to outlaw the use of hand-held cell phones while driving. Tens of thousands of drivers have put bumper stickers on their cars that read "Drive Now, Talk Later," promoted on the popular radio program *Car Talk*. Others have shown their irritation by displaying bumper stickers that command drivers to "Hang Up And Drive," or that growl, "If that phone was up your ass, maybe you could drive better." Undeterred by evidence or sentiment, most drivers who have cell phones continue to use them on the road. Fortunately, automobile accidents have not kept pace with the growth in cell phone use.

One of the primary complaints about cell phones has been the rudeness of some cell phone users. Before cell phones became ubiquitous in airports, stores, walkways, and waiting rooms, people who wanted to make phone calls from public places had to use pay phones, which were located in booths beside heavily trafficked areas. The booths allowed maximum privacy, because passersby could not hear the caller, and the caller was not bothered by passersby.

Cell phones, by contrast, sometimes sacrifice privacy for convenience and mobility. Most cell phone conversations take place in private—at home, on park benches away from others, alone in cars—out of earshot of others. But when phone calls occur close to others, people get angry. Phones ring in movie theaters, churches, concert halls, and classrooms, breaking the concentration of those who are otherwise uninvolved in the calls. To reduce the occurrence of such cell phone interruptions, local ordinances have been passed banning cell phone use in areas of public assembly. A ringing phone in a library or museum in New York can cost its owner $50.

As irritating as these interruptions can be, they end as soon as the owner of the phone can turn it off by reaching into a pocket or a purse. Not so with conversations. The most vituperative complaints about rude cell phone use come from people who have become a captive audience to one side of an interminable phone conversation. Writing in the *Christian Science Monitor*, essayist Mary Pat Kane described a train trip along the Hudson River from Albany to New York that was ruined by one man's multiple phone calls. "Like so many cell-phone people he was garrulous and loud," she recalled. "He commandeered our section of the train as his personal office, yet I wasn't on salary and he sure didn't offer to pay for my train ticket" (15). For a private, two-way communication device, the cell phone has demonstrated a remarkable capacity to influence the dynamics of public places.

CONCLUSION

The cell phone of the early twenty-first century was the fulfillment of a dream from the early twentieth. Like all electronic media of communication, the cell phone attempted to render geography irrelevant by separating communication from transportation in a novel way. To a large degree, this purpose was fulfilled, which accounts for the high degree of cell phone adoption. Cell phone users are generally pleased with their ability to be connected with others anywhere. No longer do they have to wait by a phone or get to a phone for emergencies or for everyday conversations with family, friends, and business associates.

But however much the cell phone allowed people to transcend geographical barriers, it did not remove geography altogether. Cell phone conversations are not totally ethereal. They still take place in public thoroughfares, turning some drivers into menaces and some callers into boors. The cell phone extends our range of speech and hearing, but its earthbound features have led to problems that its developers could hardly have foreseen. As cell phone technology continues to merge with other technologies of sound and sight, it will overcome geographical hindrances in new ways, but its limitations will continue to vex us in ways we cannot predict.

WORKS CITED AND RECOMMENDED

Czitrom, Daniel J. *Media and the American Mind from Morse to McLuhan*. Chapel Hill: UP of North Carolina, 1982.

Dutton, William H., and Frank Nainoa. "Say Goodbye...Let's Roll: The Social Dynamics of Wireless Networks on September 11." *Prometheus* 20.3 (2002): 237–45.

CELL PHONE

Glazer, Sarah. "Cell Phone Safety." *The CQ Researcher* 16 Mar. 2001: 203–11.

Kane, Mary Pat. "Cell Phone Culture: Who Are These People?" *Christian Science Monitor* 14 Aug. 1998: 15.

Parascandola, Mark. "Judge Rejects Cancer Data in Maryland Cell Phone Suit." *Science* 11 Oct. 2002: 338.

Wei, Ran. "From Luxury to Utility: A Longitudinal Analysis of Cell Phone Laggards." *Journalism and Mass Communication Quarterly* 78.4 (2001): 701–19.

Ray Charles

Reginald Martin

Much has been made lately of the influences Ray Charles had on multiple genres of music: jazz, blues, country, even classical (emblemized by his live performance of "Ave Maria" at the Boston Pops with Sarah Vaughan in 1984), and rightfully so. He stands, as Michael Lydon observes, with Louis Armstrong, Duke Ellington, "and a handful of others among the presiding geniuses of twentieth-century popular music," but with a difference in the breadth of his music: "Listening in the dark, he soaked up sounds and styles from every idiom, and from them wrought a personal idiom more vital than many of its sources" (Lydon 396–70). What is so often overlooked in both print and film biographies is the incredible emancipating influence Charles' music had on American sexuality. From the very first, his polyrhythmic beats, his metaphor-filled lyrics, and his church-derived, throaty, sexual growl provoked one to feel Charles' words beyond the surface narrative. An easy way to view his influence on opening sexual venues through his music is to focus on the sequential singles that Charles, himself, chose to release.

From 1950 to 1965 are pivotal years in sexual development for Charles's fans, and also in the development of Charles' own on-going sexual narrative; it should be noted that during this period radio was still segregated, so his music and lyrics for the most part were allowed only on black stations with primarily black programming. Thus, in many of the key erotic songs, in-group metaphors were used to enhance their sexual meanings. For example, in the case of Little Richard's now-familiar rock number "Tutti Frutti," Little Richard early on performed the chorus using the words "Tutti Frutti, loose booty," and the song was considered "very raucous and sexual...too suggestive for white audiences; so the words were "cleaned up" when Little Richard recorded them as "Tutti Frutti, aw Rudi" (*Songfacts*). Later, mainstream America became exposed to the original songs in concerts, then on the air, via court-legislated integration; and, due mostly to the pioneering work of jazz writers examining early rhythm and blues and rock and roll records (Nat Hentoff is a good example in his 1965 *Jazz Country*), mainstream America could understand and appreciate the in-group lyrics due to cross-referenced explications from the music writers focusing on "jazz" phrasings.

The period of 1950–1965 really brackets most of Charles's most erotic deliveries. Interestingly, in his representations during this time, erotic love can be bad or good. The number one hit, "Hit the Road Jack" (1962) clearly points out that all flames are flickering; and "Busted" (1966) holds out no promise of sex for the broke man, as it ties together financial achievement and the delights that must be afforded. But Charles's 1954 song of the benefits of eroticism, especially of female ardor, "I Got a Woman" was so vivid it tested the metaphor boundaries of black-owned stations. The title came to Charles while he was singing along with a gospel tune, on a long late-night drive with his band, and the song developed in a dialogue of playful boasting with trumpeter Renald Richard. Charles sang it in gospel style like a rejoicing preacher, changing "spiritual joy into sexual delight" (Lydon 112–13). In *Oral History Interview with Nat D. Williams: Topic: Beale Street and the Fabulous World of Entertainment* (1976), Ronald Anderson Walter notes that the lyrics were too hot even for the first black-owned radio station in the South, WDIA of Memphis. When Charles sang of his woman's eagerness for loving him in the early morning, with active tender care, alarm bells rang for even those gatekeepers on the margins of society. Nat D. Williams, the biggest disc jockey of the time for the entire South, knew Ray Charles and begged him to temper the words a bit more. Thankfully, this request was never granted.

The easy substitution of the stipulative sign "love" for the intended sign "sex" was one that from the beginning black radio found easy to program, and, generally, no one complained when "love" was made in this dyadic exchange. Even for lyrics as outrageous as those of Little Richard (Richard Penniman), the radio could always handle the stipulation, while never quite the thing itself. When Penniman screamed, "Good golly Miss Molly" and told what Molly liked to do, "ball" could be euphemized into a metaphor to mean frenetic dancing. The audience was jubilant and the radio stations and Little Richard were happy with their popularity and profits. Thus, when Ray Charles sang in "Hallelujah I Love Her So" (1953) about the coming of darkness when he is alone with his lover and stirred to cry "Hallelujah," "love" again candy-coated the raw passion that not even black radio could play.

In the same way that a simple action verb can be switched, so can nouns; in many of the songs of the 1950s, and especially in the lyrics of Charles, purposely misplaced nouns give themselves away by their incongruence with the preceding verbs. A prime example is the lyric praising nighttime as "The Right Time" (1956); Charles adapted this blues song into a duet to sing with the Raelet chorus member who was his new mistress (Lydon 149): for two lines the singer extols how his baby "rocks" him, and then invites her to begin again, by asking her to hold his "hand." The incongruence is obvious to anyone, but contained in euphemistic metaphors of dancing for sex; and the

Ray Charles, 1960. Courtesy of the Library of Congress.

song passed the censors' rules right up to the time that Charles could be played on Top 40 radio, around 1965—also the year of the federal Civil Rights Act. This song gained more fame from the 1986 *Cosby Show* episode #203, in which Cliff's parents' anniversary celebration turns into a lip-sync rendition by the whole Huxtable family of "The Right Time."

Ray's penultimate erotic song closes out the decade of the 1950s, once again turning to condensed metaphors in the lyrics and up-tempo phrasing in the music. Interestingly, when this song was performed in two extremely popular TV specials of the 1960s, one with Bing Crosby and the other with Andy Williams, the tempo was slowed down considerably by the hosts, the censors, or both. Charles can be seen clearly straining to tone down the subliminal message carried by the beat. Also, interestingly, both Crosby and Williams chose to sit on the piano bench with Charles, again disallowing the movement of any body parts. Had there ever been a song before like 1959's "What'd I Say?" With its driving bass piano beat and the response of the polyrhythmic drums, no one could sit still to listen to it. When hot, barely metaphorical lyrics were added to the gospel beat, they made the song both irrepressible and aggressively erotic, joining the singer's demonstration of stamina and his suggestions of what a girl could do with him throughout the night.

In 1960, Charles recorded the classic "Basin Street Blues" written by Spencer Williams. For anyone who didn't know before that this song was about heated interracial sex, Charles's gravelly rendering, traveling from baritone to soprano range, leaves no doubt; slowing the tempo slightly from its classic beat, Charles makes you understand why Basin Street holds a special meeting for black and white folks, nicer than anyone can know until actually coming to New Orleans. Clearly sung to reach the underground audience of blacks who were sexually involved with whites, Charles's version pulls one into the idea that only in New Orleans, the place of dreams, where race is almost indefinable by its natives, can one really enjoy what is usually taboo. Further, in the second stanza, Charles suggests that the whole taboo of cross-racial sexual exchange is what will enhance the act: in the physical embraces, and spell of the music, the ordinary staples (white rice, black and red beans) become unsurpassably better. Because this song was primarily played on "race" stations, it had to pass less censor scrutiny than if it had been played and delivered as Charles delivers it on a Top 40 station. After one listen, the insider listener would get its message about encountering sex outside the standard way.

The recording Charles made with Betty Carter in 1961 of "Baby, It's Cold Outside" can be considered "the definitive version of Frank Loesser's witty interlocked lyric" (Lydon 201). The rap dialogue and the enticement are made everything to the erotic mood, and the weather report is nothing but background. Taking the call and response technique directly from West African forms, Charles croons about the cold outside over and over, no matter the many protestations from the female respondent that she has to leave, ultimately making the female respondent croon along with him, having finally been brought to her erotic senses by the male narrator's apparently sensible advances. When it is mentioned that a bit of spirits will help to keep her warm, the foreplay is complete and the female respondent realizes, hey, it does make more sense to stay in and be warmed in every way.

"Unchain My Heart," a hit single for Charles in 1961, is an up-tempo, lamenting ballad played as a love song. However, for the intent listener to Charles's version, it is clear that the "chains" bind more than the narrator's heart: the social chains of sexual rules restrain the narrator's pulsing sexuality, keeping him from the love and lover he desires most; indeed, they try to limit even the physical desires and prowess of the narrator. Think of the image of "chains" to a segregated audience in 1965 and all of the social/sexual limitations such a symbol would connote, and you begin to get the picture the lyric would address, in confessing to be caught under the lover's spell and without any chance of loving her, unless he is freed. To be set free to do as he pleases sexually is something the male listener of the time could relate to freedoms of all sorts, and the record understandably went to number 2 on the R&B charts while at the same time becoming a staple of civil rights workers, who would slightly change the words to a more purely social meaning (See Tom Dent's *Southern Journey: A Return to the Civil Rights Movement*, 2001).

Finally, it is not coincidence that Charles' sexual period basically ends when he is allowed full radio airplay. Yet it is not cultural censorship that changes his themes from eroticism to love, standards, and the American way. It is Charles, himself, who has changed and grown, in different ways that are no better, but certainly not worse, than the themes of his earlier period. While new standards included on *Modern Sounds in Country and Western Music* (1962) came at a time when censorship on radio lists had become so porous as to be non-existent, and received cross-format airplay all over the world, one gets the feeling that this change in themes is organic, nothing forced by outside influences or infantile attempts to "cross over" to a mainstream audience. Charles, moreover, was not above inserting sexuality here and there in his later periods, with Willie Nelson in the early 1980s in "Seven Spanish Angels," and into the new millennium with his rendition of "Crazy Love" from the 2004

Genius Loves Company CD. But after 1965, Eros has become a gateway to other things, not more important than them, and still a constant in the perception of Charles. As one biographer, David Ritz, notes in *Brother Ray: Ray Charles' Own Story* (2004), even at the end, the fans wanted the erotic from Charles, a man in his seventies, and demanded every old song at each concert.

WORKS CITED AND RECOMMENDED

Charles, Ray. *Anthology*. Original Release Date: Oct. 25, 1988. Label: Rhino/Wea. Catalog: #75759. ASIN: B00000348K.

———. *The Ultimate Collection*. Original Release Date: Mar. 16, 1999. Label: Rhino/Wea. Catalog: #75644. ASIN: B00000I72B.

Crosby, Bing. *Bob Hope/Bing Crosby/Dean Martin/Jerry Lewis*. DVD. Martin Studio. Platinum Disc Corp., 2004. ASIN: B00019GHXY.

Dent, Tom. *Southern Journey: A Return to the Civil Rights Movement*. Athens: U of Georgia P, 2001.

Hentoff, Nat. *Jazz Country*. New York: Harper and Row, 1965.

Lydon, Michael. *Ray Charles: Man and Music*. New York: Routledge, 2004.

Ritz, David, and Ray Charles. *Brother Ray: Ray Charles' Own Story*. New York: Da Capo P, 2004.

Songfacts. 10 Aug. 2005 <http://www.songfacts.com/detail.lasso? id=1843>.

Walter, Ronald Anderson. *Oral History Interview with Nat D. Williams: Topic: Beale Street and the Fabulous World of Entertainment*. Memphis: Whitten Bros., 1976.

Williams, Andy. *The Best of the Andy Williams Show*. DVD. Image Entertainment, 2000. ASIN: B00004Z4V0.

Julia Child

Sara Lewis Dunne

Joseph V. Amondio, writing in the *New York Times Magazine,* says that Americans have pretty much had it with celebrity chefs, but Julia Child—one of our first celebrity chefs—is more beloved than ever, raised, in fact, to the status of icon even before her death on August 13, 2004, just two days before her ninety-second birthday. Julia Child made French food seem accessible and doable to American home cooks, many of whom had taken Peg Bracken's *The I Hate to Cook Book*, published in 1960, to heart. Before the decade ended, though, many of Bracken's followers and fans, who had accepted her advice to spend as little time as possible in the kitchen, were being inspired and entertained by America's French Chef, Julia Child. Child gained her fame through her television shows, but her first show was intended primarily to support her first book, *Mastering the Art of French Cooking*, which came out only a year after Bracken's book. Bracken, in spite of her book's popularity, has not become an icon of American culture.

Julia McWilliams Child certainly showed little promise in her early life of becoming much more than a well-educated (Smith, 1934), tall (6'2"), athletic (golf, basketball, tennis) socialite from one of Pasadena, California's, founding families. In fact, according to a newspaper note from the time quoted by Julia's biographer, Noel Riley Fitch, "She will return here after graduation and will pass the summer with her family at the McWilliams beach home at San Malo" (64). As she was expected to do, Julia Child joined the Junior League (which in 1935 was not yet famous for its fund-raising cookbooks) in Pasadena; but she returned to the East in September of 1935 and soon took a job in advertising in New York, having always been interested in writing. She showed little interest in food, according to Fitch, but subsisted on frozen foods, eating "only to defeat her hunger" (67). Her time in New York was brief, however, and she returned to Pasadena to be with her mother during Caroline McWilliams' final illness and death, in 1937. Julia spent the next five years playing golf—often with her father—seeing her friends, partying, and writing for the Junior League. She resumed her work for the Los Angeles office of the company she had worked for in New York and seemed happy to be unencumbered. She had little to do with the kitchen in her house, and most of her entertainments were cocktail parties. There were romances with young men, one in New York, another in Pasadena, a marriage proposal, but like so many young people in the early 1940s, Julia McWilliams saw World War II as her chance for an adventurous new life.

Julia McWilliams's active social life moved with her from Pasadena to Washington, D.C., where she began working as a Senior Typist in the State Department in the summer of 1942, transferring soon to the Office of Strategic Services, now the Central Intelligence Agency. She still wasn't much of a cook, but living in a tiny apartment in Washington, she did try to feed herself and her friends and continued to entertain with "'nice crowded parties'" (Fitch 85). Hungering more for adventure than food, McWilliams was transferred to Ceylon (now Sri Lanka) and then to China. Ceylon is where McWilliams met Paul Child, who would later become her husband. He was ten years older, had much experience with women, and was knowledgeable about French food and European culture. Neither was the other's ideal: she was too tall, too emotional, too funny, too outgoing, too unsophisticated, and had "no intellectual rigor"; he was too old, too bald, too bookish, too quiet, and seemed to "lack a male drive" (Fitch 122, 124). Even so, their intense friendship morphed into romance, fueled in part by their letters to one another after they had each left China. They married on September 1, 1946.

Their first home was in Washington, D.C., and Julia Child had to learn to produce meals on a regular basis. She relied on Irma Rombauer's 1943 edition of *The Joy of Cooking* in her early kitchen struggles, but she soon began to subscribe to the then-new *Gourmet* magazine. Her first cooking was amateurish, enthusiastic, and experimental, marked by occasional disasters, but always supported whole-heartedly by Paul. Her real, true, all-encompassing love of food did not begin until the Childs moved to France in 1948. One meal at LaCouronne in Rouen sparked this love: oysters *portugaises*, Pouilly-Fuisse, sole browned in French butter, salad, crème fraiche, followed by coffee. It was Julia's first French meal, eaten slowly, worshipfully, joyfully, opening a world of possibility (Fitch 155).

The next year Julia Child enrolled in the *Cordon Bleu* cooking school and was taught by Max Bugnard, who had trained with Escoffier. Child threw her heart into French cooking and began to collect recipes. Julia and Bugnard became friends and remained so. Child and two Parisian friends, Louisette Bertholle and Simone Beck, opened their own cooking school, L'Ecole des Trois Gourmandes, early in 1952. This school led eventually to the production and publication of their cookbook, *Mastering the Art of French Cooking*, a project that took nine years of writing, editing, polishing, finagling, rewriting, string-pulling, and adapting recipes for American cooks who shopped mostly in supermarkets. In the meantime, the Childs moved from Paris back to America, then to Oslo, to Germany, and finally settled in Cambridge, Massachusetts, near their friend Avis DeVoto, widow of editor and writer Bernard DeVoto. When *Mastering* was rejected by Putnam as "too unconventional," Avis DeVoto took the manuscript to her husband's publisher, Houghton Mifflin, who agreed to publish it, but later decided not to. Avis DeVoto, still the midwife of this book, sent the manuscript to Knopf, and senior editor William Koshland cooked his way through the manuscript. The book weighed three pounds when it was published (Fitch 198, 270). It was favorably reviewed in the *New York Times*, and Child's television appearances to promote it eventually resulted in her first PBS shows in Boston. Child had caught the public's eye when, in a promotional television appearance on the *Today* show, she cooked an omelet on a hotplate on the show's set. Using her vast network of acquaintances and friends, Julia Child planned and executed her own book tour, giving cooking demonstrations all over America, making friends with other food luminaries who would remain close throughout her life—James Beard and Dione Lucas to name two, and M.F.K. Fisher, to name another.

Julia Child's lucky upbringing and education, in addition to her energy, her considerable charm, and her intelligence, combined with her remarkable height and her warbly voice to make her an enduring, if unlikely, television star. She saw herself, though, primarily as a teacher, not a "personality" and certainly not a "star." Her attitude that French food could be mastered—even though it was an "art"—by anyone willing to be taught how to do it came along at a time when Americans were willing to soften their sometimes-harsh attitude toward France, the French, and French culture. The Francophile Kennedys, after all, had hired the French chef Rene Verdon as the White House chef, and other books similar to Julia Child's were appearing, such as veteran cookery scholar and writer Elizabeth David's *French Provincial Cooking* in 1960. Julia Child, in her foreword to the latest edition of David's *French Provincial Cooking* (1998), remembers the American food of the 1950s and 1960s, desserts in particular: "a jellied molded object somewhat in the shape of an upright banana (or other less innocent object). Imbedded in this structure were cubes of banana, peeled white grapes, and diced marshmallows, the whole garnished by canned whipped cream generously squirted in mounds about its base.... No. We were not yet ready for Elizabeth David" (10). Remarkably enough, though, we were soon ready for Julia Child and we were ready for the lessons she wanted to teach us about sauces, eggs, babas, batteries de cuisines, cold buffets, vegetables, aspics, quiches, and any other foods the French might cook or eat. The book has two volumes and they have sold more than a million copies since publication.

Her first show, *The French Chef*, aired February 11, 1963, on National Education Television on Boston's WGBH. Other PBS stations across America picked up the show and soon all of us knew her. Americans loved Julia Child's cooking shows first, her books second. Her shows were so popular, in part, because Child was such a thoroughly human teacher—one who burned the butter, dropped the potato pancakes, forgot key ingredients, spilled sauce, licked her fingers, and wiped them on her apron, but who always came out with something wonderful in the end. True icons are the subjects of folklore, and one

Julia Child on her cooking show, 1978. Courtesy of Photofest.

piece of folklore about Julia Child is that she dropped a chicken on the floor, picked it up, dusted it off, and carried on as usual. In a videotaped tribute to "Julia Child, America's Favorite Chef," she sets the record straight. Even though some viewers swear they saw the dropped chicken incident, it never happened. She did own up to dropping a potato pancake she was trying to flip and catch in the pan, and the footage of that occurrence backs her up, but no chicken ever hit the floor while she was on air. Nor was she the polished, perfectly coiffed, pearl-wearing TV hostess-cook. She usually wore a shirt with rolled-up sleeves, a skirt, and an apron. She didn't look anything like the TV moms Donna Reed, June Cleaver, or Harriett Nelson, or 1950s kitchen-appliances spokeswomen Julia Meade or Bess Myerson. She looked kind of like us—only taller—and she was likely to burst into giggles or make the turkey "dance" across the counter as she held it by its wings. She had a collection of large French kitchen utensils that she sometimes used for comic purposes—her giant potato ricer, for example. At another time, she unceremoniously tossed away a puny rolling pin and produced one closer in size to a baseball bat. Julia Child certainly demonstrated that cooking could be joyful, even more than her predecessor *Joy of Cooking* author Irma Rombauer had.

She appeared on the cover of *Time* on November 25, 1966, dubbed as "our lady of the ladle." She was, by this time, Fitch says, "a reassuring and familiar icon, a national treasure, cherished for her pervasive presence on television" (310). She was also lauded as a feminist role model and named by *Harper's Bazaar* as one of "100 Women of Accomplishment" in 1967. An online article by William Rice of the *Chicago Tribune* quotes Camille Paglia's claim that Child was an even more important feminist than Gloria Steinem and a transformer of American culture.

Only a few people have ever publicly admitted disliking Julia Child. One was my mother-in-law, the late Mary Mallon Dunne, who thought Julia used too many pots. Another more hateful critic was the food scholar Karen Hess who, with her husband John, wrote food columns for the *New York Times*, often trashing what they saw as American pretensions and bad imitations of European foodways, recipes, and cooking techniques. Their collected writings are contained in *The Taste of America*, and on page 174 they point out the obvious: that Julia Child was neither French nor a chef. Later, though, they take on her book *From Julia Child's Kitchen* (1975) and castigate it and her for not being authentically French and for mixing cooking traditions. The Hesses seem particularly horrified at the idea of serving lasagna with French bread or black beans with sauerkraut, although the book's title does not promise anything but Julia Child's home cooking. One appended chapter at the book's very end is spent attacking Noel Riley Fitch's biography of Julia Child (which I have found quite helpful). This review, called "Icon Flambé," only adds to the evidence that for good or ill, Julia Child is an icon of American culture, even to her detractors.

The other cook and writer who seems to have had it in for Julia Child is Madeleine Kamman, author of *The Making of a Cook* (1971) and *Dinner Against the Clock* (1973). Kamman was a French émigrée to America and had worked in the kitchen of an aunt's restaurant in France while growing up. She had studied with one of Julia's cookbook writing partners, Simone "Simca" Beck, and met the Childs, inviting them for a dinner which they described as "outstanding." Kamman, apparently, saw Julia Child as a rival rather than a colleague and, according to Fitch, demanded that the students in her cooking school in Newton, Massachusetts, neither read Julia's books nor watch her television show (351–52). Eventually, after public denunciations in such news outlets as the *Washington Post* and vituperative letters to Julia Child, Child refused to respond to Kamman, to discuss her publicly, or even to say her name, and sent all correspondence from her to her attorneys. Eventually, Kamman seemed to grow tired of her one-sided feud, while the strength of Julia Child's reputation kept the public on her side. We note now, too, that Madeleine Kamman is no icon, nor is Karen Hess.

There have been no loving television tributes to Madeleine Kamman or Karen Hess, and no genuinely mournful television wakes will mark their passing. Within a week of her death, TV's Food Network aired a tribute to Julia Child and featured many of her professional admirers: Emeril Lagasse, who had cooked with her on television; Sara Moulton, who had interned in Julia's kitchen; Paula Deen, the silver-haired chef from Savannah; the world-renowned Wolfgang Puck; and relative newcomer Bobby Flay. Emeril lauded her as one of America's most important cultural figures, and Sara Moulton claimed Julia Child as "an enormous role model," after which Emeril echoed, "She was a legend, an American icon." Paula Deen credits Julia Child with being a "pioneer of women on TV." Perhaps the comment Julia might have relished most was Puck's: "She came off just like a regular person," although her life seems to have shown that she was a most singular person. As a television cooking show pioneer, Julia Child was credited with inventing the TV cooking "process" whereby a dish is shown in its various stages of preparation, an operation that involves multiple preparations of a single dish, including the finished version. As the memorial show readily admits, Julia was not either French or a chef, but she was a revered teacher of French cooking.

Both this show and the televised biography of Child feature another important aspect of her status as an icon. When Julia Child retired and moved out of her beloved house in Cambridge that she had shared for many years with her husband Paul, the Smithsonian took her kitchen, measuring, photographing, documenting the placement of each pot, pan, spoon, spice jar, tea bag, table, chair, in short, everything in her kitchen. Television scholar Richard Thompson, of the University of Syracuse, calls the moving and meticulous reassembly of Julia's kitchen in the Smithsonian her establishment "in the canon of the most important iconic moments in American Popular Culture." The day after her death was announced, one devotee, Brian Sisolak, placed a bouquet of red roses against the plexiglass wall outside her Smithsonian kitchen, according to Manny Fernandez, a *Washington Post* writer who visited the kitchen and interviewed other visitors. One such visitor summed it up: "There's lots and lots of chefs. But there was one Julia."

WORKS CITED AND RECOMMENDED

Amodio, Joseph V. "Celebrity-Chef Backlash." *New York Times Magazine* 28 Mar. 2004: 42+.

Child, Julia. Foreword. *French Provincial Cooking*. By Elizabeth David. New York: Penguin, 1999.

Fernandez, Manny. "Seeking Comfort in Julia's Kitchen." *Washington Post* 14 Aug. 2004: BO1.

Fitch, Noel Riley. *Appetite for Life: The Biography of Julia Child*. New York: Doubleday, 1997.

Hess, John L., and Karen Hess. *The Taste of America*. Urbana: U of Illinois P, 2000.

"Julia Child: A Tribute." Narr. Sara Moulton. Food TV, Nashville, TN. 22 Aug. 2004.

Julia Child, America's Favorite Chef. DVD. WGBH, 2004.

Rice, William. "Julia Child Dies at 91." *Chicago Tribune*. Online. 28 Feb. 2005 <http://www.acepeople.com/j/Julia-Child.asp>.

Symons, Michael. *A History of Cooks and Cooking*. Urbana: U of Illinois P, 2000.

Computer Chip

Michael Bertz

Have you ever cracked open your cell phone or peeked under the hood of your personal computer (PC) at the myriad of plastic- or metal-encased devices within and wondered how these little bits of technology work? Even with their packaging removed, modern computer chips do not give up their secrets easily. The circuitry encoded on them has become much smaller (literally by orders of magnitude) than the finest human hair, and the newest versions of microprocessors can pack tens or hundreds of millions of transistors (the functional building blocks of integrated circuits) on a single piece of silicon the size of a postage stamp. Beyond your amazement at their size, however, should be the realization that these devices power some application in nearly all of our mechanized and technology-enabled products, to the extent that our society as we know it today could not exist without them. They are arguably the root of both the current triumph of our human ingenuity and the source of our now likely systemic addiction to technology. Humans have made more chips than anything else in history, and are currently building them at a rate of tens to hundreds of billions more per year (with the individual components on the chips, transistors, numbering into the *quadrillions*).

With respect to chips' current uses, the term "computer chip" is something of a misnomer. While the PC is a dominant application, in many respects the silicon-based chip (and all of the varieties it has spawned—microprocessors that power computers or game consoles, microcontrollers found in your car, high-speed digital signal processing chips in your cell phone or networking equipment, as well as ubiquitous memory chips) is the enabler for most technology everywhere. The term "computer chip" is derived from its ability to perform high speed mathematical computations—distilling the essence of the abacus, Babbage's mechanical computer, or room-sized vacuum-tube-based behemoths onto a tiny sliver of circuitry. The common denominator of much semiconductor-powered technology has become the fact that it is the semiconductors themselves that have made many of them possible, in turn generating a vast commercial infrastructure that has enabled us to produce, implement, and exploit them.

and 1990s, chip development continued in communications applications, increasing the quality and reliability of voice and data telecom connections, enabling not only a sharp decline in long-distance calling costs but also the buildout of the Internet. Today a virtually limitless array of products, from children's stuffed animal toys to flat panel high-definition televisions, have semiconductors at their heart.

In terms of the imagery of this icon, chips did not begin as the slab of silicon we currently associate them with. They started instead as a lump of another semiconducting material, germanium, as a device with a single electronic function, the transistor. From the unimpressive-looking point-contact transistor devices sprang small cans, more robust and better packaged, typically with three metal wire leads; however, these were all basically discrete devices. It was not until the late 1950s and early 1960s when integrated circuits—multiple devices built onto a single monolithic piece of silicon—became commercialized that we would truly begin to recognize the basic form factor of the chips that are prevalent today. Even though these simplistic ICs of the 1960s were quite capable for their day, we do not really observe general knowledge of the modern image of these little slabs of silicon until well into the 1970s, when one could pry open a calculator or a child's Speak 'n Spell and observe these tiny processors.

An engineer examining a computer chip. Courtesy of Getty Images/PhotoDisc.

The iconic image that we have today of chips did not really solidify until the adoption of PCs began to rise in the early 1980s, generating a new set of industry giants which, though they had existed for years, became household names—including Intel and Texas Instruments (though now for chips, and not radios or calculators or educational toys). Until then the companies had labored away in some obscurity, but they were in a position to exploit a dramatically growing market, primarily revolving around computing applications. As these companies and many others flourished, Silicon Valley became even more a magnet for innovation and engineering talent, their business success driving the American perception of the silicon chip as a powerful economic force, like oil or cars, with the image of this "wealth made from sand" solidifying around the single microprocessor (sometimes seen in stock news footage on wafers).

The chip therefore, as an icon, has become a symbol of both our ingenuity and our society's inextricable dependence on technology; few in modern society could go back to a "non-wired" civilization on a permanent basis. These small slabs of silicon not only have enabled a myriad of technological devices, but they also have created new products and applications, indeed whole new industries.

Economically, chips have changed the fortunes of individual people, companies, entire regions or even countries; would Taiwan likely be the dynamic economy it is today without its semiconductor industry? The quintessential American example, of course, is the area around San Jose at the south end of San Francisco Bay. In small cities from Fremont to Sunnyvale, Palo Alto to Cupertino, buildings flow from one technology business park to the next. The streets are littered with well-known companies, both large and small, likely the highest concentration of semiconductor design and manufacturing companies in the world. It isn't named "Silicon Valley" without good reason.

With this economic power comes both opportunity and risk. The pervasiveness of chips in technology and product applications implies that those who control their design and production will derive a significant economic advantage. Chips have already seen significant economic influence in trade disputes between the United States and Japan (the aforementioned memory-dumping disputes of the late 1980s), as well as the rise of very aggressive industry giants in South Korea and Taiwan. Here at the outset of the twenty-first century, semiconductor chips could be the central nexus of a looming geopolitical/socio-economic struggle between superpowers, as China's growing prowess with chips and its inexpensive yet educated labor force position it to challenge America's traditional dominance and design leadership in the field.

The semiconductor chip's biggest impact, however, has been how it has changed us as a society. The imprint is felt by Americans in particular, but the effects are far reaching. (Visit an Italian café and estimate the percentage of people using their cell phones.) The trend towards embedding processing power in virtually all parts of everyday life has meant that, over time, chips have changed the way that we interact with technology. For example, the enormous advances in processor power and the capabilities that they have allowed have in turn caused computers to go from being difficult-to-program black boxes to being extremely flexible tools for document creation, game playing, information gathering, or business process management.

Beyond that, however, computer chips have changed the way we interact and relate to each other. Coupled with fiber optics, chips are what make inexpensive long distance calling possible. "Reaching out to touch someone," as an old AT&T advertisement encouraged us to do, now costs on the order of one-tenth to one-hundredth of the amount it did even thirty years ago. Long-distance phone calls to grandma in Ohio are no longer quite the special occasion that they had been, but have on the other hand allowed geographically dispersed families to remain closer than ever before.

Coupled with PCs, chips enable the Internet and all that it has brought to our interactions. Surfing the Internet for information has in many ways both broadened our understanding of other peoples and places, and yet has at the same time taken away a cause for human interaction (such as taking a trip to the library to search for information). The Internet has spawned the ability for communications between far-flung people and has become a forum for almost any philosophical opinion or position. The power of the PC coupled with the Internet is in the process of revolutionizing commerce, and has recently begun to change the way some people meet and court, with online dating. Chips are now also the driving force behind digital cameras and the instant capturing and electronic sharing of memories.

As an "icon" to most Americans, chips have become a magic miniaturized black box. For Americans, they also represent an industry we started but which has been given to the world. Chips have truly become the ultimate technological icon, as the key enabler of technology, with the amount of functionality driven by the value and coding in the chip. One cannot find an item more important to the technological revolution of the second half of the twentieth century. Like the earlier processes in which the steam engine and the mechanized production equipment it drove came to signify the Industrial Revolution, and the automobile and airplane came to embody fundamental changes in transportation in the twentieth century, the computer chip stands as the seminal technology behind the Information Age. Like all great inventions, chips have revolutionized society, dramatically changing human lifestyles and changing the way humans perceive themselves and their world.

WORKS RECOMMENDED

"Bell Labs History of the Transistor." 29 Dec. 2005 <www.bellsystemmemorial.com/belllabs_transistor.html>.

Berlin, Leslie. *The Man Behind the Microchip: Robert Noyce and the Invention of Silicon Valley*. New York: Oxford UP, 2005.

Macaulay, David. *The New Way Things Work*. New York: Houghton Mifflin/Walter Lorraine, 1998.

"Microprocessors." How Stuff Works Electronic Library. 29 Dec. 2005 <http://electronics.howstuffworks.com/>.

Reid, T. R. *The Chip: How Two Americans Invented the Microchip and Launched a Revolution*. 1985. New York: Random House, 2001.

Riordian, Michael, and Lillian Hoddeson. *Crystal Fired: The Invention of the Transistor and the Birth of the Information Age*. New York: W. W. Norton, 1997.

Transistor History from Lucent. 29 Dec. 2005 <www.lucent.com/minds/transistor/>.

Coney Island

Judith A. Adams-Volpe

Coney Island made America *feel good*. These six words sum up Coney Island's past, present, and continuing influence on the collective American psyche and on the shape of our cultural environment. From the beach, hot dog, nickel entertainment, exotic architecture, appropriation of technology for fun, and sensual bombardment, to its reformatting in theme parks, Las Vegas, and an ever intensifying pursuit of pleasure, Coney Island showed us how to play. Our cultural constructs of "letting go," "feel good generation," "fast food," "sexual revolution," "people's playground," ethnic "melting pot," and "leisure" itself all had roots at Coney.

Social commentator David Brooks, in his 2004 book *On Paradise Drive* shows us that Americans continue to be driven by the spell of paradise, a myth of constant striving toward a dreamlike destiny that is "[j]ust out of reach,...the spot you can get to where all tensions melt, all time pressures are relieved and all contentment can be realized" (268–69). Coney Island actualized this place for the millions at the end of a five-cent subway ride. From the 1890s to the 1950s, the accessibility of Coney and its immediate connection to fun and amusement made it immensely powerful and enduring. Coney Island emerges as an icon far surpassing nostalgic postcard memories, what John F. Kasson describes in *Amusing the Million* as a "harbinger of modernity...a symbol not only of fun and frolic but also of major changes in American manners and morals" (8).

A small group of Dutch immigrants first settled the windblown scrub that stretched for five miles at the foot of Brooklyn, calling it "Konijn," the Dutch word for rabbit, because of the hordes of bunnies on the dunes. The events that would transform Coney into a crowded, exotic playground of pleasure began in 1829 with the building of the Shell Road and a first hotel. By the 1870s steamers carried visitors on a two-hour trip from the city for fifty cents. Increasing Coney's pleasure seekers from the thousands to the millions was the Prospect Park & Coney Island Railroad, completed in 1875. The train carried a million passengers its first year, and 2 million the second. By 1920, the subway brought tens of millions to frolic on the beach and boardwalk (Adams).

Cultural commentator Michael Immerso recognizes that it is to Coney Island that Americans, especially immigrants and middle- to lower-class urban dwellers, went to "invent their own forms of leisure" and to grasp play and leisure as a "national birthright" (11). The major trends that created a Babylon on the beach, a pyrotechnic "insanitarium," a people's playground, all endure today in altered yet easily recognizable forms: an escape destination; an architecture of feeling; technology harnessed for fun, spectacle, and sensual abandon; the nickel empire; the crowd as cultural mingler and communicator.

ESCAPE DESTINATION

Most major or mid-sized American cities in the latter part of the nineteenth century were located near a waterfront that became transformed into a leisure/excursion pleasure site. Those few urban areas without beachfronts created nearby picnic groves. With its railroad arriving by the mid-1870s, Coney Island created the forms, activities, and environment of the "resort" to be imitated by thousands of trolley parks appearing by the 1890s throughout the nation.

Coney's entrepreneurs and showmen, like their American amusement progeny to come, capitalized on demographic and economic trends, cleverly playing on the needs of an emerging social order. The population of New York City exploded between 1860 and 1940 as the result of unprecedented European immigration, rising from 700,000 to 2.5 million people. Around 1910, these New Yorkers were predominantly young, with those under 30 years old dominating the age distribution. Coney's attractions were designed to appeal to this segment of the population, especially the 15–30-year-olds. In 1909, twenty million of them frolicked on the beach, boardwalk, and Bowery enjoying spectacular fireworks, brass bands, lager, roasted clams, and amusement park dreamlands. Industrialization and the rise of labor unions reduced the hours of the work week during the years between 1890 and 1925 by nearly ten hours, so there was more discretionary income and time for leisure activities.

How did this spit of seashore land at the foot of Brooklyn lure and amuse the millions? It was a separate place, requiring a short but distinctive break away journey from the everyday to a realm that turned the respectable values of its time upside down, replacing an outmoded Victorian gentility with sexual titillation and license, and paradoxically transforming the very engines of industrialization into fun machines. Coney is escape from duty to joy permitted for a moment. The words of contemporary observers are the best conveyers of the allure and intoxication of Coney Island. Wonder, awe, and joy are irrepressible in these reactions:

> Why Coney is all the wonders of the world in one pyrotechnic masterpiece of coruscating concentration.... America has built for herself a Palace of

Illusion, and filled it with every species of talented attractive monster, every misbegotten fancy of the frenzied nerves, every fantastic marvel of the moonstruck brain...strange Isle of Monsters, Preposterous Palace of Illusion, gigantic Parody of Pleasure....the name of Coney Island is Babylon. (LeGallienne 239–46)

Maxim Gorky, postulating his intellectual disgust with Coney Island, was enraptured despite himself. Coney succeeds in transporting even him outside his gloomy, introspective persona:

A fantastic city all of fire suddenly rises from the ocean into the sky. Thousands of ruddy sparks glimmer in the darkness,...shapely towers of miraculous castles, palaces and temples. Golden gossamer threads tremble in the air. They intertwine in transparent, flaming patterns, which flutter and melt away in love with their own beauty mirrored in the waters. Fabulous and beyond conceiving, ineffably beautiful, is this fiery scintillation. (qtd. in Adams 50)

For those who couldn't visit Coney Island, this marvelous, exotic, and unique place was captured and transmitted through postcards and the new invention of the motion picture. Coney largely stimulated the postcard industry, entrancing a nation with vibrant color and static scenes of wonder and fun. This vision was made more fluid through silent film. Edison Manufacturing Company, American Mutoscope, and Biograph made more short silent films of Coney Island than any other location. From 1896 through the 1920s, films with titles like "Coney Island at Night," "Fire and Flames at Luna Park," and featuring such stars as Harold Lloyd, Fatty Arbuckle, and Buster Keaton, depicted the hurly-burley chaos of Coney (Immerso 118). The postcards and films projected the iconography of Coney to an immense national audience, generating a shared popular culture of leisure, play, and cheap thrills in a place of escape.

The cultural construct of the vacation destination continues to grow in strength and vibrancy. Today, vacation and leisure can hardly be referenced except in the context of escape destinations. Theme parks, Walt Disney World, Las Vegas, all-inclusive resorts, and historical reconstruction enclaves require a journey away from everyday temporal reality to a bordered sanctuary of illusion, indulgence, pretense, and glitz.

AN ARCHITECTURE OF FEELING

Luna Park, Frederick Thompson and Skip Dundy's lavish 22-acre amusement center appearing in 1903, became the archetypal amusement park until the advent of Disneyland in 1955. Its architecture, designed to promote wonder, chaos, awe, physical and imaginative transport to an exotic realm, and its extravaganza of lighting and color have endured and are revised in the excesses of Las Vegas and Times Square.

Luna Park and Surf Avenue, Coney Island, New York, 1912. Courtesy of the Library of Congress.

The twentieth century's architectural dictum of "form follows function" never got a foothold at Coney. Coney's architecture uses form to promote *feeling*—enchantment, dreams, exoticism, sensual stimulation. Thompson, once an architecture student, recognized the powerful entertainment potential of architectural forms, and he abandoned all restraint and convention in the creation of the sublime Luna Park, a sumptuously ornamented electric Babylon. On opening night, May 16, 1903, visitors were universally stunned by swirling pinwheels and crescents, blazing spires and turrets, minarets, sculpted fantastic animal creatures, shows depicting strange lands and peoples, all ablaze with 250,000 electric lights—at the time the greatest concentration of electric illumination ever attempted.

Thompson and Dundy set out to appeal to American desires for unrestrained extravagance, the magnetic wonder of the fantastic, and the vitality of ceaseless motion. The result at Luna Park was a sensual, enticing architecture described by one historian as "Super-Saracenic or Oriental Orgasmic" (Kasson 63). Thompson used malleable, cheap plastic staff, a plaster and fiber wall-covering, to produce marvelous curving structures and monumental grandeur. He also appropriated the popular exotic locale attractions of turn-of-the-century World's Fair midways with an Eskimo Village, Canals of Venice, and a Japanese Garden. These recreations have, of course, been reborn in the sector locales of contemporary theme parks, EPCOT Center, and progressively in theme-oriented hotels and resorts.

In Luna's second year, 1904, 4 million visitors paid for the Luna experience, and attendance continued to climb through the first decade of the new century. Thompson died in 1919, and although others took over Luna Park, it began a steady decline, succumbing to a spectacular fire in 1946. The land was secured for a large apartment complex developed by Fred Trump, Donald's father. The eventual row after row of drab square apartment buildings was the very antithesis of Luna's magic minarets.

Although Luna Park as place is gone forever, it survives in a very immediate sense in the architectural abandon, fiery scintillation, and sensual bombardment of Las Vegas. Robert Venturi, Denise Scott Brown, and Steven Izenour in their classic study, *Learning from Las Vegas*, view the Las Vegas strip architecture as "bold communication." Meaning is communicated through the "inherent, physiognomic characteristics of form." The messages are dependent on "watts, animation, and iconology" (4, 2, 15). The Las Vegas strip itself, while initially engendered by the automobile, has its formative roots in the Coney Island entertainment strip and Luna Park. While in the classic sense, Las Vegas, like Luna Park, is the embodiment of "bad" taste, people *like* it. The ceaseless sensual stimulation, the chaos of illumination and motion, and the fantasy-themed enclaves allow us to escape, play, and dream. Just like Luna Park, Las Vegas appropriates the architectural symbols of luxury and exoticism. Both places democratize the yearning for splendor in magical realms where conventional rules don't apply. Nothing could be more immediate and accessible than the primary alchemic message of Las Vegas—transforming the drab, base, and ordinary into the splendor of gold. At Luna and Las Vegas, the masses find a gilded place imbued with the irresistible promise that all of their dreams can come true.

TECHNOLOGY FOR FUN AND SENSUAL PLAY

Coney Island's amusement entrepreneurs harnessed the gears, wheels, and motors of the industrial revolution into engines of fun and sexual titillation. George Cornelius Tilyou liberally appropriated the mechanics of the factory when he opened the first major enclosed amusement park, Steeplechase Park, at Coney Island in 1897. Every element and contrivance in Steeplechase Park was designed to sweep away restraint and propel the crowds into extroverted intense motion. His fun machines threw young bodies into intimate contact, lifted long skirts to reveal shapely legs never glimpsed on a city street.

Steeplechase's emblem, the "Funny Face," was a huge devilish jester with a massive grin promising irresponsible and diabolical fun. To enter Steeplechase, visitors had to pass through the "Barrel of Love," a revolving, highly polished wooden tunnel that rolled revelers off their feet and into suggestive contact with strangers. The signature "Steeplechase" ride consisted of eight mechanical double-saddled horses that raced along an undulating track to the

Coney Island, 1997. Courtesy of Shutterstock.

finish line. The double saddles allowed couples to ride together generally with a man's arms snugly wrapped around his companion's waist, creating a rather genteel intimacy. Rides like the "Human Roulette Wheel," the "Whirlpool," and the "Human Pool Table" were more intense, physical, and sexually explicit. These rapidly revolving contrivances threw willing bodies in all directions, whisked skirts way up to reveal thighs and more, and forced bodies into intimate contact. The sensuality of these amusements is portrayed by artist Reginald Marsh in paintings that capture the ample, undulating curves and powerful muscles of out-of-control riders (Goodrich).

Thompson and Dundy took mechanical amusement to a higher level. Debuting at the Pan American Exposition in 1901, their "A Trip to the Moon" was the first virtual reality experience. They made their incredibly successful ride the centerpiece for Luna Park. This elaborate fantasy ride launched visitors in a large space ship on a voyage to the moon that combined motion, projected visual imagery, sound, and lighting. Once landed on the moon, voyagers encountered a total environment of caverns, grottos, giants, midgets, and moon maidens dispensing green cheese. Luna also featured regularly scheduled "disaster" extravaganzas, endlessly repeating the burning of a four-story apartment building (very much like the buildings where most of the onlookers resided), the eruption of Mt. Vesuvius and fall of Pompeii, the Johnstown and Galveston floods.

These illusions created at the beginning of the twentieth century are the harbingers of such technological extravaganzas as Universal Studio's "Earthquake: The Big One." Thus, generations of Americans have experienced technology outside its utilitarian bounds as spectacle and pure entertainment. In today's seemingly dangerous rides, such as mega roller coasters and free-fall contrivances, riders more intensely experience the awe, fear, and adrenalin rush of the technological sublime.

THE NICKEL EMPIRE AND CROWDS

The nickel trolley ride began transporting the masses to Coney in 1895. In 1920, the cost of the trip was the same via the five-cent subway. The millions of revelers instantly turned into the tens of millions demanding entertainment and fun at subway prices. One hot day in 1947, 2.5 million people packed the beaches. For small change, visitors could leave the dingy commonality of city streets and tenements for a colorful, exotic, ever-changing holiday milieu. Arriving as individuals, they merged into the unprecedented melting pot of nationalities, ages, interests, and sensations. They became part of the crowd and the crowd was the show. The line between performer and spectator was always blurred at Coney. Being part of the crowd gave everyone a sense of belonging, and the cultural identity of insiders.

In 1938 *Fortune Magazine* ran an anonymous lengthy article entitled, "To Heaven by Subway." This graphic and colorful piece captured the spirit of the Nickel Empire:

> For five cents Coney Island will feed you, frighten you, cool you, toast you, flatter you, or destroy your inhibitions. And in this nickel empire boy meets girl.... Some 25 million people pile into this area in a season... leaving behind them a sum estimated at anything from $7,500,000 to $35 million. But whatever the amount—and whether derived from the family on relief or from the $20 plunger and his girl friend—it is an accumulation of the smallest coins of the country.

Coney's food is fast, fun, sensual, cheap, and created for crowds on the move. The hot dog, the archetype of fast food, was invented at Coney Island by Charles Feltman, who was selling boiled sausages wrapped in pastry rolls from his pie wagon by the mid-1870s. It was Nathan Handwerker who made the hot dog an icon when he left his job slicing hot dog rolls at Feltman's Ocean Pavilion and opened a corner stand in 1916 selling hot dogs for five cents and throwing in a glass of root beer and a pickle. Nathan's Famous, established by 1925, drew incredible crowds, selling 75,000 hot dogs on weekends, with advertising slogans like "Follow the Crowd to Nathan's" and "From a Hot Dog to a National Habit." Other foods devoured in vast quantities at Coney were roasted corn on the cob, saltwater taffy, the ice cream cone (first manufactured at Coney in 1905), pizza pie first appearing at Totono's Pizzeria in 1924, and frozen custard introduced in 1927 (Immerso 131–32, 152). All of these portable, cheap, and fast foods for revelers on the go are still associated with leisure, vacation, and fun times. In July 1955, Nathan's sold its 100 millionth hot dog, and the establishment is still a monument today at Coney, open year round, a beacon of popular culture in a changed Coney.

Nathan's also holds sway today in the middle of Las Vegas as a feature of the "Coney Island Emporium" of the New York–New York hotel complex. Thus, the Coney that started it all is literally resurrected as an attraction in the heart of its spectacular desert progeny. There are a roller coaster, bumper cars, shooting gallery, and the updated technological fun of virtual reality games and laser tag. From Coney to Vegas, *feeling*, *escape*, and the lure of a *dreamlike destiny* are the intense messages.

WORKS CITED AND RECOMMENDED

Adams, Judith A. *The American Amusement Park Industry: A History of Technology and Thrills*. Boston: Twayne Publishers, 1991.

Brooks, David. *On Paradise Drive*. New York: Simon & Schuster, 2004.

Ferlinghetti, Lawrence. *A Coney Island of the Mind*. New York: New Directions, 1958.

Goodrich, Lloyd. *Reginald Marsh*. New York: Harry N. Abrams, 1972.

Immerso, Michael. *Coney Island: The People's Playground*. New Brunswick, NJ: Rutgers UP, 2002.

Kasson, John F. *Amusing the Million: Coney Island at the Turn of the Century*. New York: Hill & Wang, 1978.

LeGallienne, Richard. "Human Need of Coney Island." *Cosmopolitan* 39 (July 1905): 239–46.

"To Heaven by Subway." *Fortune Magazine* 18 (Aug. 1938): 60–68, 102–4, 106.

Venturi, Robert, Denise Scott Brown, and Steven Izenour. *Learning from Las Vegas*. Cambridge, MA: MIT P, 1972.

Couch

Dennis Hall

The couch, as the *American Heritage Dictionary* (2nd ed.) has it, is an "article of furniture, commonly upholstered and often having a back, on which one may sit or recline"—from the French nouns for bed and verbs to go to bed or lie down, presumably to rest. The sofa, "a long upholstered seat with a back and arms," warrants a picture which may illustrate its origins in *sufah*, the Arabic word for dais, and suggest its more upright character. In common American use and understanding, however, little separates these two pieces of furniture, and most people, even the writers of popular interior design books, use the terms interchangeably. Books and articles trafficking in the history of furniture, to be sure, make careful distinctions among such terms as daybed, camel back sofa, *canapé*, *canapé à confidante*, couch, chaise lounge, settee, *lit de repos*, sofa, sofa bed, among many others, detailing the evolution of furniture forms and styles, their times and locales—all of use, best I can tell, principally to collectors. But this relentless chronicle has been reluctant to attach meanings to furniture much beyond noting its obvious function as a marker of disposable income and social status, high or low, and it offers even less about the couch or sofa, as such, despite its very large footprint in the living and family rooms of most American households, and in a good many other venues.

This immediately recognizable bit of material culture, however, is filled with meaning, as is apparent to anyone reflecting upon furnished living space; watching television, a movie or a play; patronizing a coffee shop; leering at paintings of odalisques or 1940s publicity stills of Hollywood starlets (not to mention pornography); or uttering such common expressions as "couch potato," "casting couch," and "psychiatrist's couch," or reading the comics or Wallace Stevens' poem "So-And-So Reclining on Her Couch." The very commonness of the couch, as with so many elements in American popular culture, makes it easy to overlook.

The couch, however, is filled with cultural value. The presence of a couch adds meanings to the texts and contexts in which it appears: in the lived-in space of homes or offices or other private or public spaces occupied by actual people, in the possible spaces depicted in furniture showrooms or advertisements or interior designs, in the representational spaces of movies or television shows, of photographs or paintings or poems or plays or stories. The couch, I submit, occupies a distinct place in the system of furniture and in the culture which that system furnishes—furnishes as much with ideas and associations as with upholstered frames and cushions. As Mihaly Csikszentmihalyi and Eugene Rochberg-Halton found, things have their significance "not because of the material comfort they provide but for the information they convey about the owner and his or her ties to others" (239). The couch, for all its individual variation, is an immediately recognizable artifact that rises to the level of popular culture icon rich in metonymic resonance. The couch delivers meanings well beyond the simple utilitarian functions of sitting or reclining into every context in which it appears.

The couch has a long history, evolving over time from the severity of the settle, settee, and Knole sofa in the eighteenth and, in the nineteenth century, into the heavily upholstered comfort now common, all the result of such technical developments as "square stuffing," "interlaced webbing," "coil springs," and "deep-buttoning" (Boyce 307). The Victorian period "witnessed the most pronounced manifestation of this trend in over-stuffed furniture...in forms that were both massive and opulent in appearance" (Boyce 307). Comfort was the sign, if not the lived experience, of the couch in this era, as it is in the present. Indeed, couch and comfort are strongly linked associations. "The effect," as Tim Dant expresses this commonplace, "is an atmosphere of neither sitting upright nor lying down, it is rather 'the invitation to informal posture'"(80). The couch is a place and is in a place where one is bidden to make one's self comfortable. The couch suggests a comfortable home, a comfortable place to meet people, a comfortable place to be with friends, a comfortable place to watch TV, a comfortable venue for sex, a comfortable place to talk to a psychotherapist.

In cultural history, the concept of "comfort" mediates between the indulgence of excess and waste, on the one hand, and the austerity of necessity and utility, on the other; and the couch is among its most conspicuous material signs. Early in its history the couch marked aristocratic wealth and status and luxury. In the nineteenth century, upholstered furniture signed bourgeois wealth and status, but oscillated between being a token of luxury and mark of convenience; that is, a domestic indulgence morally justified by earnestness and hard work. In the twentieth century, particularly after World War II, the couch became commonplace to the point that the presence of the thing itself no longer signed wealth or status; this cultural work, then, had to be done by the design or the quality of materials or workmanship or the newness of a given couch. Indeed, not to have a couch or sofa in the house, whether it was used or not, became a mark either of extreme poverty or eccentricity. Even hippies had couches. Indeed, as Tim Dant notes, "the sofa has become a more 'democratic' seating unit, often replacing individual chairs—even when there are easy chairs, the material distinction between 'his' and 'hers' is more likely to have disappeared" (80–81).

Couches and sofas have strong associations with home and home's psychic as well as physical comforts—and, we must never forget, its dangers. When introduced into other environments, say, for example, the offices and waiting rooms of dentists, doctors, and lawyers, or coffee shops or cocktail lounges, or schools or bookstores, they mark a degree of extravagance well beyond a collection of chairs, while seeking to provide to clients and customers some of the comforts, and risking some of the discomforts, of home.

More often than not a couch symbolizes comfort in today's society. Courtesy of Corbis.

And no other cultural sign so efficiently communicates the concept of "family" as does the couch and sofa, as the sets of television soap operas and sitcoms demonstrate from *Father Knows Best* to *The Dick Van Dyke Show* to *The Brady Bunch* to *The Cosby Show*. Lest the ubiquity of this device escape our attention, every episode of *The Simpsons* opens with a variation on this motif, a parody that pays homage to the couch as cultural sign. That the *Mary Tyler Moore Show* and *Cheers* did not cast the couch in a central role are conspicuous exceptions, suggesting an effort to define the sitcom "family" in radically different terms, contra the nuclear family. *Friends*, significantly, reappropriates the couch for a redefinition of family by its conspicuous placement in the apartment and in the coffee shop, where most of the show's scenes are shot, by its incongruous placement in front of the Pulitzer fountain in front of the Plaza Hotel in the show's opening credits, and by its presence in the ensemble's picture on the program's poster and many of the web pages devoted to the program; here the couch signs a friendship that extends if not surpasses family in this carefully and successfully constructed environment. This same resonance moved the editors of the *New York Times* Sunday Styles section (November 16, 2003) to employ the couch in its effort to describe the new political style of the Howard Dean campaign; the picture of three youthful campaign workers on a beat-up three-cushion sofa infused more meaning into the story than did most of the text.

Couches, of course, have become strongly associated with viewing television, for they are commonly placed in front of television sets in living and family rooms, so to promote attention to programs and so to shape whatever conversation between or among couch sitters during the many hours a day the set is turned on in the typical American household. Couches and TVs enjoy a symbiotic relationship as household goods, one often mirrored in the programming commonly watched. Yet—with the exception of *The Simpsons* and *Beavis and Butthead*, and a few other aggressively satiric programs—the couch sitters represented on television rarely are engaged in watching television; rather, they are engaged in conversation and life, however idiosyncratically that may be represented. The "couch potato," a persona tarred with associations of routinely wasted time and attention, resulting in physical and mental atrophy, is not a character in *Seinfeld* or *Friends* or other television environments well furnished with couches.

To position a couch, in art or in life, not facing a television set is a deliberate, meaningful utterance. The couch is a necessary condition for *Friends*, for example, because the show is devoted to relationships, as are so many currently popular television narratives. And the couch, whatever else may be said of it, is a mediating device, a big piece of furniture that, for good or ill, brings people together both physically and emotionally in ways that tables and chairs and even beds do not. The democracy of seating that the couch represents in many instances serves to collapse the separate spheres of men and women common in the nineteenth and much of the twentieth century (see Attfield 156), contributing in one degree or another to a feminization of men and a masculinization of women at the dawn of the twenty-first. The increasingly shared interests and concerns of men and women are signed in much more intimately shared space, an intimacy once reserved to family.

Moreover, couches, as they bring people together physically, often vibrate between public and private space, allowing private speech and gestures in a public space and permitting expression in public of private matters. The couch is the site of the effort *Friends* makes to adjudicate between friendship and love, to negotiate degrees of intimacy, a predilection rampant in contemporary American culture.

While often involved in public and other shared use, couches can be really private, intensely personal. In most essential respects, couches are pretty much alike, but they become individuated by wear, conforming to the forms of regular sitters, in lumps and characteristics that one feels rather than sees. Use—actual or imagined, anticipated or remembered—gives a couch more resonance than do conventions of style or taste or the expense of purchasing it. Dant, citing Baudrillard, suggests "that items of furniture have 'a primordial function as vessels, a function that belongs to the register of the imaginary'; as womb-like containers they cradle and protect humans at rest" (79). Indeed, while one commonly sits "on" a chair, one often sits "in" a couch or sofa. In their study of *The Meaning of Things*, Csikszentmihalyi and Rochberg-Halton note that "chairs, sofas, and tables are most often mentioned as being special objects in the home" (58) and that "[T]hey tend to be considered special for a limited range of reasons: because they embody memories and experiences; because they are signs of the self and one's family" (62).

In his novel *The Corrections* (2001) Jonathan Franzen binds general associations of the couch to personal experience and memory and demonstrates the signal value of a particular couch to define self and relationship:

> That night...found Chip alone at Tilton Ledge pursuing sexual congress with his red chaise longue...and the digital readouts of his home electronics cast light on his carnal labors. He was kneeling at the feet of his chaise and sniffing its plush minutely, inch by inch, in hopes that some vaginal tang might still be lingering eight weeks after Melissa Paquette had lain here. Ordinarily distinct and identifiable smells—dust, sweat, urine, the dayroom reek of cigarette smoke, the fugitive afterscent of quim—became abstract and indistinguishable from oversmelling, and so he had to pause again and again to refresh his nostrils. He worked his lips down into the chaise's buttoned navels and kissed the lint and grit and crumbs and hairs that had collected in them. None of the three spots where he thought he smelled Melissa was unambiguously tangy, but after exhaustive comparison he was able to settle on the least questionable of the three spots, near a button just south of the backrest, and give it his full nasal attention. He fingered other buttons with both hands, the cool plush chafing his nether parts in a poor approximation of Melissa's skin, until finally he achieved sufficient belief in the smell's reality—sufficient faith that he still possessed some relic of Melissa—to consummate the act. Then he then rolled off his compliant antique and slumped on the floor with his pants undone and his head on the cushion. (76–77)

The sexual associations of the couch are as pervasive as the familial, to which they are related in fundamental ways. The couch has a long iconographic tradition in this regard, stretching from classical mythology to Chaucer to painting and sculpture from the Renaissance to the present, to pinup art and pornography and advertising. Hollywood starlets in the 1940s were photographed as well as cast on couches. Couches always carry with them an aura of sexual congress, if not intrigue, whether they occupy a living or family room or a hotel room or an executive office. One might argue, however, that these venereal associations are not invariably venal and that many—possibly most—families might not form, children might not be born, without the mediation of the couch.

Function as a mediating device, is, I think, central to understanding all icons, and is finally the source of their resonance. Couches, as do all icons—at least all iconic things—perform their mediating function because they foreground the material. Firmly lodged in space and time, they reaffirm the body, as Judy Attfield expresses the point, "as the threshold between the interior subjective self (the individual) and the exterior objective world (society). Put another way the body can be regarded as the traffic junction between (human) nature—that which has become absorbed into everyday life and appears unamenable to change—and culture—that which is constructed, contingent, and ephemeral" (238).

The couch, then, is a venue for the exploration, the reaffirmation, and, yes, the destruction of relationships. Sitting in a couch is palpably different from sitting on a chair or lying in a bed. While differences in degree, of course, may be very great, couches are in kind paradigmatic in their function; that is, they put existing relationships (the realm of the syntagmatic) into play and present the sitter with a structure of possible relationships (the realm of the paradigmatic). Tables and chairs imply far more conventionally fixed, unitary, relationships. The couch allows, sometimes compels, one to explore possible stories, possible lives, possible identities, even multiple identities, as, for example, those of guest or friend or date or lover or family member, and all the variations on these affinities.

For those with whom one already has a relationship, the shared couch may occasion reaffirmation or redefinition of intimacy, say for example, the move from girl or boyfriend to lover or from lover to "let's just be friends." The deeper one gets into the couch, of course, the more dangerous the game, for the couch also signs the vulnerability that attends intimacy, a structure of possible unhappy stories, lives, and identities. The venue of the kiss is often, perhaps just as often, the venue of the fight. In one set of circumstances, the shared couch might mediate between the intercourse of the dinner table and the intercourse of the bedroom; in another situation the couch might arbitrate the retreat to a separate sphere, to a chair or to a bed of one's own.

The couch is a signally loose piece of furniture, very—dare I say—postmodern. The table and chair, by comparison, are remarkably unified in their meanings and associations. So too, the bed, despite all of its associations as a venue of sexual activity. The couch, however, is always fragmented, contingent, pointing not to a unified self and fixed relationships, but to as many potential selves and relationships as actual ones. The couch, like so very many popular icons, materially signs the schizophrenia of the postmodern condition.

WORKS CITED AND RECOMMENDED

Attfield, Judy. *Wild Things: The Material Culture of Everyday Life*. New York: Berg, 2000.

Boyce, Charles. *Dictionary of Furniture*. 2nd ed. New York: Checkmark Books, 2001.

Csikszentmihalyi, Mihaly, and Eugene Rochberg-Halton. *The Meaning of Things: Domestic Symbols and the Self*. New York: Cambridge UP, 1981.

Dant, Tim. *Material Culture in the Social World: Values, Activities, Lifestyles*. Philadelphia: Open UP, 1999.

Dorenbaum, David. "Furniture Society—Three Approaches to the Couch." *Furniture Matters* (The Newsletter of the Furniture Society), October 2000. 18 Mar. 2004 <http://www.furnituresociety.org/news/article/doren.html>.

Douglas, Mary. *Objects and Objections*. Toronto: Victoria College, 1992.

Douglas, Mary, and Baron Isherwood. *The World of Goods: Towards an Anthropology of Consumption*. New York: Routledge, 1996.

[Federal Marketing Corporation]. *The New Smart Approach to Home Decorating*. Upper Saddle River, NJ: Creative Homeowner, 2003.

Fefer, Mark D. "Couch: History, Philosophy, Essence." 18 Mar. 2004 <http://www.seattleweekly.com/features/0211/features-intro.shtml>.

Franzen, Jonathan. *The Corrections*. New York: Farrar, Straus and Giroux, 2001.

Hine, Thomas. *I Want That: How We All Became Shoppers*. New York: HarperCollins, 2002.

Kron, Joan. *Home-Psych: The Social Psychology of Home and Decoration*. New York: Potter/Crown, 1983.

Leach, Edmund. *Culture & Communication: The Logic by which Symbols Are Connected: An Introduction to the Use of Structuralist Analysis in Social Anthropology*. New York: Cambridge UP, 1976.

Logan, Thad. *The Victorian Parlor*. New York: Cambridge UP, 2001.

McMillan, Patricia Heart, and Katherine Kaye McMillan. *Home Decorating for Dummies*. Forest City, CA: IDG Books, 1998.

Roche, Daniel. *A History of Everyday Things: The Birth of Consumption in France 1600–1800*. Trans. Brian Pearce. Cambridge: Cambridge UP, 2000.

Seattle Weekly Couch Pages. 18 Mar. 2004 <http://www.seattleweekly.com/features0211/features-intro.shtml>.

The Social Life of Things: Commodities in Cultural Perspective. Ed. Arjun Appadurai. New York: Cambridge UP, 1986.

Sorrell, Katherine. *The Ultimate Home Style Guide*. London: Ward Lock Books, 1998.

Courtroom Trial

David Ray Papke

During early 1995 the biggest news in America concerned the trial of O. J. Simpson for allegedly murdering his ex-wife Nicole Simpson and twenty-five-year-old waiter Ron Goldman. As jurors in the Los Angeles Criminal Courts Building listened to testimony from racist detective Mark Fuhrman and others, Americans from all around the country contemplated the same testimony on their television screens. Conversations in the workplace and over dinner involved the rulings of Judge Lance Ito, and lawyers and laymen alike used cyberspace chat lines to compare notes on prosecutors Marcia Clark and Christopher Darden and "Dream Team" defense counsels Johnnie Cochran and F. Lee Bailey. A courtroom trial had captured America's attention.

Many Americans failed to realize, meanwhile, that the O. J. Simpson trial was only the most recent trial to fascinate the nation. The twentieth century had served up numerous "trials of the century"—proceedings with defendants Harry K. Thaw, Leo Frank, Sacco and Vanzetti, Bruno Hauptmann, the Rosenbergs, Sam Sheppard, and Claus von Bulow, to name only a handful. Each of these trials provided an engaging specific narrative and, on another level, an opportunity to reflect on the principles by which society is or should be ordered. Americans were able to easily follow these trials and to use them to make sense of their world because the courtroom trial in both fact and fiction is an established icon of their culture.

During the nation's earliest decades courtroom trials were especially important civic affairs. Most of the country was rural, and judges and an accompanying band of lawyers often traveled on horseback to assorted county seats for trials. Average citizens gathered at the courthouse to watch the proceedings. These trials were among the most dramatic examples of government in action and so they were important community-building events.

In the larger cities courts were more regularly in session, and smaller percentages of the population attended trials. However, that hardly meant citizens were uninformed about courtroom proceedings. Early journals such as the *North American Review, Analectic Magazine,* and *Port Folio* covered courtroom trials extensively, and popular trial reports were for sale in Philadelphia and New York and throughout New England. Published as pamphlets, the reports traced the proceedings and often ended with only partially convincing admonitions that crime did not pay. From the start, pamphlets of this sort were as much titillating as they were cautionary.

Trial pamphlets gradually disappeared from the marketplace, but the trial coverage in the rapidly expanding daily press of the nineteenth century more than replaced them. Trial coverage was a staple in the so-called "penny press," and other daily and weekly newspapers as well provided extended coverage of courtroom trials in the middle and later parts of the nineteenth century. An exemplary journalistic extravaganza involved the trial in 1836 of Richard P. Robinson for the murder of a New York City prostitute. The New York City dailies gave front-page coverage to the trial, and the *Herald* actually tripled its circulation during the two months it covered the trial.

Fact and fiction sometimes blended together in this journalism, but nobody seemed particularly concerned. Indeed, tales with courtroom trials were also mainstays in the nineteenth century's fiction magazines, story papers, and cheap novels. In fiction with dramatic trials as well as in journalistic reports on actual proceedings, Americans found an opportunity not only to delight in well-told stories but also to reflect on social problems and values.

In the early twentieth century both the tabloids and the more respectable newspapers continued to report extensively on important trials, and the *Saturday Evening Post*, the nation's most popular magazine, published no fewer than 86 short stories between 1919 and 1945 featuring the courtroom trial exploits of Ephraim Tutt, a fictional lawyer created by Arthur Train. The *Saturday Evening Post* also serialized several early Perry Mason novels by Erle Stanley Gardner. Overall, Gardner wrote 82 Perry Mason novels and supervised or at least contributed to the 3,221 episodes of the Perry Mason radio show, seven Perry Mason movies from Warner Brothers, and the *Perry Mason* television series, which originally ran on CBS from 1957–1968 and continues to appear as reruns on many local stations. Perry Mason's composure and reasoning are legendary, but he was always at his best in the courtroom.

By the final years of the twentieth century, the courtroom trial was a staple of the American popular culture industry. Both print and broadcast journalism reported regularly on trials, a cable channel featured trials, and supermarket weeklies delighted in the courtroom dilemmas of the rich and famous. Furthermore, the fictional courtroom trial is a fixture in popular literature and the movies, and television proffers both an abundance of daytime courtroom shows and prime-time drama with weekly courtroom proceedings. Reports on actual trials and portrayals of fictional trials are so common that Americans rarely reflect on their consumption of them. The courtroom trial has long been and continues to be a familiar part of the cultural fabric.

Each trial report and each fictional story with a trial in it differs from the next, but the courtroom trial in the contemporary mind's eye is surprisingly standardized. Images reinforce one another and create conventional

Television camera filming the courtroom of the Harry Washburn murder trial, Waco, Texas, 1955. Courtesy of the Library of Congress.

expectations. Hence, the courtroom trial takes on its iconic character and enables Americans to use the icon to contemplate larger practices and beliefs of the society.

What are the features of the iconic courtroom trial? The courtroom itself is customarily wood-paneled and well-upholstered—a far cry from the dirty courtrooms with linoleum flooring in many modern-day urban courthouses. At the back of the iconic courtroom giant doors swing open and shut when key participants enter or exit. The furniture is heavy and placed symmetrically. The judge's bench stands at the exact center-front and rises well off the floor, suggesting something sacred.

Like the setting, the major players are standardized. Judges are relatively abstract, perhaps symbolizing justice or the state's neutral attempt to referee conflict, and jurors as well rarely come to life as individuals. The attorneys, meanwhile, garner a great deal of attention in media reports on actual trials and are the most developed characters in fiction, television, and the cinema. In the middle decades of the twentieth century, white, male defense lawyers tended to dominate. The Perry Mason character inspired dozens of imitators on prime time, and the American Film Institute selected defense lawyer Atticus Finch, as portrayed by Gregory Peck in *To Kill a Mockingbird*, Hollywood's all-time most heroic figure. In recent years, more and more female lawyers and lawyers of color have made their way into the iconic courtroom, and as the successful television series *Law and Order* suggests, the heroic lawyer in the present might well be a prosecutor rather than a defense lawyer.

As the prominence of defense counsel and prosecutors suggests, almost all courtroom trials reported in the press or portrayed in fiction are criminal trials. That is, they involve the state prosecuting an individual for supposed wrongdoing. Even when civil proceedings with two private parties are featured, as, for example, with the suit against a hospital in the movie *The Verdict* or with the sometimes-absurd lawsuits in *Ally McBeal*, the courtroom trial resembles a criminal prosecution. Injuries are neither accidental nor inadvertent, and one party is cast as evil like a criminal perpetrator. The case is tried before a jury, although in most real-life jurisdictions juries have virtually disappeared in civil trials.

The iconic courtroom trial, be it a criminal trial or an ersatz civil one, is presented as a narrative, and even though uncertainty may exist about the ending, the stages of the proceeding are predictable for readers and viewers. Certain parts of the real-life process—voir dire (the selection of jurors), detailed jury instructions, sentencing hearings—are rarely portrayed. Journalists, novelists, and screenwriters instead emphasize examinations, cross-examinations, and closing arguments. The average layperson might think, in fact, that courtroom trials include only these components.

Examinations and cross-examinations in the iconic courtroom trial are especially dramatic. Lawyers stand at their tables or, more likely, stride confidently into the "well"—the area immediately in front of the bench. They aggressively question witnesses, experts, and defendants. In the iconic courtroom trial (but rarely in the actual one), people break down on the stand or are exposed as conniving liars. Sometimes, as in the film *A Few Good Men* when Lieutenant Daniel Kaffee, played by Tom Cruise, subjects Colonel Nathan Jessup, played by Jack Nicholson, to blistering cross-examination, the guilty party confesses on the spot.

When the examinations and cross-examinations are complete, the prosecution and defense lawyers make their closing arguments to the jury. These arguments are also highly dramatic, albeit in a different way. The two lawyers deliver intense pieces of oratory full of passion and detail. Jurors listen carefully, apparently with their decisions still unmade. In film and television the camera frequently looks into the lawyers' faces from over the shoulders of the jurors. For at least a few moments the sight lines deposit viewers into the jury box.

After the closing arguments the jury members solemnly leave the courtroom to deliberate. Isolated works such as the film *Twelve Angry Men* take us into the jury room with the jurors, but in general journalism and fiction tell us little of what is said in jury deliberations. However, as readers or viewers we know the jury will return to the courtroom. Lawyers receive telephone calls with the news the jury is returning. Police hurriedly transport defendants from jails to the courtroom. And the jury foreman hands the judge a piece of paper with the verdict. What exactly is on that piece of paper? We never find out, but the judge, after looking intently at the paper, returns it approvingly to the foreman. He or she then reads the verdict aloud. Defendants, lawyers, in action and suggests we have a reliable process to achieve justice. In all of these ways, the courtroom trial endorses central features of the nation's dominant ideology. The courtroom trial as icon is, in the end, one of the most important vehicles through which the citizenry can recognize itself as Americans.

WORKS RECOMMENDED

Belknap, Michael R., ed. *American Political Trials*. Westport, CT: Praeger, 1994.

Breen, Jon L. *Novel Verdicts: A Guide to Courtroom Fiction*. Metuchen, NJ: The Scarecrow P, 1984.

Chase, Anthony. *Movies on Trial: The Legal System on the Silver Screen*. New York: The New P, 2002.

Harris, Thomas J. *Courtroom's Finest Hour in American Cinema*. Metuchen, NJ: The Scarecrow P, 1987.

Jarvis, Robert M., and Paul R. Joseph, eds. *Prime Time Law: Fictional Television as Legal Narrative*. Durham, NC: Carolina Academic P, 1998.

Lieberman, Jethro K. *The Litigious Society*. New York: Basic Books, 1981.

Porsdam, Helle. *Legally Speaking: Contemporary American Culture and the Law*. Amherst: U of Massachusetts P, 1999.

Joan Crawford

Claude J. Smith

When one mentions the name "Joan Crawford," images arise of a crazed woman who hated wire hangers, or of the shrew who addressed the Board of Pepsi-Cola with this tirade: "Don't [expletive deleted] with me, boys. This ain't my first time at the rodeo." Whether these events happened or not is open to question, but based on her lower-class background, her Texas origins, and her screen persona, one feels that they might well have. A key problem now exists with Crawford when we attempt to make sense of her career: most of her screen time is tinted by our knowledge of *Mommy Dearest*.

Joan Crawford occupies a special place in American popular culture, for she was a harbinger of the conflicted modern liberated woman. For American women of the 1930s and 1940s, she provided both a powerful icon of women breaking free from the constraints of a male-dominated world as well as a warning of the dangers of transgressing contemporary morality and sex roles. Her career embodied the changing conscience of women of her era and society's perception of them.

In the 1930s and 1940s Joan Crawford was, intermittently, one of the most popular actresses in America. At the time, however, she made up only one part of a trio of extremely strong mature women, the other two being Bette Davis and Barbara Stanwyck, and, in 1944, was the highest paid woman in America ("A Tribute"). Bette Davis was cut from different cloth as she had had some middle/upper-middle class advantages that the other two did not have; she was also busty/fleshy whereas they were lean. Davis's acting style, unlike theirs, was over the top in flamboyant theatricality, and she spoke an affected "stage" English.

Crawford and Barbara Stanwyck were seminal actresses in a time of dramatically changing sex roles. Their personas had both feminine and masculine traits and followed the historical feminist sweep from flapper to Depression survivor to World War II independent wage earner, only to be displaced in the 1950s by their age, by male hegemony, and by the new curvaceous ideal, the dumb blonde. Crawford and Stanwyck were naturalistic movie actresses who came from impoverished backgrounds, both having been reared initially by single parents. For working-class women, Crawford and Stanwyck illustrated the possibility of arising from nothing to being a contender. Crawford's mother was a charwoman: her father left the mother before Lucille Le Sueur (Joan Crawford's birth name) was born in San Antonio, Texas, in 1908 (Wittman); the mother of Ruby Stevens (Stanwyck, born 1907 in Brooklyn) was killed by a streetcar and her father deserted the family a few years later. She lived in foster homes (Watters). Both entered movies via the chorus line (with God only knows how much sexual exploitation). Both changed their names. Both specialized in roles involving an almost fanatical social climbing, greed, husband abuse, and love triangles in which they were unquestionably stronger than the males whom they dealt with. In a battle of wills, few men could equal theirs. Both married multiple times. Their careers followed the same trajectories with sharp declines in the 1950s. Stanwyck, described as being the best actress never to win an Oscar (Watters), managed her career better than Crawford and moved into matriarch roles on television after age pushed her out of leading movie roles.

Of the two actresses, Crawford seemed the colder, the more calculating, the one with little or no sense of humor; Stanwyck, by contrast, could play comedy. Crawford had a perpetual pout, her bottom lip petulantly thrust forward as though she had a chronic chip on her shoulder against the system and at men in general. Crawford had debuted in *Our Dancing Daughters* (1928) as a flapper, the embodiment of the liberated-from-Victorian-morality, hedonistic 1920s female (Wittman). In *Mannequin* (1938), she is enslaved again as a Depression-era worker, as a slightly horse-faced Jessie Cassidy who is what in the South is called a "linthead." The film's opening shots show dumpy women in frumpy dresses clocking out from a sewing sweatshop like the exhausted workers of Fritz Lang's *Metropolis* (1927). (The 1930s woman probably knew about the awful conditions of the historic Triangle Shirtwaist Factory; furthermore, organized labor was struggling to make its greatest gains at this time.) A depleted Jessie climbs flights of stairs to her Hester Street slum home wherein her father is an unemployed dreamer and her brother is a sponger. Despite her protesting that she "needs" stockings, the family exploits her meager salary. Her mom is drained from a lifetime of making do. Jessie begs her boxing-promoter boyfriend Eddie to take her away.

They elope and celebrate at a speakeasy where John Hennessey (Spencer Tracy) becomes infatuated with her and buys her champagne on her wedding night! She dances with Eddie (ironically) to "Always and Always." She gets a chorus-line job, one of the few open to poor attractive women at this time, and Eddie begins to sponge off of her, having lost his best fighter in "a crap game." They move in with her parents. As Jessie's feckless father bellows he's tired of waiting for dinner, her mother tells Jessie, "there's a difference between a man's world and a woman's," but that Jessie can "do things...unlike most women."

Using the few tools she has, Jessie gets a job as a mannequin, modeling fine clothes and lingerie as Hennessey obsessively pursues her. Joan Crawford's characteristic and symbolic broad shoulders are already present as Eddie pimps her by urging her to divorce him and marry Hennessey in hopes of extorting money. To foil Eddie's plan, she later leaves Hennessey, but returns in the film's finale when his first business goes bankrupt. She plans to help finance Hennessey's new business with money from her hocked jewels. She even has to slap his face to bring him around out of his own "depression." This is a strong, inspiring woman, a societal role model.

Via this movie, millions of trapped Depression women, victims of exploitation in the marketplace and at home, could vicariously escape their dead-end lives and, like Jessie, with will and physical charms, marry upwardly with men who idolize them. The film also served as warning against men such as her father or Eddie—leaches, tyrants, and ruthless exploiters. Demonstrating how popular culture can introduce new, radical ideas, this film helped rationalize divorce (i.e., ditch the loser and marry a winner) and make it more palatable.

By far, Crawford's most important role and the one for which she won an Academy Award is *Mildred Pierce* (1945), a film that parallels Crawford's own rags-to-riches journey and one in which she plays both mother and masculine breadwinner. Though the film is set during World War II, the only direct evidence in the film is that servicemen are present in a bar, and stockings are unattainable "for the duration."

Joan Crawford, 1928. Courtesy of the Library of Congress.

The tensions created by World War II's female defense worker known as "Rosie the Riveter" and her newfound independence and wealth, however, simmer barely below the surface of this marvelous film.

Again in this film, the woman is strong, hardworking, and loyal; and the men are unregenerate crooks, weaklings, exploiters, lechers. Narrating in the flashback format, Mildred says in voiceover that she married when she was seventeen and that she feels as though she was "born in a kitchen and lived there all [her] life." Her first husband, Bert (Bruce Bennett), loses his job near the beginning of the flashback story and does not seem anxious about finding another one, and he justifiably wants her to stop nagging him. Mildred is apparently the dominant force in the house, spending money they can't afford on her children, in an effort, says Bert, "to buy love from those kids." She has upward social aspirations illustrated by the piano and ballet lessons she forces on her daughters. She has never, however, boosted her husband: "Those kids," says Mildred, "come first." Her non-stop lavishing of gifts on daughter Veda turns the girl into a spoiled monster.

After Bert moves out, Wally (Jack Carter), Bert's former partner, hits on Mildred (dressed in a robe with convict's stripes), thinking she will need a strong masculine presence in her life. He bulls his way into her house and drinks Bert's whiskey, determined that he will now rule the roost, as she is part of a huge empire of "grass widows," single women with children, who will need a male friend to help them out in exchange for sexual favors. He will screw her in more ways than one. Overweight, nasal, and warty, he is one of two loathsome male leads in the film. Thousands of grass widows in the audience would knowingly observe Mildred's plight.

Struggling, Mildred waits tables during the day, one of the few jobs available to women at the time, and bakes desserts at night. Earlier she had appeared in an employment office looking for any kind of work, and was photographed behind bars, continuing the economic prisoner motif. Her rotten daughter Veda is ashamed of her mother's blue-collar job and taunts Mildred about her social inferiority, saying she understands why "You've never spoken about your people." Women's employment at this time had rigid social class divisions. Jobs typically were limited, in declining order of respectability from teacher to nurse, telephone operator, secretary, beautician, waitress, and shopgirl.

Social-class consciousness is a constant in the film as it was in *Mannequin*, an anomaly in most American popular films but omnipresent in the lives of the 1930s–1940s working-class female audience. Shamed by Veda, Mildred stops waiting tables to become a restaurant owner, an entrepreneur. Buying property from a decadent aristocrat Monte Beragon, Mildred sets in motion a tragic locomotive that will destroy her business and send her daughter to jail for murder. Zachary Scott, who plays Monte, seemed to specialize in weak male roles; in this film, he wears a wispy pimp mustache and brags that his primary career is "to loaf." Mildred, unused to the superficial ease of the idle ex-rich, finds him charming and sleeps with him although on screen there is zero chemistry between them. (Not surprisingly, Crawford had an usually cold screen persona, especially compared to Stanwyck in *Double Indemnity* [1944].) Single mothers and 1940s wives viewing this film would not have reacted negatively to the grass widow having a lover, as many of them had also had them during the war.

Though Mildred's business is successful, its déclassé menu specialty of "fried chicken" suggests Mildred cannot escape her working-class origins. Monte is soon sponging money, and Veda's non-stop demands for luxuries are a drain. In an attempt to finally "arrive," Mildred commands Monte: "Ask me to marry you." Monte demands a portion of the business (he is pimp-like), and she grants it. She buys his family mansion, and has it redone, only to have Monte soon declare he doesn't like the smell of chicken on a woman. He will soon force a crisis in her business that drives her out of the corporation. In this maneuver, her old "friend" Wally profits off her loss. One can, however, almost understand him: Mildred had put a demasculating frilly apron around his middle on the restaurant's opening night.

As Joan Crawford was in *Dearest*, the lower-class Mildred is a disaster as a mother. Veda cold-bloodedly extorts money from one young suitor by pretending to be pregnant. The suitor's rich mother pays off rather than have a former waitress as an in-law. In trying to give her daughter every benefit of an upper-class background, Mildred has turned Veda into an insatiable monster. Veda's quest for money and status is, however, only a mirror image of her mother's and probably Crawford's. At the police station, Veda accurately says to Mildred: "It's your fault I'm the way I am." The subtext of this film is that although Mildred has proved her merit in the business world, mothers still belong in the home.

Social class and women's place in the world are subtly hinted at in the film's final shot: as a reconciled Mildred and Bert leave the police station, two charwomen scrub the floor. The film suggests that a woman/mother should attend to the affairs of the home, including scrubbing the floor. She should support her husband, not nag him. She must learn her place in the world, including avoiding the mistake of filling her daughter's head with high-toned aspirations. If she does not, the results can be catastrophic. Thus, the conflicted consciousness created by Rosie the Riveter, the new independent woman, is embedded in this film.

Although Joan Crawford was not a "method" actress, she seemed to live the role of Mildred Pierce. The sense of inferior social class and ruthless ambition that drove Mildred apparently drove Joan Crawford to such an extent that her first husband, Douglas Fairbanks, Jr., soon couldn't stand her and wanted a divorce. Like Monte's dislike of the smell of chicken, Fairbanks supposedly could not stand Crawford's vulgarity (Wittman). In the film, that vulgarity and aggressive ambition are brilliantly illustrated in an early scene when Mildred is near Wally's waterfront bar wearing a gauche fur toque and a mink jacket with linebacker's shoulder pads. Although Crawford came into movies from the chorus (and, like Stanwyck, had a nice pair of legs), physical grace seemed beyond her. Crawford seemed to represent the antithesis of the Pygmalion effect.

Crawford represented the dark, fearful side of femininity, the terrible mother (literally), the siren with just enough erotic appeal to lure men to their destruction. She had an unusually cold screen persona, a result in part of a fairly impassive face. Slathered increasingly as the years passed with makeup applied, it seemed, with a trowel, her face never revealed much, although her eyes (unlike Stanwyck's that were almost slits) were large and very expressive. They helped detract the hypercritical viewer from lipstick applied like a minstrel show singer's and from eyebrows that were on the verge of being bushy. Though she supposedly photographed well from all angles, her nose in complete profile in *Mannequin* is almost a "honker." For the typical woman of her era, Joan represented the idea that attractiveness can be improved by a liberal application of cosmetics. If we remember that "painted hussies" was a popular fundamentalist perception about cosmetic usage, Joan Crawford along with other screen stars did much to tear apart that idea in the public consciousness and loose another bond of male oppression against femininity.

Humoresque (1947) was one of the final major films of Crawford's career. It signals an end to the dominating roles she had earlier played. She finally meets a male as driven as she is. Crawford plays Helen Wright, an ennui-drenched rich man's wife, who decides to make a gifted violinist, Paul Boray (John Garfield) her protégé. Eventually, she demands he pay attention to her in return for buying his clothes and arranging his career, but Paul is obsessed with his music. Paul asks her whether her husband "interferes" with her in marriage—he doesn't. The neurotic dipsomaniac Helen drowns her frustrations while Paul plays *Tristan and Isolde* at Carnegie Hall. Helen needs glasses, symbolizing her lack of outlook. Here Crawford's eyes look a little old and mean as she struggles to see him clearly. The film suggests by a slow dolly in to an extreme close-up (a surprising shot considering Crawford's vanity and age—almost 40) that what Helen probably wants to kill herself about is her lost youth. Crawford was one of the first women to age on the big screen (Garbo had retired); thus, she was a resonant icon of every aging female viewer's decline, being still attractive, but fading.

The powerful class-conscious woman that Crawford had portrayed through much of her career was reprised once again in one of her lesser known but quite amazing films, *Flamingo Road* (1949). Teamed again with director Michael Curtiz, Crawford plays a carnival cooch dancer, the clumsiest of three we see early in the film, who grows weary of that life and decides to settle down. She feels "tired and dirty" and is sick of having "people look at me like I'm cheap." Her driving goal in this film is to get respectability, which is clearly a chimera despite her later improbable marriage to a political boss who meets her while she is a tavern (brothel) singer. He moves her to ultra-respectable Flamingo Road. A clear indication of stratified social classes is shown when a "Mother's Committee" organizes a violent protest against her being there. The town is ruled by a tyrannical sheriff (Sidney Greenstreet), and the state is run by men in a smoke-filled room. In this film, men wield power almost absolutely; women's career possibilities are virtually nil. Social-class rigidity is enforced by an oppressive male power structure as well as by conservative females. Thus, in a few years after World War II, we see a dramatic shift away from empowerment that women experienced during the war.

In Joan Crawford, we see encapsulated a history of women's place in American society from the late 1920s to the early 1950s. Her career reflected the desires of millions of suppressed American women. Crawford's power as an icon is, perhaps, most important in that stars of popular culture help to normalize outré behavior. No traditional retiring female, this pushy broad from Texas had the *cojones* to wear heavy makeup, drink, smoke, use her body to attract men, divorce, sleep around, marry for money, and perhaps most importantly, to challenge male authority—a whole spectrum of nonstandard behavior for women of her generation. Having clawed her way to the top of Hollywood stardom from virtually hopeless beginnings, she was, indeed, entitled to say to the Pepsi Board, "This ain't my first time at the rodeo."

WORKS CITED AND RECOMMENDED

Flamingo Road. Dir. Michael Curtiz. Warner Brothers, 1949.
Humoresque. Dir. Jean Negulesco. Warner Brothers, 1947.
Mannequin. Dir. Frank Borzage. MGM, 1938.
Mildred Pierce. Dir. Michael Curtiz. Warner Brothers, 1945.
Mommy Dearest. Dir. Frank Perry. Paramount Pictures, 1981.
"A Tribute to Barbara Stanwyck." 14 Dec. 2004 <http://www.classicmovies.org/articles/aa011600a.htm>.
Watters, James. "Return Engagement." 10 Dec. 2004 <http:got.net/~mmills/mm_home.htm>.
Wittman, Kelly. "Joan Crawford Biography." 29 Oct. 2004 <http://ctct.essortment.com/joancrawfordbi_rxhx.htm>.

Crayola Crayon

Elizabeth Armstrong Hall

In the summer of 1990 Crayola crayon giant Binney & Smith retired eight original crayons from its flagship sixty-four-crayon box. Having learned that kids preferred bold, bright colors, the company replaced maize, raw umber, lemon yellow, blue gray, violet blue, green blue, orange red, and orange yellow with cerulean, vivid tangerine, jungle green, fuchsia, dandelion, teal blue, royal purple, and wild strawberry.

Binney & Smith had renamed crayons in the past. When teachers reminded the company that kids no longer studied Prussian history, Prussian blue became midnight blue in 1958. Prodded by the Civil Rights Movement, the company changed its flesh crayon to peach in 1962. In 1999 Indian red became chestnut to erase any perceived connection with American Indians. But the "Crayola Eight," as the retirees would be dubbed, were the first to be physically removed from the popular sixty-four-crayon pack.

Aware that crayon fans had fond memories of the old colors, Binney & Smith invited the public to a "retirement party" in the tour lobby of its world headquarters in Forks Township near Easton, Pennsylvania. The "Crayola Eight" would be inducted into a "Crayola Hall of Fame," created for the occasion. On August 7 families, political dignitaries, Binney & Smith employees, and local and national media packed the lobby for the induction ceremony. The event featured eight, five-foot crayon replicas, one for each retired color. A Binney & Smith staffer dressed as a giant crayon—the costume would be brought out for future celebrations—served "retirement cake" to the gathered throng. Then the eight replacement shades were introduced with much fanfare. Pennsylvania Congressman Don Ritter presented Binney & Smith with a document paying tribute to the company for "providing future leaders of America with brighter and bolder colors."

While the celebrants were eating cake inside, angry crayon fans, most of them adults, were staging protests outside. One group went by the name RUMPS (The Raw Umber and Maize Preservation Society). Another called itself the National Committee to Save Lemon Yellow. As quoted in a *Time* magazine article, RUMPS president Ken Lang told one reporter covering the demonstration, "Raw Umber and Maize are part of the American fabric. If you remove them, then what?"

The adults' protests and the media blitz that followed took the company by surprise. In one week alone, Binney & Smith received more than 200 letters and faxes from crayon fans. "The kids are happy," said Binney & Smith's director of art and package design, as reported in the Allentown, Pennsylvania, daily *The Morning Call*. "But some adults are taking it personally. They say, 'That's my childhood. Don't mess with it'." In *Time* magazine's August 27, 1990 issue, the writer of "Goodbye to Lemon Yellow" explained, "Any child who has ever wielded a Crayola knows the ideal color for tree trunks: raw umber. But henceforth, basic brown will have to do the job."

The following year, a vocal chorus still clamored for the old shades. They bombarded the company with letters and phone calls. Adults who had not even touched a crayon since they were kids waxed nostalgic over the old colors. "You can't draw a picture of Nebraska or Iowa without using raw umber and maize," reminded RUMP president Ken Lang. *On Good Morning America* co-host Charles Gibson asked his TV audience how anyone could draw Confederate soldiers without blue-gray ("Goodbye to Lemon Yellow").

In an unorthodox marketing decision, on October 1, 1991, Binney & Smith announced it would bring the old shades out of retirement, temporarily. "The outcry for the retired colors is an adult phenomenon," said Binney & Smith's Brad Dexler in a company press release. "To satisfy them (the adults), we are going to give them one more chance to buy the crayon colors of their childhood."

Fourteen months after the retirement party, the company rolled out fresh batches of the retired crayons and packed them inside limited edition commemorative tins. Each tin contained a box of sixty-four crayons with the eight replacement colors and a separate box with the retired crayons. The "Retired Eight" would be available only until January 1992. The president of yet another protest group, CRAYON (Committee to Reestablish All Your Old Norms), called the return of the old colors a "great moral victory."

The 1990–1991 "Crayola Eight" saga set the stage for the crayon's transformation in the 1990s from a child's coloring medium into an American icon, fueled by baby boomer nostalgia and the crayon's own 100-year-old history.

Crayola crayons started out in 1903 as America's first safe, affordable colored crayons sturdy enough for kids. When cousins Edwin Binney and Harold Smith introduced their crayons, the only other colored crayons available in the United States were pricey imported artists' crayons made with toxic organic pigments or cheap domestic brands that easily crumbled. Binney's wife Alice, a former teacher, came up with the name for the new product by combining the French "craie" (chalk or stick of color) with "ola" (oleaginous, or oily).

They were not only sturdy; they were also affordable. The first box of eight—in red, orange, yellow, blue, green, violet, brown, and black—sold for a nickel.

A box of Crayola crayons. Courtesy of Getty Images/PhotoDisc.

A box of sixteen—with the addition of light green, cobalt blue, burnt sienna, rose pink, white, gold ochre, English vermillion, and olive green—sold for a dime.

By the 1910s, the crayons were sold in boxes of 8, 12, 16, and 24. Teachers loved them. So did kids. The United States government, one of the company's first clients, distributed the crayons to its reservation schools. By the 1920s Binney & Smith was also producing a popular line of artists' crayons, including Rubens Crayola Drawing Crayons and Perma Pressed fine art crayons.

Until the late 1940s, schools and art instructors made up the bulk of the crayon market. This balance began to tilt toward consumers after World War II, as American family size ballooned and middle-class stay-at-home moms discovered that their kids could stay occupied for hours with just a box of crayons and a drawing pad or coloring book.

These baby boomer kids were the first to own their own crayons. Most preboomers had used crayons only in school. By the late 1940s, Binney & Smith refocused its attention to its burgeoning family market. And, while teachers were still the crayon's most loyal and dependable customers, much of the advertising budget was redirected toward mothers looking for creative outlets for their little ones. When the boomer kids wanted more colors, the company followed suit. In 1949 the new forty-eight-crayon box added more than twenty new colors, including boomer favorites maize, lemon yellow, bittersweet, periwinkle, violet blue, thistle, and salmon.

By the time the sixty-four-crayon box debuted in 1958 on the popular children's television show *Captain Kangaroo*, Crayola crayons were on their way to becoming one of the hottest family consumer products in America. The sixty-four-crayon box, the first with the revolutionary built-in crayon sharpener, introduced sixteen new colors to the palette, among them raw sienna, aquamarine, cadet blue, blue gray, and other memorable shades.

"The box of 64 was a watershed," says David Shayt, curator of the Crayola Collection at the Smithsonian Museum of American History, a collection that includes more than 300 boxes of vintage crayons that span most of the crayon's first 100 years. The collection got its start in 1998 when Binney & Smith donated one original sixty-four-crayon box to the Smithsonian to commemorate the product's fortieth anniversary. Binney & Smith executive Dave Hewitt, on hand for the occasion, told the *New York Times*, "At Crayola, we divide our history into the presharpener era and the postsharpener era" (Collins).

The box of sixty-four solidified a personal connection between the postwar generation and Crayola crayons, laying the groundwork for the boomers' opposition to the company's decision to make the first changes in the box a half-century later. "If you go into a restaurant with crayons on the table, it's the middle-aged adults who grab the crayons," says independent toy consultant Chris Byrne (also known as the "Toy Guy").

The American nostalgia craze, with the oldest boomers leading the charge, was taking off just as the "Crayola Eight" were heading for retirement. By the end of the 1990s, companies like Binney & Smith, Coca Cola, Hershey, Mattel, and Volkswagen of America had found a ready market in the boomers for retro and heritage products. "Middle-aged boomers obsessed with their youth and movin' down the highway to retirement clamor for retro roadsters," a *Business Week* cover story reported: "Indeed, social experts say much of the appeal of nostalgia stems from a longing to return to simpler times.... Naturally, baby boomers, ever powerful in their numbers, are driving this return to roots. The Roper survey identifies the most longed-for age as the 1950s, 1960s, and 1970s" (Naughton and Vlasic 58, 60).

"You have to credit Binney & Smith for hyping nostalgia," says Shayt. "This is a company that actually flaunts the retirement of its products." Shayt and others point out how Crayola crayons tug at layers of adult memories, including sight, touch, smell, and even taste. Long after adults put away their crayons, they can still recall the colors and names of their favorite crayons, the feel of a freshly sharpened tip, and that waxy smell that filled their nostrils whenever they opened up a new box. That aroma, according to one Yale study, is the eighteenth most-recognized scent among American adults.

With the boomers' oozing nostalgia and media attention in full throttle, after 1990, Binney & Smith pulled out all stops to keep its crayon in the national spotlight. The Hall of Fame ceremony for the retired shades foreshadowed the elaborate public celebrations, ceremonies, and crayon-naming contests that culminated in the crayon's hundredth birthday celebration in 2003. These events not only brought celebrity status to the old-fashioned crayon, but also kept its boomer fans loyal and their kids excited about crayons.

When the first boomers had entered their teens and twenties, the company paid special attention to the boomers' younger siblings. In the first breakaway from the traditional palette, in 1972 the company came out with a box of eight fluorescent crayons with names to match: atomic orange, blizzard blue, hot magenta, laser lemon, outrageous orange, screamin' green, shocking pink, and wild watermelon.

After the "Crayola Eight" saga, Binney & Smith made a point of inviting consumers to help name new crayons as the pack expanded. In 1993, Binney & Smith sponsored the first of its popular crayon-color naming contests. The sixteen new shades debuted in the biggest crayon pack ever, the ninety-six-crayon box for the crayon's ninetieth birthday. The winning names submitted by both adults and kids added even more offbeat crayons to the pack: Razzmatazz, Timber Wolf, Shamrock, Cerise, Pacific Blue, Asparagus, Tickle Me Pink, Wisteria, Denim, Granny Smith Apple, Mauvelous, Tumbleweed, Robin's Egg Blue, Macaroni & Cheese, and Tropical Rain Forest.

Five years later, when the company decided it needed to find a new name for "Indian Red," it invited the public to send in suggestions. After reading more than 250,000 entrees, a panel of company color experts chose "chestnut," a name submitted by 155 people. Each winner received an official "Certificate of Crayola Crayon Authorship" and a gift certificate for Crayola products.

With each new contest, the company revved up both its publicity campaign and public celebration to market the new crayons and infuse glamour and excitement into an old-fashioned product. As a build-up to the June 2002 opening of CrayolaWorks, a now shuttered all-Crayola retail store and family art studio outside Baltimore, the company invited the public to submit Baltimore- and Washington, D.C.–themed crayon names for two new eight-crayon packs. The contest winners (most of them adults) for the "Colors of Washington, D.C." and "Colors of Baltimore" packs won all-expenses-paid trips to the grand opening, public kudos, and giant replicas of their winning crayons.

Like the crayon-naming contests, public celebrations brought together generations of crayon fans for a shared love-fest for the crayon. On July 17, 1996, more than 45,000 people of all ages packed the streets of downtown Easton for the grand opening of the Crayola Factory, a family discovery center and museum with a giant Crayola store around the corner. The festivities featured a "ColorJam" parade of 2,000 fans with color-themed names and outfits to match. Sporting a bright gold tie, Easton Mayor Thomas Goldsmith acted as master of ceremonies.

In 1998 the Crayola crayon was officially commemorated as an American icon by the federal government, Smithsonian Institution, and American toy industry. In January the U.S. Postal Service unveiled a Crayola crayon postage stamp of the original 1903 box of eight crayons as part of its "Celebrate the Century" series. Also in January the Toy Industry Association included Crayola crayons on its much-hyped "Century of Toys" list for the twentieth century. When Binney & Smith donated its rare sixty-four-crayon box to the Smithsonian in February, the *New York Times* referred to the classic box as "an American institution, now a fixture in the collective memory of millions of adults" (Collins).

By the time the Crayola crayon reached its centennial year, fans were geared up for the much-publicized and anticipated year-long birthday party. Two years in the planning, the celebrations featured a cross-country Crayola bus, a "Name the Shade" contest for four new crayons, a chance to save one of five crayons from retirement, and a day-long street party in Easton over the Columbus Day weekend. The 100-year-old crayon was honored with a fifteen-division, color-themed parade and the unveiling of a 1,500-pound blue crayon made from stubs collected across the country. Boomers whooped it up when they learned that their beloved Burnt Sienna would be saved from retirement.

In January 2003, Binney & Smith introduced a special edition 100-crayon birthday box to kick off and promote the crayon's centennial. The box sported a new logo and bright gold wrapping; yet, that familiar waxy fragrance still wafted out of the package. And, while flashy crayons like neon carrot, hot magenta, and atomic tangerine shared the pack with the staid blue violet, cadet blue, burnt orange, and raw sienna, they were still the same Crayola crayons, sealed in the same paper wrapping one has to peel back before sharpening a crayon in the built-in sharpener.

In 2003, crayon fans could also purchase a limited edition centennial tin that contained a sixty-four-crayon box with graphics from either the 1920s, 1940s, or 1960s and a separate pack of twelve retired crayons, the infamous "Crayola Eight" plus the four shades retired in 2003. After opening the box of retired crayons, this boomer grabbed raw umber, lemon yellow, maize, and blue-gray and sketched a field of sunflowers on a cloudless day.

WORKS CITED AND RECOMMENDED

Collins, Glenn. "Crayola Box of 64 Turns 40; Can a Brand-New Crayon Color, Boomer Gray, Be Far Behind?" *New York Times* 25 Feb. 1998: B7.
"Goodbye to Lemon Yellow." *Time* 27 Aug. 1990: 49.
Naughton, Keith, and Bill Vlasic. "The Nostalgia Boom." *Business Week* 23 Mar. 1998: 58–64.

George Armstrong Custer

Michael C. C. Adams

With the possible exceptions of Abraham Lincoln and George Washington, no historical figure has more name recognition with the American people than George Armstrong Custer. Long after most of the nineteenth-century Indian-fighting army passed into obscurity, his figure continued to resonate in popular culture. The Battle of the Little Bighorn, where Custer died on June 25, 1876, has been the subject of over 900 paintings, besides numerous books and movies. The general has featured as a cardboard cutout hero on cereal boxes alongside such legendary figures as Robin Hood, King Arthur, and Cinderella. In the 1970s, he joined the Jane West line of plastic dolls in the persona of "General Custard." Interest in Custer's last stand has remained so intense that the *New York Times*, on October 27, 1991, commented that, "fascination with the battle has inspired a legion of hobbyists."

How did this particular army officer become a cultural icon, and what symbolic functions has he performed in our collective imaginations? It cannot be taken for granted that Custer has been remembered just because his life ended in a climactic last-stand encounter. Other officers who died in this manner, such as Captain William Fetterman, whose command was wiped out by Plains Indian warriors in 1866, are forgotten. Nor can it be assumed that Custer's memory remained sharp because of outstanding generalship. As Stepen E. Ambrose, one biographer, remarked: "He was a good, if often reckless, small-unit commander, no more no less" (195). The context of Custer's last battle is significant in his becoming an icon for the nation, but before we go into this issue we must observe that another important factor in preparing him for lasting fame is that he was well known to the public long before his death and was, by the 1870s, a celebrated figure who could command $200 for a public lecture, on a par with such leading literary luminaries as Mark Twain. Custer was a largely self-created media personality who worked hard to stay in the popular mind.

Graduating from West Point in 1861, the first year of the Civil War, Custer became a cavalry officer after service on General George B. McClellan's staff. He quickly established a reputation for aggressiveness in combat, a quality lacking among many opponents of the legendary Army of Northern Virginia, so that he was soon a general and a regular feature in the illustrated weekly magazines. Capitalizing on his earned notoriety, Custer affected a distinctive appearance, wearing his golden hair beyond regulation length and dressing in fancy sailor suits. When he got his own brigade, he gave his men distinctive red bandanas and made the catchy marching song "Garry Owen" his own. After the war, whenever its strains were heard on a western army post, it was known that the 7th Cavalry was present.

The death of Custer created the emotional shock waves that accompany the demise of any popular culture icon, such as Frank Sinatra or Princess Diana in our time. But several factors stopped the Custer story from expiring when the media cycle moved on to other sensational stories. First, the general's death occurred in 1876, America's centennial year, a time of gross corruption in high places that made many despair for the future of the nation. It seemed that prosperity, settling into greed, had destroyed the earlier republican virtues of honesty and selfless devotion to the public good. The deaths in action of Custer and his troopers, poorly paid servants of the state but doing their duty to the end, suggested that some civic virtue survived. Custer had just testified about corruption in the Indian Bureau, risking his career to do right seemingly; and this added to the image of nobility in a crass time.

Even then, the legend might have been short-lived if the Little Bighorn had not caught the imaginations of artists outstanding with pen or paints. The first of these, essential in setting the key elements of the Custer myth in place, was Walt Whitman, the poet of democracy. Whitman had been searching for a subject from which to mould a great American epic that would rival the ancient folk sagas of Europe. He had hoped to find his theme in the Civil War, but it had proved too sprawling, confused, and bloody. In the death of Custer, the poet thought he had his focus. He assumed that the encounter was a hard-fought last stand, brought about not by the general's bad judgment but by the treachery and cunning of opponents, the same ingredients found in such European legends as the eleventh-century epic poem, *The Song of Roland*.

In his poem, "A Death Sonnet for Custer," published in the *New York Tribune* on July 10, 1876, Whitman depicted Custer as a symbol of chivalry in a dark time, yielding up his life in a sacrificial act that suggested the culture's ultimate worth, and linking the American racial saga back to other Nordic and Anglo-Saxon heroes. Custer had died to further progress; the dusky warriors—the Native Americans—must give way and be extinguished in face of a superior civilization. As befitted so great a hero, Whitman depicted Custer as dying last amongst his determined band of followers.

This epic picture was echoed in such visual renditions of the battle as John Mulvany's painting, "Custer's Last Rally," a popular canvas first exhibited in 1881, and much admired by Whitman. The artist showed a grimly determined Custer, sword in hand, going down hard at the center of his dwindling but staunch command. This legendary image was fixed solidly in the public mind when, in 1896, Otto Becker was commissioned by Anheuser-Busch to paint

Custer's Last Charge, published in Currier & Ives, 1876. Courtesy of the Library of Congress.

a similar battle piece. Reproduced in over one million copies, the Becker print hung in bars, restaurants, and railroad stations well into the twentieth-century. At the same time, the general's devoted widow Elizabeth was immortalizing her husband in memoirs of their lives together in the west; and Buffalo Bill Cody, who bore a superficial resemblance to Custer and had taken a small part in the 1876 campaign, made the last stand the central feature of his Wild West Show, begun in 1883.

The making of an icon was complete. Custer stood for the noblest qualities of the Caucasian race and he gave his life in advancing the cause of progress, the inevitable triumph of Western civilization over inferior peoples. As the *Boston Globe*, on June 20, 1926, told Elizabeth, she could see fields of plenty thanks to her husband who had fertilized the American West with the blood of progress. This view of Custer as exemplifying the best qualities of white

GEORGE ARMSTRONG CUSTER

America was largely unchallenged in popular culture through World War II. For example, in Warner Brothers' 1942 movie, *They Died With Their Boots On*, Errol Flynn as the gallant general deliberately sacrifices his command to save a weaker army column. True to the myth, Custer cannot be allowed to die due to his own misjudgment or the superior generalship of his opponents. The movie even credits Custer with crusading to save the Native Americans and, in a totally fictitious scene, Congress moves in memory of Custer to give justice to the tribes. General Philip Sheridan says to Libbie: "Your soldier won his last fight after all."

This romantic view could not survive unchallenged into the postwar era, with the collapse of Western imperialism and with it the assumption that Western military triumph over native peoples had been inevitably good for humanity. Wars of liberation, fought viciously on both sides, marred the British, French, Dutch, and other nations' retreat from empire. The vacuum left in French Indo-China led to America's involvement in Vietnam, with its accompanying huge cost in lives and environmental destruction. In this changed climate, Custer began to look more like an anti-hero, a reverse icon, symbolizing now what was wrong with the westward movement, our bullying of weaker peoples in a greedy ravishing of the planet. In Oliver Stone's controversial 1986 movie, *Platoon*, Sergeant Elias comments that the United States has been "kicking ass" for so long, it is time we got our own back. A similar sentiment is present in the post-Vietnam bumper sticker, "Custer had it coming" and in the succinct phrase, "Custer died for your sins," which no longer meant that he had died Christ-like to atone for the nation's material sins, but that he had deserved to die as a just punishment for his part in our role as aggressors.

Much in the Custer story justified a negative image. Some officers hated him for his arrogance and perceived indifference to the needs of his men. He did respect some Native American traits and he was by no means the most brutal of soldiers, but he could be ruthless as when, in 1868, he attacked a Cheyenne winter encampment on the Washita River, killing some non-combatants and slaughtering hundreds of ponies. This episode became a key scene in the 1970 movie, *Little Big Man*, based on Thomas Berger's novel, and a classic of the anti-Custer school. Director Arthur Penn grounded the 1868 Washita scene directly on the 1968 My Lai massacre in Vietnam exactly a hundred years later, suggesting how tarnished Custer had become as an icon. The general, played brilliantly by Richard Mulligan, is arrogant, insanely ambitious, and driven by a belief in his own infallibility that is immensely destructive to all about him.

The truth about Custer probably lies somewhere between the two extremes of veneration and excoriation. He did make errors of judgment on his last day, refusing to accept he was outnumbered and fatally dividing his command in the face of superior forces. But he was not a cruel and foolish figure either. Sometimes icons disappear when their cultural relevance diminishes, but this has not happened to Custer. Debate continues to swirl around his legacy. Recently, a new aspect has been added to the Custer symbolism. The twentieth century opened with the 1912 sinking of the Titanic, a disaster we have recurred to because it told us we shouldn't place all our faith in the infallibility of technology (the last Titanic film was made in 1998). As the century ended, we suffered Y2K jitters and social critics like Neil Postman warned us that we didn't know where the revolution in media communications was taking us.

Interestingly, discoveries on the Custer battlefield at this very time also suggested that we should be careful to understand the implications of technological advance. In 1983, a range fire destroyed the wiry grass on the Little Bighorn site, allowing for archaeological digs that resulted in a starling new theory about the battle, propounded in Richard A. Fox's book, *Archaeology, History, and Custer's Last Battle* (1993). Using forensic evidence provided by battlefield artifacts, investigators determined that Custer's command had quickly lost tactical stability and gone down fast, instead of there being a grim last stand as had been previously supposed. A lack of evenly distributed shell cases where the cavalry defensive perimeter should have been and a paucity of army bullets in their opponents' positions suggested that the 7th had failed to keep control of the battlefield, losing tactical cohesion, and had even succumbed to panic, bunching together at the end in terror of death. This fit with Native American accounts saying the soldiers had not fought as hard as they expected and had even acted as though drunk, weeping and throwing down their weapons. Why? Recent innovations in military technology meant that the age-old custom of fighting shoulder to shoulder, which had lasted through the Civil War, was no longer practicable. Breach-loading, long-range weapons that could sweep the field, demanded that soldiers spread out to avoid being killed in droves. But, as French soldier-scholar Ardant Du Picq warned in his 1870 volume, *Battle Studies*, the morale of soldiers deprived of close comradely support would crumble if things started to go wrong in the isolated situation of the modern battlefield. This happened to Custer's command when the warriors pressed them hard. Du Picq prescribed careful platooning of men who would know and trust each other in a crisis. Later American commanders would compensate for the loneliness of the battlefield by encouraging this buddy system, but the vital need for human cement on the skirmish line was not realized at the Little Bighorn, where the new tactics of fighting on a thinly spaced firing line were only two years old. Thus, Custer's last battle retains an iconic significance. The dead soldiers warn us that when our technological innovations outpace our understanding of their potential consequences, we run grave dangers.

The Little Bighorn was not a great battle in terms of numbers or outcome. The Native Americans won for a change, but that did not stop their total defeat. For the army, this setback was barely a glitch in their triumphal advance. Yet the fight is remembered because talented artists memorialized it and imbued Custer's death with a symbolic quality that has continued to resonate with Americans of different generations and philosophical persuasions. So far, there is little diminution in interest; even now, Fox's hypothesis is being challenged. And controversy continues as to whose view the National Park Service should emphasize in telling the story of the Little Bighorn battle. How we interpret Custer's end still matters to many Americans.

WORKS RECOMMENDED

If you would like to know more about Custer, a good recent biography is Jeffry D. Wert, *Custer: The Controversial Life of George Armstrong Custer* (New York: Simon & Schuster, 1996). Controversial but stimulating is Evan S. Connell, *Son of the Morning Star* (San Francisco: North Point P, 1984). Stephen E. Ambrose provides a fascinating portrait of two warring cultures in *Crazy Horse and Custer: The Parallel Lives of Two American Warriors* (New York: New American Library, 1986). Elizabeth B. Custer memorialized her husband in such works as *Following the Guidon* (Norman: U of Oklahoma P, 1966). Her role in the Custer legend is detailed in Shirley A. Leckie, *Elizabeth Bacon Custer and the Making of a Myth* (Norman: U of Oklahoma P, 1993).

Custer battle art is documented in Don Russell, *Custer's Last* (Fort Worth, TX: Amon Carter Museum of Western Art, 1968); Harrison Lane, "Brush-Palette and the Little Big Horn," *Montana: The Magazine of Western History* 23 (Summer 1973): 67–80; and Robert Taft, "The Pictorial Record of the Old West: IV. Custer's Last Stand," *The Kansas Historical Quarterly* 14 (Nov. 1946): 361–90. Custer's iconic significance is explored in Bruce A. Rosenberg, *Custer and the Epic of Defeat* (University Park: Pennsylvania State UP, 1974). On Custer and Whitman, see Michael C. C. Adams, "Poet Whitman and General Custer," *Studies in Popular Culture* 18.2 (1996): 1–17.

Native American views of the Little Bighorn include R. G. Hardoff, *Lakota Recollections of the Custer Fight: New Sources of Indian Military History* (Spokane: Arthur H. Clark Co., 1991); and David Humphreys Miller, *Custer's Fall: The Indian Side of the Story* (New York: Duell, Sloan, and Pearce, 1957). Recent interpretation of the battle appears in Richard A. Fox, *Archaeology, History, and Custer's Last Battle* (Norman: U of Oklahoma P, 1993).

James Dean

Geoffrey Weiss

The 1950s' icon of rebellion without a cause was born James Byron Dean on February 8, 1931 in Marion, Indiana. When Dean was 5, his father's job took the family to California where his mother, Mildred, died in 1940. The nine-year-old Dean accompanied her body by rail to Fairmount, Indiana, and remained there with his Aunt Ortense and Uncle Marcus. At Fairmount High School, he studied speech and drama with Adeline Nall; he won the Indiana State Forensics League competition in 1949. After graduation, Dean tried to start an acting career, first in Los Angeles and then in New York. After training at the Actor's Studio and playing on Broadway and television, he made three movies in Hollywood: *East of Eden* (1955), *Rebel Without a Cause* (1955), and *Giant* (1956). Dean died on September 30, 1955, when his Porsche Spyder 550 struck a Ford sedan driven by Donald Turnipseed, who turned across the center line directly in front of Dean at the intersection of highways 41 and 466 near Cholame, California.

Dean's legend commenced forming only days later with press comparisons of his funeral to Rudolph Valentino's; both set off hysteria among fans, many of whom traveled great distances to attend. The later 1950s saw a Dean cult develop with pilgrimages to his Indiana gravesite, annual memorial services at the Quaker meeting house in Fairmount, fan clubs, and many sensational stories in the tabloid press. In May of 1956 alone, three separate articles—in *Inside*, *Rave*, and *Anything Goes* respectively—asked "Did James Dean Commit Suicide?" *Whisper* told of "The Girl James Dean Left Behind" (August 1956) while *Exposed* profiled "James Dean: God of a Morbid Cult" (September 1956). Articles through 1958 "explained" his death in supernatural terms and even purported to carry "messages from beyond the grave" and ghost sightings.

Robert Altman's *The James Dean Story* (1957), a documentary biography of the actor, explains fans' devotion thus: they "had made James Dean, and they wouldn't let him go. To keep him close they made a legend in his name." More accurately, fans created a mythology that, like any mythology, had both a more-or-less coherent narrative and a particular social function among its acolytes.

The narrative blends filmography and biography. Broadly rendered, it goes like this: a brilliant-but-misunderstood small town Everyboy attains the American dream—a combination of fame and financial success—but finds his accomplishment, somehow, unsatisfactory. Chasing a greater destiny he never fulfills, he dies tragically in his quest. Dean biographer Joe Hyams names the Dean persona "Little Boy Lost" and explains its social function: "he had the intuitive talent for expressing the hopes and fears that are a part of all young people.... [H]e managed to dramatize brilliantly the questions every young person in every generation must resolve" (Lizama et al.). Thus, Dean's legend partially reflects Dean's qualities, but much more mirrors his teen fans' struggle to understand their lives, especially their relationships with parents. Their reluctance to let Dean go derives from reluctance to part with the myth's explanatory power.

From its inception in the 1950s, the first modern era of prolonged adolescence, Dean's performances—and, indeed, press coverage of what we now call his "lifestyle"—articulated an identity for which no clear enunciation existed; his image signified teen insecurity expressed in rebellion. "Because he died young and belonged to no one," Altman's film asserts, "every girl could feel that he belonged to her alone. Because he died violently, every boy could use him as a warning to his parents, 'If you don't start understanding me, I could go the same way.'" Dean the Rebel articulates for boomer teens an opposition to Eisenhower-era social order, which blossoms into the social conflicts of the sixties.

Norman Mailer's 1957 essay, "The White Negro," defines the primary conflict as hip versus square. According to Mailer, "One is Hip or one is Square, one is a rebel or one conforms" (278). In this scheme, Eisenhower and Johnson are square; Kennedy is hip. Beer is square; marijuana is hip. Hipness and rebellion appeal because they invite the rebel to revel, "to live without roots, to set out on that uncharted journey into the rebellious imperatives of the self" (277). Translated and simplified, this appeal becomes an invitation to self indulgence. And, according to Mailer, "The late James Dean was a hipster hero" (276).

Dean's films also addressed the burgeoning generation gap between the baby boomers of his generation and the "greatest generation" of their parents. The Dean persona responded to shortcomings in the *Ozzie and Harriet* vision of the nuclear family: remote fathers, consumerism, suburban malaise. *East of Eden*, Dean's first film, dramatized a son's agony over his father's withheld love, but the central image of Dean's iconography came from *Rebel*, the film released one month after Dean's death: Dean as speed-driven juvenile delinquent, insouciantly leaning against a brick wall, wearing a red windbreaker and clutching a cigarette held at waist level in a pointing hand.

After the appearance of *Rebel Without a Cause*, Dean's portrayal of Jim Stark's bitter complaint to his distracted parents, "You're tearing me apart!" quickly became the adolescent apotheosis. Jim Stark pointed to existential questions without providing any answers. Instead, fans could dress like Dean about the Gallery—from its location directly off the highway exit (and behind a Cracker Barrel restaurant) to its gift shop lobby and its streamline moderne architecture—smacks of 1950s nostalgia and the manipulated image of Dean. Dean fans wanting to make a connection with the Little Boy Lost himself must press on.

They go to the "Authentic James Dean Exhibit" at the Fairmount Historical Museum, which tries to be the Gallery's antithesis—even in its use of the terms "authentic" and "historical" in its name. Located in a Victorian-era house in downtown Fairmount and run by the Fairmount Historical Society, the exhibit features "hundreds of rare photographs, his motorcycles, bongo drum, movie costumes, and countless keepsakes donated to the museum by his own family and close friends" (museum pamphlet). The museum's driving force is Ann Warr, a founding member of the museum's board of directors and, along with her late husband Harry, Fairmount "town historian by proclamation, July 22, 1985" (museum pamphlet). When the museum is not crowded, she greets visitors at the door and provides a personal guided tour. As you exit, she asks you to sign the guest book, which is located just under the Plexiglas cube where you may deposit the "suggested donation" of one dollar.

Eschewing memorabilia for artifacts from Dean's life, the Historical Society preserves Dean as a treasured son of Fairmount; it displays items from Dean's life in Indiana, most of which were donated by Dean's local friends and relatives. A partial list of the museum's collection: Dean's first motorcycle (purchased at a local speed shop), his metronome, alarm clock, basketball, and Santa Monica College sweaters, a pair of bull horns and a matador's cape as well as the bongos from his New York apartment, his cap pistol and drinking cup from childhood, and an orchid painted by Dean as a gift for his high school drama teacher. Here James Dean becomes a conduit to a set of small town values from an idealized past when, its creators imagine, hard work and talent ensured success. Even the merchandise in the small gift shop promotes the town of Fairmount or the annual "Museum Days" festival as much as the man himself.

Of course, the Fairmount Historical Museum's Dean is no more "authentic" than the Gallery, only authentic in a different way. In fact, they approach the same story from opposite ends. The Museum looks forward to the boy who left Fairmount for stardom; the Gallery looks backward toward the star that left too soon. As much Dean-iana as Fairmount displays to enhance the icon, the lasting impression is that the essence of the man is gone.

Yet Fairmount still draws many visitors looking to connect with James Dean. The museum's guest book lists addresses from many states and several foreign countries—England, France, Japan, and more. Red lipstick kisses, left by fans, often adorn Dean's gravestone. The Quaker meeting house still sees annual memorial services, and a mysterious character named Nicky Bazooka appears on his motorcycle to lead the procession to the graveside and place a wreath. Any pilgrim to Indiana's Dean country likely visits both the Museum and the Gallery, for anyone coming to Fairmount as a Dean tourist likely has her own idea about the star. In the end, any vision of James Dean really only represents the Rebel its inventor desires to be.

WORKS CITED AND RECOMMENDED

Alexander, Paul. *Boulevard of Broken Dreams: The Life, Times, and Legend of James Dean*. New York: Penguin Group, 1997.

Betrock, Alan, Jerry Fagnani, and David Dalton. *James Dean Revealed! James Dean's Sexsational Lurid Afterlife from the Scandal and Movie Magazines of the Fifties: From the Collections of Alan Betrock and Jerry Fagnani*. New York: Delta, 1991.

Frank, Thomas. *The Conquest of Cool: Business Culture, CounterCulture, and the Rise of Hip Consumerism*. Chicago: U of Chicago P, 1997.

Hyams, Joe. *James Dean: Little Boy Lost*. New York: Warner Books, 1992.

The James Dean Story. Dir. Robert Altman. Warner Bros., 1957.

Lizama, Dominic et al., eds. *The Official Site of James Dean*. 22 Sept. 2004. CMG Worldwide. 14 May 2005 <http://www.jamesdean.com./about/bio.htm>

Mailer, Norman. "The White Negro: Superficial Reflections on the Hipster." *Dissent* 4.3 (1957): 276–93.

"Moody New Star: Hoosier James Dean Excites Hollywood." *Life* 7 April 1955: 125–28.

Dinosaur

Mark A. Wilson

Few icons provoke as many diverse responses, or have changed meanings more rapidly, than that of the dinosaur. The plush, toothless Barney of children's shows is designed to convey love and tolerance to preschoolers, whereas the relentless raptors of the movie *Jurassic Park* represent single-minded, alien violence. Older generations remember when the epithet "dinosaur" meant giant, slow-witted, and doomed to extinction; but any third grader today can name a dozen real dinosaurs, half of whom were relatively small, quick, and destined for extinction by circumstance, not evolution. The dinosaur is a complicated icon in America, and its history as a symbol reflects deep cultural changes as well as new scientific interpretations. The image of the dinosaur provides a rich vein for anthropologists and historians of science.

THE SCIENTIFIC BACKGROUND

Dinosaurs are such fertile subjects for research and speculation that it is now even difficult to fully define them. They are reptiles more closely related to crocodiles and birds than they are to lizards and turtles. Features of their pelves and skulls distinguish them from other reptile groups. Recently developed evidence shows that birds evolved from one branch of the dinosaurs, and there are now many dinosaur fossils found with impressions of feathers which protruded from their skins. The relationship between dinosaurs and birds is now considered so evolutionarily tight that many paleontologists place birds *within* the dinosaurs, leading to the odd conclusion that dinosaurs did not go completely extinct 65 million years ago—some are still chirping on our windowsills. The dinosaurs we are concerned with here will be the "non-avian" variety, but we will see that this connection to birds continues to change the iconic meaning of the dinosaur.

The oldest dinosaur fossils are found in Triassic rocks roughly 230 million years old. Even then they were divided into two different groups which became part of the public concept of dinosaurs. The Order Saurischia ("lizard-hips") contains the bipedal, carnivorous theropods (such as *Allosaurus*) and the quadrupedal, herbivorous sauropods (such as *Apatosaurus*). The Order Ornithischia ("bird hips") was entirely herbivorous, both the bipedal forms (e.g., *Iguanodon*) and the quadrupedal (e.g., *Stegosaurus*). Dinosaurs are thus characterized both taxonomically and ecologically by four overlapping states: bipedal and quadrupedal, herbivorous and carnivorous. Each condition carries with it different models of dinosaur behavior.

All dinosaurs were extinct by the end of the Cretaceous Period, approximately 65 million years ago. (OK, all *non-avian* dinosaurs!) The reasons for their extinction are also part of the dinosaur image. Prior to 1980 there were dozens of published hypotheses explaining dinosaur extinction. Many of the earliest were intrinsic to dinosaurs: they evolved to sizes they could not maintain, their brains grew too small to function, their eggshells were too heavy to crack, and so forth. Some of the more sophisticated ideas brought in extrinsic factors, although still affecting only dinosaurs: mammals ate their eggs, new plants poisoned them, diseases swept through their populations. The best ideas for the times took into account that the dinosaurs did not go extinct alone. The end-Cretaceous extinction simultaneously affected plants and animals on the land as well as in the seas. The dinosaurs must have gone extinct in response to global events not focused on them alone. Ideas here included climate changes and massive volcanic eruptions.

In 1980, a team led by Walter and Luis Alvarez hypothesized that a comet or asteroid the size of a mountain struck the earth 65 million years ago, producing a pall of smoke, dust, and debris which shut down ecological systems so severely that mass extinctions resulted, including those of the last dinosaurs. Their evidence was a thin layer of clay found between Cretaceous and later Tertiary rocks. This clay is enriched in iridium, an element much more common in extraterrestrial bodies than in the crust of the earth. This layer must be the settled dust from the end-Cretaceous impact event. Hundreds of later studies have confirmed and augmented this extinction scenario. A "big rock from space," in the words of schoolchildren, on its journey through the solar system, happened to cross the earth's orbit and produce the cataclysm that claimed the dinosaurs (and many other organisms). The existential randomness of this event changed scientific and public images of the dinosaur almost overnight. Dinosaurs left this world because of bad luck, not bad genes.

At about the same time that dinosaur extinction ideas were dramatically changing, there was also a revolution in our concepts of dinosaur metabolism and behavior. During the 1970s, a debate among paleontologists about whether dinosaurs were ectothermic ("cold-blooded") like other reptiles or endothermic ("warm-blooded") like mammals and birds reached the public. At stake was not just how these animals maintained their body temperatures, but what behaviors could be expected to follow. Endothermic animals have higher metabolisms and are thus more active. Endothermic dinosaurs would thus not have been slow, ponderous, overgrown lizards (a common perception of them since Victorian times), but quick and agile creatures. This debate

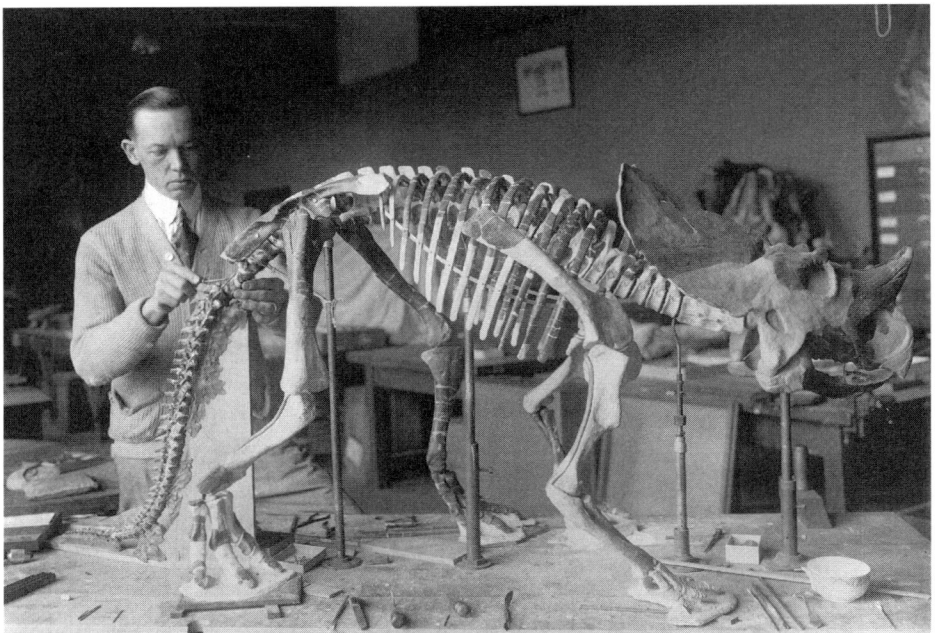

Norman Ross of the Division of Paleontology, National Museum, preparing the skeleton of a baby dinosaur some 7 or 8 million years old for exhibition, 1911. Courtesy of the Library of Congress.

continues, but the behavioral image of dinosaurs decisively changed for the public when this endothermic model was presented in the immensely popular *Jurassic Park* movie. Dinosaurs could no longer be imagined as dumb and slow beasts after watching raptors methodically hunt children in the *Jurassic Park* kitchens.

DINOSAURS AS ICONS IN THE PAST

Our earliest image of dinosaurs in popular culture comes from the Victorians. Charles Dickens may have been the first author to include a dinosaur in fiction. The first lines of *Bleak House* (1853) beautifully demonstrate the Victorian vision of a dinosaur:

> London. Michaelmas Term lately over, and the Lord Chancellor sitting in Lincoln's Inn Hall. Implacable November weather. As much mud in the streets as if the waters had but newly retired from the face of the earth, and it would not be wonderful to meet a *Megalosaurus*, forty feet long or so, waddling like an elephantine lizard up Holborn Hill.

Already by the middle of the nineteenth century Dickens could use a dinosaur to evoke an ancient, primitive time, and his dinosaur is a lumbering, awkward, gigantic beast—a lizard writ large. The seminal event for the public perception of dinosaurs was just a year later with the opening of the Crystal Palace Park in London. The sculptor Benjamin Waterhouse Hawkins, in consultation with Sir Richard Owens, the scientist who defined the Dinosauria, populated the park with life-size statues of dinosaurs and other prehistoric animals. We would not recognize most of these dinosaurs today because of the way they were reconstructed. *Megalosaurus* and *Iguanodon*, for example, were shown as quadrupedal and low-slung, whereas today they are illustrated as beautifully balanced bipeds. The models for the Victorian dinosaur were, naturally enough, living reptiles today such as lizards and crocodiles, and this imagery included not only their appearance but their behavior as well. The *Megalosaurus* of Dickens could indeed do little more than waddle in the mud.

Half a century later dinosaurs were far better known by paleontologists, but they had not yet been liberated from their slow and brutish ways. Sir Arthur Conan Doyle published *The Lost World* in 1912, and this science fiction novel reintroduced dinosaurs into the culture. The story is an account of an expedition to a South American plateau "frozen in time" and harboring living dinosaurs and other prehistoric beasts. Here is Doyle's description of a group of *Iguanodon*:

> There were, as I say, five of them, two being adults and three young ones. In size they were enormous. Even the babies were as big as elephants, while the two large ones were far beyond all creatures I have ever seen. They had slate-colored skin, which was scaled like a lizard's and shimmered where the sun shone upon it. All five were sitting up, balancing themselves upon their broad, powerful tails and their huge three-toed hind-feet, while with their small five-fingered front-feet they pulled down the branches upon which they browsed. I do not know that I can bring their appearance home to you better than by saying that they looked like monstrous kangaroos, twenty feet in length, and with skins like black crocodiles. (162)

Iguanodon is finally bipedal in this vision, although really tripedal if it is supported by its tail; and it is more placid in appearance than the menacing Crystal Palace Park version. Later Doyle makes it clear that his dinosaurs are all very stupid because of their legendary small brains.

It was when dinosaurs made it to film that their most intractable public images were formed. Winsor McCay created an affable sauropod called *Gertie the Dinosaur* (1914) in one of the earliest animated cartoons. McCay used the cartoon in a popular vaudeville show, interacting with Gertie as she did very dinosaurian things like drinking a lake dry and biting off most of a tree. The most important early dinosaur movie was *The Lost World* (1925), based on Doyle's novel. Sauropods, ceratopsians (like *Triceratops*), and theropods are featured, all monstrous, dim-witted, and excruciatingly slow-footed. The pattern was set; dinosaurs appeared in dozens of movies after this in basically the same way with only the animation improving over time. The

Gertie the dinosaur standing on a cliff edge looking at a mastodon, 1914. Courtesy of the Library of Congress.

most prominent of these movies include *One Million B.C.* (1940, but who can forget its 1966 remake with Raquel Welch?), *Journey to the Beginning of Time* (1955), and *The Valley of the Gwangi* (1969). Hollywood dinosaurs as tail-dragging, overgrown lizards persist into the 1980s.

Then came the next iconic dinosaur film: *Jurassic Park* (1993). The scientific revolution in which dinosaurs were hypothesized to have been active, upright, bird-like animals whose extinction was due more to chance than to evolution had finally penetrated Hollywood. Michael Crichton's novel of the same name, combined with Steven Spielberg's direction, changed the image of dinosaurs forever for the public. The *Jurassic Park* dinosaurs were not lizards; they were creatures unique in their own ways. Furthermore, Crichton and Spielberg showed a diversity of dinosaurs, from the small to the stupendous, from extraordinary chasing predators to swift ostrich-like herbivores. There is probably no other film which has had such a dramatic impact on science education. The modern era of the dinosaur image had begun.

DINOSAURS AS ICONS TODAY

Buy a bag of plastic dinosaurs and you'll find them roughly distributed between carnivores and herbivores, even though the latter were far more common in life. About half will be bipedal and the other half quadrupedal, again more to reflect diversity than paleontological reality. (The bag may also contain plesiosaurs, pterosaurs, and ichthyosaurs, none of which are dinosaurs!) Spread these dinosaur toys out on the floor before a group of American children and watch the kids sort them out and tell stories. The carnivores quickly become the "bad" dinosaurs, preying on the placid and friendly herbivores. *Tyrannosaurus rex* skulks around the outside of the group, pouncing on the unwary *Triceratops*, while a *Velociraptor* pack tears into a beleaguered *Iguanodon*. (You will find that most American children even know the relative ages of dinosaur taxa, so they rarely have anachronistic match-ups.) The herbivores are not without responses to the predators, though, as the children deploy them in defensive circles with "babies" protected inside, and the whip-like tails of the sauropods and the spikes of the ceratopsians do great damage on the attackers. These children have created a mythic drama with these toys. Each plastic dinosaur represents a form, a personality, a set of needs, and a reputation as fixed as those of the Greek gods. For the children it is a universal language continually modified by images from the Discovery Channel and the thousands of dinosaur books written just for them. And beneath the passion stories, growls, and mimicked mayhem are scientific concepts. Dinosaurs have become the most effective means of introducing children to science because they fit so well into cultural models of conflict and resolution, good and bad, power and weakness. This utility of dinosaur symbols as an introduction to scientific thinking is a late twentieth-century phenomenon directly traceable to the contemporaneous scientific renaissance in dinosaur studies.

We can thus understand why the poster of *Tyrannosaurus rex* in a 10-year-old's bedroom now represents power (parents, for example, would be no match for this creature!), and how it evokes the mysterious lost world of the past. But why does little brother down the hall sleep every night comforted by a soft, stuffed, purple *T. rex* called Barney? Clearly the icon of the dinosaur is not entirely controlled by scientific realism. Barney was created in 1987 by a former teacher, Sheryl Leach, who wanted to make educational videos for preschool children. She saw her toddler son's fascination with museum dinosaurs and realized the potential for a dinosaur to attract children and maintain their interest. Barney was born. In 1992, *Barney & Friends* debuted on PBS television and quickly became the number one children's show.

Roadside attraction of a tyrannosaurus rex. Courtesy of Shutterstock.

Barney was joined by his ceratopsian friends Baby Bop and BJ in the videos, and there is of course no suggestion of a predator-prey relationship! Baby Bop and BJ are even bipedal to make them more anthropomorphic and similar to Barney. The image of the dinosaur was thus transformed in Barney to that of a benign (and sometimes inane) older brother who is all about love, manners, and the primary colors. Preschool children listen to the very parental messages coming from characters very much unlike their actual mothers and fathers. It works because of that initial contact children have with much more impressive dinosaurs in museums, books, and movies. Curiously, Barney is wildly popular with young children, but among teenagers Barney is one of the most unpopular icons ever. Type "Barney the dinosaur" into a web search engine and you will see hundreds of extraordinary I-Hate-Barney Web sites.

The most enduring dinosaur in American commerce is Dino, the symbol for the Sinclair Oil Company. The company on its official

Web site (www.sinclairoil.com) says that as a trademark Dino is a symbol of "power, endurance and stamina, the prime qualities of Sinclair products." In 1930 the company wanted to find a way to convey to the public the quality of one of its crude oils which was especially old. They decided to use a dozen different kinds of dinosaurs in dramatic print advertisements to illustrate the geological past. These advertisements were very popular, and by 1932 one dinosaur stood out: the sauropod *Apatosaurus*. Curiously, the Sinclair sauropod looks very much like Winsor McCay's acclaimed *Gertie the Dinosaur*, which appeared less than twenty years before and was also seen to be powerful yet friendly and under control. The Sinclair Oil Company registered the Dino image as a trademark and for many years even supported paleontological research on dinosaurs and distributed a variety of geological education materials to schools. Dino remains in silhouette on Sinclair Oil signs much the same way he has looked for decades. All the company needs to do now is lift its tail off the ground to make it more in keeping with current interpretations of *Apatosaurus*.

The dinosaur has thus been a complicated icon for American culture because it is directly tied to a dynamic science which has changed its own image of dinosaurs dramatically. Dinosaurs were unique, diverse, instantly recognizable creatures which roamed the landscape for over 150 million years. They always represented to us great age and a mysterious past. As a cultural symbol the dinosaur has evolved, though, from an almost mythically slow and thick beast to the much more realistic animals we imagine today.

WORKS RECOMMENDED

Doyle, A. C. *The Lost World*. New York: Hodder & Stoughton, 1912.
Fastovsky, D. E., and D. B. Weishampel. *The Evolution and Extinction of the Dinosaurs*. 2nd ed. New York: Cambridge UP, 2005.
Mitchell, W.J.T. *The Last Dinosaur Book: The Life and Times of a Cultural Icon*. Chicago: U of Chicago P, 1998.
Norell, M., E. S. Gaffney, and L. Dingus. *Discovering Dinosaurs: Evolution, Extinction, and the Lessons of Prehistory*. Berkeley: U of California P, 2000.
Sanz, J. L. *Starring T. rex! Dinosaur Mythology and Popular Culture*. Bloomington: Indiana UP, 2002.
Tidwell, V., and K. Carpenter, eds. *Thunder-lizards: The Sauropodomorph Dinosaurs*. Bloomington: Indiana UP, 2005.
Weishampel, D. B., P. Dodson, and H. Halszka Osmlska, eds. *The Dinosauria*. 2nd ed. Berkeley: U of California P, 2004.

Dollar Bill

Heinz Tschachler

Every student of popular culture has his or her own personal motives for choosing a subject matter for analysis. I am old enough to admit that my relation to money is somewhat sentimental. A great deal of this is owed to my grandmother, who once gave me a stash of old German banknotes. They were emergency issues (*Notgeld*) from the inflation-plagued 1920s. Billions of those Deutschmarks together were worth less than ten bucks. By contrast, my uncle Erich's coin collection, always the object of my youthful fascination, must be worth quite a few grand. Another index to the sentimentality in my relationship to money is the fact that I always carry a one dollar bill in my wallet, for good luck. In these days of the euro I also notice that it speaks to me in a voice that is more familiar and more reassuring than that of the new currency. Why should that be so? Am I just another hapless victim of the relentless pressure to modernize? An essay on the euro's "sad symbols" and on its future as a currency "without soul or culture" (Théret) offers a more complex explanation. The gist of it is that the acceptance and legitimacy of modern currencies depend on their ability to symbolize a community based on a political territory and, at the same time, to transcend social contradictions. So much for postnationalism.

On the remaining pages, then, I want to pursue understanding the cultural work of the U.S. dollar; that is, I want to consider the meanings and associations—especially those that go beyond its function as "legal tender for all debts, public and private"—that it adds to the texts and contexts in which it appears. In order to achieve a sense of structure and coherence, I have arranged my pursuit around two issues: questions of money and value, on the one hand, and the role of the state in guaranteeing value by promising to redeem (what Marx called) "worthless tokens" at their face value, on the other.

If I focus rather narrowly on paper money, there are good reasons for doing so. Paper money is generally much more iconographically loaded than coinage. The large, rectangular shape of paper money affords ample space for expressing all kinds of ideas on a familiar canvas and thus for serving functions beyond the mere economic. Furthermore, paper money began its widespread, long-lived use in America. The absence of any precious metal in what is now the United States—gold was not discovered in any usable quantity until 1848, and silver even later—left Americans little choice. They had to rely on paper money. "Paper money alone," Richard Doty concludes, "would give the United States the peculiar capital elasticity it required" for its development as a nation (91).

Bringing together euro and dollar served to highlight a key feature of any iconic subject: as the editors of this collection found, icons generate strong reactions. People identify with them, or against them. There are undoubtedly many people carrying a $1 bill in their wallets for good luck, but who would consider doing the same with a $2 bill? If the unpopularity of that bill stems from its being the basic bet in horse-racing, the history of the national monetary icon abounds with examples of strong reactions. For the republic's founders, for instance, money had been a means to formulate and perform a national identity or, in the words of a delegate to the Continental Congress, "a new bond of union to the associated colonies" (qtd. in Goodwin 61). Indeed the notes of the Continental Currency, issued in order to finance the Revolutionary War, were "the earliest symbols of the United States.... All the power of political advertising was vested in the Continental dollar bill" (Goodwin 62–63). The actual money value of Continentals, which were redeemable in Spanish milled dollars, was beside the point. Only two years after their adoption, ten dollars in Continental Currency bills was worth only one Spanish silver dollar; by 1781, the ratio was 1,000 to 1. Ultimately the currency depreciated to a point where it cost more to print bills than they would buy so that, as Jonathan Carver observed in *Travels in America*, the "Congress paper dollars are now used for papering rooms, lighting pipes, and other conveniences" (qtd. in Newman 15). The depreciation of the notes is also perpetuated in the American colloquialism "not worth a Continental."

Dollar bills. Courtesy of Corbis.

This episode suggests the conflicted meanings surrounding the issuance of American paper currency during the Revolutionary period. But the problem of the paper money form, which unlike coins struck in gold or silver is not valuable in and of itself but only representative of value, had prompted considerable debate and given rise to much anxiety already in the colonial period. This is evident from the following practice: in order to encourage acceptance of such bills, a 5 percent premium was granted in Massachusetts (as well as in other colonies) to those who would use them for tax payments. Various colonial military needs throughout the eighteenth century were financed in the same manner, but bills of credit were also issued to repair or build jails, courthouses, harbors, lighthouses, forts, and other public works (Newman 9–10). All these measures were buttressed by the belief—held by Benjamin Franklin, among others—that an increase in the paper money would foster general prosperity. Not everyone agreed. James Madison, for instance, called the current "rage for paper money" an "improper or wicked project," which only a strong federal government would be likely to remedy (1018). Madison's vision did not become reality any time soon. On the contrary, the U.S. Constitution left to the states the power to incorporate banks that could issue notes. But with few laws to regulate banking, the situation was soon characterized by such features as wildcat banks, broken bank notes, counterfeit bills, and almost 10,000 different legal notes in circulation (Standish 124). Small wonder, then, that any business extending beyond the local was extremely risky. Edgar Allen Poe knew this well, as can be gleaned from one of his better-known tales.

This tale, written in 1843 and titled "The Gold-Bug," begins with an account of a Mr. William Legrand's bankruptcy, his forswearing of all business practices and his subsequent voluntary exile on a remote island off the coast of South Carolina. There Mr. Legrand engages in a quest of "entomological specimens," that is, of beetles. A golden-colored Scarabaeus beetle sets him off on a wild treasure hunt. Incredibly, the hunt is successful, and Legrand is finally rewarded with the real thing, gold, when he unearths an "oblong chest of wood" that contains, in coin, "rather more than four hundred and fifty thousand dollars...gold." Additionally, the hunt yields hundreds of artifacts, also in gold and exceeding "three hundred and fifty pounds avoirdupois." But not only are both the amount itself and its total value ("the entire contents of the chest [are estimated] at a million and a half of dollars" [Poe 578–80]) verging on the miraculous. The story in particular foregrounds (and implicates the reader in) the incredible ingenuity and resourcefulness that human greed—lust for gold or, again following Marx, worship of the "Lord of commodities"—is capable of spawning. Yet Poe is too shrewd and troubled a writer to tell us whether the treasure will allow Mr. Legrand to live happily ever after. What he does tell us is that the treasure may have been flawed from the beginning, may have been corrupted in several ways at once. First there is, for instance in Legrand's bug for gold, which drives him almost to madness, an echo of the traditional dislike of money in Christendom for the avarice with which it is associated. As Paul wrote to Timothy, "for the love of money is the root of all evil" (1 Timothy 6:10). Not surprisingly there is, secondly, a connection with death and violence, symbolized by the two skeletons in the pit, presumably of two associates killed by the legendary Captain Kidd when the treasure was buried. And thirdly and finally there is, via the Scarabaeus beetle, the "gold-bug" of the title, the association with dung, which is not necessarily of any intrinsic value—like paper money that is not backed by precious metal, or like the "ideal" cryptographic drawing that the treasure-hunting protagonist cashes in for "real" gold.

The paper money form may have prompted considerable debate and given rise to much anxiety, but mostly among those who were or believed themselves to be in danger of losing money. What was talked about much less frequently was that paper money also brought about the breakdown of former distinctions between high and low culture, between social elites and the common. Previously, the latter had used mainly other forms of money, like wampum, buckskin, nails, or (mostly foreign) coinage. The paper dollar changed all that. Its presence also widened the boundaries within which it circulated, from the local to the regional, and ultimately to the national. As a result, relations among people changed; they became increasingly anonymous, and the community lost its face-to-face character to become, in Benedict Anderson's famous term, an "imagined" one (Anderson 6–7).

The psychological consequences of the issuance of a national paper currency can be gleaned from Ralph Waldo Emerson's associating it with "the corruption of man," with "duplicity and falsehood," and "rotten diction" (1480). Emerson, like many of his contemporaries, located the alternative in nature. Another preferred locus emerges from Washington Irving's 1833 sketch "The Creole Village," which describes one of the villages of French and Spanish origin in Louisiana which seemed to have been bypassed by modernization. Typically in those villages the ancient trees were still standing, "flourish[ing] undisturbed; though, by cutting them down, [the villagers] might open new streets, and put money in their pockets. In a word, *the almighty dollar*, that great object of universal devotion throughout our land, seems to have no genuine devotees in these peculiar villages" (23, emphasis added). When Irving republished the sketch in *Wolfert's Roost* in 1855, he made one major addition in the form of a footnote, which reads as follows:

> This phrase [the almighty dollar] used for the first time, in this sketch, has since passed into current circulation, and by some has been questioned as savoring of irreverence. The author, therefore, owes it to his orthodoxy to declare that no irreverence was intended even to the dollar itself; which he is aware is daily becoming more and more an object of worship. (27n.)

In other words, Irving means no disrespect for religion, but expresses his contempt for those who treat money as if it were God and thus an object of devotion.

The practice of treating money as if it were God and thus an object of devotion has found a more modern interpretation in Walter Benjamin's 1921 fragment titled "Capitalism as Religion." This short text, which remained unpublished in Benjamin's lifetime, suggests that a comparison be made between religious paintings ("the images of the saints of the various religions") and the ornaments on banknotes ("the banknotes of different states. The spirit that speaks from the ornamental design of banknotes"). Such a comparison, Benjamin wrote, would reveal the ability of currency iconography to perform some kind of alchemy that transforms commodities or values into their equivalents and invests in pieces of paper values that they do not possess of their own accord (288). Furthermore, Benjamin's reference to "banknotes of different states" recalls the project, undertaken by state authorities especially in the late nineteenth and early twentieth centuries, of instilling in citizens a sense of collective identity. This goal was typically achieved by creating a wide range of memories, icons, and rituals that were capable of representing the nation's symbolic meanings. Perhaps the most obvious way in which national identity was mediated was through images that would help inculcate a sense of belonging to the national community. Such images could be found on items such as flags, stamps, murals and paintings, and statues—and on the national currency, which Eric Hobsbawm has called the "most universal form of public imagery" (281).

Throughout the second half of the nineteenth century, the national currency was adorned with classical images and allegories, such as Columbia or Victory or Concordia, or more modern ones, such as Industry, Steam, or Electricity, with vignettes pertaining to history or tradition, or with reproductions of the famous paintings of Americana hanging in the Capitol at Washington or in the Metropolitan Museum of Art in New York. As one visitor to the United States found, these (incredibly skilled and tasteful) depictions made banknote-engraving "the only true American contribution to the arts" (qtd. in Goodwin 150). Allegories were essentially feel-good images, serving the bourgeoisie well in that they concealed the worst excesses of industrialization and commodity relations. In the long run, however, images prevailed that were capable of representing the nation's symbolic meanings. This move was bound up in the shift of responsibility for note issuing from small local banks to large-scale central institutions such as the Treasury Department and, as of 1913, the Federal Reserve Bank. A crucial year was 1929, when a special committee appointed by the Secretary of the Treasury determined that "portraits of the Presidents of the United States have a more permanent familiarity in the minds of the public than any others" (Bureau of Engraving and Printing). Some exceptions were allowed, though, and thus we have portraits of Franklin (on the $100 note, colloquially called "Benjamin"), Hamilton (the first Secretary of the Treasury, on the $10 note), and Salmon P. Chase (Treasury Secretary under Lincoln, on the $10,000 note).

Also in 1929 the size of all dollar bills was reduced by 25 percent, a measure adopted in order to save paper and thus to cut down on the cost of production. The measure was also coincidental with the stock market crash and thus truly emblematic of the fall. Three years later Franklin Delano Roosevelt was elected on the expectation that he would give inspiration to a

Depression-demoralized nation. His proclamation, in the first inaugural address, that "the only thing we have to fear is fear itself" (qtd. in Lott 278) is thus particularly poignant. There was indeed much to be feared, like the fact that, following the abandonment of the gold standard in 1933, the circulation of symbolic currency was no longer related to its successful redemption. This shift meant that dollar bills had to be popular with a people who, as Roosevelt had declared, had been shamefully betrayed by the "money changers" (qtd. in Lott 279). When in 1935 the new bills began to roll off the presses, they were solidly dull-looking. Yet as Goodwin contends, the new dollar "no longer had to hoot and trumpet: America *was* the future." Uniform across America, the new dollar was also "the perfect ingredient in the corporation paycheck...an indispensable partner to Big Business" (287). Small wonder, then, that the new design was here to last. The only significant change since has been the adoption of the national motto, "In God We Trust," in 1957, a gesture by President Eisenhower to please the people who took their dollar bills seriously, like their flag and their pledge of allegiance.

Overall, dollar bills belong to those collective representations which, in the sociological tradition, provide the shared understandings which bond individuals together in society. A French commentator even remarked that "an emblematic power emanates from [the current $1 bill] and transforms it into a potent political symbol" (Goux 115–16). In a similar vein, Brian Burrell characterized the current $1 bill as at one and the same time the most familiar denomination of paper currency and "the most enigmatic of all American denominations" (181). Other commentators have gone even further, reading it as evidence of a Masonic conspiracy (Griffin). Still others connect it to big government, which undoubtedly began with the Roosevelt administration; or else to its dominance of international finance and export trading and, as well, to the preeminence of U.S. might in the global arena.

The dollar may be a sign of power both abroad and at home, but it also connects to the world of recognizable and reliable items, and, by extension, to the world of familiar things and popular culture. There are a whole set of practices associated with it which define what is culturally distinctive about it—like using it as game money, on greeting cards, or on personalized bills. Or else, referring to it in terms which have or have almost made it into standard English—terms like "greenback," "folding green," "buck" (which enshrines the fact that once deerskin went for around a dollar), "dough" (which means money because everyone "kneads" it), "grand" (meaning a thousand), and a host of other terms (Goodwin 119–20). Hip-hop has likewise valorized money throughout its existence, from Jimmy Spicer's "Money (Dollar Bill Y'all)" in 1981 to Puff Daddy's "It's All About the Benjamins" in 1997, or by using "c.r.e.a.m." ("Cash Rules Everything Around Me") as a term for money.

Also to the world of familiar things and popular culture belong the little posters one used to see in food stores, diners, gas stations, and many other establishments throughout the U.S., near the cash register, which read, "In

God We Trust, All Others Pay Cash." These posters, which seem to have disappeared with the widespread use of credit and debit cards, are a good example of the inversion of established hierarchies, when low becomes high, and high becomes low. The inversion is only temporary, though, and it does not therefore do away with Americans' "contractual relationship" with the state. That relationship, as is suggested by the phrase "In God We Trust," is legitimized by an authority beyond the state. To change these modest pieces of cotton fabric may thus be un-American. As a friend of mine remembered from watching a PBS documentary on currency about fifteen to twenty-five years ago, the United States was "pissing off European nations by refusing to change its currency." The problem was that the bills had been around so long that they were easy targets for counterfeiters. As this friend recalled, the American response was to the effect that, " 'This is the dollar,' as if one had been asked to change the teachings of Jesus because of religious counterfeits" (McNamara). Essentially, the teachings of the dollar—encoded in the verbal and visual images on the currency—serve to manufacture consent and a sense of inclusion among the American people. But as Eric Helleiner contends, the importance of the symbolic role of currencies as badges of national identity may be diminishing. There are many reasons for this, including the increasing number of everyday monetary transactions that do not involve a form of money with nationalist imagery on it. Another reason is that long-standing economic and fiscal national borders face probable dissolution, as is suggested, for example, by the introduction of the euro. But Americans are still "kindly separated" (as Jefferson would say) from the euro by an ocean, and thus the greenback remains an especially resonant American icon. To my knowledge, it is also the only currency to ever have become the subject of paintings, from John Haberle's *trompe l'oeuil* paintings of the 1890s to Andy Warhol's *Dollar-Signs* (1981), which these days sell for $50,000 apiece (Shell).

WORKS CITED AND RECOMMENDED

Anderson, Benedict. *Imagined Communities: Reflections on the Origin and Spread of Nationalism*. 1983. London: Verso Books, 1991.

Benjamin, Walter. "Capitalism as Religion." Trans. Rodney Livingstone. *Walter Benjamin: Selected Writings. Vol. 1, 1913–1926*. Ed. Marcus Bullock and Michael W. Jennings. Cambridge, MA: Belknap P–Harvard UP, 1996. 288–91.

Bureau of Engraving and Printing. "Money Facts." 15 Aug. 2001 <http://www.bep.treas.gov/>.

Burrell, Brian. *The Words We Live By: The Creeds, Mottoes, and Pledges that Have Shaped America*. New York: Free P, 1997.

Doty, Richard. *America's Money, America's Story*. Iola, WI: Krause Publications, 1998.

Emerson, Ralph Waldo. "Nature." *The Heath Anthology of American Literature*. Ed. Paul Lauter et al. Vol. 1. Lexington, MA: Heath, 1990. 1471–98.

Gilbert, Emily. "'Ornamenting the Façade of Hell': Iconographies of Nineteenth-Century Canadian Paper Money." *Environment and Planning D: Society and Space* 16 (1998): 57–80.

Goodwin, Jason. *Greenback: The Almighty Dollar and the Invention of America.* New York: Henry Holt & Co., 2003.

Goux, Jean-Joseph. "Cash, Check, or Charge?" *The New Economic Criticism: Studies at the Intersection of Literature and Economics.* Ed. Martha Woodmansee and Mark Osteen. New York: Routledge, 1999. 114–27.

Griffin, Des. *Descent into Slavery?* South Pasadena, CA: Emissary Publications, 1976, 1981.

———. *The Missing Dimension in World Affairs.* South Pasadena, CA: Emissary Publications, 1976.

Helleiner, Eric. "National Currencies and National Identities." *American Behavioral Scientist* 41.10 (1998): 1409–36.

Hobsbawm, Eric. "Mass-Producing Traditions: Europe, 1870–1914." *The Invention of Tradition.* Ed. Eric Hobsbawm and Terence Ranger. Cambridge: Cambridge UP, 1983. 263–307.

Irving, Washington. "The Creole Village." *Wolfert's Roost.* Ed. Roberta Rosenberg. *The Complete Works of Washington Irving.* Vol. 27. Boston: Twayne, 1979. 23–27.

Lott, Davis Newton. *The Presidents Speak: The Inaugural Addresses of the American President, from Washington to Clinton.* New York: Henry Holt, 1994.

[Madison, James] Publius. "To the People of the State of New York." *The Federalist* No. 10 (22 November 1787). *The Heath Anthology of American Literature.* Ed. Paul Lauter et al. Vol. 1. Lexington, MA: Heath, 1990. 1013–18.

McNamara, Kevin R. Email message to this author. 10 May 2002.

Newman, Eric P. *The Early Paper Money of America.* 4th ed. Iola, WI: Krause Publications, 1997.

Poe, Edgar Allan. "The Gold-Bug." *Poetry and Tales.* New York: Library of America, 1984. 560–96; originally published in Edgar Allan Poe, *Tales.* New York: Wiley and Putnam, 1845.

Schlesinger, Arthur M., Jr. *The Age of Roosevelt.* Vol. 2, *The Coming of the New Deal* [1958]. Boston: Houghton Mifflin, 1988.

Shell, Marc. *Art and Money.* Chicago: U of Chicago P, 1995.

Standish, David. *The Art of Money: The History and Design of Paper Currency from Around the World.* San Francisco: Chronicle Books, 2000.

Théret, Bruno. "L'euro en ses tristes symbols. Une monnaie sans âme ni culture." *Le Monde diplomatique* (Décembre 2001): 4–5. An English version is available to subscribers at http://mondediplo.com/2001/12/.

Zelizer, Viviana A. *The Social Meaning of Money.* New York: Basic Books, 1994.

Bob Dylan

Edward P. Comentale

When Bob Dylan sang "It Ain't Me, Babe," in 1964—apparently to a blinkered lover—his fans too felt the pain of rejection. The album in which the song appears—*Another Side of Bob Dylan*—marks an important turning point in Dylan's career, the first explicit rejection of his status as prophet-poet and the first of many efforts to outwit the press, the music industry, and his own supporters. Here, Dylan the folk hero dissolves into Dylan the folk trickster, shaking off his role as spokesperson for a disenfranchised America, forcing his listeners to turn inwards, to examine their aggressive neediness for a heroic icon, and to find their own damn map to a brave new world.

Yet Dylan lets himself off too easily here, disappearing behind his own invective, and refusing to address his role in an entirely new cultural phenomenon that extends far beyond this particular song, its individual singer, or its eager listeners. Put simply, his surly chorus at once signals and dismisses the emergence of an icon who so completely disavows his iconic status and who makes that continual disavowal the basis for an even more spectacular stardom. The silence that ends the album, which is also a temporary and no doubt frustrating absence of his once assuring voice, reframes the stress of its chorus, placing a perplexing emphasis not on "me" the singer or even "you" the listener, but "it," this strange configuration of need and desire, whereby a nation at large grants nearly divine status to a rebel drifter and possible con artist. Who are you, Mister Dylan? Or, better yet, *what* are you, Mister Dylan? And why does the negation of your identity—your "me"—make us want to know you even more? And then what does this singularly frustrating push-and-pull of fanatic desire and disavowal tell us about American culture today?

No doubt, Bob Dylan "made himself up" (Shelton 83). In early interviews, he describes his hometown—Hibbing, Minnesota—as a pit, a hole, the empty center of an America from which any rock star might emerge fully-formed. The old iron mines—now barren and overgrown—serve his biography both as mythic marker of a country that fails its young and as emblem of a distinctly American facility for self-creation. Early anecdotes, too, have him posing in front of mirrors or on his Harley—James Dean–style—hips out, hair slicked back. Later on, he modeled a diverse range of musical icons: he took his voice from Guthrie, his stance was all Presley, and his kinky, wildman hair was pure Little Richard. With rising fame, he quickly learned to use the press for his own shape-shifting needs. He told reporters he was an orphan, a drifter, a hobo—he hailed anywhere from Superior, Wisconsin, to Acapulco, Mexico, to Gallup, New Mexico—he claimed that as a young boy he wanted to be a movie usher, a chorus girl, and a president (but not Harry Truman). He had a long list of pseudonyms: Elmer Johnson, Tedham Porterhouse, Bob Landy, Robert Milkwood Thomas, Big Joe's Buddy, Blind Boy Grunt, Keef Laundy, Judge Magney, Lucky Wilbury, not to mention Kunezevitch or maybe Kessenovitch; he introduced himself at a Halloween concert by saying, "I got my Dylan mask on today." As one friend claimed, "Every few weeks, Bob would become a different person with a different style." Another said, "Bob is not an ordinary human being. There are two people, the cat I know and knew here and the one who's 'on' in public" (Shelton 73, 80). Apart from any obvious musical talent, political courage, or business sense, Dylan seemed to guarantee himself at least a modicum of fame with this very public form of self-creation. The mystery, the elusiveness, the incredible self-containment of his performances captivated first an intensely exclusive New York folk scene and then conquered, with each new guise, a worldwide audience. But this was not mere careerism, for Dylan always took a keen pleasure—if not a certain political stance—with this tricksterism. In fact, throughout his career, he seems comfortable only as a put-on artist, a "surly mystic tease," poking holes in his own authenticity and the sanctimony of his fans (Kael 225). As he joked in one of the first of many anti-biographies, "I's driftin' an' learnin' new lessons / I was making my own depression / ... Hitchhiked on 61 – 51 –75 – 169 – 37 – 66 – 22 / Got jailed for suspicion of armed robbery / Got held for four hours on a murder rap / Got busted for looking like I do. / An' I never done none a them things" ("My Life").

Although Dylan may have been having a hoot, each new guise served a genuine purpose; as intimates knew, with Dylan, "It really became much more than identification. He *was* the people he identified with" (Shelton 75). His endless vaudeville act—with its ad hoc staginess, its egalitarian scope, and its sexual sweep—can be aligned with a truly captivating vision of democratic America. In every dusty, impoverished incarnation, Dylan the icon nods to the rambling, gambling migrants of the country's past, present, and future, and so—more than anything else—he becomes a multitude, a voracious humanist, as big as Guthrie, Whitman, and Lincoln himself: "away away be gone all you demons," he writes in a 1964 letter to *Broadside Magazine*, "an just let me be me / human me / wild me / gently me / all kinds of me" ("A Letter").

Here, though, we are confronted with perhaps the central contradiction of Dylan's career, and perhaps the basis of his iconic status and its apparent longevity. As icon, he is at once associated with both the American folk tradition, with its emphasis on oral transmission, rural living, real labor, and rootsy authenticity, and, on the other hand, a kind of postmodern playfulness characterized by pastiche, performativity, and self-reflective irony. For him, "folklore" is also "fakelore"; the "poet-prophet" is a "profit-poet"—a "song and dance man"—a "song-thief"—or, as one fan famously shouted, a "Judas." No doubt, Dylan found this a hard line to walk, as each turn in his career—going folk, going electric, going underground, going folk again, going Christian, going Jewish, etc.—inevitably pissed off die-hard traditionalists as well as unrepentant deconstructionists. Yet, considering the arc of that career and the honky-tonk majesty of masterpieces like "Desolation Row" and "Visions of Johanna," he knew how to make the paradox work, linking both modes through their shared emphases on anti-authoritarianism and personal liberation, as well as the promise of a more fully organic community. More specifically, then, Dylan's folk is never simply or prettily folkish, for he pushes always at the tradition's tangled, degenerate ends, as it sounds on the road, played by drifters, hobos, and other hoods, as it appears in vaudeville routines or dancehall skits, as it echoes on early radio and other commercial formats. In all, this folk is aware of itself as folk—as self-conscious struggle, as impossible hope, as a crooked performance of what may never have been and what may not ever come to pass. When pressed about his music, Dylan will typically confess that "the times cry for truth," but he quickly adds that there's a whole lot more in his music: "mystery magic, truth, and the Bible" as well (Shelton 191). As he insists, his music is never simply expressive or even reflective of some greater truth; rather, it is full of lies, evasions, gaps, and obscurities, in which the listener may or may not find himself: "Folk songs are evasive," he writes; they speak

Bob Dylan, 1965. Courtesy of the Library of Congress.

> the truth about life, and life is more or less a lie, but then again that's exactly the way we want it to be. We wouldn't be comfortable with it any other way. A folk song has over a thousand faces and you must meet them all if you want to play this stuff. A folk song might vary in meaning and it might not appear the same from one moment to the next. It depends on who's playing and who's listening. (*Chronicles* 71)

Undeniably, from the start, Dylan's folksy turn was always tinged with irony and despair. "Ballad of Hollis Brown" upends rustic idealism by depicting rural life as the scene of unemployment, starvation, and squalor; the final stanza recounts a mass murder that leaves seven people dead and concludes with the equally damning notion that somewhere else there're seven new people being born. But his folk songwriting really comes into its own when it begins to tap into the ironies inherent to the genre itself. The song "Gates of Eden" proclaims nothing more than a continual deferral of paradise; with each choric reiteration, the promise of peace draws off into the distance as the singer retreats inward. Later, on *John Wesley Harding*, his understated chords and deceptively simple lyrics recall the sustaining form even as they wreck the entire folk tradition; the album's sepia-toned allegories of outlaws and drifters carry all the weight of the western experience and yet defy any easy answers his weary listeners may seek. The haunting "Ballad of Frankie Lee and Judas Priest," for example, attracts us with the apparent simplicity of its narrative style, but, in the end, it offers not one or two, but three ridiculously reductive and mutually contradicting moral conclusions.

In his recent work, Greil Marcus offers a compelling account of Dylan's folk music and its singular appeal. He emphasizes Dylan's uncanny ability to tap into an "old, weird America," to mine "certain bedrock strains of American cultural language." Dylan's songs serve as maps to an "undiscovered country" at once familiar and strange, an America that is both undeniably present yet unbearably imaginary; they point towards another version of America that is at once irretrievably lost and yet about to be born, an America that is perhaps as inauthentic as the ordinary America, yet one that follows through on its populist premises (Marcus xix–xxii). Marcus's claim—with his emphasis on the good ol' used-to-be and a god-willin' about-to-be—perhaps provides the key to Dylan's strange iconicity; as one friend from Dylan's early Minneapolis days reported, Dylan's scene is always elsewhere. "Both of us were on the edges of the scene, here, accepted but outside because of some need or difference of our own. I guess that's the real basis of our friendship then, a feeling that there was more, something else, somewhere else" (Shelton 80). As an icon, Dylan always speaks with two tongues, playing authenticity off of kitsch, presence against pose. In this, his show is all about deferral—he works in alibis, never where he pretends to be—"it," the real deal, is always truly elsewhere, just beyond the horizon. Thus, a certain emptiness, a certain mystery—perhaps like the black hole of Hibbing—lies at the center of each masked and anonymous performance, each interview, and unfinished autobiography. This emptiness is what draws the listener, demanding to be filled or fleshed out by the fan—each image is at once overdetermined and underdetermined, grounded by tangible details and yet open enough to encompass a multitude of individual desires. Frank Kermode and Stephen Spender offer a precise account of this trait:

> A preference for mystery, opacity, a sort of emptiness in his texts, a passivity about meaning, is no doubt a deep temperamental trait.... The listener provides the response, brings his own meanings; he is offered no message, only mystery.

> Dylan says the audience reaction "doesn't matter", but also that he welcomes "with open arms" people who analyse his songs. (157–58)

Pete Hammill concurs, stressing that this mystery works towards the establishment of a public:

> [B]y leaving things out, he allows us the grand privilege of creating along with him. His song becomes our song because we live in those spaces. If we listen, if we work at it, we fill up that mystery, we expand and inhabit the work of art. It is the most democratic form of creation. (Shelton 373)

But this mystery—its pliability, as the site of multiple identifications—lies at the heart of every icon. Again, Dylan's uniqueness—as a rebel icon, as a late-twentieth-century American icon—rests on an active self-negation, on his dynamic claim that the truth exists, but only elsewhere, in the beyond, with the next incarnation. It is this uncanny ability to disavow and re-create the self at will, to discard and recycle the most sacred traditions, to break the contract and yet sign another one in good faith, that seems typically Dylan and typically postmodern American. He gives his late-twentieth-century listener the distinctly cynical pleasure of holding out hope as all turns to shit in his hands—each sham or degradation also implies the possibility of authenticity, if not the possibility of a better tomorrow. In the end, "Desolation Row" is at once the most desolate street in America and the hippest place on earth. Its singular abjection—a circus-full of frauds, derelicts, and deviants—ultimately signals the possibility of a true and lush originality, not to mention human vitality and genuine community.

And yet, if this is an "old, weird America," it is also a commodified America. In fact, an object that allures by way of its inherent emptiness—serving as receptacle for a multiplicity of unrealized hopes and dreams—is nothing more than a commodity. Dylan, in his continual role-playing and self-revision—ceaselessly updating his image, his songs, his biography, his precursors, his heirs—is always also a monstrous commodity, generating capital for decades, leading on old fans, capturing new ones, synergistically selling music, books, movies, guitars, Stetson hats, sunglasses, boots, political causes, presidents, ladies' underwear, etc. His continual disavowal of his own labeling—personal, political, commercial, or otherwise—is at once a real gesture of protest against market appropriation as well as the central mechanism by which the marketplace extends itself. Indeed, Dylan's jittery dance with the commodified versions of himself is a spectacle in its own right. After 1965, when superstardom became undeniable, his work grew preoccupied with his own increasingly thing-like status, and the songs register a dizzying range of emotions from humor, irony, and anger to downright confusion and fear. "I don't want to give the impression of being a star," he stated that year, "because I don't think of myself as one. . . . I've seen all these crazes come and go, and I don't think I'm more than a craze. In a couple years time, I shall be

Albert Einstein

Anthony O'Keeffe

ALBERT EINSTEIN—ICONIC PROBLEM

The difficulty that comes with investigating Einstein's iconic status is so simple that it can be understood by invoking two short and unremarkable words: *an* and *the*. The first of those words can be shared by any number of people: James Dean is an icon of male American sexuality—as is Clark Gable, and the young Marlon Brando, and Tom Cruise, and... Eleanor Roosevelt is an icon of female American social activism—as is Susan B. Anthony, and Rosa Parks, and Gloria Steinem, and.... *An* carries with it the implication of the list. Einstein is, of course and differently, *the* icon of twentieth-century science—global and American. And in that short but decisive *the* the depth of the problem is made clear. Depth is itself the problem.

ALBERT EINSTEIN—SPECTRUM PROBLEM, MOBIUS SOLUTION

Reading Einstein's *Autobiographical Notes*, one cannot but be charmed by a passage such as this: "There were altogether only two examinations; aside from these, one could just about do as one pleased. This was especially the case if one had a friend, as I did, who attended the lectures regularly and who worked over their content conscientiously" (31). Reading further, one cannot but be charmed—differently—by a passage such as this: "Since we know from the special theory of relativity that the (inertial) mass equals the energy, we shall have to put on the right-hand side the tensor of energy density—more precisely, of the entire energy density that does not belong to the pure gravitational field. In this way one arrives at the field equation: $Rik - 1/2 gik\ R = -kTik$" (71).

Let these passages stand, for the moment, as ends of a wide spectrum, reminding us of two fundamentals of Einstein's iconic status: so human a person; so inconceivable a genius. The width of that spectrum might make any such figure seem too dauntingly, too mysteriously different to be approached or understood. But imagine that spectrum as printed on a discrete length of paper. Give it a twist—Einstein's wanderer's life can always provide one.

> If relativity is proved right the Germans will call me a German, the Swiss will call me a Swiss citizen, and the French will call me a citizen of the world. If relativity is proved wrong, the French will call me a Swiss, the Swiss will call me a German, and the Germans will call me a Jew.

Join the ends together (space does, after all, turn out to be curved). Now our spectrum is a Mobius strip; it has achieved the unity of a single surface. This playful way—scientific, mathematical—of imaging Einstein brings us back to the wholeness, the "integrity," of our icon's human self. That continuity constitutes a large part of his power as icon.

EVERY SCHOOLBOY KNOWS

Analytical commentary on the nature of Einstein's iconic status is always more a matter of reminding than of discovery. His enduring public image is tidily expressed by this link on the Web site of the Historical Society of Princeton: "Albert Einstein: Scientist, Humanitarian, Cultural Icon." As these categories imply, he was a genius whose intellectual powers, so enormous and original, did not make him coldly dismissive, analytically inhuman—qualities the popular stereotype typically applies to the scientist.

That image can be explored in more detail through the Web exhibit *Albert Einstein: Image and Impact* created by the American Institute of Physics; there such sections as "The Great Works—1905," "World Fame," and "Public Concerns" (just three of the eight available) can be accessed by clicking on a particular photographic image of Einstein. These AIP links remind us of another fundamental source of Einstein's iconic power—his appealing visual distinctiveness. The *Image and Impact* exhibit is laced with photographs that—tellingly—are available for purchase. And there would be no counting the cultural appropriations (popular and serious, consumerist and political, religious and iconoclastic) of his almost universally familiar image: the hair that seems alive with the charge of his brilliant ideas; the dark, alert, and steadfast eyes; his expression, most typically rendering him as grave sage (the striking Philippe Halsman photo on the cover of *Autobiographical Notes*) or playful mocker of his own image and reputation (his tongue stuck out in mockery of a group of press photographers). It has been used to sell everything from beer to baseball caps, from books to nesting dolls, from computers to hair gel.

And Einstein is as textually famous as he is visually, his image often being accompanied by one of his vivid aphorisms: "Imagination is more important than knowledge"; "I am convinced that God does not play dice"; "Science without religion is lame. Religion without science is blind"; "The important thing is not to stop questioning"; "One cannot simultaneously prepare for and prevent war."

Still, for all of his humanitarian concerns, and his lively anti-authoritarianism in matters both social and scientific, Einstein's iconic status naturally began with—and continues to be guaranteed by—his work in science. In *Einstein and the Rise of Big Science*, cosmologist Peter Coles deftly sketches the story of the two Royal Astronomical Society expeditions—one to Principe, off the coast of West Africa, one to Sobral, in northern Brazil—that would observe the total solar eclipse of May 29, 1919. Einstein's theory of general relativity predicted that the sun's enormous gravitational force would "bend" light rays passing close to it, deflecting by a measurable amount the known position of stars close to the sun's circumference. A day after the expedition teams presented their data, to a joint meeting of the Royal Astronomical Society and the Royal Society of London, confirmation of Einstein's correctness—and thereby of his genius—struck the world full force with this *London Times* headline of November 7, 1919: "REVOLUTION IN SCIENCE. NEW THEORY OF THE UNIVERSE" (Coles 57). Even though few people could follow the mathematics of Einstein's ideas (or even hold them in mind in familiar conceptual ways), all could manage a sense of the genius it must have taken to create them.

Yet the depth of Einstein's genius does not alone account for the permanence of his fame, and the growth and persistence of his stature. His genius was also, as luck would have it, timely; wedded to it was the exponential growth of science in the twentieth century. In *The Search for Solutions*, historian Horace Freeland Judson argues that science "is the most interesting, difficult, pitiless, exciting, and beautiful pursuit that we have yet found. Science is our century's art" (12). And he dates the beginning of its rise to such status precisely: June 30, 1905—the day Einstein submitted his "On the Electrodynamics of Moving Bodies" to the *Annalen der Physik*. In the realm of high theory, Einstein marks the defining step forward in twentieth-century science. After that, the historical march of theory and technology will carry him forward with it.

It is crucial, of course, that Einstein worked within physics, the hardest of the so-called "hard sciences." Physics typically combined deep theoretical thinking with experimental procedure under controlled conditions, to yield the most precise, wide-ranging, and

Albert Einstein, 1931. Courtesy of the Library of Congress.

predictive truths. Within that science, Einstein worked in an unusually pure way: deriving his brilliantly revolutionary insights through "thought experiments," only pursuing mathematical proofs after. And then, of course, as the century unfolded, physics added to its image as the very emblem of pure thought (relativity, quantum theory) its new status as the source of raw inconceivable power (nuclear weapons).

The historical arc defined by the years from Hitler's rise to power (January 1933) to the development of the first atom bomb (August 1945) marks the period in which Einstein became a specifically *American* icon. On October 17, 1933, Einstein arrived in Princeton, taking up his appointment as the first faculty member of Abraham Flexner's new Institute for Advanced Study. It was to Einstein's Princeton home that fellow physicists Leo Szilard and Eugene Wigner made their way in July 1939, bringing him the news that German scientists had established the possibility of splitting the uranium-235 atom—making the creation of a fission bomb feasible. On August 2, Einstein sent to President Franklin Delano Roosevelt the now-famous letter, drafted by Szilard, alerting him to the possibility that the creation of "a nuclear chain reaction in a large mass of uranium" will likely lead to the creation of "extremely powerful bombs of a new type." Einstein's paradigm-smashing theoretical work in physics was already behind him; nor would he, as the Manhattan Project unfolded, become directly involved in its work—given his avowedly leftist politics, the U.S. government would not grant him security clearance to do so. But this letter alone linked him inextricably to the history of nuclear weapons development—and thereby to the growth of his adopted home country as the century's dominant superpower.

Einstein's American life played directly into several of the important narratives by which the country has traditionally hoped to define its best self. His arrival proved America to be—as its Statue of Liberty advertised—a haven for the persecuted and dispossessed. Einstein's image as a revolutionary genius who had worked out his astonishingly deep ideas on his own fit nicely with the American icon of the lonely, courageous hero—popularly reproduced and celebrated in any number of movie westerns. Living now in a country marked so enduringly by frontier awareness, he had proved his credentials at the "frontiers" of science. And having spoken forcefully and repeatedly as a pacifist, his embrace of necessary violent resistance to the march of Nazi power revealed in him the kind of pragmatism so central to America's self-image.

Einstein's towering intellectual achievements connected him publicly and indissolubly with the history of thought and the unfolding of technological power that define the twentieth century. In physics, he proceeded in the purest of deductive ways toward discoveries of universal importance. As befits ideas so fundamental and wide-reaching, his most famous formula, $E = mc^2$, provided both the universal relation of energy and matter *and* a step toward dangerous enormities of human power. And as befits his humanitarian nature, he worked relentlessly against the technological and political misuses of what his pure theories had handed an unthinking and violence-prone humankind. Iconic as scientific genius, iconic—because iconoclastic—as social thinker, iconic as visual image that can represent both playfulness and almost tragic wisdom, Einstein remains a lively—perhaps even dominating—presence fifty years after his death.

CLOSER ENCOUNTERS

Near the end of Steven Spielberg's *Close Encounters of the Third Kind*, those human beings who had been taken aboard the enormous alien spaceship over several decades are returned to earth; they emerge un-aged by their years of faster-than-light-speed travel, prompting one of the awestruck scientists to comment, to a colleague, "Einstein was right!" The answer he receives—"Einstein was probably one of *them*"—provides a particularly well-placed pop-culture confirmation of Einstein's iconic status, grounded as it is in his seemingly otherworldly intelligence.

Since his first appearance in the *New York Times* yearly index, Einstein was never absent from it a single year in his life (Coles 57). I write this essay during the official World Year of Physics, an initiative of the United Nations—whose posters and Web site feature as their presiding eminence Einstein, of course (2005 being the hundredth anniversary of the year in which his four papers that reinvented physics appeared in the *Annalen der Physik*). Though dead fifty years, Einstein remains, in the words of the *New York Times* article "Brace Yourself! Here Comes Einstein's Year," "still the scientist most likely to have his picture on the front page of the newspaper." And he remains an enduring icon of anti-violence social wisdom, and *the* enduring icon of scientific genius, possessing a mind so capacious and freshly far-seeing as to appear almost alien to us. In an anticipatory "echo" of the comment in *Close Encounters*, the *Washington Post*, upon his death, printed an editorial cartoon by Herb Block that shows Earth, floating amid the universe's vastness, sporting an enormous plaque that reads "ALBERT EINSTEIN LIVED HERE." It seemed only fair to advertise to any alien intelligences inclined to notice us, and even to the universe at large, a thinker whose ideas were so vast that only the universe itself could confirm them (as in the 1919 expeditions designed to observe the bending of light).

Inevitably—and perhaps soon—the Einstein that lingers so forcefully as legend and image will be returned to more human, and thereby richer, status. As the Hebrew University of Jerusalem and Princeton University Press work through the enormous task of publishing *The Collected Papers of Albert Einstein* (projected to run more than twenty-five volumes), we will be forced to encounter the more complex figure briefly presented in Alan Lightman's essay "The Contradictory Genius." The Einstein that Lightman allows us to glimpse is more deeply shadowed by the personal than any public image can be: a young man who can strenuously defy his parents and marry Mileva Maric, only to prove "a remote and insensitive husband and father"; a genius whose "stubborn self-confidence and willingness to strike out completely on his own" lead him to profoundly revolutionary insights into space, time, and matter, but then isolate him when he turns his back upon quantum physics to pursue—unsuccessfully—his own stubborn search for a non-quantum unified theory; an enormous public presence who remains, at heart, "above all else a loner" (97, 108, 87).

All of which is not to say that Einstein will lose his iconic status—only that it will be transformed. His extraordinary achievements may come to seem even more brilliant as we gain—especially through personal letters—a more sharply detailed sense of the realities of the very human life within which they were so laboriously pursued. In contradiction of the clever line in *Close Encounters*, our sense of Einstein's greatness—and perhaps the certain foundation of our continued awed response to him—is that he was very much one of us.

WORKS CITED AND RECOMMENDED

Albert Einstein: Image and Impact. American Institute of Physics. Nov. 2004 <http://www.aip.org/history/einstein/>.

Albert Einstein: Scientist, Humanitarian, Cultural Icon. Historical Society of Princeton. Mar. 1995 <http://www.princetonhistory.org/einsteinindex.shml>.

Coles, Peter. *Einstein and the Birth of Big Science*. Cambridge: Icon Books, 2000.

Einstein, Albert. *Autobiographical Notes*. Ed. Paul Arthur Schilpp. La Salle, IL: Open Court Publishing, 1979.

Judson, Horace Freeland. *The Search for Solutions*. Baltimore: Johns Hopkins UP, 1987.

Lightman, Alan. "The Contradictory Genius." *A Sense of the Mysterious: Science and the Human Spirit*. New York: Pantheon Books, 2005.

Overbye, Dennis. "Brace Yourself! Here Comes Einstein's Year." *New York Times* 25 Jan. 2005: D1+.

Emergency Room

Robert Wolosin

One of the most successful television shows of its genre, NBC's *ER* was nominated for twenty Emmy awards in its inaugural season. Ever since, its weekly episodes have entertained millions of viewers with a good cast and slick production values.

ER portrays a fast-paced emergency room life. Scenes cut between multiple story lines, creating a sense of breathlessness. The show prides itself on its "realism." Writer/director Jack Orman assures us that emergency physicians review the show "to make sure that everything is accurate" (Barrett). Realism is suggested by sounds such as beeps, loud shouts, screams, sirens, and simultaneous speech. A chaotic, impersonal ambience is conveyed visually by choppy camera work, quick scene changes, and frequent, brief shots of unidentified personnel between the camera and main actors. We see emergency medical technicians wheel patients in on gurneys; we glimpse cops, orderlies, nurses, doctors. The physical trappings of real emergency rooms, including florescent lights, pneumatic double doors, charts, electronic equipment, oxygen masks, and defibrillators, abound.

Nonetheless, this is fiction, not reality. From my own visits to real hospital emergency rooms, I know that they differ markedly from their TV counterparts; real ERs are relatively quiet, long waits are common, and patients without life-threatening problems constitute much of the caseload. In a real ER, patients are more likely to get stitches than CPR. These "reality checks" have been reinforced through a course I teach as a social psychologist. Preparing for medical careers, my undergraduate students observe local emergency rooms and write about their experiences. They say, for instance, that when a "real emergency" arises, the scene reflects an efficient, focused team effort.

As part of an ongoing dialogue between contemporary medicine and American culture, television shows, movies, comic books, jokes, and stories portray emergency rooms in particular ways. Such portrayals are digested and compressed, ultimately to coalesce into a mental representation, or icon. This imagined place represents ideas, values, and feelings about ourselves vis-à-vis modern medical care.

EMERGENCY ROOM

The positive image of the ER in popular media today is a recent development, and scarcely resembles its history. The idea of organized emergency medical care in the United States goes back to at least 1807, when Philadelphia's Pennsylvania Hospital was urged to hire a salaried "house surgeon" to treat emergency cases. In the mid-1800s, Boston's Massachusetts General Hospital had "admitting physicians" who attended emergencies; and New York City's Mount Sinai Hospital treated, emergently, wounded Union Army soldiers as well as victims of riots, fires, and accidents. The earliest reference to an actual emergency room appears to have been in Mount Sinai's Annual Report for 1888, "when the House Staff treated 301 emergency cases. This tiny ER was often referred to as 'the accident closet,' and was located in the entrance hall" (Aufses and Niss 200).

In the mid-twentieth century, several factors increased the use of hospital emergency rooms dramatically. The burgeoning population dispersed to suburbs; and general practitioners, whose numbers were already dwindling, ceased making house calls; instead, they sent patients in dire need directly to an ER. Insurance policies indemnified hospital-based services to a far greater extent than services obtained in offices. Thus, in addition to its continuous availability, patients had a financial incentive to seek ER care. It did not seem to matter that the physicians who staffed the ERs of the day inhabited the lowest rungs of the medical ladder. In teaching hospitals, ER duty was often relegated to interns and residents, and in non-teaching hospitals, the situation was even worse: "Foreign medical graduates, impaired physicians, and those disenchanted with their own practice" worked ERs (Society of Academic Emergency Medicine).

To deal with the personnel problem, a new medical specialty with its own training programs was created, and in 1979 emergency medicine became a full-fledged medical specialty. ERs now employ Board-certified emergency physicians.

From this recent establishment, emergency medicine has risen through media portrayals to dominate the public image of medical care, with its center in a drama-packed ER. I turn now to the prominent features of the iconic ER.

SPEED

Portrayals of ERs constantly emphasize the race against time. In the desperate attempt to save a life, seconds count. We know the drill: rushing through city streets with lights flashing and siren blaring, an ambulance careens toward the scene of a critically injured person. Cars pull over; curious bystanders gawk, wondering where it is going, what the matter is, who is in need. At the accident scene, the crew quickly assesses the patient, immediately applies first aid, gets the patient into the ambulance, and whisks him off to the nearest ER. The ambulance arrives at the hospital's ER bay and the breathless crew bursts through the doors and hustles the patient—now strapped to a gurney and connected to IVs—to a trauma room. Rushing in, the crew barks out the patient's status to the trauma team. Intravenous lines sway, the patient

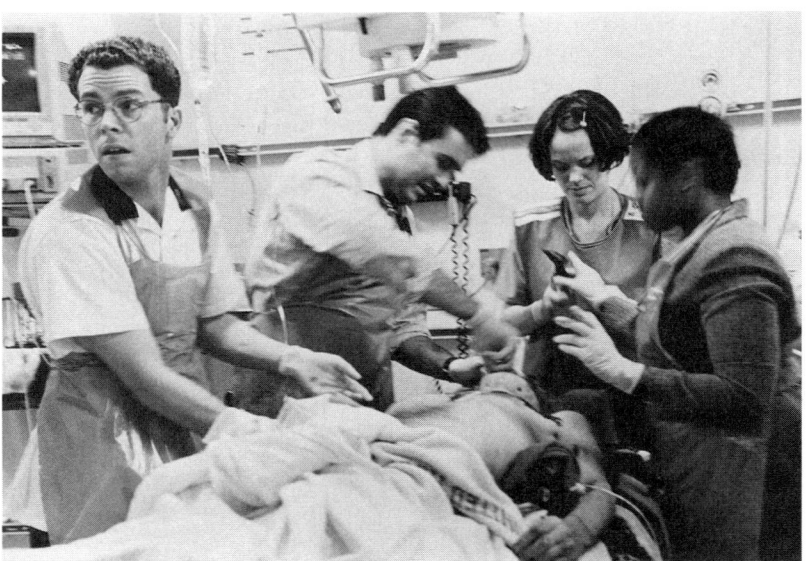

Doctors and nurses fight to save a life in an Illinois emergency room. Courtesy of Corbis.

is disrobed; the trauma team quickly assesses what must be done and goes to work. Packages of medical supplies are ripped open; an oxygen mask is applied, monitors are hooked up: Will the patient's life be saved?

CPR: THE HEART OF THE MATTER

At some point during treatment, the patient may require cardiopulmonary resuscitation (CPR). CPR is a staple of TV emergency room shows. According to one source, over 60 percent of episodes of the TV shows *Chicago Hope*, *ER*, and *Rescue 911* aired in 1994–1995 featured CPR (Diem, Lantos, and Tulsky). Unlike CPR in the real world, most of these attempts succeeded without serious complications. Full CPR includes chest compressions and inflating the patient's lungs. But cardiac defibrillation through electrical shock is CPR's most vivid manifestation. The dramatic application of paddles to the patient's bare chest, the cry of "Clear," and the sudden, convulsive jump of the patient's body at the moment of shock give CPR a visual and emotional impact other medical inventions can't approach.

CPR is powerful because it proclaims our willingness, nay, eagerness to defy death, to bring someone back from the Beyond; to play God. Through CPR depictions, we congratulate ourselves for marvelous technology and its skillful application. This is serious business. Like drawing up a will that directs the disposition of our property, we draft "Living Wills" and "Advance Directives" that routinely include instructions about the use of CPR, hoping to specify how this most extreme of medical interventions is applied to our own bodies.

CPR inhabits an ambiguous moral ground and evokes ambivalence. Even when obviously futile, CPR is considered a symbolic ritual, a sometimes literal "goodbye kiss" valued because "everything possible" was done to save the patient. But CPR has a dark side: a work by the UK cartoonist "KES" highlights the ultimately horrifying connotations of CPR's ability to cheat death. It shows CPR being applied to a Frankenstein-type monster in a subterranean laboratory. The ancient and the modern are mixed: a torch lights the winding staircase, while machines with dials and gauges line the walls. Three medical personnel are present: a doctor at the controls of the shock apparatus, a paramedic holding the paddles, and an anxious bystander wearing a surgeon's smock. The monster lies face up on a table, an oafish companion at his side. The caption reads, "Clear!" (Smith).

MIRACLES AND SALVATION

CPR is part of the conception of ERs as places where miracles occur. Severed limbs are reattached; well-being is restored to critically ill patients. Most miraculous is the saving of seriously-endangered lives. On *Rescue 911*, the word "miracle" itself was often used to describe a successful outcome of emergency treatment.

Formerly, religion was the proper venue of miracles; concern with miracles is but one modern parallel between religion and medicine. Both institutions respond to birth, decline, suffering, and death; medicine is our secular bulwark against existential facts. Like religion, medicine gives meaning to the chaotic and incomprehensible, invokes "higher powers," and takes place in specialized institutions where highly trained personnel use powerful procedures and enact elaborate rituals. We call upon physicians, like priests, for salvation. As priests mysteriously summon supernatural forces, so contemporary emergency room doctors call upon esoteric skills and recondite technology to save lives.

If doctors are the priests, nurses are the nuns. Intermediaries between patient and doctor, nurses comfort the former and obey the latter. Popular culture portrays nurses contradictorily "to evoke issues of work, death, dependence, sexuality, and womanhood." They simultaneously enact and defy traditional women's roles (Melosh 58). If TV has emphasized nurses' sexuality, it is because that aspect is most likely to resonate with male viewers' fantasies about the physical intimacy that nursing practice often involves.

ERs resemble secular temples whose specialized personnel use potent but obscure processes, hidden from public view by geographic isolation and carried out through cryptic jargon, for example, "Bag him!" or "I need some epi, stat!" Salvation imagery ("Rescue Squads," "saving a life") surrounds emergency treatment and imbues it with religious fervor. The "Jaws of Life" is an apparatus used by emergency crews to extract crash victims from mangled wreckage. If only we can keep the crash victim alive at the scene, the logic goes, we can apply further interventions aboard the ambulance and in the ER. We can, perhaps, salvage another life.

And what are we being saved from? Ourselves! A look at ERs through the lens of stories suggests that it is mankind's follies that most result in ER care. The following, billed as a "true" emergency room story, was taken from the Internet:

> A 28-year old male was brought into the ER after an attempted suicide. The man had swallowed several nitroglycerin pills and a fifth of vodka. When asked about the bruises about his head and chest, he said that they were from him ramming himself into the wall in an attempt to make the nitroglycerin explode. ("Emergency Room True Stories")

Stupidity and dumb luck excepted, such stories show us as hapless victims of our own indiscretions, many of them formerly considered sins, particularly the sins of gluttony and lust. Tales with sexual content—the more bizarre, the better—are commonplace. Ultimately, the purpose of the ER as a secular religion is to save us from paying the price of sin.

TECHNOLOGY AND SCIENCE

And what saves us? High-tech science! "The popular image of healthcare organizations is high-tech. Stopped hearts are restarted, airways are reopened, arteries are sewn, babies are rescued, and rampant infection is overcome" (Griffith and White 47).

Today, it is difficult to imagine medicine as anything other than scientifically based, but it was only in the twentieth century that medical practice became firmly established as such. The doctor's white coat—symbol of the laboratory scientist—and the trappings of the doctor's office, which included stethoscopes and other scientific gear, ultimately established medical practice as scientific in the public's mind (Blumhagen).

Doctors regard themselves as scientists. Medical students spend countless hours memorizing biological facts. One observer declared that the point of the first year of medical school is to replace the lay idea of persons and the human body with a conception grounded in science (Good 70). Perhaps catering to public hope, or fear, of this superior knowledge, television and movies emphasize medicine's scientific technology in displays of machines with meters, tubes, and CRT's. Such apparatus, recognizably "medical," but whose functions and operations are unknown to the audience, adds to the mystique of the ER as a place where Nature is trumped by Science.

HEROISM

The medical scientists who apply ER technology represent the hero; their magic words, "He's going to be fine," fix a world gone awry. As a descendant of battlefield medicine, the ER evokes images of struggle culminating in triumph. Strong, dramatic images of physicians as heroic fighters are perfect for TV action shows where doctors are the commanders of the defense amid the battleground of the ER. They fight time and grievous injury and display the combat values of bravery, perseverance, and valor in the face of overwhelming odds while the patient's life teeters on the brink.

The doctor-hero is a familiar theme of popular media; in the 1940s, movies such as *Dr. Kildare* depicted fictionalized physicians fighting to save lives, while comic books portrayed the lives of historical physicians alongside those of other heroes such as Dwight Eisenhower (Hansen). A basic premise of TV doctor shows is that the doctor-hero can command whatever resources (hospital bed, rare drug, costly procedure) are necessary to accomplish the task of restoring the patient to health or alleviating the patient's suffering (Turow).

HUDDLED MASSES: MEDICINE FOR EVERYMAN

In reality, ERs are uniquely open to their surroundings. Emergency room care is constantly available; street level entry gives necessary access to ambulances, and also offers a public portal to the hospital. For those who can't obtain hospitalization through regular admission, the ER offers an alternative "back door." Consequently, it becomes the medical care of last resort for persons who can't or won't find it elsewhere. This brings a motley array of patients, including the uninsured, homeless, or mentally ill. Some patients indeed come to the ER with a hidden agenda—they seek drugs, shelter, or companionship, rather than medical care.

These facts have been reflected in media portrayals, but rarely. The inner-city ER in the movie *Bringing Out the Dead* is old, understaffed, and overcrowded with street people. Its staff is cynical and burnt-out. It is guarded by a tough cop whose major duty is to turn away additional patients. The destitute lie on gurneys that line the corridors; fights break out. In one scene, a restrained, drug-addicted patient screams for water and flees half-naked into the night at his first opportunity. If this is not Hell, it is at least Purgatory.

The ER as a cultural icon, on the other hand, displays an idealized relationship with medical care: we want a place where someone will take care of us, no matter what or when. We want miraculous cures for everyone in need, and we want them now. In the popular conception, the ER is simultaneously a place of chaos and a restorer of order, a place of suffering and of redemption: our secular Purgatory.

WORKS CITED AND RECOMMENDED

Aufses, Arthur H., and Barbara J. Niss. *This House of Noble Deeds: The Mount Sinai Hospital, 1852–2002*. New York: NYU P, 2002.
Barrett, Amy. "Playing Doctor." *New York Times Magazine* 16 Mar. 2003: 13.

Blumhagen, Dan. "The Doctor's White Coat: The Image of the Physician in Modern America." *Annals of Internal Medicine* 91 (1979): 111–16.

Diem, Susan, John D. Lantos, and James A. Tulsky. "Cardiopulmonary Resuscitation on Television: Miracles and Misinformation." *New England Journal of Medicine* 334 (1996): 1578–82.

"Emergency Room True Stories." 4 July 2004 <http://www.tech-sol.net/humor/true4.htm>.

Good, Byron J. *Medicine, Rationality and Experience: An Anthropological Perspective*. Cambridge: Cambridge UP, 1993.

Griffith, John R., and Kenneth R. White. *The Well-Managed Healthcare Organization*. 5th ed. Chicago: Health Administration P, 2002.

Hansen, Bert. "Medical History for the Masses: How American Comic Books Celebrated Heroes of Medicine in the 1940's." *Bulletin of the History of Medicine* 78 (Spring 2004): 148–91.

Melosh, Barbara. "Nursing Illusions: Nurses in Popular Literature." *Popular Culture in America*. Ed. Paul Buhle. Minneapolis: U of Minnesota P, 1987.

Smith, Kevin. "Clear!" Cartoon. 4 July 2004 <http://www.cartoonstock.com/directory/e/emergency_ room.asp>.

Society of Academic Emergency Medicine. *The History and Future of Emergency Medicine*. 13 Mar. 2004 <www.saem.org/download/01marx.pdf.>.

Turow, Arthur. *Playing Doctor: Television, Storytelling, and Medical Power*. New York: Oxford UP, 1989.

Flea Market

Michael Prokopow

The suggestion has been made that on any given summer Sunday in the United States more people can be found at flea markets than attending church. Now while very possibly an apocryphal account, the idea of millions of women and men searching for old and new treasures is compelling. And whether located in a borrowed farmer's field, the parking lot of mammoth sports arenas, the broad and artificially bright aisles of some suburban shopping malls, or a high school gymnasium seemingly unchanged since the Cold War, the contemporary American flea market constitutes a remarkable cultural and social phenomenon (Carbone; LaFarge; Rinker). The idea of so many Americans examining the plethora of goods that mark modern consumer culture or browsing the detritus of their fellow citizens—both alive and dead—constitutes a compelling and complicated variant of the idea that the United States is the land of opportunity. Serving most obviously as places of economic exchange, flea markets also operate as sites of pilgrimage and memory, not to mention entertainment, emotional sustenance, and the occasional good investment.

But how best to assess the cultural meanings of the flea market in contemporary American society, or the kindred phenomena of the yard, rummage, and garage sale? What roles do these loosely regulated gatherings of buyers and sellers play in North American society in terms of late capitalism and social culture? As sites of the distribution of goods (or sites of the redistribution of used or second hand goods), flea markets offer both sellers and buyers opportunities to participate in the theater of capitalism, but to do so with considerably more freedom than the familiar, and predictable, shopping conditions of late capitalism (Gregson and Crewe). Operating at both the actual and symbolic edges of the nation's gargantuan economy, flea markets not only generate billions of dollars in annual sales—with some estimates suggesting that as many as 100 million people frequent such markets annually—but they also serve a vital role in both the recirculation of used goods and the distribution of low-cost and bargain goods. And while other venues such as dollar stores, clearance centers, thrift stores, and charity shops and the like may perform similar functions and may offer similar products, the flea market constitutes a unique commercial form. Not only does it celebrate unfettered commerce, but it also affirms personal freedom and individuality. For whether it is the freedom of vendors to sell what they want or the freedom of buyers to seek out whatever pleases, the jumble and bustle of the hundreds of thousands of flea markets across the United States operate as constant reminders and confirmations of the idea and fact of America as a land of opportunity (Harmon; Rinker).

PROVENANCE

By definition, flea markets are gatherings of vendors and potential customers where the goods for sale range from the readily available to the rare to the unique. Flea markets are places where prices (at least in theory) are low, and flea markets are places where there exists a real and palpable sense of material promise; that is, there is never any way of knowing what will be found on the tables or stands that make up the market. Rather, holding true to their ancestry as gatherings of merchants selling whatever happens to be available for sale, the flea markets of contemporary America represent exercises in free enterprise at its most liberated, while also affording shoppers the chance to treasure-hunt, bargain-shop, and participate in nostalgic musing. In these ways, flea markets are different from most other arenas of commerce. They tend not to be defined by a particular type of commercial character, they do not have to cater to a specific consumer demographic, and they do not need to remake a corporate brand—to use contemporary business parlance—in order to stay current and commercially viable. If anything, the popularity and success of flea markets turn on their anomalous, quirky, and safely unpredictable character as emporia of possibilities.

And yet, despite the immense popularity and cultural importance of flea markets in American society, no formal history has been written that traces the development in the United States (or North America) of this ubiquitous commercial model. For although there have been numerous studies of early commercial activity in the early settlement period—or studies in which country and town markets were assessed as critically important in the distribution of goods—and studies about the economic transformation of the countryside in the nineteenth century where market gatherings served vital roles in community development, there has been no investigation of the American flea market as a vernacular commercial form.

Contemporary flea markets in the United States trace their evolution from the town markets of the early colonial period, where goods of all kinds, including livestock, foodstuffs, slaves, and chattels of all sorts—old and new—were offered for sale, and through the expansion of the nation to the west. And whether weekly or monthly gatherings—from the early established markets of Boston and New York to the horse auctions of the frontier west—public markets facilitated the necessary exchanges of goods, capital, and information. But more than arenas that served the economic needs of local communities, flea markets also embodied long-standing and distinctly Anglo-American ideas about the rights of property. Operating on the premise of a citizen's right to engage freely in commercial activity, the flea market is arguably a place of unencumbered exchange, marked by negotiation and largely free of state intervention. Thus, as arenas for the open exchange of goods, from new wares to the discarded possessions of the living and the dead, the flea market in the United States has been central in the growth of capitalism, community, and the idea of the nation as a land of plenitude, liberty, and material opportunity.

Taking its English name from the French phrase *marche aux puces*—quite literally a 'market of fleas' because of the old, bug-infested upholstered furniture that was offered for sale—flea markets in the United States are probably best characterized as vernacular and idiosyncratic adaptations of old commercial forms. As Albert LaFarge has suggested, "today's American flea market is the modern incarnation of a feature common to civilized societies throughout history—wherever there is a high concentration of people, there will be market days when they assemble for the exchange of goods and services" (LaFarge ix–x). Acknowledging that the contemporary flea market in the United States can trace its lineage back to the *agora* of ancient Greece, the forum of ancient Rome, and the market days of feudal Europe and Asia, LaFarge makes the important point that the phenomenon of merchants gathering in central locations in order to do business is a part of economic history found the world over. Marked by the sale of new and used goods, flea markets operate as sites of unfettered *laissez-faire* capitalism. For while transactions may well include the writing of a receipt, and while detailed records of inventory and business flow may or may not be kept, most flea market business turns on the counting out of crumpled dollar bills dug from a pocket or purse or the discrete transfer of crisp, newly-minted twenty-dollar bills recently dispensed from some ATM (Harmon).

In this way, the modern American flea market, with its eclectic mix of goods, owes a debt both to the work of waste pickers or itinerant traders and the small capitalists of the early modern world. In the case of the rag and bone traders of medieval and early modern Europe, this denigrated laboring class provided a vital service to their society's economic well-being by removing waste of all kinds from urban areas (Burrows). Marked by stamina and business sense, the highly organized and stratified world of scavenging constituted a profession dedicated to the recycling of waste products. In fact, the instantly familiar and catch-all term "junk dealer"—a notion closely allied to the rag and bone trade—comes from the word *juncus*, the name of a species of bulrush used in the making of cordage and rope and for which there existed a brisk second-hand trade throughout the seventeenth, eighteenth, and nineteenth centuries (Dolan; Kline; Richardson).

If, however, contemporary flea markets are places defined by the more or less random assortment of used and new goods that are for sale, flea markets are also defined by the personal contact that accompanies the smallest and most insignificant of transactions. In the age of corporate capitalism and e-commerce, the haggling and often good-humored negotiations that result in a sale are an increasingly rare throwback to an earlier, perhaps even simpler, time. The conversations that take place about price are modern versions of the negotiations that were standard in the past, whether between a vendor and customer at a market or a peddler and backwoods farmer at the door of a log cabin. And while not wanting to put too romantic a spin on the idea of the face-to-face negotiations over price, what is now identified as "direct selling" or contact between the vendor and the customer does recall the type of vital personal relationships that marked the economic development of the nation. Thus, the twenty-first-century flea market represents both an anachronistic commercial model—a holdout of sorts against the rationalized, usually impersonal, business practices that define contemporary and global commerce—and one that clearly resonates with the buying public because of its humanity.

GO QUEST, YOUNG MAN

Human history has always been marked by famous quests, spiritual and otherwise. From Augustine's search for the City of God to Pizarro's hunt for the City of Gold, human beings have projected their longing—their desire—for enlightenment, discovery, and reward onto the unknown but experiential world. In seeking both the seen and unseen, the disembodied and the tangible, the quest has existed as a type of projection of the physically and metaphysically possible, of a mystery solved and the world as it might be. Such narratives of questing appear across cultures, social classes, and experiences. One thinks, for example, of the search for the Holy Grail, perhaps the most famous of all material quests. Vastly important in religious terms, the idea of the grail has come to embody very broadly the quest for an elusive, cherished, even coveted thing. For the popularization—the secularization—of the idea of the grail speaks to the capacity of the known but absent object to create a powerful longing that arguably requires the things to remain unfound. Arguably, it is the search that matters, and not necessarily the discovery. It is as if the process of the hunt is sufficient reward (Belk; Muensterberger). And while the discovery of a desired thing may well bring joy, the hunt is for many people reward in itself.

In this light, it is obvious that flea markets in the United States do more than provide fertile ground for the frugal, the curious, and the acquisitive. As depositories of tangible goods, most of which are used, flea markets cater to social, personal, aesthetic, and psychological needs. There is, to be sure, a sense of community and camaraderie when wandering around a flea market, as one sees countless other fellow travelers. Likewise, in a consumer culture so preoccupied with the latest styles and trends and instantly familiar products, the chance encounter with the never-before-seen or long-forgotten thing is a powerful experience. As Harry L. Rinker has suggested, the flea market is a place where one can mine older used objects (Rinker ix). Accordingly,

FLEA MARKET

America's fascination with flea markets turns on the shared premise that a trip to the flea market will yield some type of find, physical and emotional.

Arguably, the ongoing search for meaning in life by way of the past drives many Americans to the flea market. Now this is not to deny that many North Americans seem to derive great pleasure from the abundance of the consumer economy and their access to a remarkable and ever-changing world of new consumer products. On the contrary, shopping is obviously one of the central national pastimes. However, it is striking that in the face of a consumer culture that constantly promotes the new and improved, millions of people annually turn to flea markets for an alternative consumer experience, namely shopping for history. For many people flea markets provide an anti-consumerism consumer experience. Beyond the aesthetic and status values of antiques and collectibles that experts suggest are the staples of most flea markets (Rinker iv–viii), lurks the value of the past. In a nation that prides itself on consumer choice and innovation, people paradoxically pursue old objects, things that are no longer current in style or function, the two pillars of contemporary product design and marketing. Indeed, old objects, whether labeled antiques or memorabilia or whatever, defy notions of progress and change.

In this light, the broad appeal of the American flea market lies in its function as a cross between the museum and the midway. Here, the experience of going to the flea market is never solely about acquisition but, rather, about the process of looking, discovering, reflecting, mourning, remembering, and perhaps possessing. It is, in short, about a knowable and needed encounter with the past and a past that may well be unknown, inchoate, or plain forgotten. As such, the encounter with history or what remains of history provides both amusement and diversion in light of the often-mindless consumerism of North American society and a world of cheap products. But more, the flea market encounters with the past also offer succor and the opportunity to acknowledge forbears, familial and national. Indeed, the flea market is in large part about a willing and wanted encounter with history; and consistently flea market devotees acknowledge that it is the lure of the unimaginable discovery—an object of reckoning—that is moving. The significance of the discovery lies not necessarily in its monetary value (although there may well be rarified market demand for the thing), but rather in the message the thing delivers, the memory it evokes or the associations it conjures. For such people—and clearly their numbers are immense in the United States—the flea market is the one place where the present can mingle with the tangible which may well teach lessons about life. Absent glass cases, absent security guards, and usually absent prohibitions on the handling of the merchandise, flea markets take the principles of shopping and combine them with all the emotional and sensory opportunities of museums. At the flea market—any flea market—the visitor-traveler-purchaser is at once pilgrim and patron, and all the while possessing the opportunity not only to look and to find, but also to behold, cherish, and possibly claim the object of affection.

Thus, in operating simultaneously as temporary morgues of the discards of contemporary society and as sites of economic exchange, flea markets occupy the unusual position of manager to consumer society because they facilitate the redistribution of used goods. Things unwanted by one individual may well strike the fancy of another. One person's obsolete object may be the most splendid thing for someone else. For while it has been said many times that "one's man trash is another man's treasure," and while there is significant truth in this notion, it is both the complex psychology of the relationships human beings establish with things and the mandatory disposable nature of consumer capitalism that combine to make flea markets more than simply places where old things end up (Csikszentmihalyi and Rochberg-Halton). Rather, in thought-provoking ways, flea markets serve American society as sites of reckoning and reclamation, both material and spiritual. While antique stores and consignment shops function in similar ways as depots for the recirculation of older things, arguably the levels of aesthetic discernment are considerably higher in such establishments; that is, not every object that is disowned or about to be disowned would be eligible for sale. In contrast, flea markets—in ways similar to thrift stores and charity shops—operate as the only places of commodity redistribution where things of all kinds, of all pedigrees and origins, can coexist without material incident.

And perhaps it is the very capacity of the flea market to jumble time, collapse distance, and obliterate the historical context of things that gives it power. As places where objects of diverse kinds and distinct histories are brought together (and brought together because of the frequently harsh truths about how used objects enter the post-consumer or second-hand market). They are at once optimistic and baleful places: places of optimism because of what they might hold and do hold, and baleful places because of what they do hold and because of the circumstances that lead to things being loosed from their one-time moorings of meaning.

DISCARDS AND DISMANTLINGS

In July 1999 an article in the *New York Times* made the powerful point that over the course of the next two decades the North American middle class would witness the largest transfer of wealth and property in history (Karlen). Acknowledging the unavoidable mortality of the parents of the baby-boomer generation, the *Times* rightly noted that no generation had every previously accumulated so much material wealth, and that their children, faced with parental loss, nonetheless stood to inherent vast riches. But what the *Times* did not discuss was that for most of the beneficiaries the acquisition of the household goods of their parents—treasured family items from across several generations, wedding presents that established the making of new families and the myriad domestic goods purchased proudly in the those post-war decades of rising affluence—posed the difficult but unavoidable question of what to do with it all? For though the retention of family "heirlooms" might never be in question—Grandma's china cabinet or Great Aunt Millicent's painted wedding trunk from the old country regarded as the treasures of lineage and history never to leave the family—the other contents of a house or apartment or cottage or storage facility pose different challenges. Indeed, given that inheritance is one of the rather predictable details of the cycle of life, then the question of how to negotiate the surplus of unwanted things becomes an exercise in determining the emotional capital of each object and proceeding to keep or dispose of one's family history.

Now, these same types of calculations apply to almost any instance where a possession is no longer needed, regarded with fondness, or desired. For whatever reasons—taste, commodity fetishism, faddism, and so on—people are constantly letting go of things. They give things to charity, they leave possessions on sidewalks for takers walking by, they take perfectly good things to the dump, and they sell functioning, usable things to dealers in second-hand goods all in order to be rid of them. As such, the process of distancing that needs to take place closely resembles that of the patterns that can mark social relationships: attraction, possession, familiarity, waning interest, and departure. In the context of flea markets—the repositories of things that existed some place else before ending up on the vendor's table—it comes down to the basic fact that certain things long cluttering a house are finally gathered up and dispersed. Whether it is the dismantling of the house or the emptying of a cupboard or closet, the excision of possessions represents a powerful act. It is the sundering of a relationship, the casting off of something that at some point mattered. Indeed, the sentimental or utilitarian relationships that human beings have established with things can always be terminated, with the end of one relationship potentially providing the basis for the establishment of another. Thus flea markets operate as archives of sorts. They represent countless stories of dispersal or "narratives of dismantling," to borrow Cynthia Wall's poetic phrase, and they provide meaningful places for once meaningful things (Wall).

DONE DEAL

Writing on matters of collectibles, that category of acquired objects that are not in traditionally active use, Chandra Mukerji has suggested that these things "seem to be commodities on the brink of extinction, saved by people who saw in them some lasting importance" (Mukerji 353). And in truth, every old thing in a flea market holds the potential of being discovered and possessed and cherished by some one. The discarded or loosed thing lies in wait for the person who will rescue it. As such, flea markets, yard sales, and the like are sites where objects are in transition or suspended, as it were, between one set of contextualized meanings and another set of emerging meanings. For every old and used thing in a flea market faces one of two possible futures: first, the thing may be purchased and incorporated into a new setting, where new meanings and associations will accrue to it; or, second, the thing will end up never being sold and at some point will be discarded, once and for all, as trash to be buried in a landfill.

Thus contemporary flea markets in the United States serve an invaluable role in the economic and cultural life of the country (LaFarge; Rinker). Flea markets operate as places for the distribution of new merchandise and they serve as the sites that permit and encourage the redistribution of many types of used goods. However, more than these strictly economic functions, flea markets simultaneously operate as the temporary and changing storerooms of society and history. That Americans flock to flea markets at all times of the year in all parts of the country speaks to the way that a journey into the unknown is part of the national psyche—a legacy from history—and that the past, while so easily forgotten in the press of the moment and the promise of the future can always be found, even if it takes the shape of the most seemingly simple, innocuous, and familiar thing.

WORKS CITED AND RECOMMENDED

Belk, Russell W. *Collecting in a Consumer Society*. London: Routledge, 1995.
Burrows, Hermann. *A History of the Rag Trade*. London: Maclaren, 1956.
Carbone, G. G. *How to Make a Fortune with Other People's Junk: An Insider's Secrets to Finding and Re-selling Hidden Treasures at Garage Sales, Auctions, Estate Sales, Flea Markets, Yard Sales, Antique Shows and eBay*. New York: McGraw-Hill, 2005.
Complete Directory of General Flea Market Merchandise Wholesalers, Distributors, Manufacturers and Importers. Bay Pines, FL: Publishers Distributing Company, 1988.
Csikszentmihalyi, Mihalyi, and Eugene Rochberg-Halton. *The Meaning of Things: Domestic Symbols and the Self*. Cambridge: Cambridge UP, 1981.
Dolan, J. R. *The Yankee Peddlers of Early America*. New York: Bramhall House, 1964.
Gregson, Nicky, and Louise Crew. *Second-Hand Cultures*. Oxford: Berg, 2003.
Harmon, Charlotte. *The Flea Market Entrepreneur*. Babylon, NY: Pilot Books, 1987.
Karlen, Neal. "And the Meek Shall Inherit Nothing." *New York Times* 29 July 1999: F1.
Kline, Priscilla Carrington. "New Light on the Yankee Peddler." *New England Quarterly* 1 (1939): 80–98.
LaFarge, Albert. *US Flea Market Directory: A Giude to the Best Flea Markets in All 50 States*. New York: St. Martin's Griffin, 2000.
McCracken, Grant. *Culture and Consumption: New Approaches to the Symbolic Character of Consumer Goods and Activities*. Bloomington: U of Indiana P, 1988.
Miner, Robert. *The Flea Market Handbook*. Radnor, PA: Wallace Homestead, 1990.
Muensterberger, Werner. *Collecting, an Unruly Passion: Psychological Perspectives*. Princeton, NJ: Princeton UP, 1994.
Mukerji, Chandra. "Artwork: Collection and Contemporary Culture." *American Journal of Sociology* 84 (1978): 348–65.

[Public Broadcasting System]. "A Flea Market Documentary." WQED, Pittsburgh, PA, 2005.

Richardson, Wright. *Hawkers and Walkers in Early America*. Philadelphia: J. B. Lippincott Company, 1927.

Rinker, Harry L. *Official Guide to Flea Market Prices*. New York: The Crown Publishing Group, 2001.

Wall, Cynthia. "The English Auction: Narratives of Dismantling." *Eighteenth Century Studies* 31.1 (1997): 1–25.

the oft-cited protean utterances in an advertisement that "cements its Mustang's status as an American icon..., in which the car sings the national anthem, using various pitches of engine noises" ("Ford Mustang Anthem").

The humanity ascribed to the Mustang is distinctly American in character, and by design. The immensely successful fortieth anniversary Mustang of 2005 repeats elements of the original, especially the short, raised back and long, lowered hood, which the anniversary model's designer saw in Saigon in 1971 when it paraded with GIs on a morale-boosting tour. To him as a 5-year-old the car brought positive images of America in its size, power, and association with freedom (Sauer). Now, the Mustang's allure of freedom has a range: for Europeans, that of cowboy boots and the "open roads of America"; for the CEO, the style statement "to inject a bit of rebel chic into the parking lot"; for the middle-aged, indomitable youth and the cool glamor of Steve McQueen in *Bullitt*, as an appropriate attitude at age 50 (Sauer). Significantly also, the middle-aged Mustang itself, in its retro get-up, appeals to actual youth, the teens and twenties who never saw the 1968 *Bullitt* but take the car's "aggressive posture" for a token of its acceleration time zero to sixty. Notably, the 0–60 motif pervades Mustang reviews as consistently as it does articles on drag racing, street rods, and muscle car history; yet the Mustang retains its original, larger status, its class among the classic cars it originally rebelled from "as the ugly American of sports cars." Its power to transcend generational differences in style suggests that its appeal amounts to much more than a sum of parts, and that it informs perceptions of it and has become a taste-maker. Its "American" identity is acclaimed insistently yet without consistent basis; its media presence may attract and drive its success more than any other aspect of this hybrid, as *Time* magazine's review implies: "The Mustang is an American icon, with more movie cameos, hot-rod clubs and fanzines than any other vehicle" (Fonda).

In its 1964 cover story hailing the Mustang, "Ford's Young One," *Time* participated in the media campaign managed by Lee Iacocca that built wide-scale public curiosity about Ford's new model, and spurred anticipatory competitive designs in Detroit; but *Time* also pointed out the car's appeal to Americans, and its response to their changing circumstances. The Mustang spoke to the country's basic motoring urge, and to the new style of this desire: it was "destined to be a sort of Model A of sports cars," available to the masses. The car had useful practicality in its four-passenger seats, many options, and moderate price; but it incorporated European features; with, for example, "its Ferrari flare and open-mouthed air scoop, the Mustang resembles the European racing cars that American sports-car buffs find so appealing." Its designs had reminders of

A classic Ford Mustang. Courtesy of Shutterstock.

its European heritage—and competition—in the Austin-Healey, Triumph, and MG, and some resemblances to their U.S. imitators the Thunderbird and Corvette; but the Mustang was much cheaper and could accommodate a small family (92). Iacocca intended it to rival directly the Chevrolet Corvair Monza, and be more of a "sports car" with its standard bucket seats, floor shift, and leather-like vinyl upholstery (101). *Sports Illustrated* greeted the Mustang as the same, "A Sports Car for Everyone," and supplied its qualifications: it was "raceable," especially fast in its optional V-8 acceleration; in other versions it was a "plush road car" that could be "dolled up" for attractiveness (Grossman 38).

The racehorse component of the Mustang, thus heralded from its debut, and into today's fandom, was carefully prepared, with attitudes of the public being the primary object of attention. Major automotive companies had, for several years, agreed not to promote racing, but Lee Iacocca demurred from such "hypocrisy" and, to change the public image of Fords, promoted the cars onto stock car tracks. More people, Iacocca reasoned, watched auto racing than baseball and football combined ("Ford's Young One"). Ford began "its massive racing program in 1962," and positioned itself at the head of a highly popular American sport (Grossman 38). Other automakers felt the pressure of Ford's racing stake and intention to market a sporty model; and their advertisements, as in the early 1964 *Sports Illustrated*, reflected the competition for favor in an area little known to the magazine's adult middle-class audience. A Chrysler ad posed the quandary—"This car set 26 dragstrip records. What's a drag?"—and explained the quarter-mile drag race, "a million-fan sport, sanctioned by national organizations," along with the photograph of a Plymouth and its winning driver. An ad for Buick promised, "You too can be a rally driver...in the first Buick Sports Car Rally. Really" (27 January 1964). When the Mustang appeared, it offered "the aspiring young sport...a reasonable facsimile of a European rally car" for a cheap price; and for $400 more "a real rally car" that "will peel off 555 feet in ten seconds from a standing start." Its customers would be young—the "post-war babies coming of age" ("The Mustang—A New Breed Out of Detroit" 97). Iacocca had targeted teenaged baby boomers as the forward movement he saw in the new market of suburban, multi-car families. His opponent the Corvair Monza overshot the target age; its ads pictured courting couples, such as a naval officer and his date, and new families, such as the husband at the bus stop and young wife shopping in the family car, while the Mustang in ads sat waiting for the imaginations to people it—as baby boomers' would.

The keys to their imaginations, and pockets, were the fifty options, including the racing package, although perhaps the front-end design Iacocca favored also caught their liking with its "pointed, mouthy appearance" ("The Mustang—A New Breed Out of Detroit" 99–100). With the many options, a buyer could nearly individualize the car to a self-expression and self-assertion. Also, with the options the buyer could assemble a race car, and become a stock-car driver or dragster, at least potentially. The Mustang enabled fulfillment of the civic rebellions dramatized in youth culture in the 1950s: remaking a standard car into a hot rod which could compete in striking looks and action with others; showing off such loud cars by "cruising" the streets, boulevard, or parking lots; and preparing at any stoplight for a drag race, at least by revving the engine. This scenario occupied teenagers in cities, suburbs, and villages across the country, and extended into the movies they gathered to watch in couples or carloads at the drive-in theaters, such as *Rebel Without a Cause* (1955), which featured a deadly car game of "Chicken," *Hot Rod Girl* (1956), and *Hot Rod* (1957).

This teen car culture seems, in hindsight, neither so delinquent as adults feared it, nor very serious as a rebellion; but it did enact and promote the hybrid force of car and driver, personally and socially. Customizing the car spurred a teenager's creative cleverness and confidence, and produced an "animated" vehicle that demanded experimental driving despite risks. The customized car also starred in displays of teen fashion, music, and dancing such as the 1963 Teen Fair which Tom Wolfe reported in "The Kandy-Kolored Tangerine-Flake Streamline Baby." The cars crafted by these California "kids" demonstrated their automotive sophistication, their values—"freedom, style, sex, power, motion, color"—and their impressive access to money. The sponsor of this musically rocking exposition? The Ford Motor Company's "Custom Car Caravan": as Wolfe speculated, "Even the kids who aren't full-time car nuts themselves will be influenced by which car is considered 'boss'" (64–65). Here was Ford's dual entry in the youth market, and perfect lure for the coming Mustang's customizing options. The true basis of the Mustang's visual appeal was probably not the Italian features alluded to in "sports car" guise, but the lowered roofline and drop of the body over the wheels reminiscent of the chopped and channeled 1950s hot rod. Tom Wolfe, like Lee Iacocca, foresaw that "teen-age styles" had created a new economy and a new, anti-elite aesthetic that would influence "the life of the whole country" (Wolfe, Introduction xiv–xv). Enthusiasm for the 2005 Mustang emphasizes values Wolfe identified with the teens' aesthetic: the "raw power," the "verve, guts and bravado to inflate the old ego," freedom in the almost inevitable customizing done by owners of even a brand-new Mustang, and myriad loud or sultry colors (Sramik 88–90). Sex? Add a body kit for "the updated boy racer we've come to lust for" (Gritzinger).

Cruising endures, from the lonely village street to the 2-million crowd at Detroit's Woodward Dream Cruise. The Mustang and its fellow travelers now host "cruises" in a city or region on almost every fair-weather evening. Sponsored by a car club, in a store or restaurant parking lot, the restored cars and their drivers gather, the cars sparkling for display, the drivers lounging on lawn chairs in the shade, unless keen to tout a vehicle on sale. Children, dates, and business are entertained. Restoring and maintaining these vehicles is a leisure craft for enjoyment and admiration, but it has ties to commerce, both in its expenses—there's an industry from corporate to informal internet dealers supplying replacement and custom parts of all kinds—and its rewards—even if the astronomical prices of collectors' cars do not motivate car restorers, as they claim, an increase in market value justifies their labors of love, or a disparagement of money wasted on a worthless model looms. The hobby almost necessarily entails commerce, like the 1966 Mustang a young man was showing and selling this summer at a Corvette Open Cruise at a Home Depot. His photo album showed the rusty ruin as it was found behind a Tennessee barn, and through its many phases to its gleaming customized features. Why had he worked on it? The young owner's father "grew up" with Mustangs, and his grandfather also owned and worked on them. So this Mustang was one of three the family now had, and its sale, for $11,000, would bring another into their garage. They also had a rarer 1965 fastback, worth $35,000. He liked working on Mustangs, the young man observed, because so many parts and options are readily available; in fact, solely from parts you can get through catalogs, you could completely build one.

Here's a side of the Mustang–hot rod icon with little resemblance to Hollywood's alienated *Bullitt*, and opposite *Rebel Without a Cause*. Hot-car culture unites this son and his father in leisure, learning, and a bit of successful business, and connects them with a sponsoring and cooperating social and commercial network, of car fans everywhere. The radio in their family work space probably plays oldies rock and roll and latter-day imitators, same as the loudspeakers at the open cruise. There's no generational rift. The car stars; and it sheds its values (style, power, etc.) on its attendant, who could as well be a woman driver, as in *Charlie's Angels*. When the car takes precedence in the hybrid, language is more technical than personal, and illustration doesn't show muscled men or leggy women. In the hard-core magazines of car culture, only hands, usually grease-ringed, appear, for the proper manipulation of shining chrome parts. This aspect of Mustang iconolatry hearkens back to *Popular Mechanics* of the past mid-century and beyond, to the charm of mechanics, invention, and tinkering for Americans. I was persuaded of the Mustang's transformative aura when searching for Mustang articles on a public library computer. With a glance at some print-outs beside me, the young man at the next computer asked me, seriously, if I was going to build one. I've been a person who could build a Mustang ever since.

WORKS CITED AND RECOMMENDED

"Drivers Log." *AutoWeek* 13 Dec. 2004: 8. *Business Source Premier*. EBSCO. Louisville Free Public Library, 6 June 2005 <http://web23.epnet.com/>.

Fonda, Darren. "A Galloping Stallion." *Time* 1 Nov. 2004: 101. *Business Source Premier*. EBSCO. Louisville Free Public Library, 8 June 2005 <http://web23.epnet.com/>.

"Ford Mustang Anthem." *Creativity* Dec. 2004: 48. *Business Source Premier*. EBSCO. Louisville Free Public Library, 6 June 2005 <http://web23.epnet.com/>.

"Ford's Young One." *Time* 17 Apr. 1964: 92–102. *Business Source Premier*. EBSCO. Louisville Free Public Library, 8 June 2005 <http://web23.epnet.com/>.

Gritzinger, Bob et al. "Kit Cars, Kitsch Cars, & Incredibly Fast Cars." *AutoWeek* 15 Nov. 2004: 14. *Business Source Premier*. EBSCO. Louisville Free Public Library, 6 June 2005 <http://web23.epnet.com/>.

Grossman, Robert. "A Sports Car for Everyone." *Sports Illustrated* 20 Apr. 1964: 38–45.

Michael, Mike. "The Invisible Car: The Cultural Purification of Road Rage." *Car Cultures*. Ed. Daniel Miller. Oxford: Berg-Oxford International Publishers, 2001. 59–80.

Miller, Daniel. "Driven Societies." *Car Cultures* 1–33.

"The Mustang—A New Breed Out of Detroit." *Newsweek* 21 Apr. 1964: 97–101.

Neff, Natalie, and Mike Ditz. "Bring on the Dancing Horses." *AutoWeek* 10 Jan. 2005: 20+. *Business Source Premier*. EBSCO. Louisville Free Public Library, 6 June 2005 <http://web23.epnet.com/>.

Piller, Ingrid. "Extended Metaphor in Automobile Fan Discourse." *Poetics Today* 20 (1999): 483–98.

Quiroga, Tony. "Goat and Pony Showdown." *Car and Driver Road Test Annual 2005*: 17–22.

Robinson, Aaron. "The Jury Deliberates over Four New Convertibles on Our Most-Selfish List." *Car and Driver Road Test Annual 2005*: 6–13.

Sauer, Patrick J. "At 40, the Ford Mustang Still Hasn't Lost Its Cool." *Inc.* Sept. 2004: 62. *Business Source Premier*. EBSCO. Louisville Free Public Library, 8 June 2005 <http://web20.epnet.com/>.

Sramik, Tim. "Middle-Age Muscle." *Aftermarket Business* Nov. 2004: 88–92. *Business Source Premier*. EBSCO. U of Louisville, Ekstrom Library, 21 Aug. 2005 <http://web10.epnet.com?>.

Winfield, Barry. "The Latest Generation of Mid-Size Luxury Sports Sedans Will Spoil You as Never Before." *Car and Driver Road Test Annual 2005*: 66–78.

Wolfe, Tom. Introduction. *The Kandy-Kolored Tangerine-Flake Streamline Baby*. New York: Bantam, 1977. xi–xvii, 62–89.

Gettysburg

Randal Allred

Ask any American to name a famous American battle; the likelihood is that Gettysburg may be the most frequently named. Not only has it become the climactic battle and symbolic microcosm of the American Civil War, but the place itself has become the archetype of American military shrines, and the locus of memorialized heroism in American culture. The study of this battle and the way we have memorialized the site necessarily becomes also a study of how we choose to remember the past.

No American battle is more debated than Gettysburg, nor any battle more tantalizing with the potential of "what if," near chances, and potential turning points, within the battle itself. This battle has always been represented in the popular imagination as the crucial juncture of the war's plot itself—the tragic climax—especially as it came at almost the exact halfway point in the war as it did. Geographically, it represents the apex of the Confederate enterprise. The place also has a mystic drawing power in its quiet pastoral setting's stark contrast to the fury and slaughter of July 1, 2, and 3 in 1863. The hushed, parklike grounds attract over 2 million visitors a year, and the town's name has become synonymous with pilgrimage—a "byword for Americana" as Jim Weeks puts it (4). The battlefield's location makes it a natural stop on a tour of America's early historic sites, and its site has been revered and preserved from early on, unlike many other battle areas.

Gettysburg immediately impresses the visitor with a panoramic view of things—an almost amphitheatrical view to the coherence of the entire conflict. The fact of the battle's taking place in three days, and each stage of the battle occurring on fresh ground, argues to even the casual observer a coherent narrative thread in a battle that seemingly was conducted according to cause-effect logic, if not by a God-ordained script. And unlike visitors at Shiloh, Chickamauga, or Manassas, one can stand in many places on the Gettysburg battlefield with its low hills and gently rolling farmlands and easily see the landscape and topography that figured so crucially in the way the events played out. The names of features on the field also are embedded in the national memory, with the grimly appropriate Cemetery Hill and

Cemetery Ridge, Devil's Den, and the ironic Seminary Ridge. The appeal of simple names is also there: Oak Ridge, the Angle, the Copse of Trees, Little Round Top, the Wheat Field, and the Peach Orchard.

Gettysburg is generally seen as the turning point in the war that we see as the defining point in our history. Although Antietam was a significant conflict—the bloodiest day of the war—and became even more politically important because it provided a pretext for Lincoln's issuing the Emancipation Proclamation in 1862 (even though it was, for McClellan and the Union, a tactical defeat), the plot of Antietam as narrative is rather muddled, full of missed chances and miscues for the Union forces; besides, the vainglorious McClellan, the victorious Union general, was sacked by Lincoln some few weeks later for failing to destroy Lee's already-weakened Army of Northern Virginia when it was at its most vulnerable. The 1862 invasion of Kentucky by Bragg and Kirby-Smith, and its repulse, was too disjointed and full of miscommunication and almost comic misapprehension, before and after the battle of Perryville, Kentucky, to figure largely in the memorable story of the war.

But Gettysburg was the most significant Confederate invasion of the North. In the summer of 1863, as Lee headed north again, the Army of Northern Virginia, at 75,000 strong, was the largest it would be during the war since the outset of the Seven Days Battles, when Lee took command of nearly 90,000 men. Lee was following up what some call his most brilliant victory at Chancellorsville. Gettysburg was the largest battle in the war in some respects: it had the most men engaged, by some counts, and had the most casualties. Its three days of combat stand as a motif-like trinity of horror, but full of Christian significance. Of battles as single, sustained conflicts, rather than a series of actions like Cold Harbor, only the Battle of Spotsylvania lasted longer among the major battles.

Gettysburg was the biggest battle of the few fought in the North, and consequently the one that Northerners have paid attention to. It was also the most significant battle for the Army of the Potomac, that proud, hard-luck unit whose war experience had been an odd mixture of continual defeat and a grand esprit de corps. After successive defeats at the hands of Lee, this army finally defeated him at his biggest and best. In later campaigns, even though the Union army drove the Army of Northern Virginia into the Petersburg entrenchments, most of the stand-up battles after Gettysburg were also won tactically by Lee: the Wilderness (which some argue to be a draw), Spotsylvania, the crossings of the North Anna, and Cold Harbor. So Gettysburg remains as the grand victory, the magnum opus, the best performance of the Federal army in the East, and perhaps the most poetic for the Union cause: you have the moral high ground if your enemy is the invader.

This battle on the other hand provided the South's biggest hurrah, if not its last. It was the conflict with the most at stake for the South; European recognition, although less likely than it had been in 1862, was a distinct hope driving this campaign for the Confederates. If Lee's army could defeat the Army of the Potomac convincingly, and capture a major city such as Philadelphia,

GETTYSBURG

Baltimore, or (most hopeful yet) Washington, it would be hard for Europe to avoid the conclusion that the Confederate States were a viable enterprise. Militarily, it portended the South's finest hour: the effort to drive the Yankees from their positions with sweeping attacks suggests that a Southern victory would likely have been a significant one. It has seemed, in the American imagination, the most desperate and hopeful moment for the Rebels' fortunes: this is, we feel, where they almost won it all. Southerners often take a perverse pride in their performance in this battle, for these reasons: it was Lee's only significant loss (and that on unfamiliar ground); it was the best performance of the Army of the Potomac at its peak and yet the South, still outnumbered and on the attack, nearly won.

Yet the defeat has added a poetic and poignant aura to the "Lost Cause"—that it was only barely lost, and lost in such a dramatic and gallant manner, along with natural sympathy for the underdog, has enhanced the Lost Cause in popular culture. Many observers and scholars have noted that although the North won the military war, the South won the war of national sympathies in the sense of dictating the terms, forms, paradigms, and images by which the story of the conflict has been told in the years since: the *Gone with the Wind* syndrome. A postbellum (1888) comment by Confederate General Daniel Harvey Hill, who had served under Lee, is revealing:

> I love to hear the praises of the wonderful deeds of McClellan, Grant, Meade, and Hancock, for if they were such great warriors for crushing with their

The cemetery gatehouse at Gettysburg, Pennsylvania. Courtesy of the Library of Congress.

massive columns the thin lines of ragged Rebels, what must be said of Lee, the two Johnstons, Beauregard, and Jackson, who held millions at bay for four years with their fragments of shadowy armies?...

Suppose the tables had been turned, and that either of the five Southerners named above had been superior to his antagonists in all the appliances and inventions of war, and had been given, moreover, an excess of two millions of men over them, how many statues, think ye, my countrymen, would there be of bronze warriors and prancing chargers?

The logic here, of course, dictates that if the Army of the Potomac required all that might and material, and so many tries over those first two years of war to finally defeat Lee, how much more do Lee and his ragged troops deserve praise? Hence we have the myth of the Southern soldier being a nobler and better fighter than the Yankee, with Gettysburg their High Water mark in valor.

Was it the turning point of the Civil War? This is one of the issues debated still. Thomas Goss posits that even had Lee "succeeded in smashing the Army of the Potomac at Gettysburg, the war would not have ended with Southern independence," and that it would not have been a fatal blow to the Northern will to fight (14). Yet Goss also admits that the physical impact of battlefield defeat "[is] not what makes a battle decisive; it is the psychological effect on confidence in eventual victory that determines the significance of a battlefield defeat" (15). With this in mind, it is difficult to calculate the effect of a Rebel victory at Gettysburg. Northern war weariness would manifest itself within days in the New York draft riots. Had Lee won, and Stuart been in place to push the pursuit of the retreating Yankees, keeping the roads and routes of retreat compromised, Lee very well could have marched into Washington. True, the city's fall would have not have destroyed the Northern capacity to wage war, but it may easily have been discouraging enough to the North for a cease fire or treaty, leading to probable foreign recognition for the Confederacy and eventual nationhood.

As it was, the actual battle's overall effects on the war were extensive: the defeat sapped Southern war spirit, according to Jefferson Davis and others. It prompted increased enlistments in the North, far outstripping the number of draftees. The Confederate government experienced increased internal dissension and fraction. And, combined with the fall of Vicksburg on July 4, Gettysburg convinced many Northerners that the war could indeed be won.

The recent blooming of alternative history in popular culture and speculative fiction springs from this kind of seed. Gettysburg seems to bristle with more near chances than other battles, inviting the imagination to engage in "What If" speculation. Many recent books, including a collection of short fictional pieces called *Alternative Gettysburgs*, offer many scenarios of what might have been. Many events in the battle invite this thinking: General Buford's decision to defend the high ground; the nick-of-time arrival of the First Corps; the fateful decision of Ewell not to attack Cemetery Hill and Culp's Hill; Stuart's failure to screen Lee's army and keep it informed; the

Battle of Franklin, a lithograph published in 1891. Courtesy of the Library of Congress.

crucial time wasted by Longstreet's countermarch on Day Two; the sheer chance of General Warren's being on Little Round Top in time; the arrival of Vincent's brigade barely in time to save that hill for the Union; the undying controversy of Sickles' unauthorized advance to the Peach Orchard; the near chance of the Hoke-Avery assault on Cemetery Hill; the empty trenches on Culp's Hill that General Edward Johnson's Rebels nearly captured; and finally, most of all, the desperate and audacious attack led by Pickett, over open ground, on Day Three—all of these have provided endless grist for armchair generals and students to debate. The theatrical potential of Pickett's Charge, best articulated by William Faulkner's narrator in his novel *Intruders in the Dust*, demonstrates how this moment seems still viable and malleable:

> For every Southern boy fourteen years old, not once but whenever he wants it, there is the instant when it's still not yet two oclock on that July afternoon in 1863, the brigades are in position behind the rail fence,... and it's all in the balance, it hasn't happened yet, it hasn't even begun yet, it not only hasn't begun yet but there is still time for it not to begin... and that moment doesn't even need a fourteen-year-old boy to think *This time. Maybe this time* with all this much to lose and all this much to gain: Pennsylvania, Maryland, the world, the golden dome of Washington itself to crown with desperate and unbelievable victory the desperate gamble, the cast made two years ago. (194–95)

This scenario has played in the mind of anyone who has contemplated deeply those circumstances while visiting the battlefield park and walking the same ground—especially that long stretch across to Cemetery Ridge, the path of Pickett's assault, which the National Park Service keeps mown for walking. The tantalizing possibilities must surely exert more power than mere history.

The most significant single factor in making Gettysburg forever a shrine to American patriotism was the delivery of Lincoln's address there at the dedication of the Cemetery on November 19, just four months after the battle. The 272-word speech which, as argued by Garry Wills and others, has done more to shape the concept of nationhood and American political rhetoric than any other text, was fundamentally designed to shape the meaning of the recent battle. Lincoln's rhetorical triumph lay in imbuing the slaughter of American boys with the sanctity of the most sacred of public causes—the "new birth of freedom" for mankind, by preserving the Union. His argument, we remember, is that the sacrifice of the soldiers killed there would be dishonored by our failure to carry on the war to a victorious conclusion. In so few words, the entire American experiment—past, present, and future—was tied up in that three-day battle. If the field was not hallowed ground before, Lincoln's speech has certainly made it so. The full ramifications of this speech are still being explored in our time, for Lincoln defined the meaning of military sacrifice in all wars where America's interests are at stake.

Pickett's Charge, July 1903. Courtesy of Getty Images/PhotoDisc.

Another significance of Gettysburg rose in the veterans' reunions and reenactments that began there with the 1887 event, on the twenty-fourth anniversary of the battle, when members of the Philadelphia Brigade invited members of Pickett's division to a commemorative celebration. Larger than anyone anticipated, this event hosted 9,000 visitors—veterans and their families. The largest of these events was the fiftieth anniversary of the battle in 1913, when Virginia-born President Woodrow Wilson spoke to nearly 50,000 veterans who camped on the field, greeted former adversaries, and staged mock battles. One participant expressed the meaning of the event:

> Not only were there veterans of Gettysburg, but men who had fought under McClellan at Antietam, Jackson in the Shenandoah Valley, Sherman in Georgia,... This was the largest gathering of former soldiers who had changed the face of a nation, torn it apart, and now delighted in its reunification. ("The Great Reunion of 1913")

In 1938, President Franklin D. Roosevelt, in the presence of only a few hundred surviving Civil War veterans but many thousands of spectators, on the 75th Anniversary of the battle dedicated the Eternal Light Peace Memorial in the spirit of ending all wars. Gettysburg's landscape itself had thus been revisioned into a space for the worship of peace.

In the last decade or so, we cannot underestimate the impact of Michael Shaara's 1974 novel *The Killer Angels* on our collective construction of the Gettysburg myth. The novel has gained in popularity as the years go by, and is more widely read today as an expression of the meaning of the Civil War than when it won the Pulitzer Prize for Literature in 1975. Its focus, among the multiple narrators, is the Battle of Gettysburg as a microcosm of the entire struggle—the clash of all of the social, racial, spiritual, intellectual, political, and military issues that inform the Civil War as a whole. The subsequent movie based on the novel, Ron Maxwell's four-hour-plus epic *Gettysburg*, produced by Ted Turner, has had an even wider reach. It has done much to change the way the public reads the battle, giving rise for example to renewed critical debate over Longstreet's conduct and the feud between his adherents and Lee's, as well as fostering a whole new cult of Joshua Lawrence Chamberlain admirers. More people visit Little Round Top than ever before, and interest in the film (which was filmed in the park and surrounding areas) has stimulated more reenactment and living history programs in the area.

Criticism of the film, on the other hand, summarizes opposition to Gettysburg in all its aspects. Philip Beidler admits up front that, being a native of Gettysburg, he is "no fan of the Civil War industry," and that he resists "any attempt to render war attractive—the Civil War, the Vietnamese war, any war... particularly as regards the perverse spectacle called reenactment." In targeting the film *Gettysburg*, he attacks the "packaging and marketing of the Civil War as part of a larger commodification of cultural desire" which Turner's film exemplifies, and reenactors' aid in its making (489). The problem with *Gettysburg*, Beidler argues, is that it is "handsomely done," with almost none of the bloodshed and maiming that actually occurs in war, understating the destructive potential of the .58 caliber Minie ball and canister in cannon, showing the picture-perfect reenactors' authenticity rather than realistic carnage (496–97). His voice joins those of other cultural critics who join an increasingly heated debate about how we should memorialize the past.

Recent arguments on Gettysburg's planned new Visitor Center, which would discuss slavery and put the battle into an historical context, indicate that the revising of the battlefield text is a continual dialogical process, driven by the needs and imperatives of our times. The town of Gettysburg today boasts more sensitivity to the history than it did earlier, although there are also many museums, restaurants, ghost tours, and other industries that capitalize on the tourist trade, including General Pickett's Buffet, Farnsworth House, the Lincoln Battle Theater, O'Rourke's, and a major supplier of reenactor gear, the Regimental Quartermaster. The popular and famous Cyclorama painting (360 feet long and with a 360-degree view of Pickett's Charge) by Paul Dominique Phillippoteaux also remains an important feature of the Gettysburg heritage industry, and has been included in plans for the new Museum and Visitor Center, after a $9 million restoration.

Overall, though, recent trends have answered visitors' increased demand for authenticity. Preservation efforts have acquired more of the original battlefield. National Park battlefield rehabilitation plans include removing trees not there during the battle, burying power lines, and as much restoring of the landscape to its 1863 state as possible. In 2000, the famous privately-owned observation tower near Culp's Hill was purchased and demolished. The "shifting flow" of cultural authority is at work, according to Weeks, once again revising the text of what the battlefield means, now in the trend of increased preservation, while maintaining some of the commercialism that has always been part of the mix of the sacred with the secular. A few decades ago, for example, reenactors would have been considered "too vulgar" to be included in any Gettysburg activity; now they are a staple. They, like "guided tours, museums stuffed with relics, the cyclorama," and other things, "emerged from the marketplace and in time were embraced by the battlefield's custodians" (Weeks 220).

It is perhaps the deeper significance of Gettysburg that may account for its impact on American lives and culture. Robert Penn Warren reminds us that our national impressions of the war are a representation of life rather than being life itself: a "condensation of many meanings." "There is no single meaning appropriate to our occasion," adds Warren, "and that portentous richness is one of the things that make us stare at the towering event" (80–81). Perhaps the most profound appeal of the Civil War—and of Gettysburg, of course, because we have "read" it to encompass the whole conflict—is the picture of human will enduring in the face of incomprehensible suffering. The stories of soldiers and townspeople caught up in this battle, and the narrative of its myriad conflicts also satisfy our yearning for epic heroism and patriotic spectacle. Experiencing the memorialized battlefield invites us to join the action.

WORKS CITED AND RECOMMENDED

Beidler, Philip. "Ted Turner et al. at Gettysburg; Or, Reenactors in the Attic." *Virginia Quarterly Review* 75 (Summer 1999): 488–503.

Faulkner, William. *Intruder in the Dust*. New York: Modern Library, 1948.

Goss, Thomas. "Gettysburg's 'Decisive Battle.'" *Military Review* July–Aug. 2004: 11–16. July 2005 <https://calldpb.leavenworth.army.mil/scripts/>.

"The Great Reunion of 1913." *Voices of Battle: Gettysburg National Military Park Virtual Tour*. July 2005 <http://www.nps.gov/gett/getttour/voices.htm>.

Hill, Daniel Harvey. "The Old South." *Southern Historical Society Papers* 16 (1888). Richmond, VA, Janu.–Dec. 1888.

Warren, Robert Penn. *The Legacy of the Civil War: Meditations on the Centennial*. New York: Random House, 1961.

Weeks, Jim. *Gettysburg: Memory, Market, and an American Shrine*. Princeton, NJ: Princeton UP, 2003.

GI

Michael Smith

The prevailing factor in the psychological make-up of the legendary American GI figure is his fatalism. This is a slightly different thing from his pessimism, or his cynicism, or even his sense of irony. He may certainly possess any of those qualities in abundance. We need only consider the grizzled GI who, after a wide-eyed, trembling recruit (a "greenhorn," in the GI's parlance) has taken a bullet through the head in the first five minutes of his very first combat patrol, looks down at the red mash of obliterated brain, shakes his head, and says, "Well, I guess his cherry got popped." (The GI may even take off his helmet first, and deliver this line solemnly, in the manner of a prayer.) Another GI, after discovering that a bullet has passed neatly through his hip and exited cleanly through his buttock instead of blowing off the entire cheek (a much-hoped for circumstance, one that would have provided him with the Holy Grail every soldier is looking for, the elusive "Million-Dollar wound" and ticket home) is likely to gripe, "Ah, shoot. Lookit that. Just my rotten luck."

Still another GI may ask just what it is about this particular hill that makes it more important than, say, the one right next to it. Is it simply because one is fortified and the other is not? Or is it the view? Because if it's a question of the view, well, all things being equal, the GI much prefers the unfortified hill, because it seems like you'd certainly be able to see more of the river from up there, and oh, yeah, didn't they cross a neat little bridge on their way here and wouldn't you be able to look back and *see* that neat little bridge better from the nice, clean, *unfortified* vantage point than the one that's all cluttered up with mines and barricades and trenches and barbed wire and pillboxes and, well, *Germans,* who seem always to be getting in the way with their *"Achtungs!"* and Schmeisser submachine guns whenever a fella is just looking to take in a little scenery?

But while the GI's fatalism might be expressed in this kind of resigned, doomed humor, his particular fatalism is not, exactly, an acceptance of his fate. It is, rather, the existential sense that he is there to do a job, and that other than fulfilling that job, his life (and death) could scarcely be said to matter at all. And that job? The American GI should be a patriot, yes, he should, if at all possible, be brave and strong and handsome and self-sacrificing and reverent—he should be, in effect, an exceedingly well-armed Boy Scout. But above all of that—far, far above that—the American GI's job is to be a *weapon*. He is, first and foremost, something that can be pointed and fired at the enemy, like an M-1 or an M-16 rifle. So, like those standard-issue weapons, he finds himself bought and paid for, manufactured (maybe at a considerable discount, owing to the large quantities in the purchase order) by means of mass production, and rolling off the line, one after the other. While there might be slight differences or infinitesimal variations and even occasional flaws in the line when you are producing weapons at such speed and in such large numbers, one finished weapon is still expected to fire pretty much the same as another, given that they are all of the same type.

Now, if the GI is a weapon, those who aim that weapon know it must be respected if it is to function properly and reliably. It must be taken care of, attended to. Mud has to be kept off the sights. It must often be cleaned and occasionally polished. It must have its grooves checked, and its firing mechanism must be evaluated regularly. You must look down, along, and inside the barrel.

Left in the water too long, the weapon will rust. Left too long in the sand, it will seize. And fired too long, in a sustained burst, it will melt.

Still, as in the case of the M1 or M16, the owners of this particular weapon know it doesn't pay to get too attached to your weapon. Oh, you may have a favorite or lucky piece for a while. One weapon may have served you particularly well. You may even have carved some notches in the stock to mark or commemorate this service, but still, the eventual loss or necessary replacement or upgrading of this weapon is hardly a thing to bring tears the eyes.

Abroad, this functioning is the American GI's only job, really, and he can be forgiven if he is not particularly well mannered or clean-shaven so long as he does that job effectively. He can be forgiven if he loses his faith in the cause or the flag or in his commanding officers so long as he can be pointed and, when his trigger gets pulled, he fires.

The GI knows this, senses it, has had the idea engrained in him by his training and his experiences on the field of battle, and still he carries out his orders. He is a weapon, and in a way, that makes it easier. Weapons

A pair of GIs camouflaged for forest conflict. Courtesy of Shutterstock.

don't have to think. They don't have to debate the morality of their actions. War is nothing personal, he will tell himself, and only a fool (a fool who is likely to die, and soon) insists on making it personal, in believing himself important.

The GI's acceptance of these ideas, and his reliance on them, transforms him, for all his wisecracks and his recalcitrance, into an engine of destruction. He becomes someone who approaches war in the manner of Ulysses S. Grant. Grant stunk of the twenty-plus cigars he inhaled a day, he was invariably covered in dust, he wore his ratty coat unbuttoned and without insignia, but he was primarily—as Shelby Foote describes him in *The Civil War, A Narrative*—a "killer-arithmetician" (2: 962). He may not have been a particularly honorable man, or even an articulate one (he had the laconic tendencies of the abstaining alcoholic, and he was notoriously uncomfortable amid ceremony and pomp). He was not considered particularly brilliant—although he could be tactically clever, even daring, as in his Mississippi campaign. But he did have one strength: Grant did not love war, but he absolutely did not fear it, either (2: 218–20). When Grant looked at war, when he viewed the battle to come or its aftermath, when he considered the cost, he did not see a human (or even a political) cost. What he saw was an equation: numbers, not people. And so he could shrug off 35,000 casualties in his two first weeks in charge of the Army of the Potomac, write it off as a natural consequence of the new, aggressive stance he was inculcating in that legendarily lethargic army. He could endlessly hurl his men at the earthworks at Cold Harbor in 1864 (he lost approximately 4,500 men in about 90 minutes) and then refuse a truce, leaving wounded soldiers to anguish for days in the hot sun on the field of battle because he did not relish even the smallest perception that he might have somehow given an inch by treating with Lee (3: 281–99).

It was Grant's calculation that originated, and in a sense installed, the American GI's fatalism. But there is no single figure that best illustrates the sheer annihilative power of this fatalism, once it has been embraced, better than World War II's Audie Murphy, the most decorated American soldier in history. Murphy appears, at first consideration, to be anything but a stony killer. To look at his photograph is to see the very essence of the picture-perfect Johnny Soldier Boy Scout, brought to life. In one postwar army publicity headshot, he is skinny, his head seemingly too big for his neck. His brow and cheeks are smooth, his eyes perfectly clear, and his lips are full, almost sensuous. His hair looks, more than anything, *clean* and nourished. You might guess his age as barely 18, except there are so many medals piled over his left breast that the sheer accumulation would stop a bullet from reaching his heart.

To read a short blurb of Murphy's online biography is to scan the quintessential American story. He appears as the very son of the American Dream: from Kingston, Texas, born of sharecroppers, his family abandoned by his father, his mother dying when he is young, he makes for an unlikely (and so, because of that very improbability, near perfect) war hero. At first rejected from the marines and the paratroopers because he was too small, he enlists in the army infantry, 3rd Division, and fights in Sicily, Italy, France, Germany. He is awarded the Congressional Medal of Honor and anywhere from 21 to 33 other medals and decorations; there seems to be some disagreement as to the exact number, and so it appears his acts of heroism are numerous and large enough that it is hard to pinpoint exactly how many different honors he received. After the war, Murphy becomes something of a matinee idol, starring in a series of war films and westerns starting in 1948 and continuing through the 1960s. John Huston directs him in an adaptation of Steven Crane's *The Red Badge of Courage* (1953) and in *The Unforgiven* (1960). At various times, he finds himself working alongside movie stars like Cagney, Stewart, and Hepburn (Rodgers). He makes a great deal of money, and eventually, he achieves what is the ultimate dream of everyone in Hollywood (and perhaps in America): in 1955's *To Hell and Back,* which chronicles Murphy's experiences in World War II, he gets to star in a movie about himself, as himself.

It is in the autobiography on which this movie is based, however, that Murphy's other side, the fatalism that, in a sense, opened the door to these later successes, can be seen. Murphy's body count in World War II was almost demonic: 240 German casualties were attributed to him. Reading *To Hell and Back,* we come to suspect that the actual number is probably much, much higher. Murphy is given to scrambling onto tanks and assault vehicles, opening hatches, and dropping in grenades and gasoline cocktails. He blasts machine gun nests with mortars and exploding shells, and sneaks up on dug-in enemies and then shreds them at close range with a large-caliber, heavy machine gun. He calls in artillery fire on positions he triangulates from angles of fire, but cannot see. It is hard to imagine exact figures being possible under such conditions.

The oddly detached, clinical tone of the book (for it is anything but proud, or even filled with the kind of false modesty that invites us to think we are being treated to an exaggeration) doesn't leave us feeling that Murphy is the sort inclined to keep count. He takes no pleasure, no real satisfaction, in the facility with which he deals death. At the same time, he expresses an absolute lack of feeling for the men he kills. Indeed, they are usually not men at all, but "krauts." (In the book, there are two kinds of krauts: "krauts"—not even "live krauts," but simply "krauts"—and "dead krauts.")

The moment when he rounds a bend in a gully, and runs headlong into two startled Germans, is fairly representative of just how mechanically he views and presents his own actions in combat: "For an instant they recoil in surprise; and that is their mistake. My combat experience has taught me the value of split seconds. Before the Germans can regain their balance, I kill them both with a carbine" (174). Again and again, we are given stripped, detached descriptions like these: "I lob the grenade and grab the carbine trigger with one movement. Before the grenade has time to burst, two krauts fall with carbine slugs in their bellies" and "I squeeze the trigger. The helmet jumps. The man falls as if struck in the head with a club" (209–10) and "As he frantically reaches for the safety on his rifle, I fire twice. He crashes backwards.

I throw two hand grenades to take care of any companions lurking in the area" (215). The closest Murphy comes to analyzing his approach (and brilliance) in combat is when he tells us that in battle, his brain is "coldly alert and logical. I do not think of the danger to myself. My whole being is concentrated on killing" (177). On days when the lines are quiet or the platoon is idle, he says that he is "bored with the lack of activity, which breeds the kind of thinking that I try to avoid" (209). That kind of thinking, presumably, is anything—anger, fear, thoughts of home, or of exacting vengeance for a downed friend—that takes him out of his role as weapon.

If he even recognizes that his ability to deal death is startling, or that he seems to have a particular affinity for the work, or even just that he happens to leave an impressive number of obliterated bodies wherever he goes, Murphy does not once indicate it. Only *once* does he report any of his fellow soldiers remarking on his actions as if they are unusual ("What are you trying to do? Win a wooden cross?"; 175). For the most part, his fellows do not, it seems, see Murphy as anything out of the ordinary, or that he is doing much of anything they couldn't—or, rather, *wouldn't,* if they shared his technique. They are all engines, after all. Murphy might be a more efficient engine, but they share the same function.

Still, it seems the GI cannot bring himself to embrace completely his particular brand of fatalism. For alongside it, he also carries a deeply held and occasionally voiced suspicion, one he cannot ignore: he eventually suspects that he is become a toy gun, a plaything in the hands of idiot-child generals—that he is a pawn for lunatics who get their jollies moving those pieces willy-nilly across the chessboard battlefield. It's fairly typical for the GI to grumble, for example, about just what in the hell the "Invisibles" (those never-seen commanding officers whose presence is nevertheless always felt) are thinking about. As he finds himself packing his gear for yet another mindless patrol, the GI may idly wonder just what it is the "Old Man" is doing in that tent of his, located oh-so-many miles behind the front lines. Is he simply drunk? Insane? Senile? ("I'll lay you even odds on all three," the platoon's sergeant is likely to mutter. "Now shut up, all you dogfaces, and keep packing.")

The sense of this suspicion is strong throughout *To Hell and Back,* but particularly when Murphy's platoon fights for endless weeks to take Hill 193, only to be suddenly given an unexplained reprieve. As they limp off, one of Murphy's comrades—the man's name is Snuffy—looks back on the valley and snorts. "What was all the shootin' about?" he wonders, unable to imagine a more disadvantageous piece of ground. "I wouldn't give one turnip patch in Tennessee fer the whole damned [thing]." Mulling the *reason* for their mysterious reprieve, which seems to have come just when they were approaching a breakthrough, the platoon ultimately decides they are either to be checked for venereal diseases or that "the gravediggers ran out of mattress covers." Once behind the lines, they are assigned "a period of rigorous training. Twice daily we have hot chow, and we sleep on cots in pyramidal tents." Later, when Murphy and a friend are walking down a road, they shoot a chicken and must hide it in the grass for later retrieval, lest they be caught and formally charged. Murphy ponders the incongruity: "In combat, we can destroy whole towns and be patted on the back for our efforts. But here in the rear, the theft of a chicken is a serious offense indeed. Army regulations say 'No looting'" (51–56).

The GI's recognition of the absurdity of his own predicament—the relentlessly indiscriminate orders of imbecilic or paranoid superiors, the haphazard application of rules and niceties to war—has become a staple of almost every piece of literature or popular entertainment involving him. We need only consider Joseph Heller's novel *Catch-22* and the television show it inspired, *M*A*S*H*, to begin to get the sense of this absurdity.

But it is not just his superiors—the generals, and their bosses, the politicians—that the GI comes to believe have lost sight of his essential humanity and have instead transposed something in its place. It is also those the soldier has left behind, the public, Mom and Dad and Betty Sue, home. On the home front, the role of "weapon" is replaced with "hero." It is a role made all the more discomfiting because the GI knows there's nothing particularly ennobling about having once been a weapon. The reflective GI wonders what will happen after Johnny comes marching home, and after they throw the parade? What will they think when he lies in bed for two weeks, the lights out and the shades drawn, but not sleeping? And what will Johnny do with his life when he ventures outside again?

In *To Hell and Back*, one of Murphy's fellow soldiers properly sums up the dilemma caused by the GI's fatalism: it is the knowledge that you can't go home again. Pinned down in a cave, the platoon has spent the night listening to the labored breathing of a group of gut-shot Germans who survived when a member of the platoon took the cave (it's worth noting that Murphy, with his efficiency, is not the one who assaulted this position, or else the Germans would doubtless have been dispatched immediately). When the last German dies, the platoon leader, Kerrigan, speaks:

> "Home is the place where they send you when you lose an arm or a leg. I've read all about it in the papers. You ride in a hospital train, with beautiful nurses and Red Cross Dames drooling all over you. With newspapers writing how you gave your all for your country. With the train stopping at little towns, where the people are waiting at the depots to cheer....
>
> "Sure. Just like a picture. Your mama cries and calls in the neighbors to see her hero. You sit around the old store with your chest full of ribbons and tell the people about the war. You say, 'It wasn't so bad; and we're beating hell out of the krauts.'...
>
> "You forget about nights like this. All you do is eat hot dogs and drink coca-colas, the absence of which has mostly occupied your mind in the field....
>
> "For a while, you miss the old gang. And you feel like a fish out of the water in civvies. You won't have to go back clerking in a grocery store, because the good old army has trained you for a better job....
>
> "Sure. You've learned a lot of useful things. You can pick off a man at three hundred yards with an M-1. You can toss a grenade further than anybody else

in town. You can sleep among corpses, bathe in ditch water without any complaint a-tall. As civilians, we'll be in great demand." (50–51)

There's no greater proof of the essential truth of this feeling—and of the GI's appreciation of it—than one of the platoon's muttered reply to this monologue: "Horse Manure."

Recognizing the truth of one's condition, though, and reconciling with it are two very different things, especially for the GI on the home front. For Audie Murphy, it is clear that playing the role of hero was never quite comfortable. He was reportedly haunted by shrieking nightmares, and he struggled with alcoholism and an addiction to painkillers. There is general clinical agreement that Murphy simply could not have avoided suffering from what is now characterized as "post-traumatic stress disorder." Already uncomfortable in the role of hero, his movie roles—in which he, as the genuine article, tried to bring a Hollywood version of heroism to life—could only have contributed to the sense of his own dislocation and disorientation. He suffered financial setbacks in the 1960s, and his acting career declined. He died in a private plane crash—on Memorial Day—in 1971. Just the year before, he'd returned to the public eye, when a friend of Murphy's reportedly asked him to intervene after a dog trainer had done what she believed was a less than satisfactory job with her dog. In the bizarre case, Murphy was charged with threatening and even shooting at the man. He was acquitted, but his response to a reporter asking about the incident helps illuminate just how deeply engrained the GI's fatalism remained in him. In a recent preface to *To Hell and Back*, Tom Brokaw reports that Murphy, when asked "Did you shoot at that guy?" simply stared blankly at the questioner, as if he could not fathom the reason for the question. Then he shrugged. "If I had," he said. "Do you think I would have missed?" (viii).

U.S. marine from the 3/5 Lima company carries his "GI Joe Action Man" as he walks past the destruction in Fallujah, 2004. Patrick Baz/AFP/Getty Images.

For the contemporary GI, Murphy's brand of fatalism remains a necessary fact of his existence, both in real life and in our fictions. The undefined Korean war (or "police action"), the apparent futility of Vietnam, the stalemate of the Cold War, and the seeming ease but inscrutable end of the first Gulf War have done nothing but reinforce the GI's conviction that he exists only to fulfill two roles: he must be weapon abroad, and hero at home. At home, the figure must smile for the camera and wave during the parade. Abroad, the figure *must* maintain his absolute competence when it comes to dealing death. Today, the fighting GI can be as philosophical about these roles, as profane or angry or circumspect or even as blind to their implications, as he prefers. His feelings are, as ever, entirely beside the point.

WORKS CITED AND RECOMMENDED

Brokaw, Tom. Preface. *To Hell and Back*. By Audie Murphy. New York: Henry Holt & Co., 2002. i–viii.

Foote, Shelby. *The Civil War, A Narrative*. 3 vols. New York: Vintage, 1986.

Heller, Joseph. *Catch-22, a Novel*. New York: Simon and Schuster, 1961.

Murphy, Audie. *To Hell and Back*. New York: Henry Holt & Co., 2002.

Rodgers, Richard L., ed. *The Audie Murphy Memorial Web Site*. 28 Apr. 2005 <http://www.audiemurphy.com>.

Golden Gate Bridge

Kenneth M. Sanderson and Laura Kennedy

As you drive south on U.S. 101 approaching San Francisco, the ridge of Mount Tamalpais rises on your right and ahead, and San Francisco Bay lies on your left. You cannot see the Golden Gate Bridge at all, even though you know it has to be near. The road rises and curves upward to the mouth of the Waldo Tunnel.

Your car enters the tunnel, the road begins to slope downward, and the bright arc of the tunnel's far end appears ahead. As you run through the tunnel, the opening ahead becomes larger and larger, lighter and lighter, and then suddenly the opening frames red towers: your first glimpse of the Golden Gate Bridge. You are already almost at the bridge; it appears so suddenly and is so large as to be surreal, almost shocking. You have plunged down the rabbit hole, and while you are still underground the huge, beautiful structure looms before you.

You emerge from the tunnel and swoop down toward the bridge, which grows ever taller in your vision as your car rounds the last bend of the highway and the entire north tower of the bridge soars above you, framing the south tower ahead, more than a mile away on the other side of the Golden Gate.

What is so fascinating about the Golden Gate Bridge? Why does it evoke such wonder and delight? The size of the bridge is both breathtaking and absolutely appropriate to the surrounding headlands and cliffs. This elegant man-made thing complements the stunning landscape, neither subdued by it nor challenging it. Without the bridge, the Gate—the strait connecting bay and ocean—would be immense, impressive. The bridge is an artwork on the scale of nature's creation, but it isn't nature—it's art and engineering and labor. The Gate just is; the bridge is imagination cast against a vast natural canvas.

Why do so many people come to this bridge, to walk across what has been called the largest Art Deco sculpture in the world? Walk with them—families, couples (lots of couples), solitary strollers, joggers, bicyclists—and feel the wind on your cheek. It is cool despite the bright sunshine, and passing clouds bring a chill. Gulls wheel below you and flocks of brown pelicans patrol above the strait. Fleets of paddling and diving black cormorants scatter when a seal surfaces in their midst. Huge container ships, barges towed by seagoing tugs, oil tankers, and a mammoth car carrier pass under the bridge with their escorts of harbor tugs. With the rising breeze of late afternoon, windsurfers and sailboarders course back and forth just inside the bridge, which defines the entrance to San Francisco Bay.

Always above your head are the huge, ornamental towers and the thick catenary cables that curve up to the top of one tower, then down, up again to the other tower, and down to the far anchorage. The heavy suspension cables hang from the catenaries in rigid pairs just outside the railing at your elbow. The color of the bridge is called International Orange, a deliberate choice of the designers, who were mindful of the striking setting and wanted their bridge to stand out, to define and be defined by the precipitous headlands to the north and the city and the forest of the San Francisco Presidio to the south.

These men were not only skillful and meticulous engineers, they were also visionaries. They thought as deeply about the meaning of the bridge as about the details of its materials and construction. Joseph Strauss, the chief engineer and for almost twenty years the driving force behind the planning and building of the bridge, was also a poet. When the bridge was completed in 1937, Strauss wrote a poem that began, "At last the mighty work is done; / Resplendent in the setting sun" (qtd. in Petroski 284). Only an engineer who was a poet could have built the Golden Gate Bridge.

The bridge represents perfection in an imperfect world. It tells us that no matter how flawed, tawdry, unreliable, petty, or frustrating life may sometimes be, there is one thing—one huge, useful, beautiful, gracefully aging thing—that can be relied on, that we can see, visit, touch, and use. The bridge is beautiful in a world that is often superficial and ugly. It raises our spirits; it is a work of art that speaks to us.

The Golden Gate Bridge probably does not mean the same thing to everyone, and there may be some for whom it is merely a way to get from here to there. But it is there, for you to make of it what you can, what you wish. It asks nothing (except a $5 toll when you drive across it southbound into the city; northbound it's free). The crowds walking on the bridge on a sunny day are proof that many people want what the bridge offers them, whatever that may be. A sizable number of those walkers are speaking languages other than English. The Golden Gate Bridge is an icon to people from all over the world.

An icon is more than just an object of admiration. It represents something beyond itself, and beyond the person admiring it. It is part of some bigger, communal reality: a culture or a religion. By focusing on the icon, the individual identifies with the larger truth, and locates himself within the community that recognizes the icon. For some, the bridge is an icon for what it makes them think. For others, it is an icon because of how it makes them feel.

The Golden Gate Bridge. Courtesy of Corbis.

Close up or far off, the bridge invites the eye and stirs the imagination. It is visible from many points and in many aspects. From the ridge of Mount Tamalpais closest to the north tower, you see the top of the tower almost on eye level as you look down on the bridge deck and across the Gate to the south tower and the city in the distance. This aspect, like the view of the bridge from across the bay, emphasizes the structure's gracefulness and elegance. From below, on the seawall at Fort Winfield Scott under the south end of the bridge (used to great effect in Alfred Hitchcock's movie *Vertigo*), you look up at the great towers and the underside of the span. It looms above you, heavy, almost threatening, and impossibly large. You can take a harbor tour on a boat that goes right under the bridge and be struck anew by how far above the water even the deck is, let alone the towers, lost far above in the clouds.

When the weather is clear, the Golden Gate Bridge is a presence in your field of vision, even from the opposite shore of the bay, ten miles away: a dividing line between heaven and earth during daylight hours and a string of golden lights at night. Often, however, the Bay's fog hides the bridge. Sometimes the towers vanish up into the overcast, and sometimes they are all of the bridge that can be seen, as a low fog swallows the bases of the towers and the deck.

The fog, like the strait, the city, and the bridge, plays its own part in the history of the region. For more than 200 years, that fog concealed the Golden Gate and San Francisco Bay from explorers and others sailing along the coast, including Francis Drake. Finally in 1769 members of the Portola expedition, coming overland from the Spanish settlements in the south, were the first Europeans to see the strait and the bay when they reached Point Lobos, the westernmost point in what is now San Francisco. A day or two later, other members of the party saw the southern end of the bay from Montara Mountain. The history of the region had begun.

In 1846 the scout and explorer John Charles Frémont named the strait the Golden Gate, inspired by a fancied comparison with the Golden Horn, the harbor of Byzantium. In naming the strait in homage to a geographical icon of the old world, he was the first to acknowledge the iconic aspect of this waterway in the new world. The ancient Greeks had called their harbor the Golden Horn because of its shape and its advantageous location for trade with Asia. The Golden Gate, Frémont wrote, was a fitting name for the strait because of its shape and its suitability for trade, especially with Asia. His rationale was either prescient or breathtaking in its presumption, in view of the fact that at the time Yerba Buena (not yet called San Francisco) was a mere village at the edge of a continent largely unexplored and sparsely inhabited.

The promise of riches, fame, and dreams come true is a key element of the iconic meaning of the Golden Gate Bridge. It exists at the farthest end of the continent that so many immigrants would come to believe had streets paved with gold. Frémont was lucky in his timing. Two years after he gave this bit of landscape its legend-infused and poetic name, gold was discovered in California. The following year the gold rush transformed the hamlet of Yerba Buena into a bustling city, and the Golden Gate truly became the gateway to riches.

The name "Golden Gate" caught on quickly. In mid-August of 1849, Bayard Taylor, a reporter and man of letters, arrived in California after a journey, typical for the time, down the east coast of the United States, across the Isthmus of Panama, and up the Pacific coast in the steamer *Panama*. He wrote, "At last we are through the Golden Gate—fit name for such a magnificent portal to the commerce of the Pacific!" (43). Not only did he use the name provided by Frémont just three years earlier, but he shared Frémont's sense of what the place meant: a commercial opportunity.

Because it is striking and beautiful, the Golden Gate Bridge is endlessly depicted in all sorts of places, for all sorts of reasons. It appears on the dust jackets of books and in advertisements for airlines, car rental firms, tour companies, even supermarkets. It provides the very name for the Golden Gate National Recreation Area and of course its image is a regular feature in GGNRA literature. Especially in the San Francisco Bay Area, the image of the bridge is omnipresent. Elsewhere, it appears far less often, but it is still relatively common and always instantly recognizable. It means excitement, travel, adventure, freedom.

It may contribute to the bridge's iconic status that many people from elsewhere first encounter it when they are in their late teens or early twenties, the age when their lives are becoming independent and are opening up, an age that is often full of possibilities (and sometimes full of angst). California has long been a destination for the young. Before the bridge was even imagined, many of those who came for the gold rush were of that age. Nowadays, the young often first really encounter it as college-age "runaways" from somewhere else. For them, the bridge means sunshine, freedom, open sky, and possibilities. For them, the bridge still has the aura of the "Summer of Love."

Others, who may also have come to the bridge in their youth, may now be old enough to remember when ships went to sea under the bridge in the early nineteen-forties, bound for the war on the other side of the Pacific Ocean, or later steamed into the bay victorious. In those days, the bridge had a special and potent place in the hearts of familes, wives, and sweethearts who clustered at the railing of the bridge, hoping for a last glimpse of loved ones as the ships departed, or a first glimpse as they returned home.

If the bridge represents the promise of a dream fulfilled, what happens when the dream fails? Every year, some eighteen or nineteen people leap from the bridge to their deaths. Even this shocking number may be too low, though, for some suicides may not be observed, and the bodies of some who leap are never recovered. In addition, an unknown number of people presumably contemplate committing suicide by jumping from the bridge; some of these probably never actually go to the bridge, and some perhaps walk out on the span and then change their minds. It is clear that suicide is a dark aspect of the bridge's status as an icon. Perhaps even as a heartbroken soul contemplates leaving this world, the choice of this monumental structure as a place to die is an unconscious response to something transcendent, larger than the individual, that is represented by the bridge. If so, the contemplated suicide could be interpreted as a last attempt to grasp meaning or a sense of belonging.

People need dreams, and symbols, and icons. The Golden Gate Bridge is one of the more potent icons of the modern world. The bridge is very much a part of our time, the age of machinery, steel, and the automobile. It has fed the longings of modern people for most of the last century. As we move out of the industrial age that created the bridge and into a new world, with new kinds of commerce, new kinds of longing, what dreams will this twentieth-century icon inspire in the young people of the twenty-first century?

WORKS CITED AND RECOMMENDED

Frémont, John Charles. *Geographical Memoir upon Upper California*. Washington, DC: Wendell & Van Benthuysen, 1848.

Jenkins, Dorothy G. "Opening of the Golden Gate." *Geologic Guidebook of the San Francisco Bay Counties: History, Landscape, Geology, Fossils, Minerals, Industry, and Routes to Travel*. California Department of Natural Resources. Division of Mines. Bulletin 154. 1951. 11–29.

Petroski, Henry. *Engineers of Dreams: Great Bridge Builders and the Spanning of America*. New York: Alfred A. Knopf, 1995.

Taylor, Bayard. *Eldorado: Adventures in the Path of Empire*. 1850. Rev. ed. Santa Clara, CA: Santa Clara University; Berkeley, CA: Heyday Books, 2000.

Billy Graham

David Fillingim

The crowd in the packed stadium bursts into applause at the final note of the song, then a hushed anticipation settles over them as the time for the main event arrives. But this is not an athletic contest. On a stage in the middle of the field at the twenty-five yard line, a man in a dark gray suit slowly makes his way to a simple lectern and begins to speak in a familiar, deliberate, baritone voice. Billy Graham is delivering his simple gospel message of salvation, and the capacity crowd hangs on every word.

If asked to name one person who stands as an icon of American Christianity, Billy Graham is the first name that would come to most people's minds. But Billy Graham represents different (and even opposite) things to different people. To some, Graham represents reactionary conservatism; to others, liberal compromise. He has been called both a prophet and a bulwark of the status quo against which prophets rail. Perhaps the varying perceptions of Graham and his legacy demonstrate that he has successfully embodied the Apostle Paul's ideal of becoming "all things to all people." Or perhaps they constitute yet another indication that iconic is in the eye of the beholder.

Graham is an icon both within and beyond the revivalist and evangelical strands of American Christianity, and one's perception of exactly what Graham represents depends in large measure upon one's position in relation to the various subgroups that comprise American evangelicalism. To "insiders" Graham will represent various theological and political substrata within evangelical Christianity. To "outsiders" he will tend to represent Christianity, evangelicalism, or American civil religion as a whole.

Born in 1918, Billy Graham was raised on a dairy farm near Charlotte, North Carolina. At age 16, Graham had his experience of being "born again" at a crusade led by traveling evangelist Mordecai Ham, and was ordained to the ministry five years later. He attended Florida Bible Institute and earned a bachelor's degree from Wheaton College in Illinois, where he met and married Ruth. After serving as a pastor in Illinois, he joined the ministry of the parachurch organization Youth for Christ, from which he launched his own evangelistic ministry through a successful 1949 Los Angeles crusade.

Most broadly, Billy Graham is an icon of American Christianity in the electronic era. To insert Billy Graham's name into a song lyric or his image into a work of art is to evoke immediately whatever the listener/viewer associates with being Christian in America—respectability, influence, power, stability, hope, peace, quaintness, prejudice, backwardness, and so on. More specifically Graham represents several strands of American religious history in which his ministry has played a pivotal role, and he symbolizes several major conflicts in American religion as evidenced by conflicting views of various facets of his own ministry.

First and most obviously, Billy Graham exemplifies the revivalist tradition that is endemic to American Christianity. As numerous observers have noted, the individualistic frontier mentality that has shaped American culture is uniquely suited to a religious mindset emphasizing rational decision and individual conversion (see my essay on "Self-Help and Popular Religion" in *The Greenwood Guide to American Popular Culture*). The revivalist tradition in America, beginning with Jonathan Edwards and George Whitefield, and extending through Charles Finney, Dwight L. Moody, and Billy Sunday, shows a progressive emphasis on the rational decision to follow Christ as the most prudent choice an individual can make. With his plain presentation of the gospel—always concluding with a simple appeal for a decision to follow Christ—Billy Graham stands at the zenith of this tradition.

One dynamic within revivalism that Graham especially exemplifies is the effort to control the emotional excesses sometimes associated with religious fervor. In other words, Billy Graham is an icon of religious respectability. During the first Great Awakening, which burst forth in late-seventeenth-century Puritan New England, many were critical of the revivals for their excessive emotional displays. Puritanism had tended to emphasize a more rational and orderly approach to religion and all of life. Revival leaders were concerned to demonstrate that the conversions brought about in the revivals were deeper than mere emotional excitement. Jonathan Edwards (1703–1758) wrote *On Religious Affections*, an exploration of the behaviors associated with conversion and a precursor to social science methodologies, in an effort to differentiate authentic religious emotion from excessive emotionalism.

As the Revivalist tradition developed, a sort of science of soul-winning developed with it. In the urban revivals of the mid-nineteenth century, Charles G. Finney (1792–1825) pioneered many of the elements that would become associated with mass evangelism, most notably the citywide crusade with publicity, trained volunteers, and local clergy support. Finney also pioneered the notion of the "evangelist" as a specialized minister, and was known for a colloquial preaching style that appealed to the common person. Finney's successors as leading evangelists, Dwight Moody (1837–1899) and Billy Sunday (1862–1935), also appealed to the common folk and increased the showmanship associated with revivals. Finney, Moody, and Sunday were all self-taught, lacking formal theological training. Moody's partnership with songleader Ira Sankey gave birth to the "gospel song" tradition of sacred music, in which songs about heaven and personal friendship with Jesus are prominent. Sunday's songleader, Homer Rodeheaver, introduced new dynamics to gospel song performance and congregational singing styles.

Finney, Moody, and Sankey all presented a populist, anti-elitist, and anti-intellectual version of Christianity. With the advent of the Pentecostal movement at the dawn of the twentieth century, evangelists such as Aimee Semple McPherson (1944) took the revival movement farther from the cultural mainstream with healing ceremonies and other new and strange ritual practices. Revivalist Christianity was again criticized for its excessive emotionalism. McPherson's ostentatious ministry was also criticized for its commercialism, and scandals in her personal life brought accusations of outright hypocrisy. As the biting satire in Sinclair Lewis's novel *Elmer Gantry* demonstrates, by the mid twentieth century the figure of the evangelist was an icon of everything that was wrong with American Christianity. So how has Billy Graham come to be an icon of honor, integrity, and serenity?

Billy Graham, 1966. Courtesy of the Library of Congress.

From early in his ministry, Graham attracted support from the cultural mainstream. During Graham's 1949 Los Angeles tent crusade, news publisher William Randolph Hearst made the decision to give Graham positive press, perhaps because Graham's gospel seemed more palatable than the city's Pentecostal revivals that had preceded it. Graham's 1957 New York crusade filled Madison Square Garden for sixteen weeks. The years between included a successful crusade in London. Graham attended several meetings of the World Council of Churches from its founding in 1948 and sought to make evangelism a higher priority within the ecumenical movement by sponsoring the World Congress on Evangelism in Berlin in 1966. One reason for Graham's broad appeal is simply that, unlike some earlier evangelists, he did nothing that would separate himself from the mainstream. He lacked the isolationist, anti-intellectual, and anti-elitist impulses sometimes associated with conservative Christianity. Graham's meticulously staged crusades avoid excess of any kind, thus providing a suitable frame for the simple gospel message and appealing to an audience given to moderation and rational decision-making.

William Martin's definitive biography of Graham is entitled *A Prophet With Honor*. To admirers Graham is an icon of both honor and the prophetic.

Graham represents the honorable in religion in part because of the previously mentioned avoidance of emotional excess and other extravagances, and also because of his reputation for financial integrity. Graham's organization is governed by a board of directors which approves Graham's moderate (by celebrity/televangelist standards) salary. During the 1980s, sex scandals involving televangelists Jim Bakker and Jimmy Swaggart rocked the world of religious broadcasting; Bakker's opulent and self-indulgent lifestyle had already been a matter of some controversy. Graham managed to stay above the fray, keeping intact his reputation as a man of personal integrity and financial responsibility, never prone to the dishonorable and embarrassing antics of some of his peers.

The idea of Billy Graham as prophet is more problematic. To some, Graham represents the prophetic dimension of Christianity in that he proclaims a simple, uncompromising message of salvation that posits Jesus as the true solution to all personal and social problems. But to those who identify prophetic Christianity in the twentieth century as the religion of people like Dorothy Day, Martin Luther King, Jr., and the Berrigan brothers, Billy Graham is an icon of all that is wrong with the church. His simple individualism is seen as working against an adequate response to the great social issues of the day. For example, during the Cold War, Graham would often mention or allude to the anxiety brought on by nuclear proliferation, then conclude with the appeal that true peace in one's heart can be found only through Jesus Christ. The more radical prophetic wing of Christianity sought a more comprehensive solution to the nuclear arms race than individual conversion.

A similar dynamic revolves around Graham's stance on race relations. Admirers portray Graham as an advocate of racial reconciliation because of his insistence in the 1970s and 1980s that his crusades be open to all, which was indeed an improvement over the practices in many Southern churches (I personally witnessed white attendees walk out in protest when Graham stated his belief in racial equality from the podium of a 1986 crusade). But critics—most notably Reinhold Niebuhr, perhaps the most influential theologian of the twentieth century—have criticized Graham's failure to speak out on racial segregation in the Bible Belt during the earlier years of the Civil Rights movement. In reality, Graham had tried to desegregate his crusades in the early 1950s, but opposition from local crusade organizers in southern cities forced a difficult decision. Faced with the choice between evangelizing an audience with separate seating for black and white listeners and not evangelizing at all, Graham chose to make a difficult compromise.

Graham's relationships with United States presidents are iconic of the place of religion in American public life. Graham participated in the inauguration services of presidents Johnson, Nixon (twice), Reagan (twice) George H. W. Bush, and Clinton (twice). He also attended the inauguration of President Eisenhower and stayed overnight at the White House and participated in a prayer breakfast during the early days of the Carter presidency. To some,

Graham's role as the presidents' de facto chaplain reinforces the myth of America as a nation uniquely blessed and perhaps even chosen by God. To others (including Niebuhr), Graham's friendships with presidents compromise the integrity of the gospel through association with corrupt power and political agenda.

Though sometimes associated by critics with narrow, partisan agenda of the Religious Right, Graham's friendships with politicians differ markedly from the political friendships enjoyed by other television preachers like Jerry Falwell and Pat Robertson. Graham was accused of political partisanship in mid-career because of his close relationship with President Richard Nixon and his open disdain for communism. But Graham's subsequent friendships with Jimmy Carter and Bill Clinton demonstrated that he was not captive to a particular political ideology. By contrast, the new Religious Right led by Falwell and Robertson rose to prominence during Ronald Reagan's 1980 presidential campaign and has unashamedly pursued specific policy goals. Falwell and Robertson have associated only with Republican leaders, despite the fact that the one Democratic president during their years of political involvement is the only president to share their Baptist denominational background. Graham, on the other hand, was one of the ministers Bill Clinton met with privately seeking counsel regarding his marital infidelity.

To most observers perhaps, Graham represents conservatism. But to some Christian fundamentalists, Graham is the prime example of the dangers of compromise with liberalism. While Graham was bringing respectability to revivalism by moderating its anti-intellectualism, the fundamentalist reactionary stance against evolution and higher criticism of the Bible intensified the anti-intellectualism of the far right wing of American Christendom. In the middle of the twentieth century, at the zenith of the fundamentalist reaction against modernism, Graham was among a group of Christian leaders who launched the current movement in American Christianity known as "Evangelicalism" in an effort to forge a middle way between rabid fundamentalist backwardness and the drift toward liberalism and secularism. Throughout his career, Graham has been criticized in arch-fundamentalist publications for adulterating the gospel by associating with the doctrinally impure.

Graham also represents serenity. His book laying out the gospel he preaches is entitled *Peace with God*. In a preaching career that spanned the Cold War and the constant threat of nuclear annihilation, Graham has always presented Jesus as the only source of true peace. When Graham would appear at public ceremonies, particularly in times of national crisis or disaster, his presence and demeanor exerted a calming influence. Graham's son, Franklin, apparently did not inherit this gift, as indicated by his inflammatory remarks about Islam in the wake of the atrocities of September 11, 2001. One of the functions of religion, including civil religion, is to nurture a sense of inner peace among its adherents. Billy Graham's steadiness and consistency, along with the simplicity of his message, have allowed him to be a visible symbol of the serenity that people seek from religion.

Several factors help to explain Graham's popularity. Graham and his contemporaries rose to fame on the tide of the growth of radio, and later television. The Roman Catholic Church had pioneered religious broadcasting. Father Coughlin, the radio priest, pioneered the use of radio to broadcast religious teaching in the 1930s, while Bishop Fulton Sheen was the first widely successful religious figure on television. Charles Fuller pioneered radio evangelism in the mid-twentieth century, paving the way for Graham and serving as a mentor of sorts for the younger evangelist. Though Father Coughlin's message had included harsh invective, television tended to favor more moderate voices—at least until the advent of cable TV with enough channels for every voice to find a niche. Graham's message of inner peace and rational decision-making was well-suited for the new medium.

Graham's career also bracketed with the Cold War and its anxiety-producing doctrine of nuclear deterrence. The acronym MAD (mutually assured destruction) for the era's major weapons policies bespeaks a culture crying out for a message of peace and tranquility. Graham's assurance that "peace with God" could cure the anxieties of an age of rapid cultural change found receptive ears.

Certainly Graham's own talents and character play a significant role in his popularity. His straightforward preaching style is accessible and engaging. His personal integrity has seldom been questioned. And his single-mindedness of purpose in placing the simple message of salvation above all other concerns allowed his ministry to carve a straight path through the tumultuous social environment of the second half of the twentieth century.

WORKS CITED AND RECOMMENDED

Fillingim, David. "Self-Help and Popular Religion." *The Greenwood Guide to American Popular Culture*. Ed. M. Thomas Inge and Dennis Hall. Vol. 4. Westport, CT: Greenwood, 2002. 1665–98.

Graham, Billy. *Peace with God*. Dallas: Word Publishing, 1994.

Martin, William. *Prophet with Honor: The Billy Graham Story*. New York: William Morrow and Company, 1991.

Niebuhr, Reinhold. "The King's Chapel and the King's Court." *Christianity and Crisis* 4 Aug. 1969 <http://www.religion-online.org>.

———. "Proposal to Billy Graham." *Love and Justice: Selections from the Shorter Writings of Reinhold Niebuhr*. Ed. D. B. Robinson. Louisville: Westminster/John Knox Press, 1992.

Grateful Dead

Nicholas Meriwether

When Grateful Dead guitarist Jerry Garcia died in 1995, the *New York Times* eulogized him as an " Icon of 60's Spirit" (Pareles). Nor were they alone: the term icon cropped up repeatedly, applied to both Garcia and the Dead, as well as to their tie-dyed fans, the Deadheads. Though used then in the broadest sense, the idea of an icon is actually quite apt in getting at what has made the Grateful Dead such a colorful, complex, and enduring phenomenon in American culture.

Of all the American bands to emerge from the heady ferment of the 1960s, the Grateful Dead cast the longest cultural shadow. Considered avatars of—and spokespersons for—the Haight-Ashbury, San Francisco's famous bohemian neighborhood, the band coalesced in Palo Alto in 1965 with lead guitarist Jerry Garcia, drummer Bill Kreutzmann, bassist Phil Lesh, organist and lead vocalist Ron "Pigpen" McKernan, and rhythm guitarist Bob Weir. Their backgrounds—and aggregation—reveal much of the cultural currents that made San Francisco the "Liverpool of the West," as columnists called it then. Garcia was a veteran of a number of folk and bluegrass groups, already considered the best banjo player in the competitive Bay Area folk scene. Weir and Pigpen were also part of that scene, though Pigpen's forte was the blues. A former jazz trumpeter with perfect pitch, Lesh had studied with famed composer Luciano Berio and spent the past four years writing avant-garde classical music when Garcia tapped him to play bass for the fledgling group. After a brief apprenticeship playing peninsula bars, they performed at a party thrown by Ken Kesey and his circle of bohemians, nicknamed the Merry Pranksters. It was not just another party, though: this one featured the still-legal psychedelic drug LSD, and everyone—musicians included—participated. When Kesey decided to take the parties public, the Dead were tapped as the house band for what was called the Acid Tests, immortalized in Tom Wolfe's memoir, *The Electric Kool-Aid Acid Test*.

Later the band would attribute much of their approach to music to the lessons they learned during this brief period. As they saw it, by breaking down barriers, psychedelics reinforced their ability to listen to each other, laying the groundwork for the freeform improvisation that would become a defining aspect of their performances. It also broke down patterns of thinking and helped them view their music as almost infinitely expansive, able to absorb whatever influence or inspiration they might have. This eclecticism was bulwarked by the competitive nature of the jazz and folk scenes that birthed San Francisco rock: musicians were judged not only by their chops, but also by how deep—and esoteric—their musicology was. In a scene that produced the Jefferson Airplane, Big Brother and the Holding Company (Janis Joplin's first band), Quicksilver Messenger Service, Country Joe and the Fish, Santana, Creedence Clearwater Revival, and dozens of others, the Dead were considered the best, by common consent.

Part of their appeal was the bond they managed to establish with their audiences. Some of this was purely kinetic: they were a tight dance band. But the spiritual quality of their performances was commented on from the outset: this was not three-chord rock, moaning about teen-aged love. Some of that spirit they brought with them from the Acid Tests; some of it, though, was imbued in the lyrics and in the warm, communal glow of group improvisation. It was an approach that made the audience a participant; indeed, the band would say that on a good night, the audience was another member of the band. Their first album, released in early 1967, featured their own arrangements of blues and jugband classics like "Good Morning, Little Schoolgirl" and "Don't Ease Me In." Though the band quickly ceased playing the originals on the album, songs like "The Golden Road (To Unlimited Devotion)" captured the burgeoning ethos of the Haight, with its catchy refrain, urging everyone to join the party. Sadly, that happened, and the Haight scene collapsed under the influx of young people. After living in what one band family member called "the Haight's unofficial community center," the Dead grew tired of Grayline tour buses driving by to gawk, and moved out shortly after 1967's Summer of Love (Scully and Dalton 74).

The band would always be associated with the Haight, however, and for the rest of their career, their songs would continue to explore those rich origins as well as steadily expand to encompass musical traditions from the rest of the world. They added another impetus for that diversity with second drummer Mickey Hart, who joined in the fall of 1967. A student of the drum in all its cultural guises, Hart was already practiced in Eastern rhythms and added both power and color to their percussion. Their sophomore album, released in 1968, blended live and studio recordings to capture a series of originals, designed to showcase their formidable reputation as a live band. From the Beat-inflected surrealism of "New Potato Caboose," set to a madrigal-flavored melody, to the gut-bucket blues of "Alligator," this was another document of the high seriousness and dazzling array of influences that informed the San Francisco scene. For fans, the standout was the thundering riot of "The Other One," which captured another important chunk of the band's mythos: their relationship with the Pranksters, epitomized by Neal

The Grateful Dead, 1968. Courtesy of the Library of Congress.

Cassady, the legendary Dean Moriarty in Jack Kerouac's *On the Road*, and their notorious patron and sound engineer, Augustus Owsley Stanley III, better known as Bear. A famed underground LSD chemist, Bear was responsible for helping establish the band's sound system, and began the practice of taping each show, so that the band could critique themselves afterwards. Later on these tapes would produce a gold mine of releases, and reinforce the precedent for fan taping as well.

It was with the pair of albums that followed, though, that the band's place in the mythology of the Haight-Ashbury was cemented. With the addition of lyricist Robert Hunter, the words took on the kind of learned, literate sophistication that already defined the music. From the allegorical "St. Stephen" to the slashing psychedelia of "Cosmic Charlie," Hunter was the final ingredient. His words for "Dark Star" clinched what would grow into the band's signature anthem, the centerpiece of their last album of the Sixties, *Live/Dead*. Over the next twenty-three years, Hunter would continue to pen words that Garcia thought captured his way of thinking, even his history, with an uncanny precision. Their last composition together, "Days Between," hearkened back to their days in the Palo Alto folk scene and the early days of the Haight, in a gem of a ballad that finally settled the issue of whether rock music could age gracefully. Much of his work with Garcia can be found on the band's dozen studio recordings, though along with the band's second lyricist John Perry Barlow (who mostly worked with Bob Weir), many of their gems only appear on the band's more than fifty live releases.

Many critics have commented on the intelligence, beauty, and power—the "larger-than-lifeness" in Steve Silberman's words—of the music and lyrics of the Dead; some have begun to describe how these combined to outline a coherent vision (Silberman xx). One academic has called this a "lifeworld," and one aspect of this is its ability to sustain and generate an iconography whose symbols are among the best known in popular culture (Ganter 176). The most famous of these were created by the small group of original Haight-Ashbury artists whose posters advertised early Fillmore and Avalon Ballroom shows. Like the Dead's concert repertoire, some of these early images drew on older traditions: Stanley Mouse and Alton Kelley found an illustration by Edward Sullivan for *The Rubaiyat of Omar Khayyam*, and it became one of the most recognized images for the band, the skeleton surrounded by roses—the perfect pictorial representation of the words "grateful dead." Other images were as startling and original as the band's own songs, and often drew on their imagery: Rick Griffin listened to Hunter's lyrics, where roses feature prominently, and created a seminal poster of a gorgeous blue rose, one of horticulture's holy grails. Most famously, Bob Thomas created the stylized image that graces the band's 1975 album, *Steal Your Face*: nicknamed steallies or Lightning Jacks, the skull with a thirteen-point lightning bolt through it became the band's best known symbol, and a trademarked logo. In time, these artists and others would add dancing bears, terrapins, skeletons, and dozens more to the iconography of the Dead, a process Deadheads joyfully participated in as well. Emblazoned on handcrafted teeshirts, stickers, and posters, Deadheads' iconography drew on and embellished these and added their own, eventually earning their own gallery exhibition (Cole and Stallings).

There was a practical aspect to these icons: the Lightning Jack—colorful, simple, easily recognized—made it instantly possible to separate the band's equipment from others, an important consideration in crowded backstages and festival situations. Likewise, fans could recognize each other when they spotted a bumper sticker emblazoned with a chain of dancing skeletons or the cryptic phrase, "nothing left to do but smile, smile smile," one of the hundreds of lyric couplets that became touchstones of Deadhead philosophy. That identification carried risks as well, when law enforcement agencies began to use Deadhead insignias as probable cause to stop cars and perform contraband searches (Fraser and Black 24). For Garcia, whose bearded beaming visage and signature handprint, with its missing middle finger—chopped off in a childhood accident—became visual icons, fame became a trial and a burden.

With appearances at the Monterey Pop Festival in 1967 and Woodstock in 1969, the Dead's centrality in the broader folklore of the Sixties was enshrined. Their historicity would also provide an enduring source of appeal for later fans, as well as for academics. Indeed, the ways in which the band both shaped and were shaped by their times would become one of the challenges facing academics trying to explain the Grateful Dead experience and phenomenon, terms that embrace both the band's work and the fans' sense of involvement. While the band members' erudition and virtuosity made them appealing subjects, it was the bond they shared with their audience that would ultimately arouse even more commentary.

That audience showed no signs of diminishing after the sixties. Moreover, they remained loyal despite the band's refusal to conform to music industry norms and expectations. Touring without the benefit of a radio hit or massive record company promotion, the Dead soon became legendary for playing hours on end, and never repeating a show. With a repertoire that encompassed hundreds of songs, by 1990 a diehard fan could hear six consecutive shows featuring more than 100 songs, with none repeated.

That the band was still innovating, still improvising, after so many years was part of their continual appeal. In every era, critics noted that the band's audience renewed itself with young recruits, even as the older ones continued to come. By the 1980s fans could see three generations at every show, proof that the scene was healthy and that the Deadhead identity was not a negation but an affirmation. Like the original hippies of the Haight, Deadheads viewed themselves as artists of their lives, charged with the responsibility to find a meaningful, spiritually aware way of contributing to their community—even if that community was defined as being as far removed as possible from the mainstream society that condemned and misunderstood them.

All of this exuded a sense of authenticity that coils through much of the literature on the band. Just as the band recognized that what they were doing was tied into older, deeper knowledge, so too did the fans: being a Deadhead not only carried with it the challenge of understanding an exceptionally dense, wide-ranging musical corpus, it also entailed learning the band's musical antecedents and historical genesis. When Deadheads read Garcia's reaction to finding Harry Smith's folkways anthology, they too were turned on to what Greil Marcus called "the old, weird America." Hidden, suppressed or forgotten knowledge ran throughout the Dead scene, from Hart's forays into tribal drumming to the ritual use of psychedelics. Nor were they anti-academic: Dead shows were famous for attracting favorable attention—and participation—from luminaries such as Joseph Campbell and Owen Chamberlain, Nobel laureate in physics, who said he liked sitting between the two drummers on stage "because it gives me interesting ideas" (McNally 387). And the band was explicit about their sense of indebtedness to their artistic, musical, and cultural antecedents; in a late interview, Garcia reflected, "I feel like I'm part of a continuous line of a certain thing in American culture, of a root.... My life would be miserable if I didn't have those little chunks of Dylan Thomas and T. S. Eliot. I can't imagine life without that stuff. Those are the payoffs: the finest moments in music, the finest moments in movies. Great moments are part of what supports you as an artist and a human" (Henke 40). Deadheads who listened and read those interviews learned much about folk music, blues, jazz, classical, the Beats, modernism, and the cornerstones of Western civilization (plus a few from the East).

Deadheads may have felt alienated from mainstream America, but they felt rooted in much deeper human cultural traditions.

This helps explain why the band and fans have already generated so much academic work. There is the monumentalism of so many well-played shows, each one unique, most of them recorded and traded among fans; and there is the spectacular range of sources, musical and literary, informing their work. But what emerges as the most slippery and compelling aspect of the whole Grateful Dead phenomenon is the way that all of this translated into what one critic called "a union with their audience that was unrivaled and unshakeable" (Gilmore 96). It has also proven to be complex enough to merit a sizable amount of academic work, including a bibliography, several collections of essays, dozens of articles, five Ph.D. dissertations, more than two dozen master's theses, and over 130 conference papers (Meriwether). Most remarkable is the percentage of papers and theses that have been published, a statistic that includes a surprising amount of undergraduate work as well. For knowledgeable academics, this is less surprising: but as Deadheads, these authors measured their effort against a very real and intensely personal experience; that passion, as Rebecca Adams has pointed out, is a critical component of Deadhead scholarship (Adams, "What Goes Around, Comes Around" 37).

Academics have approached the Dead phenomenon from a variety of disciplines: musicology, literary criticism, history, sociology, anthropology, philosophy, religious studies, communication theory, business theory, and others have all made contributions. There is a certain propriety in this attention: the academy has always had a certain tolerance for eccentric, learned excellence, which could easily describe the Dead. But the real appeal of Dead studies for academics is that it offers unusual opportunities to address longstanding issues, from fundamentals such as a workable definition of rock music, to more theoretical concerns such as connecting a work of art to its audience, from creation to consumption (both thorny and still confounding issues, despite decades of work). The fact that all of these disciplines can provide compelling insights also suggests that Dead studies may well offer a unique basis for interdisciplinary work, grounded in a single phenomenon. Perhaps even more, the band and its subculture offer compelling models for such work: the band exemplifies the ideal of participating in the traditions you study. This has implications for the academy: as one anthropologist maintained, "the study of phenomena such as the Grateful Dead in American culture is not only justifiable, but requisite for the development of the discipline" (Bradshaw ix). And Deadheads believe in emulating the band's standards—and ideals—of excellence, cooperation, and open-mindedness in their own work, which Rebecca Adams has hailed as uniquely laudatory in the academy (Adams, Foreword). The collaboration that lies at the heart of the book she coedited with Robert Sardiello, *Deadhead Social Science*, is at the forefront of educational theory, and it has also produced fine work.

From the outset, the band and their reluctant figurehead were called icons of hippiedom in general, and of the Haight-Ashbury and San Francisco rock in particular. It was no surprise then to see the term pressed into service again after Garcia's death, and not just by commentators, but by fellow musicians. Jazz saxophonist Branford Marsalis, who played with the band on several occasions, said: "Most rock shows are just like versions of MTV, but not the Dead—they're into jazz, they know Coltrane, they're American musical icons.... They're *fantastic*" (Pooley). Ornette Coleman, who had invited Garcia to play on one of his later albums, put it more succinctly: "Jerry Garcia was one of the original American icons. He played very naturally and beautifully" ("And We Bid You Good Night" 67). Both remarks chart the unlikely course the band pursued—or more properly, the improbable destination that emerged during their quest. In the more than 2,000 unique concerts they played over thirty years, playing more shows to more listeners than any other band in history, the Dead became much more than just symbols of the Sixties or the Haight-Ashbury. Indeed, as one academic commented in the early 1990s, "The Grateful Dead have become an American cultural icon, even for those who don't listen, or no longer listen, to rock music" (Tillinghast 188). Their place was cemented when the remaining members decided to retire the name, though they would continue touring in various aggreggations and even partially resuscitate the name, as simply The Dead, a few years later. Cynics dismissed the continuation, but staying power was always a central part of the band's ethos. After all, they had outlived three keyboard players, though the rest of the band's lineup had remained stable.

While academics and the rest of America argue today over the meaning of the Sixties, one of its greatest cultural artifacts and legacies quietly transcended those tangled, turbulent origins to become an icon of America itself, in all its oft-misunderstood complexity. Novelist Robert Stone, an alumnus of that early Palo Alto bohemian scene, put it best: "The art and the thought and the spirit of liberation of the sixties flourished in their way. But of that holistic magic vision of the garden set free, the music of Jerry Garcia and the Grateful Dead is the purest single remnant. It was supposed to be an accompaniment to the New Beginning. In fact, it was the thing itself, all that remains with us" (Stone 67). It is a true icon, embodying a complicated, challenging, uniquely American artistic and social phenomenon.

WORKS CITED AND RECOMMENDED

Adams, Rebecca. Foreword. *Perspectives on the Grateful Dead: Critical Writings*. Ed. Rob Weiner. Westport, CT: Greenwood, 1999. xiii–xiv.

———. "What Goes Around, Comes Around: Collaborative Research and Learning." *Deadhead Social Science: You Ain't Gonna Learn What You Don't Wanna Know*. Ed. Rebecca Adams and Robert Sardiello. Walnut Creek, CA: AltaMira P, 2000. 15–50.

"And We Bid You Good Night: Artists and Colleagues Pay Tribute to Garcia." *Rolling Stone* 21 Sept. 1995: 31+.

Bradshaw, Geoffrey W. *Collective Expressions and Negotiated Structures: The Grateful Dead in American Popular Culture, 1965–95*. Ph.D. Diss., U of Wisconsin, 1997.

Cole, Chris, and Tyler Stallings. *Dead on the Wall: Grateful Dead and Deadhead Iconography from 30 Years on the Bus*. Exhibition Catalog. Huntington Beach, CA: Huntington Beach Art Center, 1996.

Dodd, David, and Robert Weiner. *The Grateful Dead and the Deadheads: An Annotated Bibliography*. Westport, CT: Greenwood, 1997.

Fraser, David, and Vaughan Black. "Legally Dead: The Grateful Dead and American Legal Culture." *Perspectives on the Grateful Dead* 19–40.

Ganter, Granville. "'Tuning In': Daniel Webster, Alfred Shutz, and the Grateful Dead." *Dead Reckonings: The Life and Times of the Grateful Dead*. Ed. John Rocco. New York: Schirmer Books, 1999. 172–80.

Gilmore, Mikal. "Jerry Garcia, 1942–1995." *Rolling Stone* 21 Sept. 1995: 44–51+.

Henke, James. "Jerry Garcia: The Rolling Stone Interview." *Rolling Stone* 31 Oct. 1991: 34–40+.

Marcus, Greil. "The Old, Weird America." Liner notes to *Anthology of Folk Music*. Ed. Harry Smith. U.S. Smithsonian Folkways, 1997. 5–25.

McNally, Dennis. *A Long Strange Trip: The Inside History of the Grateful Dead*. New York: Broadway, 2002.

Meriwether, Nicholas, ed. *All Graceful Instruments: Writings on the Grateful Dead Phenomenon* (forthcoming).

Pareles, Jon. "Jerry Garcia of Grateful Dead, Icon of 60's Spirit, Dies at 53." *New York Times* 10 Aug. 1995: A1+.

Pooley, Eric. "Raising the Dead." *New York* 16 Apr. 1990: 24.

Scully, Rock, and David Dalton. *Living with the Dead*. New York: Little, Brown, 1996.

Silberman, Steve. "Introduction: Gathering the Sparks." *The Grateful Dead Reader*. Ed. David Dodd and Diana Spaulding. New York: Oxford UP, 2000. xix–xxi.

Stone, Robert. "End of the Beginning." *Rolling Stone* 21 Sept. 1995: 63+.

Tillinghast, Richard. "The Grateful Dead: Questions of Survival." *Michigan Quarterly Review* 30.4 (1991): 686–88.

Wolfe, Tom. *The Electric Kool-Aid Acid Test*. New York: Farrar, Straus and Giroux, 1968.